Private Real Estate Markets and Investments

FINANCIAL MARKETS AND INVESTMENTS SERIES
H. Kent Baker and Greg Filbeck, Series Editors

Portfolio Theory and Management
H. Kent Baker and Greg Filbeck (Co-Editors)

Public Real Estate Markets and Investments
H. Kent Baker and Peter Chinloy (Co-Editors)

Private Real Estate Markets and Investments
H. Kent Baker and Peter Chinloy (Co-Editors)

Private Real Estate Markets and Investments

EDITED BY H. KENT BAKER

and

PETER CHINLOY

OXFORD
UNIVERSITY PRESS

OXFORD
UNIVERSITY PRESS

Oxford University Press is a department of the University of Oxford.
It furthers the University's objective of excellence in research, scholarship,
and education by publishing worldwide.

Oxford New York
Auckland Cape Town Dar es Salaam Hong Kong Karachi
Kuala Lumpur Madrid Melbourne Mexico City Nairobi
New Delhi Shanghai Taipei Toronto

With offices in
Argentina Austria Brazil Chile Czech Republic France Greece
Guatemala Hungary Italy Japan Poland Portugal Singapore
South Korea Switzerland Thailand Turkey Ukraine Vietnam

Published in the United States of America by
Oxford University Press
198 Madison Avenue, New York, NY 10016

Library of Congress Cataloging-in-Publication Data
Private real estate markets and investments / edited by H. Kent Baker and Peter Chinloy.
p. cm. — (Financial markets and investments series)
Includes bibliographical references and index.
ISBN 978–0–19–938875–2 (alk. paper)
1. Real estate investment. I. Baker, H. Kent (Harold Kent), 1944– II. Chinloy, Peter, 1950–
HD1382.5.P765 2014
332.63'24—dc23
2014003349

9 8 7 6 5 4 3 2 1

Printed in the United States of America on acid-free paper

Contents

Acknowledgments

We are pleased to have this book published by Oxford University Press as part of the Financial Markets and Investments Series. Many others contributed to the success of *Private Real Estate Markets and Investments*. The chapter authors deserve special appreciation for their substantial efforts writing highly informative chapters. Our expert team at Oxford University Press deserves thanks for the high level of professionalism demonstrated throughout the process. Special thanks go to Claudie Peterfreund from Cover-to-Cover Indexing Services for providing the index. We also want to recognize the support provided by the Kogod School of Business at American University. The authors dedicate this book to Linda Baker, Chris Chinloy, and Diana Hancock for their ongoing support.

About the Editors

H. Kent Baker is a University Professor of Finance in the Kogod School of Business at American University. Professor Baker has authored or edited 23 books. Among his most recent books with Oxford University Press are *Portfolio Theory and Management* (2013), *International Finance: A Survey* (2013), and *Survey Research in Corporate Finance* (2011). His most current books with John Wiley & Sons, Inc. are *Investor Behavior—The Psychology of Financial Planning and Investing* (2014), *Market Microstructure in Emerging and Developed Markets* (2013), *Alternative Investments—Balancing Opportunity and Risk* (2012), and *Socially Responsible Finance and Investing* (2012). As one of the most prolific finance academics, he has published more than 150 refereed articles in such journals as the *Journal of Finance, Journal of Financial and Quantitative Analysis, Financial Management, Financial Analysts Journal, Journal of Portfolio Management,* and *Harvard Business Review*. He has consulting and training experience with more than 100 organizations, serves on six editorial boards, and is the past president of the Southern Finance Association. Professor Baker holds a BSBA from Georgetown University; MEd, MBA, and DBA degrees from the University of Maryland; and an MA, MS, and two PhDs from American University. He also holds CFA and CMA designations.

Peter Chinloy is Professor of Finance and Real Estate in the Kogod School of Business at American University. His teaching experience includes managerial economics and corporate finance, as well as all types of real estate courses at graduate and undergraduate levels including income properties, mortgage securities, development, residential, and commercial real estate. Professor Chinloy serves on the editorial boards of *Real Estate Economics, Journal of Real Estate Finance and Economics,* and *Journal of Real Estate Research*. He has also served on the board of directors of business firms, including for the entity that operates the MRIS multiple listing service in the Washington, DC, area. He received a BA in commerce from McGill University and an MA and PhD in economics from Harvard University.

About the Contributors

John S. Baen is Professor of Real Estate at the College of Business, University of North Texas. Professor Baen is an internationally recognized oil and gas researcher, expert witness, appraiser, and investor. He has been interviewed or quoted in the *Wall Street Journal, Boston Globe, Dallas Morning News, Fort Worth Star Telegram, ABC News,* and many other news outlets. He has authored more than 70 published articles, two books, and has taught or delivered lectures in many oil-producing countries. Professor Baen has served as an officer or held position in the International Real Estate Society and American Real Estate Society. He currently is the Vice President of the Texas Land and Minerals Association. He has an undergraduate, master's, and doctoral degrees, all in real estate and planning from Texas A&M University.

Sandy Bond is the Professor of Property Studies within the Commerce Faculty at Lincoln University in New Zealand. She is a Registered Property Valuer and Senior Member of the Property Institute of New Zealand, has served as the President of the Pacific Rim Real Estate Society (PRRES), and is the President for the International Real Estate Society (2014). Professor Bond received the Property Institute of New Zealand Academic Award in 2010 and the PRRES Achievement Award in 2002 for her significant contributions to property education and research. Her research is of an applied, multidisciplinary nature that aims to solve globally important property issues. Her current focus is on sustainability of the built environment. However, as a result of the 2011 earthquakes in Christchurch, New Zealand, her research now encompasses the impact of natural disasters on property values. Her academic credentials include a PhD in property studies from Curtin University in Western Australia and an MBS in property and BBS in valuation and property management from Massey University in New Zealand.

Man Cho is Professor of Public Policy and Management at the KDI (Korea Development Institute) School of Public Policy and Management who teaches real estate finance, asset securitization, and other related courses. He also has a joint appointment as Director of Real Asset Research Team at KDI and is currently managing various research projects on real estate market and policy issues in Korea and other countries. Before joining the KDI School, he worked at Fannie Mae holding both research and management positions. His other professional appointments include being a consultant at the World Bank and an adjunct professor at Johns Hopkins

University. He holds a PhD in applied economics and managerial science from the Wharton School, University of Pennsylvania.

François Des Rosiers is an urban and real estate economist. Since 1976, he has been teaching urban and real estate management at the Faculty of Business Administration, Laval University. Over the past decades, Professor Des Rosiers has authored or co-authored more than 100 articles, papers, monographs, research and consulting reports as well as book chapters in the field of urban and real estate management and planning issues. He has received several distinctions and awards. His main research area deals with hedonic price modeling and the measurement of urban externalities. Professor Des Rosiers holds a PhD in urban and regional planning studies from the London School of Economics.

William G. Hardin III is the Director of the Hollo School of Real Estate and the Jerome Bain Real Estate Institute and Professor of Real Estate and Finance, Florida International University. He is a full professor and directs the MSIRE and BBA in real estate programs. He has an extensive publication record in the top real estate journals, including *Real Estate Economics, Journal of Real Estate Finance and Economics,* and *Journal of Real Estate Research.* Professor Hardin was ranked eleventh globally in academic real estate research during 2000–2006. He is Co-Editor of *Journal of Real Estate Practice and Education,* a board member of the American Real Estate Society, and serves on the editorial board of *Journal of Real Estate Research, Journal of Housing Research,* and *The Appraisal Journal.* He worked in commercial banking and development before earning a PhD from Georgia State University.

Douglas Hough is an Associate Scientist and Program Director in the Department of Health Policy and Management at the Bloomberg School of Public Health Johns Hopkins University. His research interests are in identifying the optimal size and structure of a physician practice and in the application of the emerging field of behavioral economics to contemporary healthcare issues, including a book on the topic published by Stanford University Press. He has published in the *Journal of the American Medical Association* and *Journal of Human Resources* and served as the editor of the business of medicine column in *Advanced Studies in Medicine.* He earned an MS and PhD in economics from the University of Wisconsin.

G. Donald Jud is Professor Emeritus of Finance in the Bryan School of Business and Economics at the University of North Carolina at Greensboro. He is author of more than 80 academic articles and three books. Professor Jud's research has appeared in numerous academic and professional journals including the *Appraisal Journal, Journal of Real Estate Finance and Economics, Journal of Real Estate Research, Journal of Financial Economics, Land Economics, and Urban Studies.* He is a past president of the American Real Estate Society and former editor of the *Journal of Real Estate Research.* He is a research fellow at the Homer Hoyt Advanced Studies Institute and the National Association of Industrial and Office Properties Research Foundation. He received BA and MBA degrees from the University of Texas and a PhD from the University of Iowa.

John A. Kilpatrick, MAI, FRICS, is the Managing Director of Greenfield Advisors and a Visiting Scholar in Real Estate Finance at the Zichlin School of Business, Baruch College, in New York City. Dr. Kilpatrick is the author of four books and a contributing author to three others including *Brownfields,* 3rd edition. He is an MAI-Designated member of the Appraisal Institute, a nationally certified Appraisal

Standards Instructor, a Fellow of the Faculty of Valuation of the British Royal Institution of Chartered Surveyors, and a Principal Member of the Real Estate Counseling Group of America. He also serves on the editorial boards of the *Journal of Sustainable Real Estate* and the *Appraisal Journal* and the review board of the *Journal of Real Estate Research.* Dr. Kilpatrick earned a PhD in finance from the University of South Carolina.

Kyung-Hwan Kim is President of Korea Research Institute for Human Settlements (KRIHS). He is on leave from Sogang University where he is a Professor of Economics. He is also a research affiliate of the Center for Asset Securitisation and Management in Asia at the Sim Kee Boon Institute for Financial Economics at Singapore Management University. Professor Kim is a member of the board of directors of AREUEA and serves on the editorial board of the *Journal of Housing Economics* and the management board of *Housing Studies.* Previously, he taught at Syracuse University, University of Wisconsin-Madison, and Singapore Management University. He also served as an urban finance advisor at the UN Habitat, and president of the Asian Real Estate Society. His research areas include land and housing markets, government regulations, and local public finance. He has published in the *Journal of Urban Economics, Journal of Real Estate Finance and Economics, Journal of Housing Economics,* and *Urban Studies.* Professor Kim received a PhD in economics from Princeton University.

Peter Linneman is Professor of Real Estate, Finance, and Public Policy, Emeritus, Wharton School, University of Pennsylvania and Chief Executive Officer of the American Land Funds, KL Realty, and Linneman Associates. He is widely recognized as one of the leading strategic thinkers in the real estate industry and was recently cited as one of the "25 most influential people in real estate" by *Realtor* Magazine. For nearly 30 years he has provided strategic and financial advice to leading corporations. He is the founder and principal of a series of private equity funds that invest in long-term land developments and also served as Chairman of the Board of Rockefeller Center Properties. Professor Linneman has published over 80 articles during his career and more than 40 universities have adopted his book, *Real Estate Finance and Investments: Risks and Opportunities.* He holds master's and doctorate degrees in economics from the University of Chicago.

Ming Kai Low is the Chief Information Officer at Baen and Company, which provides consulting, valuation, and appraisal services to the oil, gas, and minerals industry. Mr. Low was a second-generation student of Professor Baen and his academic and professional work assistant. He was born in a real estate family in Malacca City, Malaysia, where he is a fourth generation real estate investor. He has an MBA from the University of North Texas.

Isaac F. Megbolugbe is an Associate Professor at the Carey Business School, Johns Hopkins University. He is also the managing principal of GIVA International, LLC. His expertise is in the areas of hedonic pricing in real estate economics, regional economic development, and healthcare real estate. He is a Fellow of the Royal Institute of Chartered Surveyors, American Real Estate Society, and a member of the editorial board of the *Journal of Real Estate Research.* He has published in *Real Estate Economics* and *Journal of Real Estate Research.* Professor Megbolugbe received a PhD in real estate economics and finance from the University of Pennsylvania.

Glenn R. Mueller is a Real Estate Investment Strategist at the Dividend Capital Group and a Professor in the F. L Burns School of Real Estate and Construction Management at the University of Denver. He has 38 years of real estate industry experience. Professor Mueller has published more than 86 articles. He received the Richard Radcliff Award for Groundbreaking Research in Real Estate Market Cycles by the American Real Estate Society in 2010, the Graaskamp Award for Research Leadership from the American Real Estate Society in 2004, and the Graaskamp Award for Research Excellence from the Pension Real Estate Association in 2001. He has been a co-editor of the *Journal of Real Estate Portfolio Management* since 2001. Professor Mueller has held top research positions at Legg Mason, Price Waterhouse, ABKB/LaSalle Investment Management, and Prudential Real Estate Investors. He was also a developer/builder in New England. Professor Mueller holds a B.S.B.A. from the University of Denver, an MBA from Babson College, and a PhD in real estate from Georgia State University.

Graeme Newell is Professor of Property Investment at the University of Western Sydney. He has more than 30 years of experience in property research and education mainly in Australia, the United States, United Kingdom, Hong Kong, Malaysia, and China. His research covers the areas of property investment vehicles and the role of property in portfolios. He has numerous publications in the property and infrastructure areas in a wide range of international journals including the *Journal of Real Estate Research, Journal of Real Estate Portfolio Management, Journal of Property Research, Journal of Property Investment and Finance,* and *Pacific Rim Property Research Journal.* Professor Newell received a PhD from the University of Western Sydney.

Hsu Wen Peng is Assistant Professor in Property at the National Taipei University, Taiwan. His research covers infrastructure, emerging property sectors, and property investment vehicles. He has numerous publications in the area of infrastructure investment and emerging property in international journals including the *Journal of Property Research, Journal of Real Estate Portfolio Management,* and *Pacific Rim Property Research Journal.* He received a PhD from the University of Western Sydney and was a PhD scholarship holder.

Michael J. Seiler is the founding Director of the Institute for Behavioral and Experimental Real Estate (http://www.IBERE.org) and Professor and K. Dane Brooksher Endowed Chair Professor of Real Estate and Finance at the College of William and Mary. Professor Seiler is an internationally recognized behavioral real estate researcher whose studies have been cited in the *Wall Street Journal, New York Times, Los Angeles Times,* and *Washington Post.* Professor Seiler has published more than 100 research studies, has written several books, and serves as the editor of *Real Estate Finance* and the co-editor of *Journal of Real Estate Literature.* In 2009, he received the William N. Kinnard Young Scholar Award, a national recognition for making significant contributions in his field. More recently, he received the Governor's Technology Award in the area of modeling and simulation in the state of Virginia for his work on strategic mortgage default and foreclosure contagion. Professor Seiler earned a BS in finance and economics at the University of South Florida, an MBA at the University of North Florida, and a DBA at Cleveland State University.

Marius Thériault is a geographer, who taught transportation, GIS, spatial analysis, applied statistics, applied computing, and climatology since 1976. He was Director of the Land Planning and Regional Development Research Centre at Laval University from 2000 to 2006. Professor Thériault has authored more than 100 articles, papers, and book chapters. His research interests are about combining GIS, spatial statistics, GPS, spatio-temporal modeling, and simulation to further studies related to real estate markets, mobility behavior, urban studies, transportation, environmental impacts, health and urban planning. Professor Thériault holds a PhD in climatology from Laval University.

Elaine Worzala is the Director of the Carter Real Estate Center and a Professor in Real Estate at the College of Charleston. Professor Worzala has served as the President of both the American Real Estate Society and the International Real Estate Society. She has completed research grants for numerous organizations including the National Association of Realtors, Royal Institution of Chartered Surveyors (RICS), International Council of Shopping Centers (ICSC), Pension Real Estate Association (PREA), and Real Estate Research Institute (RERI). Professor Worzala believes strongly in bringing relevancy to her classroom from her research projects. She has published in mainstream real estate academic journals and industry-based publications. Several of these publications focus on sustainability and the built environment. Her academic credentials include a PhD in real estate and urban land economics, a Masters in real estate appraisal and feasibility analysis, and a BBS in marketing with a minor in international business.

Private Real Estate Markets and Investments

1

Private Real Estate Markets and Investments: An Overview

H. KENT BAKER

University Professor of Finance, Kogod School of Business, American University

PETER CHINLOY

Professor of Finance and Real Estate, Kogod School of Business, American University

Introduction

Investment in real estate can take a direct form in the private debt and equity markets, as opposed to those where public trading occurs. *Private real estate* is where an investor is a direct owner or lender to a property. Investing in private real estate is widespread in the United States. According to the U.S. Department of the Treasury, Internal Revenue Service (2013), individuals filed 142 million returns for 2010. Of these, 18 million (13 percent) submitted Schedule E principally for rental income as landlords. Thus, private real estate is an extensive activity among U.S. households. At the large-scale institutional level, Colony Capital owns more than 10,000 houses and Blackstone more than 30,000 in 2013 (Bloomberg News 2013).

Conventional investable real assets include retail, office, apartments, hospitality, and industrial properties. Apartments include large-scale properties and exclude the small assets owned by individual investors. According to Standard & Poor's (2013) in its S&P/GRA index SPCREX, total investable commercial real estate was worth $5.3 trillion in 2013. These are investments owned by entities solely in the real estate business and exclude properties owned by entities including corporations not in the sector. Retail accounts for $1.9 trillion (36 percent) of the S&P/GRA SPCREX; office is $1.5 trillion (29 percent); and apartments are $1.3 trillion (24 percent). Hospitality is $0.4 trillion (7 percent) and industrial properties are $0.2 trillion (4 percent).

Other less conventional real estate assets involve healthcare, infrastructure, and resources. Healthcare consists of facilities at hospitals, nursing homes, biotech labs, and doctors' offices. Infrastructure consists of projects involving roads, bridges, airports, and public facilities. Resources include agriculture, land and timber, oil, gas, and mineral assets.

According to the American Hospital Association (2013), the United States has 4,973 community hospitals with 797,403 beds. Of these, 2,903 hospitals (58 percent) are owned by non-profit non-government entities, but still available for private property and asset management. Another 1,025 hospitals are operated for profit. State and local governments hold the remaining 1,045 hospitals (21 percent). Consequently, public sector entities with no investable right in the property or management own only one of every five U.S. hospitals accessible by all-comers.

On the demand or buy side for physical or real assets, three factors seem to dominate. First, the share of real estate in institutional portfolios has risen because low interest rates have allowed investors to leverage properties. Allocations to real estate have risen at the expense of bonds. Second, the world's wealth is shifting to emerging markets where real estate is already a dominant asset class and public securities markets are limited. Third, institutions with very long horizons and limited demand for liquidity often eschew publicly traded markets. They do not need immediate exit strategies offered by public markets for stocks, bonds or real estate investment trusts (REITs).

El-Arian (2008) proposes that institutional investors should place 6 percent of their portfolios in real estate. For example, the Norwegian Government Pension Board, the pioneering sovereign wealth fund adopted a similar strategy. Its holdings are 60 percent of its assets in stock equities, 35 percent in bonds, and 5 percent in physical real estate. Buying large properties in stable markets leads to a core real estate strategy. Real estate can be leveraged up to 50 percent, increasing the gross holding to as high as 10 percent of the portfolio.

A portfolio with 35 or 40 percent in bonds at low interest rates barely above inflation leads to risks of no real income flow and capital losses. The capital losses come from interest rate increases. That is, as interest rates rise, the price of low yielding bonds falls. This situation has led some institutions to raise their holdings of real estate at the expense of bonds, regardless of the location. Funds outside of the United States have incentives to increase their proportions invested in real estate given the local dominance of real estate and limited public capital markets.

Real estate is a larger investable asset class outside of Western nations. Davies, Lluberas, and Shorrocks (2012) construct annual estimates of world wealth. For 2012, they estimate world wealth at $220 trillion in U.S. dollars, with $70 trillion each in Europe and North America. Unlike most other countries, financial assets such as stocks and bonds dominate wealth in the United States. In Indonesia, for example, real estate constitutes 90 percent of total wealth.

Private real estate has two characteristics that can result in investment advantages: illiquidity and active management. One characteristic is that private real estate is priced at a discount to comparable, more liquid assets yielding similar cash flows. Ibbotson, Chen, Kim, and Hu (2013) estimate this illiquidity discount to be between 25 and 40 percent in financial asset markets.

Liquidity enables exiting an asset during a crisis. Investors are willing to pay higher prices for this ability to divest an asset from their portfolios. Even in relatively liquid markets for stocks and bonds, assets with lower liquidity earn a higher return. Ibbotson et al. (2013) find that the bottom quartile of firms by liquidity or trading volume as a proportion of shares outstanding earns total annual returns 8 percent higher than those in the top quartile with a lower standard deviation. A dollar invested in the most illiquid quartile of stocks in 1971 grew to $204 in 2008. By contrast, a dollar invested in the most liquid stocks in 1971 grew only to $12 in 2008. Restricted illiquid stock sells for a discount of 25–40 percent even when having similar claims on the firm.

The *bid-ask spread* is the difference between what the seller is willing to accept and the buyer is willing to pay. Returns are increasing and concave for the bid-ask spread (Amihud and Mendelson 1986) with investors having longer horizons capturing the benefit from holding length. Amihud (2002) constructs a measure of liquidity as the ratio of the return in absolute value to the trading volume and this measure is positively correlated with excess returns. For a bid-ask spread of 3 percent, an investor trading once a year with a 10 percent hurdle rate is paying 0.03/0.1 or 30 percent for liquidity over a long horizon. The investor holding the illiquid asset should expect an initial 30 percent price discount in exchange for not having access to trading.

The illiquidity discount also occurs in the bond market. Longstaff (2004) finds that investors pay a premium for U.S. Treasuries over similar assets issued by a federal agency with comparable federal guarantees. The premium ranges from 3 basis points on 3-month issues to 500 basis points for 30-year bonds.

In real estate where transaction costs are 6 percent of an asset's price or even higher for brokerage fees on house sales, the benefit from holding illiquidity is potentially even greater. As Riddiough, Moriarty, and Yeatman (2005) point out, the premium is reduced if illiquid investors hold better quality assets, differ in management incentives or have lower leverage, when comparing the non-traded National Council of Real Estate Investment Fiduciaries (NCREIF) index with one for REITs.

The real estate illiquidity premium rises during times of crisis because selling these assets becomes more difficult. According to Yale University (2011, p. 18), "investors frequently encounter the opportunity to earn excess returns from accepting illiquidity." Not surprisingly, Yale has placed a target of 28 percent of its portfolio in real assets including real estate, oil and gas, and timberland. The holding ranged between 27 and 30 percent over the period 2006–2010.

Another characteristic that can result in an investment advantage is that private real estate relies on asset management. Real estate managers in the highest quartile of performance over the period 2000–2010 have annual returns of 20 percent compared with those in the bottom quartile of –4 percent. Some performance differences that address agency issues or conflicts include whether managers focus only on real estate, put equity into each deal, and have "skin in the game" constituting a large portion of their total wealth. Thus, real estate offers an advantage over other assets involving a return to active management.

Purpose and Key Topics

The purpose of this book is to provide an overview and synthesis of private real estate markets and investments. This review primarily focuses on privately held properties and debt and equity positions in these markets. Some chapters concern both private and public real estate marketsbecause no complete separation exists between them. The book also examines the impact of regulation on these markets including the requirement for appraisal of properties before lenders make loans, licensing of brokers and agents, and such issues as sustainability and the green footprint. Additionally, the book presents research evidence. This book serves as a companion to *Public Real Estate*

Markets and Investments, which is also published by Oxford University Press as part of the Financial Markets and Investments Series.

The scope of the coverage focuses on three areas: (1) foundations of private real estate, (2) private assets and properties, and (3) agency, sustainability, and regulation.

- *Foundations of private real estate.* The first section provides an overview of real estate, its role in portfolio diversification, and the type of institutional or large-scale investors who hold the properties. The real estate market is cyclical and strategies of large-scale investors and others vary. The differences in strategy suggest that behavioral issues permeate these markets.
- *Private assets and properties.* The second section examines various property types in three subareas: (1) conventional property types such as commercial real estate, apartments, and retail, (2) healthcare, and (3) emerging markets in real estate including oil and gas, mineral rights, and infrastructure.
- *Agency, sustainability, and regulation.* The rules governing land ownership, property rights, transfer, protection, and financing are determined locally. By comparison, the capital markets for mortgage debt and real estate equity are national or international. These local fundamentals may have similar roots and solutions. Owners as *principals* are delegating managers as *agents* to carry out transactions resulting in potentially conflicting compensation goals. Agency includes brokerage, asset and property management in real estate, and the role of investors as third party limited partners. Real estate addresses issues of energy conservation and sustainability. Commercial real estate tenants are increasingly demanding that buildings be certified to meet standards such as those mandated under the Leadership for Environmental and Engineering Design (LEED).

Distinctive Features

Private Real Estate Markets and Investments has several distinctive features.

- The book provides a detailed discussion of private real estate markets and investments in a global context.
- It offers a synthesis of important, recent, and relevant research in a straightforward manner.
- The book contains contributions from a diverse array of authors including academics and practitioners.
- Chapters 2 through 14 each contain discussion questions that reinforce key issues and concepts. Guideline answers are presented at the end of the book.

Intended Audience

Private Real Estate Markets and Investments is of interest to various parties. These include real estate investors and professionals such as accountants, property and asset managers, appraisers, attorneys, leasing and sales brokers, mortgage and bank lenders, and financial analysts. Public sector professionals such as planners, regulators, and those at government-sponsored enterprises will find the book of interest. Real estate professionals can target how their services affect transactions. Investors can use the book to provide guidance on carrying out investment strategies. Real estate academics and students will also find this book helpful. The book's 14 chapters fit well into an academic system operating on a semester basis and also courses of shorter duration such as real estate training programs.

Organization of the Book

The remaining 13 chapters are organized into three sections. A brief synopsis of each chapter by section follows.

PART ONE FOUNDATIONS OF PRIVATE REAL ESTATE

Chapters 2 through 4 examine the foundations of private real estate. Chapter 2 explains the strategies of institutional investors involving existing income-producing assets or core, versus value-added or opportunistic capital gains. Chapter 3 discusses the cyclicality of real estate markets. During market booms, prices rise and properties more easily qualify for lending within a given set of underwriting standards. Loosening standards as a consequence of lenders competing for borrowers results in more properties qualifying. During down markets fewer properties satisfy underwriting criteria as these criteria tighten. Chapter 4 examines behavioral issues involving real estate investors.

Chapter 2 Institutional Real Estate Markets (Glenn R. Mueller)

Institutional real estate investors consist of defined benefit pension funds, endowments, insurance companies, and publicly traded real estate companies, mostly REITs. Their investment processes and financing decisions differ markedly from individual investors. Institutional investors typically have large portfolios of real estate and use investment managers and consultants in their investment process. Strategies include core, value added, and opportunistic. Core strategies involve holding stabilized or highly occupied buildings. Value added strategies offer capital improvements to reposition a property. Opportunistic strategies include buying with cash. This chapter gives an overview of investment allocation, investment strategy, pricing, property quality level, performance measurement, manager compensation, consultant duties, and global investments. A cycle analysis shows markets go through phases of growth, maturity, and decline.

Chapter 3 Real Estate Cycles: International Episodes (Man Cho and Kyung-Hwan Kim)

A strand of literature contends that the housing market is cyclical. Evidence in recent episodes of housing price boom-busts from the United States and Europe supports this belief. This chapter documents housing price cycles from three countries—Korea, China, and the United States—in terms of their underlying determinants, empirical evidence, and public policy implications. The comparison shows that, along with market fundamentals such as household income and demographic shifts, policy-driven cycle amplifiers are important. The major ones are urban land use, housing supply, and residential mortgage lending. The chapter discusses specific policy issues to combat a contagious housing price cycle. These include resolving a chronic housing shortage involved with rapid urbanization, balancing macro-prudence and financial inclusion in regulating mortgage lending, and monitoring and regulating sources of excessive market volatility.

Chapter 4 Behavioral Real Estate (Michael J. Seiler)

This chapter discusses the burgeoning implementation of behavioral and experimental approaches to modeling real estate phenomena. Behavioral and experimental techniques are additional tools to understand problems when datasets and procedures do not exist, are inappropriate, or ineffective. Many of these behavioral and experimental designs have been established in fields such as medicine, natural sciences, and psychology. The question is not, "Why is real estate using established techniques from other disciplines?" Instead, it is "Why has so much time passed to adapt established techniques to the specific problems faced by real estate researchers?" In the future, instead of referring to "behavioral real estate," the time will come when researchers simply refer to "real estate", as the distinction between behavioral and non-behavioral approaches becomes increasingly indistinguishable.

PART TWO PRIVATE ASSETS AND PROPERTIES

Chapters 5 through 11 discuss various property types. The first two chapters examine conventional asset types. Chapter 5 involves multifamily properties and chapter 6 focuses on retail and shopping centers. Chapters 7 and 8 discuss healthcare facilities and the costs and incentives in the health sector. The remaining three chapters deal with alternative real estate owners and investments: chapter 9 focuses on corporate real estate; chapter 10 examines mineral rights; and chapter 11 centers on infrastructure.

Chapter 5 Multifamily Investment (William G. Hardin III)

This chapter refines the definition of multifamily properties and outlines the characteristics that make investment in this type of real estate unique. In the United States the term is closely associated with single ownership of a property with a substantial number of units leased to end-users. A single ownership group owns a building or group of buildings that may have anywhere from two to thousands of units. The property generates a scalable cash flow that can be valued and supports a capital structure including debt and equity. Multifamily investment is also associated with the development of multi-unit projects with units sold to individual owners who then either occupy or lease these specific units. This is a condominium-based market. The multifamily property type further includes senior housing, affordable housing, and other forms of ownership characterized by multiple units within a single physical structure.

Chapter 6 Retail Real Estate (François Des Rosiers and Marius Thériault)

This chapter summarizes two research studies on shopping centers. With regard to spatial competition among shopping agglomerations, commercial streets, and community centers are only competitive at the local scale. Big-box stores have a smaller market area when compared to regional and super-regional shopping centers. Commercial streets remain highly efficient for attracting trips for grocery, restaurant, and leisure activities where they do better than regional centers. Strong differences in destination choices are linked to gender, age, and car ownership. Retail concentration reduces regional and super-regional shopping mall base rents. This is a result of the bargaining power by dominant tenants, although retail concentration varies among store categories. For stores in higher-order goods categories, the economies generated outweigh the bargaining power, with a higher level of retail concentration resulting in higher base rents. Stores in lower-order goods categories benefit from a rent discount as retail concentration increases.

Chapter 7 Healthcare Facilities (Isaac F. Megbolugbe and Douglas Hough)

This chapter examines the critical role of real estate as an expense in the delivery of medical services. In the United States, healthcare facilities for hospitals and nursing homes are largely owned outside of the government and generate revenue at each location. They are investable real estate assets and are subject to extensive regulation. The demand for beds and occupancy depends on income, prices, and insurer restrictions. Regulatory constraints limit the supply of hospital beds, while the supply of nursing homes has fewer restrictions. A paradox is that despite increasing healthcare spending and population growth, the number of hospital and nursing beds in the United States is declining. Explanations include holding excess capacity to meet demand surges, reimbursement restrictions, and user response to prices.

Chapter 8 Healthcare Providers (Douglas Hough and Isaac F. Megbolugbe)

The healthcare delivery system in the United States is unlike any other business. Those who intend to work in real estate should understand its peculiarities. The hospital sector is largely not-for-profit, and driven by forces often unrelated to market conditions. Physicians are largely organized as a cottage industry with relatively small, autonomous units. Patients, who are the ultimate consumers of healthcare, are largely unaware of the true characteristics of the services that they consume and often do not make rational purchasing decisions. Third parties pay for the care and often do not fully understand what the services for which they are paying. These are insurance companies for most of the population and government through Medicare and Medicaid for the elderly and the poor. The result is a system that generates high expenditures but uncertain outcomes.

Chapter 9 Corporate Real Estate (Peter Linneman)

Operating companies around the world have generally owned their real estate assets. In the United States, corporate users own $2 trillion or roughly half of all commercial property. Companies own production facilities as well as offices, warehouses, and retail outlets. Although many of these properties are suitable for a broad range of users, companies frequently choose to commit their scarce capital to the ownership and operation of real estate, rather than deploying it to their core businesses. But this capital tied up in real estate drains capital from core expertise. By leasing their real estate, particularly general-use properties, operating companies can generally enhance shareholder value.

Chapter 10 Mineral Rights (John S. Baen and Ming Kai Low)
This chapter examines the subsurface rights that owners hold with the land. Surface rights allow an owner either to grow crops or prepare for development. Subsurface rights have the potential for minerals including oil and gas. The United States generally assigns subsurface rights to property owners. This chapter examines these subsurface rights, which can be bought, sold, and transferred. Because all or a fraction of the mineral rights can be retained or sold, they can be stripped, securitized, and offered as a bundle. Mineral rights are an emerging class of real estate alternative investments. They qualify for tax-deferred exchanges, have very long lives, and trade in secondary markets.

Chapter 11 Infrastructure (Hsu Wen Peng and Graeme Newell)
Real estate-related assets provide potentially enhanced returns and diversification benefits in an investment portfolio. As such, infrastructure has taken on increased investment importance in listed and unlisted funds and as a separate asset class. This chapter discusses the general concepts of infrastructure investments including characteristics, vehicles, and markets. Recent evidence shows substantially enhanced returns for infrastructure. These returns have come from reduced risk due to the increased demand for infrastructure and maturity of the market. Increased returns have also resulted from enhanced portfolio diversification benefits as compared with all major asset classes. The chapter presents an empirical analysis of infrastructure investment based on the Australian experience including the risk-adjusted performance, portfolio diversification benefits, and the impact of the global financial crisis.

PART THREE AGENCY, SUSTAINABILITY, AND REGULATION

The last section consists of three chapters that examine agency, sustainability, and regulation in real estate markets. Chapter 12 discusses appraisal and valuation. Chapter 13 involves brokerage and transaction costs and chapter 14 explores the topics of sustainability and green building. Each chapter contains regulatory aspects.

Chapter 12 Appraisal and Valuation (John A. Kilpatrick)
The valuation of a mortgage-backed security requires numerous real estate skill sets, particularly appraisal. Appraisal standards include a maximum debt-to-income (DTI) ratio and loan-to-value (LTV) ratio for a residential property. For a commercial property, the appraisal standards include on a minimum debt service coverage ratio of net operating income to debt service and a maximum LTVloan-to-value ratio. The appraisal process not only validates the collateral in the case of default but also drives the LTV ratio, which in turn drives the rating of the security. This chapter explores the regulatory scheme in the United States and provides an overview of the methodological paradigm that defines appraisal in most countries. It concludes with a discussion of current efforts to globalize appraisal standards.

Chapter 13 Real Estate Brokerage (G. Donald Jud)
This chapter explores the real estate brokerage industry. It examines trends in employment and income and traces the historical development of the industry and outlines the

legal and regulatory environment. The industry includes agents and brokers involved in intermediation of residential and commercial property. In the United States, all states impose licensing requirements for collecting fees for selling or leasing properties by an agent or broker who is not the owner. The chapter looks at the firm structure of the industry, examining recent trends in franchising and the use of information technology. It surveys the competitive structure of the industry and the impact of the industry on housing market transactions. Employment in real estate brokerage is pro-cyclical. Lastly, the chapter examines how the industry functions outside the United States and the growing effect of globalization.

Chapter 14 Green Buildings (Sandy Bond and Elaine Worzala)

Worldwide initiatives to address climate change, specifically the reduction of greenhouse gas emissions, have been a major driver for the increased focus on sustainable buildings. This chapter reviews the international environmental movement and its impact on commercial real estate. It summarizes the green building rating and certification systems that have been developed around the world and highlights current regulations developed to control energy use in buildings. Regulations include mandatory disclosure of energy performance data to investors and tenants. Finally, the chapter reviews recent research investigating the business case for green buildings. In the majority of cases, investors and tenants are willing to pay a premium for high performance buildings. Recent case studies support this by indicating that these buildings have lower occupancy costs and vacancy rates, proving further incentives to invest in green buildings.

Summary and Conclusions

Real estate markets cover a wide range of assets. When portfolio managers include real estate in their allocations, sometimes using publicly traded assets such as REITs and mortgage-backed securities, any inefficiency from differences in management strategy and agency or illiquidity is priced into the market. The alternative is to invest directly in private real estate to capture these features. This is what the 18 million rental property owners filing tax returns are doing, along with institutional investors. The direct investment includes conventional and traditional real estate assets such as retail, office, apartments, hospitality, and industrial properties as well as other assets including healthcare, infrastructure, and resources.

Investors such as Yale University are attracted to real estate because these assets offer opportunities to pay lower prices for illiquidity and to adopt management strategies that mitigate agency costs. More than a quarter of the university's portfolio is in direct, private real estate. The strategy is to gain from buying illiquidity and to manage agency costs by hiring asset management companies that only focus on real estate.

Corporate entities not focused on real estate hold other private or non-traded real estate assets. Although corporate entities own real estate, the typical capitalization (cap) rates of 6–8 percent annually are below the hurdle rates of 10 percent or more that such firms use to allocate capital. The implication is that firms will sell real estate to unlock shareholder value. The problem is even more acute internationally where corporate entities use real estate as a vehicle to access the capital markets through mortgages.

Consequently, corporations own extensive real estate even in advanced countries such as Japan. Opportunities exist for these firms to unlock the equity and raise capital by selling real estate in order to focus on their core objectives.

References

American Hospital Association. 2013. *Fast Facts on U.S. Hospitals.* http://www.aha.org.

Amihud, Yakov. 2002. "Illiquidity and Stock Returns: Time–Series and Cross–Section Effects." *Journal of Financial Markets* 5:1, 31–56.

Amihud, Yakov, and Haim Mendelson. 1986. "Asset Pricing and the Bid–Ask Spread." *Journal of Financial Economics* 17:2, 223–249.

Bloomberg News. 2013. "Blackstone Raises $5 Rental Bet with Lending Arm." http://www.bloomberg.com/news/2013-2007-08/blackstone-raises-5-billion-rental-bet-with-lending-arm.html.

Davies, James, Anthony Lluberas, and Anthony Shorrocks. 2012. *Credit Suisse Global Wealth Databook.* New York: Credit Suisse.

El-Arian, Mohamed. 2008. *When Markets Collide.* New York: McGraw-Hill.

Ibbotson, Roger, Zhiwu Chen, Daniel Kim, and Wendy Hu. 2013. "Liquidity as an Investment Style." *Financial Analysts Journal* 69:3, 30–44.

Longstaff, Francis A. 2004. "The Flight-to-Liquidity Premium in U.S. Treasury Prices." *Journal of Business* 77:5, 511–526.

Riddiough, Tim, Mark Moriarty, and P. J. Yeatman. 2005. "Privately Versus Publicly-Held Asset Investment Performance." *Real Estate Economics* 33:1, 125–146.

Standard and Poor's. 2013. S&P/GRA Commercial Real Estate Indices. http://www.the-commercial-group.com/uploads/19_SPCREX_Index_Factsheet.pdf.

United States Department of the Treasury, Internal Revenue Service. 2013. "2010 Estimated Data Line Counts: Individual Tax Returns." http://www.irs.gov/pub/irs-soi/10inlinecount.pdf.

Yale University. 2011. *The Yale Endowment Portfolio, 2010.* New Haven, CT: Yale University.

Part One

FOUNDATIONS OF PRIVATE REAL ESTATE

2

Institutional Real Estate Markets

GLENN R. MUELLER
Real Estate Investment Strategist, Dividend Capital Group, Denver, Colorado
Professor, F. L. Burns School of Real Estate and Construction Management, University of Denver

Introduction

Real estate as an industry consists of two major groups: home building and income producing. The home building group is most akin to a manufacturing process. Builders use raw materials and labor to construct homes and must sell finished products to make a profit. Then the process starts over. This group, which produces single-family homes, townhomes, and condominiums for sale, depends on consumers to buy the homes and banks to finance the purchases. The National Association of Realtors (2013) estimates that the value of all owned housing in the United States reached a peak of $20 trillion in 2006 after 40 years of continuous average yearly price appreciation. The S&P/Case-Shiller home price index decreased by 42 percent from 2006 to 2012 causing a home equity wealth loss of more than $8 trillion. Home building has contributed between 2 and 8 percent of annual U.S. gross domestic product (GDP) over the years, and represents a major catalyst in most economic recoveries. The recent economic recovery following the 2008–2009 recession has been much slower than most previous recoveries due in part to the lack of home building.

The second group is income producing real estate, which combines building production with the long-term investment process. Income producing real estate has many property sectors. The major or core five sectors are office, industrial, retail, hotel, and apartments. The first four are also known as commercial real estate. Apartments are sometimes referred to as multifamily, but this term is also used for condominiums and townhomes. Thus, this term is inappropriate here although single-family housing for rent is emerging as a potential asset class itself. Once a new building is constructed, the investment and operations process begins. Each building is similar to a business that must be marketed and operated and financed with tenants as clients and must face competitors who own similar buildings in the local market.

Although many specialized property sectors exist, most can be categorized under the five core property types. Student and senior housing fall under apartments and mini warehouses and manufacturing facilities fall under industrial. Malpezzi (2006) estimated that the income producing U.S. real estate properties had an equity value of

$10.6 trillion in 2006 or about half the size of the home ownership market in the United States. CoStar conducted a more comprehensive study that estimated the value of commercial real estate equity at $11.8 trillion (CoStar Group Inc. 2010). The Federal Reserve Board's *Flow of Funds* (2013) showed houses had capital structure of about half debt and equity. Therefore, income producing real estate asset value was about equal to home asset values in the United States in 2010.

The purpose of this chapter is to give an overview of the steps institutions follow in their investment process. The rest of the chapter has the following organization. The next section discusses types of real estate investors, followed by sections on investment allocation, investment strategy, pricing, property quality level, performance measurement, manager compensation, consultant duties, and global investments. The final section provides a summary and conclusions.

Types of Real Estate Investors

Individual investors own most of the housing and the majority of income producing real estate in the United States and globally. They typically use relatively limited down payment cash for their investments in real estate. These investors rely on large loans with high leverage and are willing to take risks in their investments. Therefore, their purchase and development decisions are highly dependent upon financing from banks and other debt sources. Many of these investors have short investment time frames because they hope to sell the property for a profit and invest in additional or larger properties.

Institutional investors consist of foreign and domestic pension funds, endowments, insurance companies, and public companies that invest in real estate. The majority of public companies in the United States are real estate investment trusts (REITs). Institutional investors usually have considerable cash, use lower leverage, and take less risk than individual investors. Their investment time frame is longer. Because they answer to a large group of people that they represent, institutional investors must provide periodic performance measurement. They usually report on a quarterly basis.

Analysts use two major indexes to monitor and report real estate performance. The National Council of Real Estate Investment Fiduciaries (NCREIF) operates an index of real estate performance that tracks data back to 1978. All members of the organization must provide quarterly income and price data. Income yield and capital appreciation are combined to provide a total return on each investment. The price change is calculated from an internally or externally appraised value of properties that members must report each quarter. NCREIF members are required to have an outside independent appraisal done at least once every three years. Many believe that appraised values do not reflect the true volatility of the real estate prices, creating a smoothing effect. The information is reported as though the properties have no debt in order to make comparisons on different properties.

The NCREIF index consists of regional, property type, and city sub-indexes so that investors can benchmark their properties against peers. The individual building information is kept confidential so that proprietary property data are unavailable to competitors. Sub-index return information is also available, but requires a minimum of five buildings and three different advisors or owners contributing information. The Pension Real Estate Association (PREA) has started a similar index with the international firm Investment Property Databank (IPD).

The National Association of Real Estate Investment Trusts (NAREIT) index, which was established in 1972, provides the historic returns of all publicly traded REITs. It is unique in that an index is normally a sample of a population, but the NAREIT index is actually a census of all publicly traded REITs. Because all the REITs in the index are publicly traded, the NAREIT index reports the closing price at the end of each day. Most REITs pay a dividend each quarter. A total return is easily calculated from the dividend income plus price change on a quarterly basis. The NAREIT total index includes equity REITs, mortgage REITs, and hybrid REITs that hold both properties and mortgages. This discussion only uses equity REIT returns. The NAREIT equity return is for the company's full portfolio of properties after using leverage. The NCREIF and NAREIT equity indexes are not fully comparable. The NCREIF contains unleveraged returns for individual properties. The NAREIT equity return includes both leverage and the reinvestment of equity when a property is sold.

Figure 2.1 shows the historic returns for NCREIF, NAREIT, and inflation as represented by the U.S. consumer price index (CPI). The NCREIF direct, unleveraged return is twice that of inflation. This result substantiates the studies that show real estate has been a good hedge against inflation. The NAREIT return is three times the rate of inflation and the NAREIT return is 50 percent higher than that of NCREIF. The results show the positive effect of leverage on real estate equity investments. The NAREIT index return is also higher as it accounts for management reinvesting funds from sold properties while NCREIF does not. Additionally, the NAREIT return is much more volatile than the NCREIF return, as public stock prices are emotionally driven in the short run.

This chapter focuses on institutional investors and their motivations and methods for adding real estate to their portfolios. Insurance companies have invested in real estate for many decades in both equity and debt because the long-term cash flow returns matched policy payout liabilities. Until the 1940s the only investment allowed

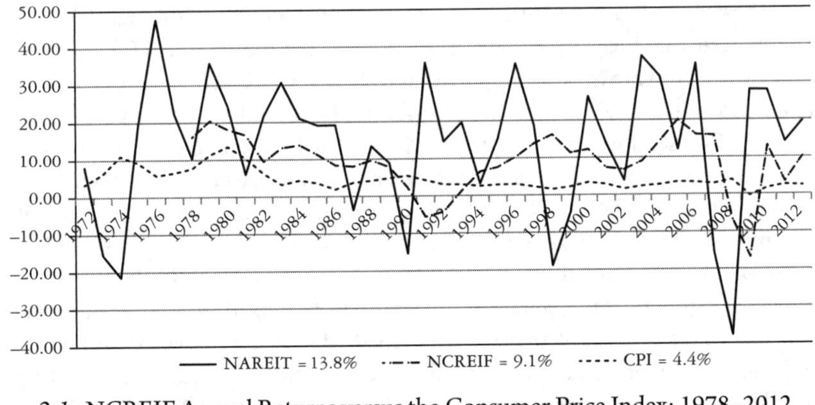

Figure 2.1 NCREIF Annual Returns versus the Consumer Price Index: 1978–2012.
Source: NCREIF.

by the government for pension funds was bonds. Once the Dow Jones stock index was established and historic returns were available to analyze, pension funds were allowed to invest in stocks.

The first pension funds began investing in real estate in the 1960s. Most of these pension funds used insurance companies to advise them for investing and operating their real estate investments. In 1974, the U.S. government passed the Employee Retirement Income Security Act (ERISA) that required all pension funds to diversify their investment holdings. Although this act did not specify the amounts, real estate was one of the asset classes that pension funds could use. However, with no information about the historic returns and risks of real estate investments, many funds did not add this asset class at that time. Institutional investors started adding alternative investments to their portfolios in the 1960s and 1970s, including private equity, venture capital, and real estate.

By the mid-1980s many pension funds were having problems. The returns in the stock market from 1975 to 1985 were negligible. Institutions had used the assumption of a 10 percent annual return for the stock market, which was the long-term average return over 50 years. As they looked for better investments, they saw that the NCREIF Index had produced a return above 15 percent annually since its inception. The increased demand for real estate provided the opportunity for insurance companies to offer their services to others. Users included pension funds and endowments. Soon after, small startup firms started to offer investment management services. Eventually investment banks and developers entered the investment management arena. In the 1990s, investment managers started promoting real estate as a separate asset class and thus it received a separate allocation in portfolios. Based upon the $11.8 trillion size of real estate in the United States in 2010, it makes up about 20 percent of the investible universe when compared to stocks and bonds. Most institutional investors have allocations ranging from 5 to 20 percent for real estate with a few as high as 33 percent. According to Institutional Investor's Sovereign Wealth Center (2012), sovereign wealth funds in 2012 placed 26 percent of their allocations that year to real estate. Fund allocations to bonds declined as those in real estate increased.

Although legislation created REITs in 1960, this public group did not start to grow until the start of the 1990s. In 1992 the creation of the Umbrella Partnership Real Estate Investment Trust (UPREIT) was a catalyst in the growth of REITs. UPREITs allowed real estate owners to move their properties into REITs while deferring their capital gain tax liability to a later date. The UPREIT legislation had a similar effect on deferring taxes as the 1929 IRS section 1031. Under section 1031, investors can take proceeds of a sale, place them with a qualified intermediary, and buy replacement properties with tax deferred proceeds. Under an UPREIT, by exchanging property into a REIT's umbrella partnership investors can liquefy their investment while deferring capital gains tax to a later date when they liquidate for cash.

REITs have grown from a public equity market capitalization of $10 billion in 1990 to more than $600 billion at the end of 2013. REITs in 2013 owned and controlled more than $1 trillion in real estate assets in the United States, which is about 10 percent of all real estate in the country (NAREIT 2013). In the late 1990s, REITs also started to become managers of properties for other institutional investors. They typically co-invested with institutional investors in properties at a much higher percentage of 50 percent, thus aligning the REIT managers' interests with investors. By comparison, traditional institutional managers may have only a few percent of the equity invested in a property, if any at all.

Investment Allocation

Institutional investors must allocate between investments in an effort to maximize long-term risk-adjusted returns and determine the role real estate will play in their portfolios. First, this requires defining the roles and responsibilities of the board, staff, consultants, and managers. Next, the investment strategy, return objectives, and risk levels should be set along with diversification targets and limits. With these guidelines, institutional investors can select the investment vehicles for public, private, equity, and debt along with the property types and the managers who will target the markets, property size, quality, and ages.

How much to allocate to real estate is a macro portfolio question that should be answered by real estate's expected return. The institutional investor compares the expected return on real estate with the other asset classes as well as the diversification benefits. Figure 2.2 shows the historic returns for the major stock, bond, and real estate indexes as well as the volatility of the return as measured by standard deviations. The graph shows that publicly traded securities have much higher volatility and a longer history of negative return years. Only bonds and direct real estate do not show negative returns within one standard deviation of the mean.

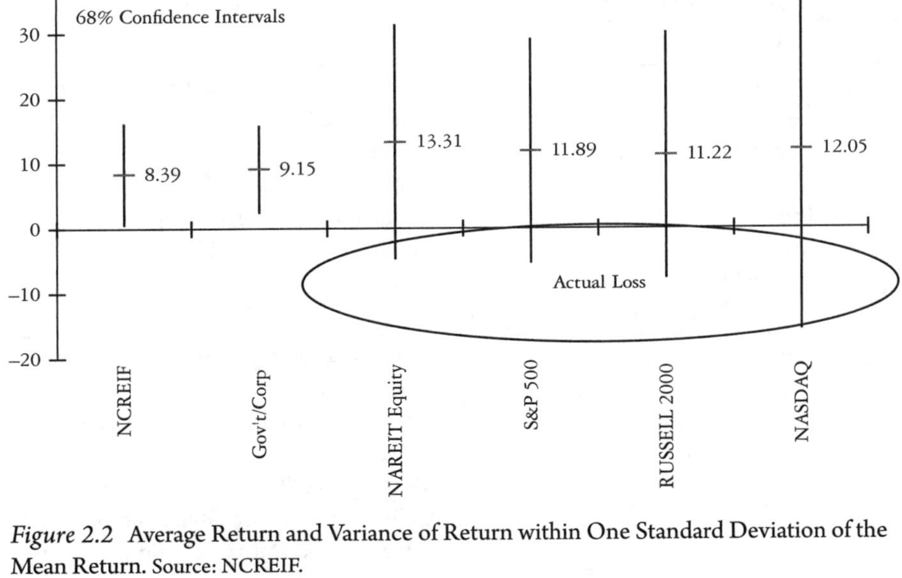

Figure 2.2 Average Return and Variance of Return within One Standard Deviation of the Mean Return. Source: NCREIF.

A comparison of real estate with stocks and bonds for the United States from 1934 to 2013 reveals that real estate has less downside risk. This comparison examines up years when returns are positive and down years when returns are negative. In only 5 of 79 years did real estate produce negative returns versus 20 of 78 years for stocks and bonds.

Direct real estate is usually considered to fit in the middle of the investment spectrum on a risk versus return basis. It usually fits in between different types of bond and stock investments.

Timing strategies might suggest when to invest in real estate versus other investments. Institutional investors may want to enter and exit real estate at different times. However, when real estate is a separate asset class with a given proportionate allocation, institutional investors should be invested at all times. This strategy involves maintaining the 5–20 percent portfolio allocation to real estate. Investors make this allocation decision analyzing the prospective return of real estate relative to that of the alternative investment classes.

Investment Strategy

Once institutional investors have made an allocation to real estate, they must develop a strategy to place the funds within the asset class. The most used strategy is the four-quadrant approach, which involves choosing among public and private into debt and equity. Table 2.1 shows the different forms of investment available in the quadrants.

In most cases, institutional investors focus on equity investments. The majority of the allocation has historically been into private real estate equity investments shown in the upper left quadrant of Table 2.1 REITs or public equity are the second most popular

Table 2.1 **The Four Quadrants of Investing in Real Estate with Forms of Ownership for Each**

	Private	*Public*
Equity	Individual General Partnership (GP) Limited Partnership (LP) Corporation Private REIT Trust Limited Liability Company (LLC) Limited Liability Partnership (LLP)	Real Estate Investment Trust (REIT) Real Estate Operating Company (REOC) Public Corporation Publicly Traded Partnership Public Non-Traded REIT
Debt	Mortgages • Secured • Unsecured • Participating Structured Financing	Residential Mortgage Backed Security (RMBS) Commercial Mortgage Backed Security (CMBS) Mortgage REIT Collateralized Lease Obligation (CLO) Collateralized Debt Obligation (CDO)

form of investment. They typically receive between 1 and 20 percent of the real estate allocation. Some institutional investors hold real estate debt. This debt is usually managed by the fixed income or bond group of the institutional investment team. This section focuses on the private equity investment area. Most of the concepts are also applicable to the REIT and debt areas for investment decisions.

The first step in the investment strategy is to make target allocations to the five major property types: office, industrial, retail, apartment, and hotel. Many institutional investors allocate to the four largest property types and leave out hotels, as hotels have the highest volatility and lowest historic return. Agency issues regarding management affect the return and hotels are an operating business, not pure real estate. The usual method for making allocations is to examine the weightings within the benchmark being used as starting point. One strategy is an allocation that mirrors the benchmark. As the most widely used benchmark, the NCREIF Index had approximate weightings of 35 percent office, 14 percent industrial, 22 percent retail, 25 percent apartment, and 4 percent hotel at the end of 2013.

The goal of an active investment manager is to provide a higher return than the benchmark or beat the index through better research, investment, and management practices. Most managers receive a base fee for investing and managing the portfolio plus a performance fee above a certain percentage return or above the benchmark return. Figure 2.3 shows the historic returns and risks of the property types in the NCREIF Index. Based upon the historic returns and risks a manager may decide to overweigh retail and industrial, given that these assets produce the highest returns with the lowest risks. Then the strategy would be to equally weight apartments and underweight office and hotels because they exhibit the lowest returns and highest risks. The problem is that this strategy does not take into account the current fundamentals and prices in the market.

Real estate is a hard, immobile asset trading in a private marketplace. Adding to new supply and creating more competition is much more difficult. Yet, anticipating new

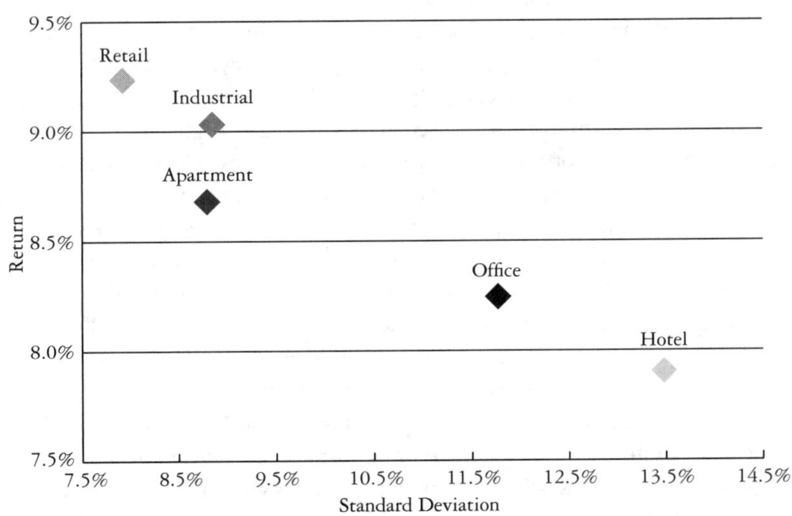

Figure 2.3 NCREIF: Average Risk and Return Rates during 1978–2013. Source: NCREIF.

competition is relatively easy because one can see the projects being built. Increases in both occupancy and rents drive income from real estate. Real estate is also very local in nature. The demand and supply of office space in New York City and Boston differ. So the next step in an institutional investor's process is to select cities to target for investment in each property type. Many such investors prefer to be only in the largest institutional quality markets where they can choose from many large buildings and numerous transactions.

Investors can choose among 363 Metropolitan Statistical Areas (MSAs) in the United States. However, most institutional investors focus on the largest 12 as core markets and the next 20–30 as second-tier markets. Opportunistic investors may also enter third-tier markets. According to research firm Real Capital Analytics (RCA) (2013), the top 10 cities in order of 2011 transaction values are New York, Washington, DC, Los Angeles, San Francisco, Chicago, Boston, Dallas, Houston, Miami, and Atlanta. Most institutional investors buy data and forecasts on market fundamentals to help in this decision-making. The three top data providers are Property & Portfolio Research owned by CoStar, CBRE Global Research, and REIS Reports. These firms all provide data on the five major property types and also have submarket information. These data providers look at fundamental demand using employment growth and supply growth from new construction to estimate occupancy and rent changes.

Figure 2.4 shows the Dividend Capital's Market Cycle Monitor concept of occupancy cycle and rent growth developed by Mueller (1995), a graphic example of how markets move differently. The cycle monitor analyzes occupancy movements in five property types in more than 50 MSAs. Market cycle analysis should enhance investment-decision capabilities for investors and operators. The five property-type cycle charts summarize almost 300 individual models that analyze occupancy levels and rental growth rates to provide the foundation for long-term investment success.

Real estate markets are cyclical due to the lagged relationship between demand and supply for physical space. The long-term occupancy average differs for each market and property type. Long-term average occupancy along with occupancy changes are key factors in determining rental growth rates and real estate returns. Rental growth rates differ at each point in the market cycle. Demand and supply interaction is important to understand. Starting in the recovery phase at the bottom of a cycle at point 1 in Figure 2.4, the marketplace is in a state of oversupply from previous new construction or negative demand growth. At this bottom point, occupancy is at its trough.

Typically, the market bottom occurs when the excess construction from the previous cycle stops. As the cycle bottom is passed, demand growth begins to slowly absorb the existing oversupply and new supply growth is nonexistent or very low. As the marketplace absorbs excess space, vacancy rates fall, allowing rental rates in the market to stabilize and even begin to increase. As this recovery phase continues, positive expectations about the market allow landlords to increase rents at a slow pace, typically at or below the rate of inflation. Eventually, each local market reaches its long-term occupancy average at point 6 whereby rental growth is equal to inflation.

In the expansion phase (points 6 through 11) on Figure 2.4, demand growth continues at increasing rates, creating a need for additional space. When occupancy is above the long-term average, it signals that supply is tightening in the marketplace, and rents begin to rise rapidly. Rents rise until they reach a cost-feasible level that allows new construction to commence at point 8. In this period of tight supply, rapid rental growth

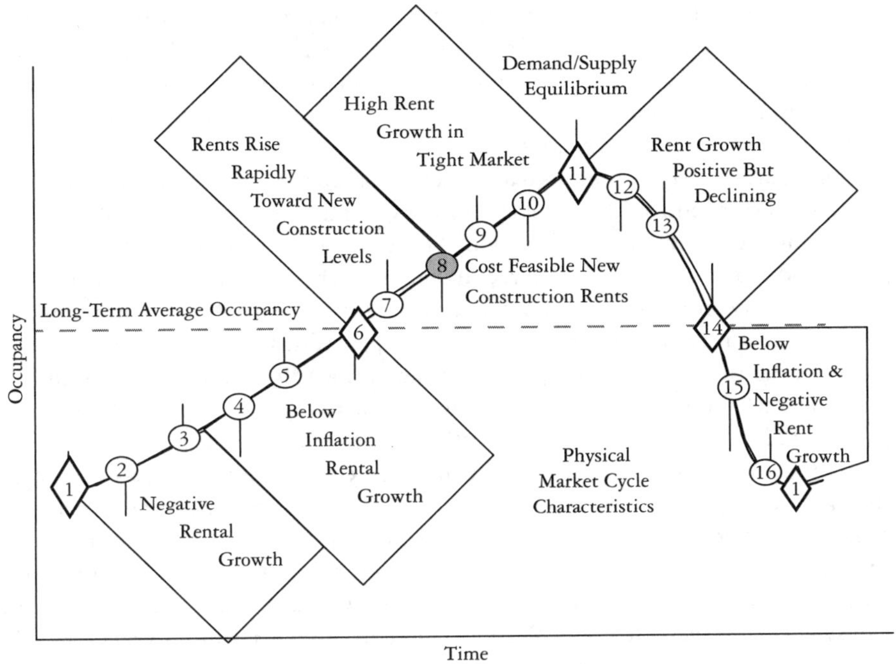

Figure 2.4 The Physical Occupancy Cycle and How Different Points in the Market Cycle Affect Rents.

can be experienced, which some observers call rent spikes. Some developers may begin speculative construction in anticipation of cost-feasible rents if they can obtain financing.

Once the marketplace achieves cost-feasible rents, demand growth is still ahead of supply growth. Supply growth lags in providing new space because of the time to construct. Long expansionary periods are possible. Many historical real estate cycles show that the overall up-cycle proceeds with long periods of rising rents and occupancy rates. As long as demand growth rates are higher than supply growth rates, occupancy rates continue to rise. The cycle peak point 11 is where demand and supply are growing at the same rate or market equilibrium. Before equilibrium, demand grows faster than supply; after equilibrium, supply grows faster than demand. The hypersupply phase of the real estate cycle commences after the peak or equilibrium point 11.

Most real estate participants do not recognize the peak or equilibrium's passing, as occupancy rates are at their highest and well above long-term averages, a strong and tight market. During the hyper supply phase supply growth is higher than demand growth or oversupply, causing occupancy levels to fall back toward the long-term occupancy average. While no painful oversupply occurs during this period, new completions compete for tenants in the marketplace. As more space is delivered to the market, rental growth slows. Eventually, participants realize that the market has turned down and commitments to new construction slow or stop. If new supply grows faster than demand once the long-term occupancy average is passed, the market falls into the recession phase at point 13. The market moves past the long-term occupancy average, with high supply growth and low or negative demand growth. The difference between the market supply growth and demand growth determines the extent of the market down-cycle. Massive oversupply, coupled with negative demand growth, sent most U.S. office markets into the largest down-cycle ever experienced up to that time in the late 1980s.

During the recession landlords realize that they may lose market share if their rental rates are not competitive. They then lower rents to capture tenants, even if only to cover the marginal cost of the lease. The marginal cost of the lease is for variable operating expenses and capital costs involved in recruiting the tenant. The cycle eventually reaches bottom as new construction and completions cease, or as demand growth turns up and begins to grow at a rate higher than that of new supply added to the marketplace.

Figure 2.5 shows a summary graphic of the industrial occupancy levels in the 54 largest markets in the United States for the first quarter of 2013. New Orleans occupancies are low and rental growth is negative. The New Orleans market may not have many attractive investments. On the other hand, three California markets—Los Angeles, San Jose, and San Francisco—along with Indianapolis have high enough occupancy rates to justify new construction. Investments in these markets should have more occupancy and rental growth in the near term, making them much more attractive. Also note that 12 markets are in bold and italics (Atlanta, Chicago, Dallas, Detroit, East Bay, Houston, Los Angeles, Memphis, Northern New Jersey, Philadelphia, Riverside, and St. Louis). Within the industrial property type, these 12 are the largest and therefore considered core institutional markets. These markets include warehouse and flex industrial that most institutional investors target for investment. Memphis is on the list because it serves as the base for FedEx air cargo. These 12 markets make up 50 percent of the square footage in all 54 markets.

A large institutional investor might hold properties in 10 different markets for each of the five property types for a total of 50. Most of these would be in the largest core markets. Once investors target a market, they then need to select acceptable submarkets within the MSA. For instance, one strategy is to focus on downtown central business

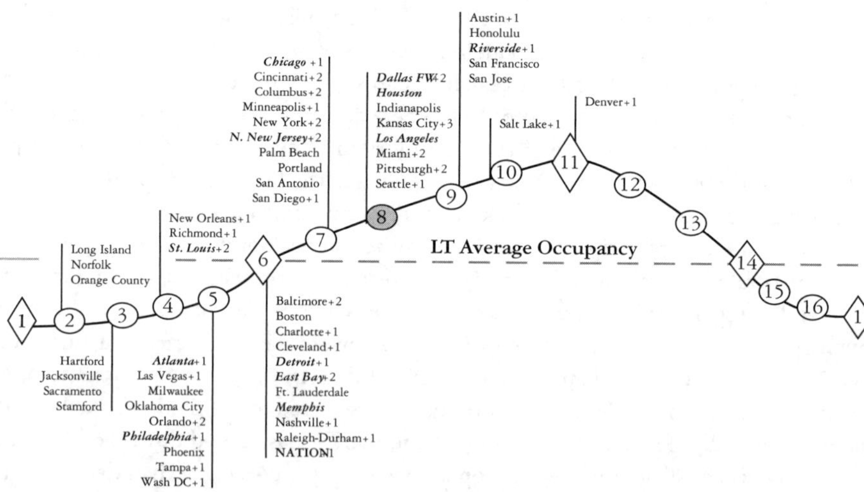

Figure 2.5 Industrial Market Cycle Analysis: 1st Quarter, 2013.

district (CBD) offices only and not suburban markets. The next step is to select the target building type, such as the top quality or class A high rise office only. The last step is to underwrite potential building purchases. Underwriting involves examining the physical building and the tenants, and then estimating potential returns and risks over the projected holding period with a discounted cash flow (DCF) analysis. The process is labor-intensive and requires an experienced team of researchers and acquisition personnel plus portfolio, asset, and property managers.

Pricing

One matter not discussed above is the price to be paid for properties. High-quality core buildings in institutional markets may have a dozen or more bidders on the property. Property prices are normally expressed in terms of capitalization (cap) rates. The *cap rate* is the ratio of net operating income to the price. Real Capital Analytics (RCA), founded in 2000, collects data on every commercial real estate transaction in the United States over $2.5 million. RCA's data also includes the buyer and seller of properties, the price per square foot, and the cap rates for each property. With these data, institutional investors can determine if properties are selling for premiums or discounts to the current market cap rate average.

Figure 2.6 shows that institutional investors were focusing on the top six core markets for their investments during the economic recovery period of 2010–2012. Because institutional investors consider the core markets to be less risky, they focus on these markets during difficult economic times. As the prices in the six largest core markets rose, institutional investors began to expand into the other core markets and then the second-tier markets to achieve higher cap rates on their purchases and expected higher returns.

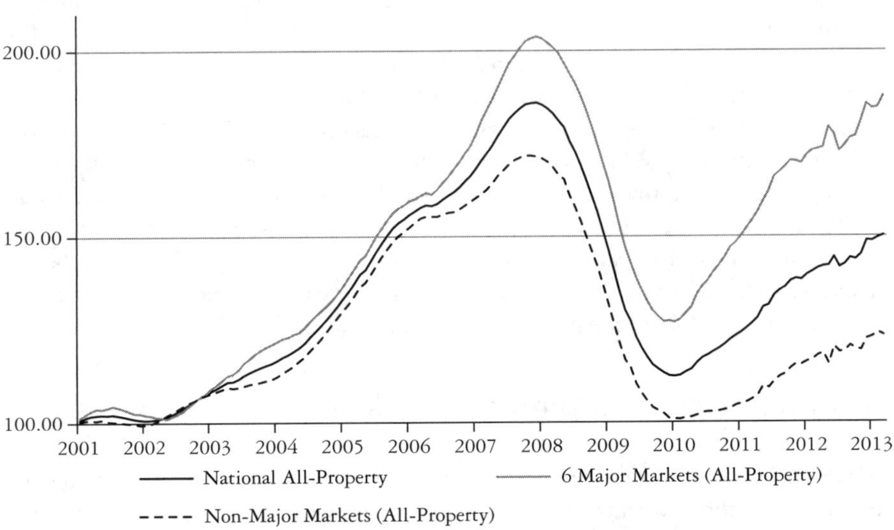

Figure 2.6 Transaction Price Trends in Major and Non-Major Markets. Source: Real Capital Analytics.

Quality Level

The next step in portfolio allocation is to select different risk levels in real estate properties. The main property-type risk categories are core, core plus, value added, and opportunistic. A core property strategy focuses on the five major property types in the 10–20 largest markets and may include some of the 30 secondary markets. Institutional investors usually require positive market conditions and properties with stabilized income and good credit tenant leases. Because these tenants have been in business long enough to have an established credit rating, the risk of not paying rent is low. In some cases, a very good credit tenant agrees to pay operating expenses for property taxes, insurance, and maintenance known as a *triple-net lease*. Some investors specialize in these situations and many are known as triple-net-REITs.

Core properties are managed to have staggered lease rollovers so no future year has large re-leasing risk. No more than 10–15 percent of leases should expire in any given year. Buildings normally use standard management practices and managers and conduct an annual buy-hold-improve-sell analysis on the property. Managers have a strategic plan for tenant retention, rent increases, and capital improvements. Performance on properties is measured with quarterly income and valuation metrics. The property carries little debt. In 2013 the target return for institutional investors on these core properties was in the range of 6–8 percent with no leverage (Institutional Real Estate Investor 2013).

A core plus strategy also focuses on the five major property types in the largest markets but includes leverage on the property with a debt range of 20–50 percent. In 2013 the target return on these core plus properties was in the range of 8–10 percent (Institutional Real Estate Investor 2013). A value added strategy takes on more risks including: repositioning a property, developing excess land, expanding existing buildings, assuming lease-up risks from currently low occupancy levels, re-tenanting space by removing low-quality tenants, and replacing with higher quality credit tenants. Investment strategies include positions in smaller markets and older or lower quality buildings. This strategy usually includes leverage up to 60 percent debt and has a target return range of 10–15 percent annually (Institutional Real Estate Investor 2013).

An opportunistic investment has few constraints on strategies employed. It focuses on achieving property value increases from making improvements and usually means lease-up risk after improvements are finished and targets higher rents. Such an investment may also include new development properties. Many opportunistic strategies use loan-to-value (LTV) ratios of 60 percent or higher and may include complicated financial structures. These opportunistic strategies have a target return range of 18–20 percent or higher (Institutional Real Estate Investor 2013).

Performance Measurement and Manager Compensation

Most institutional investors use outside managers instead of inside personnel to make their real estate investments and operate the properties. Consequently, they want to measure and analyze the returns received from their managers. The different performance measurements include:

- Simple annual rate of return
- Compound annual rate of return
- Time-weighted rate of return
- Internal rate of return
- Risk-adjusted rate of return (Sharpe ratio)
- Inflation-adjusted (real) rate of return
- Return before and after fees
- Return before and after leverage

The annual rate of return received may be the simplest way to measure performance. It would not take into account the cyclical nature of returns that occur in all types of investments. One would not expect a manager to produce a high return in a year when all markets are down. Therefore, institutional investors must have some benchmark against which they can measure their managers' performance. The common benchmarks in the private direct real estate area are the NCREIF Property Index (NPI) in the United States and Investment Property Databank (IPD) in the United Kingdom, Europe, and Asia. In 2010 IPD entered the U.S. market in a joint venture with the Pension Real Estate Association (PREA).

Additionally, a group promulgated by NCREIF and PREA established a set of real estate information standards (REIS) on terminology, performance calculations, and methods for presenting real estate information and performance data. These standards help to provide meaningful comparisons for all investors. Analysts evaluate performance at the property, manager, fund, and portfolio levels. An institutional investor with multiple investment advisors or managers compares them using these standards. Comparing managers with different mandates such as core and opportunistic can be difficult. The appropriate comparison for performance is the benchmark that most closely matches the investment strategy. In some cases, institutional investor consultants build custom benchmarks to match the manager's given strategy to make a meaningful comparison possible. For instance, consider a manager hired to invest in core real estate in four of the five major property types excluding hotels. Using the entire NCREIF index is inappropriate because it includes hotels. Instead, using a custom benchmark that excludes hotels would be appropriate. In many instances, managers' compensation is based on how they perform versus their benchmark.

Institutional investors should do an attribution analysis. Such an analysis determines whether the manager performed well based on portfolio-level allocations by type, city, submarket, property, and management. As an example, a manager could provide only market average returns on each property. This manager outperformed the index by overweighting the two best performing property types of industrial and apartment in 2012. This outperformance could occur even though the owned properties produced market average returns. Another possibility is that the manager held property types in the same proportion as the benchmark index but selected better cities in which to invest or better properties that outperformed their peers. Knowing the reasons for performance can help the institutional investor make better decisions about hiring managers.

Evaluating managers on the public real estate investment (mainly REIT) side is easier. Numerous indexes are available in the United States. The most widely used benchmarks in the public real estate area in the United States include the National

Association of Real Estate Investment Trusts (FTSE/NAREIT) Index, Wilshire REIT Index, Morgan Stanley REIT Index, and Bloomberg REIT index. These indexes focus mainly on equity REITs as mortgage REITs make up less than 10 percent of all public REITs. Some institutional investors include REITs in their real estate allocation while others place REITs in their stock allocation and have it managed there. Internationally, REITs exist in 30 countries including the United Kingdom, France, Japan, and Hong Kong. While not all countries have the REIT structure, they still have publicly traded real estate companies. Thomson Reuters/Global Property Research (GPR) tracks them with a worldwide real estate securities index. For inclusion in the GPR index, a company must have a minimum equity size and stock trading volume, which varies by country.

Most institutional investors ask their investment managers to provide returns and to provide comparisons to the appropriate benchmark. The goal is to beat the selected benchmark and most managers are paid a performance incentive fee when they do. Various structures are available for different types of accounts and these fees are defined in an offering circular or are negotiated when a large separate account is established.

Real estate investment is an expensive process. Key components of the fee structure for managers include commitment, acquisition, asset management, onsite property management, development, and financing fees for procuring debt as well as lease commissions and origination costs. The parties may also negotiate incentive fees that have minimum return hurdle rates for the investor before paying the manager or paying out on a profit-sharing arrangement. These fees can be negotiated on a deal-by-deal or on a programmatic basis where each investment fee is structured the same. In many cases, institutional investors require partial fee reserves or *claw-back* provisions that allow them to receive previous fees paid if future returns are below a targeted minimum. *Catch up* provisions could also be available in which previous underperformance returns are made up from current high performance before the manager receives any incentive compensation. For example, a contract has a 1 percent base management fee for assets under management with a 7 percent investor return hurdle. Once the return hurdle is met, the manager receives 20 percent of any return above the 7 percent minimum hurdle rate.

In the typical fund arrangement, the institutional investor is a limited partner (LP) in the deal, with the manager as the general partner (GP). The maximum loss for a LP is typically the initial capital invested. What most investors want from their contractual arrangements with investment managers can be found by reviewing the Institutional Limited Partner Association (ILPA) policies regarding structuring of limited and general partner relationships. These include investor-friendly terms, stronger investor rights provisions, the right to terminate the GP with or without cause, simple majority voting rights for LP fund investors, and better alignment of interests between the GP and LPs. They also support simplicity of fee structures where the majority of compensation is based on performance. The rules include eliminating or reducing fees not based on performance, especially for larger funds, a more reasonable basis for establishing hurdle rates for performance fee splits, eliminating or reducing investment manager catch up provisions, incentive fees paid on a programmatic versus deal-by-deal basis, and eliminating the need for reserve set asides or claw-back provisions.

Consultants

Institutional investors use general and real estate specific consultants. When institutional investors are looking for new managers, they usually use a consulting firm that compares the focus and historic performance of managers and helps to make manager selections. General investment consultants consider stock, bonds, real estate, and private investments. Their services include: advising staff and board on investment related matters; evaluating total portfolio mix and risk tolerances; conducting asset, liability and asset allocation studies; developing investment policy guidelines; evaluating investment products, structures, and fees; designing and conducting investment manager searches, monitoring investment manager activities and performance; preparing and delivering performance reports, managing funds of funds; and serving as manager of managers.

These consultants help the chief investment officer (CIO) make the decision on how much to allocate to real estate. Some major institutional general consultants in 2012 include Callan Associates, Rogers Casey, William M. Mercer, DeMarche, Ennis Knupp, Cambridge Associates, and Evaluation Associates.

Real estate consultants focus on real estate as a separate asset class. Their services include designing real estate investment policy guidelines; maintaining real estate investment manager databases; evaluating real estate investment products, structures, fees; designing and executing real estate investment manager searches; monitoring performance; operating as independent fiduciaries or acquisition advisors; advising on new market or product opportunities; helping resolve property or product-related problems; recommending changes in investment managers, when warranted; and managing real estate fund of funds and manager of manager products. Some major institutional real estate consultants include Russell R. E. Advisors, Townsend Group, Pension Consulting Alliance (PCA), Opportunity R. E. Group (ORG), Callan Associates, Wilshire Associates, and Courtland Partners.

The manager selection process is both complex and intense. The institutional investor and consultant first establish selection criteria and then identify the universe of potential managers. Next, the consultant issues a request for proposals (RFPs), qualifications, or information. After reviewing submissions, they rank manager responses by their selection criteria. Together the institutional investor and consultant interview potential manager candidates and select finalist manager candidates for due diligence. Typically, they visit the final three candidates onsite to conduct manager due diligence. This is where the due diligence team looks for a good strategic fit, examines management team quality, and reviews execution, reporting, and relationship management capabilities. They want to understand how conflicts might compromise the manager's alignment of interests and to discuss fee structures. This lengthy process culminates in ranking the final candidates. In most cases the institutional investor staff and consultant provide their rankings to the fund's board of directors to make the final selection decision. These requirements have created a large and complex institutional investment industry in the real estate space. Acquiring, owning, financing, and operating real estate has become a large business.

Global Real Estate Investment

Most institutional investors have grown to a size that allows them to consider worldwide commercial real estate investments. This creates a new challenge because they still need local knowledge to make intelligent investments, but it also adds to the complexity and risks of their decisions. A few investment advisors have a global presence including Jones Lang LaSalle and CBRE Global Advisors. These firms provide local market information on many major markets around the world. Having local offices with local market knowledge remains a key to good investment performance.

The largest risk in foreign investments is currency risk. The possibility exists of making a return in a local currency but having a loss if the local currency depreciates against the dollar, for a U.S. investor. In other sectors such as stocks and bonds, hedging currency risk is feasible for periods up to a year. Given that real estate is a long-term and illiquid investment, hedging currency risk is much more difficult and expensive. Hedging the cash flows from a 10-year lease is also difficult and expensive. Some institutional investors may decide to hedge a single year of lease payments if they expect a major risk of currency devaluation. Yet, institutional investors often assume that currency exchange rates average out over the entire investment period. Institutional investors can also hedge some of their principal investment risk by placing a mortgage on the property in the local currency. This strategy reduces the equity investment and allows local currency lease payments to pay the mortgage payment.

Another important risk is political. If the government is unstable or has the potential to confiscate, tax or re-appropriate properties or businesses, this total loss of investment can be a large risk. Emerging markets may change property rights they have given to foreign and local investors. These risks increase the required returns for global investors even when historic returns in these fast-growing markets have been high. Nevertheless, global real estate investments have grown substantially since 2000. These capital flows move both in and out of the U.S. markets. Historic information also shows that global investing might improve risk-adjusted returns.

Summary and Conclusions

Institutional investors have determined that real estate is a separate asset class that deserves its own allocation in their portfolios. As highly sophisticated investors, they require considerable analysis and reporting on their investments. Several factors justify their investment. For example, real estate follows the economic fundamentals of GDP and employment growth. Real estate has stable earnings and value growth potential due to predictable risks and returns and market cycle characteristics. It provides positive cash flow on long-term leases, though less predictably in multi-tenant buildings. Real estate offers diversification and inflation hedging benefits to an overall investment portfolio.

As large investors, institutions have many choices available in both public and private vehicles as well as equity and debt investments. Because the majority of institutional investors do not have enough staff to run their own real estate investments, they employ consultants and investment managers to help them. History shows that active portfolio management can reduce risk. The manager, market, and property selection are critical to developing a disciplined approach to investing. Institutional investors have many benchmarks available to evaluate their investment results, including those that specialized real estate consulting firms use to determine the reasons and attributes for performance. Institutional real estate investing provides career opportunities within the investor, manager, and consultant fields.

Discussion Questions

1. Outline the major steps that institutional investors take in developing a real estate strategy.
2. Explain the major players in the institutional real estate investment process and their functions.
3. Identify the major reasons institutional investors include real estate to their portfolios.
4. List and describe the main property-type risk categories institutional investors might consider in their real estate portfolios.

References

Board of Governors of the Federal Reserve System. 2013. *Flow of Funds*. http://www.frb.gov.
Costar Group Inc. 2010. http://www.costar.com.
Institutional Investor's Sovereign Wealth Center. 2012. http://www.institutionalinvestor.com.
Institutional Real Estate Investor. 2013. The Institutional Real Estate Letter, 2013. http://www.irei.com.
Malpezzi, Stephen. 2006. "Size of the US Commercial Real Estate Market." Working Paper, University of Wisconsin.
Mueller, Glenn R. 1995. "Understanding Real Estate's Physical and Financial Market Cycles." *Real Estate Finance* 12:3, 51–64.
NAREIT. 2013. Index Data Tables. http://www.reit.com.
National Association of Realtors. 2013. "Annual Price Changes Data Table 1968–2012." data@Realtors.org.
NCREIF. 2013. NPI data tables 2013. http://www.ncreif.org.
PREA. 2013. *The PREA Newsletter*. http://www.prea.org.
Real Capital Analytics. 2013. *Commercial Transaction Data*. http://www.rcanalytics.com.

3

Real Estate Cycles: International Episodes

MAN CHO
Professor of Public Policy and Management, The KDI School of Public Policy and Management and Director, The Real Asset Research, Korea Development Institute (KDI), Seoul, Korea

KYUNG-HWAN KIM
President, Korea Research Institute for Human Settlement (KRIHS), Professor of Economics, Sogang University

Introduction

Evidence shows that housing prices are positively serially correlated in the short run, or autocorrelated, but negatively serially correlated in the long run, or mean-reverting (Case and Shiller 1989; Abraham and Hendershott 1996; Chinloy, Cho, and Megbolugbe 1996; Capozza, Hendershott, and Mack 2004; Mian and Sufi 2011; Pavlov and Wachter 2009). While the former implies that the housing market tends to be informationally inefficient, the latter points to the tendency that a sustained deviation from its equilibrium level reverts to a long-term mean. The recent episodes of housing price boom-busts in the United States and Europe, as well as the past similar cases in Japan, Sweden, and other countries, suggest that mean-reverting housing prices are in action. Furthermore, as shown during the global financial crisis (GFC) in 2007–2009, fallouts of large-scale housing price corrections are contagious. The impact goes beyond housing markets by contracting real economic activity and by compromising soundness of financial institutions. The main objective of this chapter is to document the experience with housing price cycles in Korea, China, and the United States and to identify policy implications for emerging market countries.

Evidence also shows that the mortgage credit cycle works as an amplifier of the real estate price cycle (Duca, Muellbauer, and Murphy 2009; Geanokoplos 2010). The ratio of mortgage debt outstanding (MDO) to gross domestic product (GDP) rose substantially in the United States and Europe between 1994 and 2008. The ratio rose from 57 to 98 percent in the United Kingdom, 42 to 94 percent in the United States, 22 to 82 percent in Australia, 22 to 75 percent in Ireland, and 14 to 60 percent in Spain (Lea 2010). In these countries, housing price appreciation was relatively high compared to other Organization for Economic Cooperation and Development (OECD) countries during the boom of 2000–2006 (Crowe, Dell'Ariccia, Igan, and Rabanal 2011). However, both house price and GDP declines were deeper during the bust in 2008–2010.

Besides the volume of lending, the microstructure of the mortgage finance system also plays an important role. To illustrate, the Danish MDO-to-GDP ratio was 90 percent in 2008, a similar level to that of the United States, but experienced a milder default ramp-up during the downturn. That lower default rate came even though the Danish prevailing mortgage products involved a higher interest rate risk to lender-investors. The Danish fixed rate mortgage has embedded two call options to borrowers—one to refinance with the market interest rate in a declining interest rate environment and another to refinance with the original contract rate in a rising rate environment. However the Danish system generally employed more conservative mortgage underwriting criteria (Lea 2010).

Emerging markets often experience high levels of housing price volatility in the course of rapid industrialization and urbanization. Furthermore, the liberalization of mortgage lending amplifies the cycle, generating spillovers to the macro-economy and financial system. This chapter offers a critical survey of two emerging market countries—Korea and China—by using the U.S. experience as a benchmark.

The tri-country analysis shows that different market fundamentals are at work. The typical drivers include demographic shifts, macroeconomics, demand-supply mismatches in local or national housing markets, mortgage credit availability, and regulations. Nonetheless, several policy implications emerge.

First, as the Korean case shows, a fast resolution of chronic housing shortages is an important but challenging public policy task. The two million housing unit construction initiative in Korea from approximately 1989–1993 that resolved the housing shortage in Seoul and other urban areas serves as a milestone event. This strategy may offer useful lessons for other emerging market countries attempting to launch a similar large-scale government-driven construction project. According to the Korean experience, such a large-scale construction initiative involves negative side effects. These include poor building quality, inflated costs of building materials and construction labor, excess capacity in the construction sector, and a lack of diversity in building design. A careful policy design is called for to minimize such effects.

Second, in building a residential mortgage finance system, explicitly defining what a conforming loan constitutes in product types and underwriting criteria is important. These conforming loans can serve as a benchmark in extending mortgage finance to marginal borrowers, and can also work as a stabilizer to reduce leverage-driven real estate volatility if lenders and regulators change the underwriting standards in a counter-cyclical fashion. As a result of financial liberalization after the Asian financial crisis (AFC) in the 1990s, the residential mortgage sector in Korea greatly expanded and became more market-oriented. The dominant mortgage product has a short maturity typically of three years and is non-amortizing with an adjustable rate. The instrument is vulnerable to a market-wide stress event such as a housing price bust or an interest rate hike. A more stable loan product that can serve as a conforming mortgage in Korea and other emerging market countries will have to be longer in maturity (e.g., 10 to 20 years), fixed in contract rate for a reasonable time period (5 to 10 years), amortized in principal repayment, and funded preferably via a whole-sale funding method.

Third, in combating contagious housing cycles implementing the macro-prudential policy tools for DTI and LTV limits, going directly to the source of volatility would be better than imposing more broad-based restrictions. If the source of volatility is speculative borrowers with multiple housing units, the appropriate action is to restrict leverage by loan purpose for residence versus investment or by the number of housing units owned. If the source of volatility is high risk-taking developers, the appropriate action is to increase down payments or to impose other lending restrictions. If the source of volatility is pro-cyclical lenders, the appropriate action is to strengthen loss provisions and capital requirements. Determining whether LTV or DTI is too high—both analytically and operationally—is important for both regulators and investors. Loans in excess of around 60-80 percent loan-to-value is a conventional threshold for determining a high-risk loan. But one should consider volatility of housing prices and other key state variables to determine an appropriate level in a given country.

Fourth, pro-cyclical mortgage lending should be a subject of proper policy response in taming real estate cycles that can inflict contagion. Mortgage volume tends to increase, and non-price terms in underwriting such as LTV and DTI to be relaxed, during housing price booms because the rising asset prices reduce perceived default risk. The lending raises the share of optimistic buyers and will bid up asset value, creating an endogenous interaction between housing prices and mortgage lending (Geanakoplos 2010; Herring and Wachter 1999). Instituting counter-cyclical regulatory measures, either through a capital charge or DTI-LTV regulations, warrants consideration. In so doing, timing of policy action and specific policy instruments to combat the contagion cycle represents further research issues.

Finally, balancing macroeconomic stability with financial inclusion should be a policy priority. Ensuring macroeconomic stability via micro or macro-prudential regulations and expanding financial inclusion to marginal borrowers are two competing policy objectives to consider. Defining and expanding a conforming loan is one way to achieve these dual policy objectives. In imposing DTI and LTV limits, proper levels in a given country should also be determined by weighing both policy objectives. Differentiating by the number of residential properties owned is one method. Accurate, credible, and transparent market data including loan issuance, transaction prices, price indexes, and loan performance are a must to further empirical research and fact-based policy decision-making.

Theoretical Underpinning

The asset price of housing, at a given location and given time period, H_t, consists of its fundamental value (F_t) and a shock or a bubble (B_t):

$$H_t = F_t + B_t \tag{3.1}$$

When the shock is positive ($B_t > 0$), the housing asset is overvalued, and vice versa. Some view its persistence as the main cause of cyclical housing price movement, following an autocorrelated process:

$$B_t = \delta \cdot B_{t-1} + \varepsilon_t \tag{3.2}$$

where δ and ε represent a regression coefficient and white noise.

A rational investor is willing to buy with positive B so long as there is an expectation of over-valuation growing at a rate at least equal to the time value of money. Here $E_t[B_{t+1}] = \hat{\delta} B_t \geq (1+i_t)B_t$, where i is the appropriate discount rate in a rational bubble. This interpretation of the bubble-building process has a long history in mainstream economics (Samuelson 1958; Tirole 1985). Englund and Ioannides (1997), Malpezzi (1999), and Ortalo-Magné and Rady (2001) empirically test this idea in the housing market. Two general points are worth mentioning on a rational bubble. First, it is a Ponzi scheme in which the first period participants receive a windfall gain from subsequent buyers. That return is never promised but only expected by the first period participants. Second, excessive credit works as another bubble-builder because it can reinforce expectations about the return to holding an asset.

The fundamental value represents the discounted present value of expected rental income, R, in all future time periods:

$$H_t^* = \sum_{t=1}^{\infty} \frac{E[R_t]}{\prod_{j=1}^{t}(1+i_j)}. \tag{3.3}$$

Under the assumptions of a constant rent, R, a non-time varying discount rate, i, and permanent asset holding, Equation 3.3 becomes the perpetuity $H_t^* = R/i$ or $H_t^* = NOI/c$ where c is the capitalization (cap) rate. However, when the rent is expected to grow at a constant per-period growth rate, g, this equation is the Gordon growth model (GGM):

$$H_t^* = {R_t} \big/ (\bar{i} - g^e) \tag{3.4}$$

where g^e represents the expected constant rental growth rate at time t and R_t is the observed rent at time t.

The expected rental growth rate, g^e, can be construed as a depository of all demand- and supply-side housing market fundamentals or their expected trends at time t. Realized and expected changes in demographic characteristics such as aging, baby boomers retirement and fertility, macroeconomic conditions, demand-supply mismatch either nationally or locally, credit supply, and government regulations impact g^e, which changes H_t^*.

Several specific factors affect this housing price and mortgage lending linkage. First, changes in common macroeconomic factors such as declining market interest rates or rising real GDP growth rates influence housing price and mortgage credit cycles. This common economic channel can be empirically tested in two ways. One is by directly including them in a testing model. The other is by employing a Consumer Credit Index (CCI) as an indirect measure of their influence. As termed by Fernandez-Corugedo and Muellbauer (2006), CCI is a proxy of the credit supply function faced by borrowers.

Second, the availability of mortgage credit will reduce constraints faced by marginal borrowers, increasing housing demand and its price. This linkage or tenure choice channel assesses lending constraints on LTV and DTI faced by first-time home buyers or other marginal borrowers. Relaxing lending constraints can happen alongside rising mortgage volume or be independent of it.

Third, as Geanakoplos (2010) and Herring and Wachter (1999) contend, mortgage lending volume and borrowing constraints measured by LTV and DTI react to changes in housing prices. This will change the bidding price for housing by the marginal borrower. Being referred to as the marginal investor channel, this linkage has some assumptions. Lenders pro-cyclically change lending constraints by raising lending volume and relaxing borrowing constraints during ebullient times. The rising asset prices reduce perceived default risk. This lending increases the share of natural or optimistic buyers and bids up asset value. Endogenous effects occur between housing price and mortgage credit cycles. Expanding mortgage credit availability influences not only asset values but also the cost of capital for owning. The leverage-driven optimism elevates expected future rental cash flow, $E_t[g]$ during a booming period, which raises the equilibrium asset price in Equation 3.4. The issue is how to measure expected rental growth g^e. Campbell, Davis, Gallin, and Martin (2009) offer an empirical model. Here g^e is a residual between the realized rent-price ratio R/P and the predicted return i. The predicted return is the sum of the risk-free interest rate and expected housing premium.

On the supply side, the mortgage lender will determine two equilibrium lending conditions for each borrower. These are the lending interest rate and LTV. Fostel and Geanakoplos (2008) and Geanakoplos (2010) describe how the interaction between pro-cyclical lending by financial institutions and heterogeneous borrowers can result in a leverage cycle. In ebullient times, lenders relax credit constraints by increasing the equilibrium leverage rate, which increases the share of natural or optimistic buyers. This rise of optimistic buyers, who are more risk-tolerant, bids up asset prices. When the market has more optimistic buyers, marginal buyers exhibit a greater willingness to pay for the asset. In a downturn, the opposite occurs. Facing bad news from the market place, lenders lower the equilibrium leverage, which reduces both the share of optimistic buyers and collateral value.

MEASUREMENT ISSUES

Several modeling issues arise in fitting a dynamic area-wide housing price equation. Mean reversion may be caused by model specification error rather than by speculative forces. An example of a specification problem is omitting hard-to-capture supply-side constraints such as zoning and other land use regulations. Exceptions include Glaeser, Gyourko, and Saks (2005a, 2005b, 2006), Glaeser and Gyourko (2005), Glaeser, Gyourko, and Saiz (2008), and Glaeser and Ward (2009). Measuring time- and location-varying regulatory restrictiveness is highly difficult and time-consuming. Nonetheless, this is a key driver of housing price dynamics, and its omission will lead to a classic case of bias caused by excluding a relevant variable.

Most housing price equations are reduced forms that include various demand and supply market fundamentals. Nonetheless, several sources of simultaneity bias exist between housing price dynamics and mortgage finance variables (Pavlov and Wachter 2004, 2009), and between price changes and macroeconomic variables (Leamer 2006; Case and Quigley 2008). The user cost is the conventional measure to capture conditions of mortgage market. However, the volume of lending and mortgage product types also influences housing price dynamics. Subprime mortgage lending boosted the explosive housing price appreciation in the United States between 2003 and 2006.

Another source of bias in projecting future home prices includes time-varying volatility, which requires fitting a generalized autoregressive conditional heteroskedasticity (GARCH) model (Chinloy, Cho, and Megbolugbe 1997; Crawford and Fratatoni 2003). Other biases relate to index construction and geographical and intertemporal aggregation (Calhoun, Chinloy, and Megbolugbe 1995). The appraisal outcome in the residential mortgage lending is biased upwards, which can result in an under-prediction of credit risks borne by mortgage applications (Cho and Megbolugbe 1996; Chinloy et al. 1997; Leventis 2006).

Econometric testing of an asset price bubble involves testing statistical significance of *B* in Equation 3.1 assuming a correct specification of prices based on an appropriate set of market fundamentals. Gurkaynak (2008 surveys various empirical methods for testing the bubble primarily focusing on the equity market. Researchers typically assume that the bubble term, *B* is independent of market fundamentals *F*. Froot and Obstfeld (1991) and Driffill and Sola (1998) relax this assumption. They test the intrinsic bubble that is correlated with market fundamentals. Overall, this strand of empirical studies does not generally offer a definitive answer as to the existence of bubbles because testing represents a joint test of a misspecified market fundamental *F* and bubble *B*.

In the housing market context, Glaeser and Gyourko (2005), Glaeser et al. (2008), and Davidoff (2013) show asymmetric supply elasticity between upturns and downturns. Glaeser et al. (2008) examine the nature of housing price bubbles, instead of testing for their existence. Rational bubbles exist when the supply of housing is fixed but not when it is elastic and when a finite number of homebuyers exist. Under the assumption of adaptive expectations by households, more inelastic places have bigger and longer bubbles.

International Episode: The United States

Figure 3.1 shows real annual home price growth rates in the United States between 1890 and 2011. Various price cycles appear over this 120-year period. The first price cycle occurred at the end of the nineteenth century, showing a housing price boom-bust combined with the ramping up of the unemployment rate from 4 percent in 1891 to 12 percent in 1897. Between then and the early 1970s, a number of upturns and downturns occurred. Around the Great Depression, cyclical price movements coincided with the macroeconomic shock.

After the 1970s, three more pronounced price cycles occurred. During the first two cycles (1975–1983 and 1983–1993), the principle of what goes up comes down seems to apply. In real terms, total price growth during the boom is followed by a similar decline in the downturn. In the last cycle (1997–2011), the cumulative real growth rate of

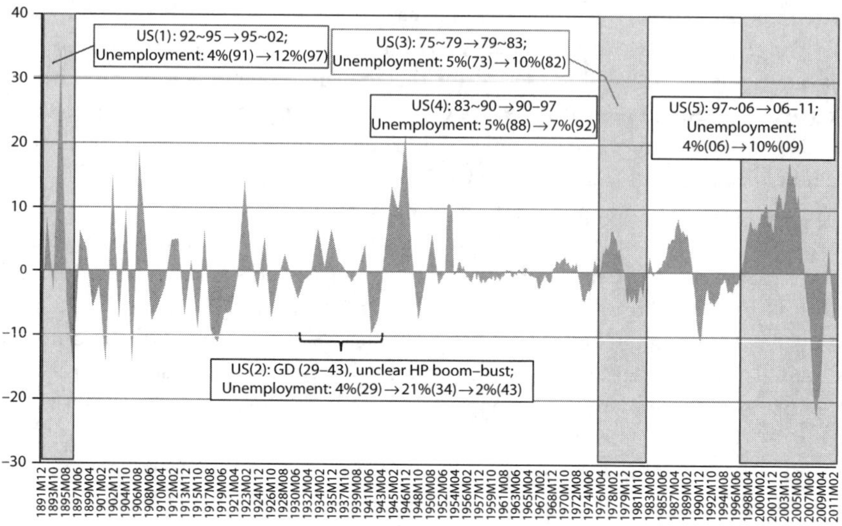

Figure 3.1 Real Home Price Growth Rates in the United States, 1890–2011. Source: Cho and Song (2011).

prices is 87 percent, amounting to several times that from the earlier booms. This boom is followed by a deep downturn of 34 percent price decline up to 2011. Overall, the price cycle in the United States has become amplified over time.

In the context of the credit cycle, the fact that price growth accelerates more from 2003 is worth noting. The price boom from 2003 and the precipitous bust from 2006 coincide with the private label MBS issuance pattern in Figure 3.2. Mortgage origination started picking up rapidly after 2001, followed by a sharp reduction in 2004. Origination volume rose after 2004. Figure 3.2 shows co-movement with the rise and fall of private label issuance. The dramatic rise and fall of private label issues seemingly reflects the highly favorable and unique interest rate environment between 2003 and 2005.

As Gorton (2008) discusses, other non-price terms in mortgage underwriting continuously weakened in the early to mid-2000s. This is evidenced by incrementally high delinquency rates from more recent origination-year loan cohorts. Geographical areas with high subprime and Alt-Loan originations during the boom experience higher frequency defaults and distressed sales of foreclosed homes (Mian and Sufi 2009).

Evidence shows similar episodes of large and contagious housing price cycles in other countries in different time periods. The price boom in the United States during 1997–2006 surpasses the prior two cycles both in terms of the average annual growth rate and the duration. Nonetheless, it is not an outlier when compared with other international cases. The two price booms during similar time spans—Ireland in 1995–2007 and Great Britain in 1998–2008—show higher average growth rates and longer durations. Some of these price booms interacted with a surge in residential mortgage lending.

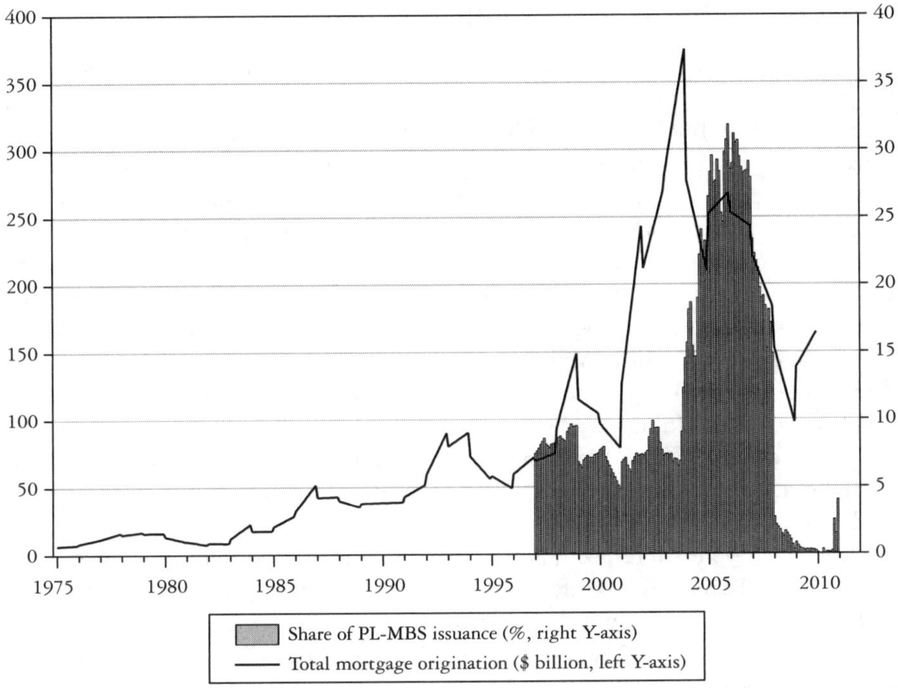

Figure 3.2 U.S. Residential Mortgage Origination and Private-Label MBS Issuance.
Source: Cho and Song (2011).

LINKAGES OF HOUSING PRICE AND MORTGAGE LENDING

Cho and Song (2011) test causal relationships between housing price dynamics and mortgage lending indicators in the United States. Housing price and mortgage credit cycles exhibit a statistically significant and explainable co-movement pattern in the recent period (1997–2010), but not in prior cycles. A regime shift is observed in the causal relationship between recent housing price movements and the mortgage credit cycle. Indicators to reflect behavior of three key cycle generators—exuberant borrowers, pro-cyclical lenders, and yield curve playing investors—appear to be useful in assessing cyclical price and lending patterns.

Cho and Song (2011) conduct pair-wise Granger causality tests among six variables separately for the United States for 1980–1997 and 1997–2010 to check for a regime shift. These variables are: (1) real annual home price growth rate residual of a fitted rent-to-price ratio, (2) annual growth rate of residential mortgage origination, (3) average LTV (Duca et al. 2009), (4) share of private label mortgage backed security issuance, (5) 10-year versus one-year constant maturity yield spread, and (6) real GDP growth rate. The mortgage lending variables Granger-caused home price growth in 1997–2010, but not in the prior two cycles; and so did the interest rate spread in 1980–1997 but not in the later period. A regime shift occurs between the two periods in terms of causal relationships among the included variables, and an endogenous linkage between the price cycle and mortgage market variables. A vector autoregressive analysis confirms the findings from the causality tests.

PRO-CYCLICAL MORTGAGE LENDING

Pro-cyclical mortgage lending to home buyers, which is often termed as *endogenous leverage*, works as a cycle amplifier (Fostel and Geanakoplos 2008; Geanakoplos 2010; Haughwout, Lee, Tracy, and van der Klaauw 2011). An argument favoring the leverage-driven asset price cycle hinges on heterogeneous borrowers. Borrowers differ in their degree of optimism about future rent growth, g^e, in Equation 3.4. Credit market conditions influence consumer psychology in upturns and downturns. Price volatility increases depending on conditions in the consumer credit market. Mortgage lenders relax underwriting constraints in ebullient times to increase LTV. These actions raise the share of optimistic buyers. The higher LTV and lower DTI ratios increase the bidding price of housing by the marginal buyer. In the face of bad news during a downturn, the asset price starts declining. Lenders lower the equilibrium leverage ratio, which reduces the share of optimistic buyers as well as the collateral value.

The experience of the U.S. subprime mortgage sector between 2003 and 2006 demonstrates that the interest rate environment played a critical role in funneling liquidity to the residential mortgage lending sector. This particular period was unprecedented in recent history in two respects, notably between August 2002 and September 2004. First, the real Federal Funds rate was negative. Second, the spread between the long and short rate, measured by the 10-year Treasury note less the one-year Treasury bill, continuously exceeded 200 basis points. These two phenomena had not occurred in any two-year period since 1950.

The situation offered a fertile ground for yield curve playing on the part of mortgage-backed security investors. Investors with access to the money market issue short-term securities including asset-backed commercial paper. They obtain a windfall gain by investing in the long-term bonds such as residential MBS. That favorable environment abruptly ended when the Federal Reserve rapidly increased the short rate beginning in 2005. The situation generated an inverted or negatively sloped yield curve starting in July 2006.

The average LTV among first-time home buyers in the United States sharply increased from 87 percent in the early 2000s to almost 95 percent in 2005, dramatically reducing the down-payment requirement. The average LTV rapidly reverted to its 1980s level after the housing price decline in 2006. Duca et al. (2009) empirically show that the increase in LTV reduces the user cost of housing. The user cost is the difference between the mortgage rate and expected capital gain, and in equilibrium equals the rent-price ratio. The higher LTV raised asset prices and capital gains, lowering the user cost and rent-price ratio. The LTV closely tracks the rise and fall of private-label MBS, which represents a unique mortgage market phenomenon in the 2000s.

By using micro data, Haughwout et al. (2011) document the surge of investor-borrowers in the U.S. mortgage market during the latest housing price boom. Multi-unit owning investors default more frequently than single-unit homeowners during a downturn. These investors are more optimistic or intend to buy and flip. During the boom, weakened underwriting conditions enabled the flippers' investment behavior in terms of not only increasing LTV but also lowering DTI. Other favorable non-price terms in mortgage underwriting include lower credit scores and reduced documentation requirements.

Other factors including the uncertainty caused by product complexity help to explain the cyclical behavior of subprime mortgage-backed security investors. Private-label MBS issuers packaged the subprime mortgage loans into subprime asset-backed securities (ABS). They re-securitized the ABS tranches into subprime ABS collateralized debt obligations (CDOs). Issuers pooled the tranches of the subprime ABS CDOs into subprime ABS CDO². These complex re-securitized subprime MBS products became the sources of the liquidity spiral after Lehman's bankruptcy (Ashcraft and Schaumann 2008; Brunnermeier 2009; Fender and Mitchell 2009). Pro-cyclical bond ratings by rating agencies exacerbated the downturn beginning in the second half of 2007 (Benmelech and Dlugosz 2009; Griffin and Tang 2010).

International Episode: Korea

Figure 3.3 shows that since the onset of the economic boom in the 1960s, land and housing prices in Korea exhibit pronounced cycles. In terms of correlation with the growth of the macro economy, housing prices in Korea are highly correlated in downturns, but not in other periods. A negative real GDP growth rate occurred during the Asian and global financial crises in 1997–1998 and 2007–2009, respectively. The series show close co-movements, but the correlation gets weaker during other periods. One milestone event in Korea was the drive to build two million housing units between 1989 and 1992. In response to rampant housing price growth in major cities, the Korean government initiated a massive supply response. About 30 percent of the housing stock was constructed within a four-year time span. After the positive supply shock, housing prices increased at below the rate of inflation between 1991 and 1996.

Another milestone event was the expansion of mortgage lending after the AFC. Mortgage debt outstanding (MDO) as a share of GDP grew from 10 percent before

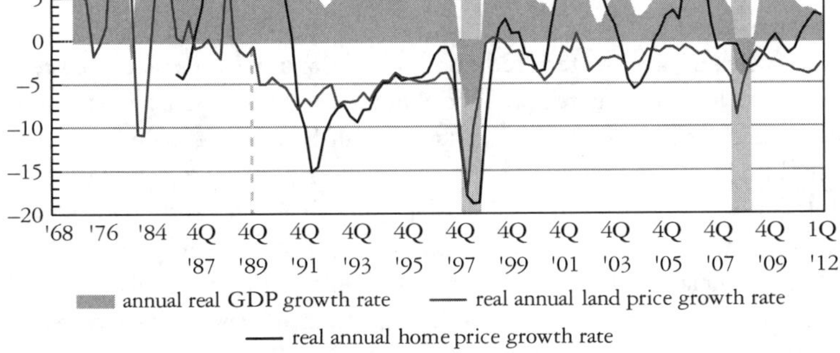

Figure 3.3 GDP and Real Estate Cycles in Korea, 1968–2012. Source: Cho (2012).

the AFC to more than 30 percent by 2010. This ratio is similar to Japan at 37 percent and France at 41 percent. Being propelled by the post-AFC recovery and the growth of credit supply, house prices show twin peaks in 2001–2003 and 2005–2006.

A bigger cycle occurs in construction. With the surge of construction financing from the mid-2000s, the quantity of new housing supply exhibited a boom-bust before and after the GFC. This resulted in a large number of unsold new housing units as an overhang in the post-GFC period. After the GFC, the cross-sectional dispersion in housing price dynamics became more marked. Price dispersion exists across locations, such as between the country's capital city and other regions. Price increases vary across submarkets and by unit size.

EXPANSION OF THE MORTGAGE MARKET

Before the AFC, the Korean housing finance system was underdeveloped. Access to mortgage credit was limited to selected groups of target households. The government set lending rates at a subsidized, below-market level. After the AFC, two deregulations were catalysts in expanding mortgage finance.

First, the government previously directly regulated lending and deposit rates charged by financial institutions. Realizing that the regulation was an obstacle to creating competitive and efficient financial markets, the Korean government announced a four-phase interest rate liberalization plan in 1991. The deregulation started from short-term lending rates and long-term (three plus years) deposit rates. The final stage initiated in July 1997 was completed in February 2004. The government liberalized all lending and deposit rates including demand deposits and short-term savings accounts.

Under the interest rate regulation, lending institutions had no incentive to issue high-risk loans. Furthermore, wholesale funding from the capital market was infeasible because of the negative interest rate spread in the mortgage intermediation process. The controlled lending rates were lower than market-based funding costs. A discussion started during the 1980s about establishing a mortgage securitization system, but it was not possible until the interest rate liberalization. Due to the phased deregulation and to the overhaul of the financial system after the AFC, KoMoCo, the first mortgage-backed security issuer was created in 1999. That was later merged with the Korea Housing Finance Corporation (KHFC) in 2003, a wholly government-owned MBS issuer. By 2012 KHFC was the sole issuer of MBS sold domestically, although some private MBS issuers such as the Korean affiliate of Standard Chartered Bank sold the securities in the international markets.

Second, as a part of the directed credit policy, the Bank of Korea restricted real estate lending by private lenders. The regulators did not allow banks to make loans to finance land or to purchase and construct houses larger than 100 square meters of floor space. Government lifted the regulation in February 1998 during the AFC. That deregulation, plus the interest rate liberalization, induced private financial institutions in Korea to enter mortgage lending. The institutions include large commercial banks and non-bank deposit-taking financial institutions. Commercial banks with a national branch network quickly dominated the residential mortgage market, with a 70 percent share in mortgage debt outstanding by the end of 2008. The two public sector institutions—the National Housing Fund as a lender of affordable mortgage loans and KHFC as a securitizer of

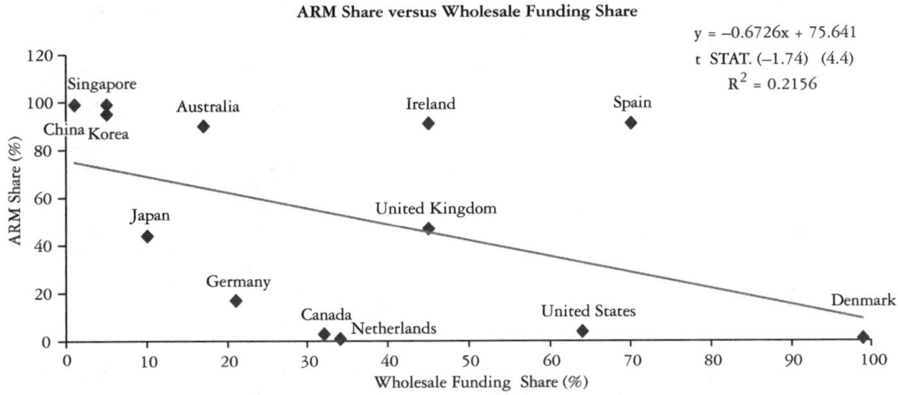

Figure 3.4 International Shares of Adjustable Rate Mortgages and Wholesale Funding.
Source: Cho, Kim, and Renaud (2012).

long-term fixed-rate mortgages—had less than a 5 percent market share. The remainder is private lenders including insurance companies and cooperative financial institutions.

Korea represents a typical adjustable rate mortgage (ARM) market. As an additional risk factor, the majority of ARMs in Korea have less than a three-year maturity with non-amortizing principal. ARMs represent more than 90 percent of outstanding mortgage contracts. Korea has the highest ARM share among OECD countries. As Figure 3.4 shows, the ARM share declines and the share of fixed rate mortgages increase as wholesale funding rises. Wholesale funding comes from MBS or mortgage-backed bonds. Wholesale funding rises with per capita income. Similar to the problems with ARMs in the U.S. subprime mortgage market, short-maturity bullet mortgage loans in Korea incur severe payment shock and rollover risk. The risk increases when housing and mortgage markets head to a downturn (Gorton 2009).

One similarity between the two countries is that the securities backed by real estate loans have a majority share. In the United States, commercial and residential MBS outstanding account for 74 percent of GDP at the end of 2008. Securitized construction loans and residential MBS have a 72 percent share in Korea at the end of 2007. The main difference is that the maturity of securities is much shorter duration in Korea than in the United States. The securitization of residential mortgages has not helped expand the long-term bond market in Korea due to the short-term securities issued.

FUNDAMENTALS AND EXTENT OF OVER-VALUATION

In order to identify key market fundamentals and to gauge the extent of over- or under-valuation of housing prices in Korea, Cho (2009) estimates a two-stage error correction model using city-level data from Korea and the United States. Market fundamentals include the user cost of capital for owning, real GDP growth rate, and construction volume. The user cost becomes significant and has a much larger impact for 2000–2007. A one percentage point decrease in the user cost increases house prices by 6.68 percent. This evidence indicates a regime shift in the Korean housing market after the AFC. A large and market-oriented mortgage lending sector is a possible reason. City-level variables are either not statistically significant or do not have the expected signs.

Table 3.1 **Second-Stage Results, Serial Correlation, and Mean Reversion in the United States**

	α	β	R^2	*Convergence*	*Oscillation*
Boston	0.7858	0.0161	0.6763	Yes	Yes
Charlotte	0.1786	0.0049	0.0448	Yes	No
Cleveland	0.5098	−0.0220	0.2577	Yes	No
Denver	0.7800	0.0199	0.6162	Yes	Yes
Los Angeles	0.9495	0.0170	0.8248	Yes	Yes
Miami	0.9503	0.0166	0.7503	Yes	Yes
New York	0.8444	0.0161	0.7842	Yes	Yes
Portland	0.6044	0.0066	0.3447	Yes	No
San Diego	0.9290	0.0166	0.7762	Yes	Yes
San Francisco	0.7870	0.0181	0.5798	Yes	Yes
Tampa	0.8502	0.0166	0.6960	Yes	Yes
Las Vegas	0.7862	0.0200	0.5550	Yes	Yes

"Convergent" if $\alpha < 1$; "Explosive" otherwise.
"Oscillate" if $(1 + \alpha - \beta)^2 < 4\alpha$, otherwise non-oscillating.

Table 3.2 **Second-Stage Results, Serial Correlation, and Mean Reversion in Korea**

	α	β	R^2	*Convergence*	*Oscillation*
Busan	0.9530	0.0409	0.8148	Yes	Yes
Daegu	0.9925	0.2536	0.7654	Yes	Yes
Daejeon	0.9964	0.2463	0.8452	Yes	Yes
Gangbuk, Seoul	0.8983	0.0421	0.7349	Yes	Yes
Gangnam, Seoul	0.9367	0.1864	0.6822	Yes	Yes
Gwangju	0.9195	0.1090	0.8081	Yes	Yes
Incheon	1.0979	0.4036	0.8770	No	Yes

"Convergent" if $\alpha < 1$; "Explosive" otherwise.
"Oscillate" if $(1 + \alpha - \beta)^2 < 4\alpha$, otherwise non-oscillating.

Two adjustment parameters α for autocorrelation and β for mean reversion are estimated for cities in both countries. Wide ranges of α occur in the United States from 0.17 for Charlotte to 0.95 in Los Angeles and Miami. More serial correlation exists in coastal cities including Los Angeles, San Diego, San Francisco, and Boston. The serial correlation α for Korean cities is higher than for the United States, and tightly distributed, ranging from 0.89 for Gangbuk to 1.09 for Incheon. The U.S. cities exhibit low β

estimates for mean reversion, with a 1–2 percent range. Those in Korea are much higher and widely dispersed, between 4 and 40 percent. This outcome may reflect the Korean government's aggressive policy actions for the last 30 years to stabilize home prices.

As an indicator of how a mortgage lending sector serves the housing market, Cho, Min, and Kim (2012) estimate a CCI similar to those for European countries (Fernandez-Corugedo and Muellbauer 2006; Goodhart and Hofmann 2007; Jansen and Krogh 2011). CCI closely tracks residential mortgage lending in Korea. The one-period lagged index of consumer credit has a positive and significant effect on home price changes but not the other way around. The flow of impact is from mortgage credit availability to housing prices. The index reduces the user cost. The marginal investor channel in terms of transmission of mortgage credit availability appears to be at work in Korea.

International Episode: China

The housing prices in China have risen sharply since 2009 (Figure 3.5). Regarding market fundamentals in Chinese housing markets, Cho (2012) identifies four major factors driving price dynamics. First, the high sustained economic growth since the 1970s combined with the rapid pace of urbanization are the key demand-side pull factors. Given the favorable environment for international trade, GDP growth in China was explosive from 2003 to 2008, averaging 17 percent nominally a year. The growth rate dropped to a 5 percent annual range in early 2009, but quickly recovered since the second half of 2009 to an annual rate of 15 percent. The urban population, which is 25 percent of the total in 1975, has been steadily growing to more than 50 percent as of 2013. By 2025, the share of the population that is urban is expected to grow to 64 percent, from 570 million to 930 million (McKinsey Global Institute 2009).

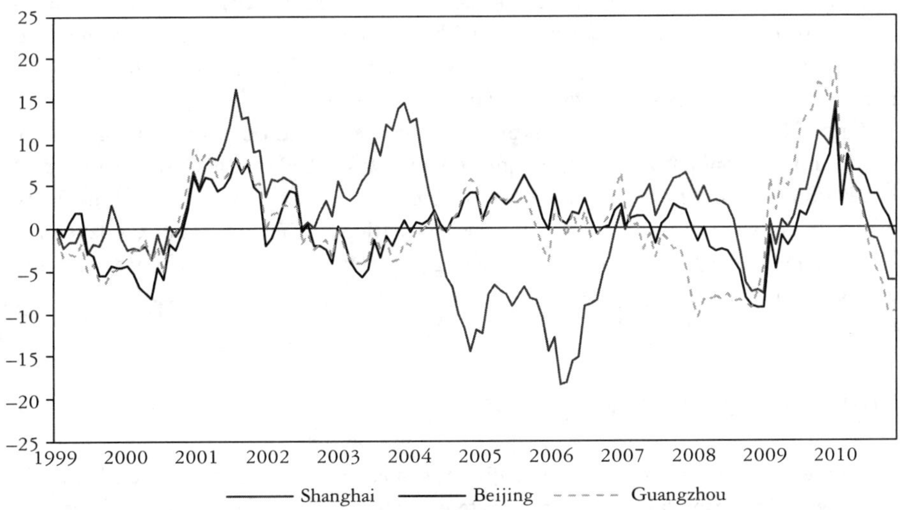

Figure 3.5 Real Housing Price Growth Rates in Major Chinese Cities (Percent, Annual).
Source: National Bureau of Statistics of China (2013).

Second, residential mortgage lending in China expanded rapidly since the late 1990s. Mortgage originations in China, which were 19 billion yuan in 1997, increased to 7.2 trillion yuan by the end of 2011. The ratio of mortgages to GDP in China was 15 percent in 2011. Four major commercial banks have more than 90 percent of mortgage originations. As in Korea, typical loans are ARMs with a maximum LTV of 80 percent, a maximum DTI of 70 percent, up to 30-years maturity, and principal amortization being required for loans with more than a one-year term. As in Korea, new housing units are sold via presale; at which point the mortgage loans are issued to the ultimate owner (Deng and Liu 2009).

Third, as a result of low and declining interest rates and the rapid increase in mortgage credit, the user cost of capital in major cities declined. This effect works as a demand push in recent years. Wu, Gyourko, and Deng (2010) estimate price-monthly rent ratios in seven large cities in China as 26 in 2007, which rises to 46 in 2010. The inverse rent-to-price ratio, or user cost is only 2.2 percent.

Fourth, Wu et al. (2010) find that land prices rise very rapidly. A constant quality land price index for seven Chinese cities increases by eightfold between 2003 and 2010. The shares of land cost in new housing units have substantially increased. As a related supply-side indicator, the value of housing construction to GDP increased from 1.0 percent in 1998 to 5.8 percent in 2010.

RESULTS OF ERROR CORRECTION ESTIMATION

Cho (2012) estimates panel regression models for the five regions in China based on publicly available housing price indexes. Real GDP is a highly significant positive determinant of housing prices. The mortgage-GDP ratio is also a significant positive explanatory factor in all five regions. Among city-specific variables, rent-to-price ratios are an important negative determinant of housing price levels. While the macro and financial variables are more significant in the two East coast regions, land price indexes influence housing prices in the Mid-Western region. The user cost becomes statistically more significant in the latter period, possibly as consumers become more reactive to changes in home ownership costs such as financing or real estate taxes.

Cho (2012) measures the extent of under- or over-valuation in housing prices. The maximum over-valuation among major cities between 1998 and 2010 is 10 percent. Market fundamentals explain large portions of housing price variations in China. However, Liu, Lejot, and Arner (2013), who use alternative housing price indexes developed by Tsinghua University, report that three large cities in the Eastern seaboard—Beijing, Shanghai, and Shenzhen—show significant levels of over-valuation.

Summary and Conclusions

The three-country housing price dynamics indicates that different market fundamentals are at work in these countries during different periods. Therefore, monitoring market fundamentals is important to detect and respond to a contagious housing cycle that can have spillover to the macro-economy and financial markets.

In the context of emerging markets, a fast resolution of a chronic housing shortage is an important but challenging public policy task. That is the case of the two million-unit housing construction initiative in Korea from 1989 to 1992. Although this expansion helped stabilize the Korean housing market in the 1990s, it created some negative side effects. Hence, a careful policy design is needed to minimize such side effects. As a related issue, developing an active and affordable rental housing sector for low-income and middle-income households should be a high-priority policy concern. In terms of designing a mortgage finance system, developing a conforming or prime mortgage lending sector with conservative underwriting parameters, sound products, and efficient funding arrangements is important. The mortgage insurance industry and other risk-sharing arrangements can be a part of this conforming loan sector. In terms of macro-prudential regulation in mortgage lending, balancing macroeconomic stability with financial inclusion of marginal borrowers is another important issue that policy designers should consider.

Much advancement has occurred in providing more dynamic housing price indexes, including repeat sales indexes and index-generating methodologies along with various time-series econometric models for testing asset price dynamics. Nonetheless, several specific research areas merit investigation, such as modeling the interaction between house prices and new construction cycles and endogenous relationships between the housing market and macro-economic variables. Other areas include expected or forward-looking home price distributions and co-movement and contagion of housing price dynamics. Building accurate, credible, and transparent market data on new loan issuance, transaction prices, price indexes, and loan performance is critical to advance quality research and to make sound policy decisions.

Further, a framework for sound banking supervision is also needed. Besides the lending institution's portfolio-level risk indicator or Basel-type capital requirement, researchers should consider special assessment on particular loans with high risk. Gramlich (2007) contends that the subprime mortgage debacle could have been averted had the existing regulation on high-cost loans been applied properly.

As required by the Home Owner Equity Protection Act of 1994, U.S. mortgage lenders are obliged to perform a set of special risk assessment for high-cost loans, defined in terms of spreads between lending rates and benchmark Treasury rates. Specific tests required include the level of payment shock, documentation, amount and duration of prepayment penalty. All of these represent typical risk attributes in the subprime and Alt-A lending sectors. The problem was that the threshold spread was set too high at 8 percent, so that this regulation covered only 1 percent of subprime loans issues. If the cutoff were 5 percent, about 50 percent of subprime loans would have been covered. At 3 percent, virtually all would have been covered. Another regulatory proposal is that going-in or teaser rates should not count for underwriting or the purposes of regulation.

Discussion Questions

1. Discuss the determinants of housing price movements in a particular country or geographical area.
2. Compare and contrast the housing markets in the United States, Korea, and China.

3. Identify the main contributing factors to the contagious housing price cycles from the real or non-financial side of the housing sector.
4. Explain how financial deregulation and pro-cyclical mortgage lending amplify housing price cycles.

References

Abraham, Jesse, and Patric H. Hendershott. 1996. "Bubbles in Metropolitan Housing Markets." *Journal of Housing Research* 7:2, 191–207.

Ashcraft, Adam, and Til Schuermann. 2008. "Understanding the Securitization of Subprime Mortgage Credit." Federal Reserve Bank of New York Staff Report 318.

Benmelech, Efraim, and Jennifer Dlugosz. 2009. "The Alchemy of CDO Credit Ratings." *Journal of Monetary Economics* 56:4, 617–634.

Brunnermeier, Markus K. 2009. "Deciphering the Liquidity and Credit Crunch 2007–2008." *Journal of Economic Perspectives* 23:1, 77–100.

Calhoun, Charles, Peter Chinloy, and Isaac Megbolugbe. 1995. "Temporal Aggregation and House Price Index." *Journal of Housing Research* 6:3, 419–438.

Campbell, Sean D., Morris A. Davis, Joshua Gallin, and Robert F. Martin. 2009. "What Moves Housing Markets: A Variance Decomposition of the Rent–Price Ratio." *Journal of Urban Economics* 66:2, 92–102.

Capozza, Dennis R., Patric H. Hendershott, and Charlotte Mack. 2004. "An Anatomy of Price Dynamics in Illiquid Markets: Analysis and Evidence from Local Housing Markets." *Real Estate Economics* 32:1, 1–32.

Case, Karl E., and John M. Quigley. 2008. "How Housing Booms Unwind: Income Effects, Wealth Effects and Feedbacks through Financial Markets." *European Journal of Housing Policy* 8:2, 161–180.

Case, Karl E., and Robert J. Shiller. 1989. "The Efficiency of the Market for Single Family Homes." *American Economic Review* 79:1, 125–137.

Chinloy, Peter, Man Cho, and Isaac Megbolugbe. 1997. "Appraisals, Transaction Incentives, and Smoothing." *Journal of Real Estate Finance and Economics* 14:1, 89–112.

Cho, Man. 2009. "Home Price Cycles: A Tale of Two." KDIS Working Paper.

Cho, Man. 2012. "Empirical Testing on Housing Price Bubble in Chinese Cities." Korea Development Institute Research Paper Series.

Cho, Man, and Isaac Megbolugbe. 1996. "An Empirical Analysis of Property Appraisal and Mortgage Redlining." *Journal of Real Estate Economics and Finance* 13:1, 45–55.

Cho, Man, and Inho Song. 2011. "Housing Price and Mortgage Credit Cycles: Tales of Two Countries." Presentation at the KDI Conference on a New Paradigm in Housing Policy after the Global Financial Crisis.

Cho, Man, Kyung-Hwan Kim, and Bertrand Renaud. 2012. "Real Estate Volatility and Economic Stability: An East Asian Perspective." *KDI Policy Study.*

Cho, Man, Insik Min, and Hyun Ah Kim. 2012. "Housing Price and Mortgage Credit Cycles: An Investigation of Alternative Transmission Channels." Presentation at the 2013 AREUEA Annual Meeting, San Diego, CA.

Crawford, Gordon, and Michael Fratantoni. 2003. "Assessing the Forecasting Performance of Regime-Switching, ARIMA and GARCH Models of House Prices." *Real Estate Economics* 31:2, 223–243.

Crowe, Christopher, Giovanni Dell'Ariccia, Deniz Igan, and Pau Rabanal. 2011. "Policies for Macrofinancial Stability: Options to Deal with Real Estate Booms." IMF Staff Discussion Note SDN/11/02.

Davidoff, Thomas. 2013. "Supply Elasticity and the Housing Cycle of the 2000s." *Real Estate Economics* 41:4, 793–813.

Deng, Yongheng, and Peng Liu. 2009. "Mortgage Prepayment and Default with Embedded Forward Contract Risks in China's Housing Market." *Journal of Real Estate Finance and Economics* 38:3, 214–240.

Driffill, John, and Martin Sola. 1998. "Intrinsic Bubbles and Regime-Switching." *Journal of Monetary Economics* 42:2, 357–373.

Duca, John, John Muellbauer, and Anthony Murphy. 2009. "House Prices and Credit Constraints: Making Sense of the U.S. Experience." Presentation at the 2010 ASSA Meeting, Atlanta, Georgia.

Englund, Peter, and Yannis M. Ioannides. 1997. "House Price Dynamics: An International Empirical Perspective." *Journal of Housing Economics* 6:2, 119–136.

Fender, Ingo, and Janet Mitchell. 2009. "The Future of Securitization: How to Align Incentives." *BIS Quarterly Review* September, 27–43.

Fernandez-Corugedo, Emilio, and John Muellbauer. 2006. "Consumer Credit Conditions in the United Kingdom." Working Paper 314, Bank of England.

Fostel, Ana, and John Geanakoplos. 2008. "Leverage Cycles and the Anxious Economy." *American Economic Review* 98:4, 1211–1244.

Froot, Kenneth A., and Maurice Obstfeld. 1991. "Intrinsic Bubbles: The Case of Stock Prices." *American Economic Review* 81:5, 1189–1214.

Geanakoplos, John. 2010. "Solving the Present Crisis and Managing the Leverage Cycle." *FRBNY Economic Policy Review* 16:1, 101–131.

Glaeser, Edward, and Joseph Gyourko. 2005. "The Impact of Zoning on Housing Affordability." Harvard Institute of Economic Research Discussion Paper 1948.

Glaeser, Edward, and Bryce Ward. 2009. "The Causes and Consequences of Land Use Regulations: Evidence from Greater Boston." *Journal of Urban Economics* 65:3, 265–278.

Glaeser, Edward, Joseph Gyourko, and Albert Saiz. 2008. "Housing Supply and Housing Bubbles." *Journal of Urban Economics* 64:2, 198–217.

Glaeser, Edward, Joseph Gyourko, and Raven Saks. 2005a. "Why Have House Prices Gone Up?" *American Economic Review* 95:2, 329–333.

Glaeser, Edward, Joseph Gyourko, and Raven Saks. 2005b. "Urban Growth and Housing Supply." Harvard Institute of Economic Research Discussion Paper 2062.

Glaeser, Edward, Joseph Gyourko, and Saks Raven Saks. 2006. "Urban Growth and Housing Supply." *Journal of Economic Geography* 6:1, 71–89.

Goodhart, Charles, and Boris Hofmann. 2007. *House Prices and the Macroeconomy: Implications for Banking and Price Stability*. Oxford: Oxford University Press.

Gorton, Gary. 2008. "The Panic of 2007." In *Maintaining Stability in a Changing Financial System*. Presented at the 2008 Jackson Hole Conference, Federal Reserve Bank of Kansas City.

Gorton, Gary. 2009. "Securitized Banking and Run on Repo." NBER Working Paper 15223.

Gramlich, Edward. 2007. *Subprime Mortgages: America's Latest Boom and Bust*. Washington, DC: The Urban Institute Press.

Griffin, John M., and Dragon Yongjun Tang. 2010. "Did Subjectivity Play a Role in CDO Credit Ratings?" Presentation at the 2010 ASSA Meeting, Atlanta, Georgia.

Gurkaynak, Refet S. 2008. "Econometric Tests of Asset Price Bubbles: Taking Stock." *Journal of Economic Surveys* 22:1, 166–186.

Haughwout, Andrew, Donghoon Lee, Joseph Tracy, and Wilbert van der Klaauw. 2011. "Real Estate Investors, the Leverage Cycle and the Housing Market Crisis." Working Paper, Federal Reserve Bank of New York.

Herring, Richard J., and Susan M. Wachter. 1999. "Real Estate Booms and Banking Busts: An International Perspective." Center for Financial Institutions Working Papers 99–27, Wharton School Center for Financial Institutions, University of Pennsylvania.

Jansen, Eilev S., and Tord S. H. Krogh. 2011. "Credit Conditions Indices: Controlling for Regime Shifts in the Norwegian Credit Market." Discussion Paper 646, Statistics Norway.

Lea, Michael. 2010. "Alternative Forms of Mortgage Finance: What Can We Learn from Other Countries?" Paper for the Harvard Joint Center for Housing Studies National Symposium, Harvard Business School.

Leamer, Edward E. 2006. "Homes and Jobs and Bonds." UCLA Anderson Forecast, June.

Leventis, Andrew. 2006. "Removing Appraisal Bias from a Repeat–Transactions House Price Index: A Basic Approach." OFHEO Working Paper 06–1.

Liu, Qiao, Paul Lejot, and Douglas W. Arner. 2013. *Finance in Asia: Institutions, Regulation and Policy.* London: Routledge.

Malpezzi, Stephen. 1999. "A Simple Error Correction Model of House Prices." *Journal of Housing Economics* 8:1, 27–62.

McKinsey Global Institute. 2009. "Preparing for China's Urban Billion." McKinsey & Company, March.

Mian, Atif R., and Amir Sufi. 2009. "The Consequence of Mortgage Credit Expansion: Evidence from the U.S. Mortgage Default Crisis." *Quarterly Journal of Economics* 124:4, 1449–1496.

Mian, Atif, and Amir Sufi. 2011. "House Prices, Home Equity Based Borrowing, and the U.S. Household Leverage Crisis." *American Economic Review* 101:5, 2132–2156.

National Bureau of Statistics of China . 2013. "Sales Price Indices of Residential Buildings in 70 Large and Medium–Sized Cities." http://www.stats.gov.cn/english/statisticaldata/.

Ortalo-Magné, François, and Sven Rady. 2001. "Housing Market Dynamics: On the Contribution of Income Shocks and Credit Constraints." Discussion Paper 470, CESIfo.

Pavlov, Andrey, and Susan Wachter. 2004. "Robbing the Bank: Short-term Players and Asset Prices." *Journal of Real Estate Finance and Economics* 28:2/3, 147–160.

Pavlov Andrey, and Susan Wachter. 2009. "Mortgage Put Options and Real Estate Markets." *Journal of Real Estate Finance and Economics* 38:1, 89–103.

Samuelson, Paul A. 1958. "An Exact Consumption-Loan Model of Interest with or without the Social Contrivance of Money." *Journal of Political Economy* 66:6, 467–482.

Tirole, Jean. 1985. "Asset Bubbles and Overlapping Generations." *Econometrica* 53:5, 1071–1100.

Wu, Jing, Joseph Gyourko, and Yongheng Deng. 2010. "Evaluating Conditions in Major Chinese Housing Markets." NBER Working Paper 16189.

4

Behavioral Real Estate

MICHAEL J. SEILER
K. Dane Brooksher Endowed Chair Professor of Real Estate and Finance,
The College of William & Mary

Introduction

The scope of behavioral research spans disciplines such as real estate, finance, economics, and psychology. This chapter begins with a simple definition of behavioral real estate. Utility maximization is a long-standing maxim in the traditional field of economics. People will behave and make choices in a way that maximizes their expected utility. The same starting point is true in behavioral real estate. The difference is that in economics, utility is often defined as a person maximizing an expected level of wealth. While behaviorists agree that money is a strong motivator of underlying behavior, they believe additional factors should be considered. For example, if people care about lifestyle, free time with family, or fitting into a social network of friends, models that attempt to explain their choices should incorporate these considerations. Any model that does not incorporate these factors is subject to specification error.

Many academic researchers have denied the need to incorporate these additional considerations. That is surprising given that academics have made non-monetary choices by working in educational institutions as opposed to industry. Reasons cited for academic employment preference include flexible work schedules, time off in the summers, intellectual freedom, and the rewards of teaching students and watching them learn. All these reasons are non-monetary, yet the traditional viewpoint is to exclude them in models that explain behavioral choices. Behaviorists incorporate a more inclusive definition of utility maximization into their models.

Misconceptions about Behavioral Real Estate

Debates abound attempting to reconcile behavioral analysis with the efficient markets hypothesis (EMH) as explained by Fama (1970). While a discussion about the efficiency of the capital markets is valid and needed, the positions taken by both sides in the argument are misdirected.

Possibly the greatest misconception surrounding behavioral real estate is that these studies are tests of rationality. The notion that behavioral studies assume everyone is irrational is simply untrue. A truer statement is that behaviorists believe that expected utility maximization proxied by wealth alone is too limited. Traditionalists solve problems using the tools and assumptions they learned. Behaviorists recognize that traditional tools cannot always solve the current problem. As a result, they look to other fields for tools that have long been developed to solve similar problems in other contexts. Abraham Maslow, an American psychologist, once remarked, "If you only have a hammer, you tend to see every problem as a nail." Of course, behaviorists can get into trouble if they find a new tool such as in psychology that they view as a panacea. Try turning a screw with a wrench. It simply makes no sense. The trick in behavioral real estate is to identify the problem first and determine whether the traditional tool works. If not, go in search of a new tool. Failure to adhere to this process causes unnecessary confusion and conflict between the two camps of researchers.

The Need for a Behavioral Approach

There are several instances where a behavioral approach to research should be taken. This section lists a few of these circumstances.

INACCURATE OR MANIPULATED FIELD DATA

Another reason to employ a behavioral technique when solving a real estate problem relates to data. Transactions data from secondary sources do not always provide researchers with valid and reliable field information (Bloomfield and Anderson 2010). Take residential real estate transaction data. Traditionalists and behaviorists alike use transaction data because they give market participants a chance to have their voices heard. Because buyers' and sellers' actions are directly related to their underlying wealth, transactions data are relevant to real estate researchers.

However, residential real estate data such as through local multiple listing services (MLS) are often intentionally biased. The listing agent has a goal to maximize the selling price and minimize time on the market (TOM), not provide researchers with reliable data. Benefield and Hardin (2013) summarize the literature surrounding transaction prices versus TOM. Their results show disparate findings surrounding the relationship in magnitude and direction between price and TOM. Such differences stem from inconsistent measurement and intentional agent manipulation. Agents intentionally pull listings, wait a few days, and relist the property in order to reset the TOM clock to zero. This is an effective marketing strategy because many systems alert buyers' agents to new listings.

Other selling agents use the reset to make a listing appear fresher due to the stigma associated with a property that has been on the market too long. As a result, a transaction-based price is potentially matched with an artificially shorter TOM number skewing research results. MLS data providers inconsistently measure TOM. Some local MLS systems reset the TOM clock when any change is made to the property listing, while other local MLS data providers do not.

Measurement errors can occur innocently. When agents list a property, they often insert home characteristics contained in previous listings without verifying their accuracy. Over time, these listing errors can result in a compounding of mistakes meaning that what researchers measure as the characteristics of the home can often be far from the home's true characteristics. Moreover, field data are generated from events that occurred at a specific time and place making the generalization of results difficult (Yavas and Sirmans 2005). Listing information on houses is subject to seller disclosure rules and requirements. Yet incentives operate in the opposite direction. Sellers and their agents have incentives to present the property in its most favorable light, and they have asymmetrical information.

In sum, listing information is often far from accurate. Still, this information makes its way into traditional studies on a regular basis.

DO TRANSACTION PRICES REVEAL EVERY ASPECT OF A DECISION?

When examining residential real estate transactions data, researchers know what price is ultimately paid. Little insight is available about the process by which the buyer arrived at a willingness to pay. Allen and Dare (2004, 2006) and Palmon, Smith, and Soprazetti (2004) examine the effect that list price has on the ultimate selling price of a home.

The traditional view of an efficient market is that listing price should have no effect on ultimate selling price. The market uses supply and demand to establish an equilibrium price for each property. Yet, both sets of authors find that psychological list pricing significantly affects the final selling price with conflicting results. Palmon et al. (2004) find that homes listed with round-pricing sell faster and at a higher price, while Allen and Dare (2004, 2006) find the opposite.

To understand these pricing effects, Beracha and Seiler (2014) perform two experiments. The first examines preference for one property over another based solely on list price differences. In order to isolate the effect of pricing strategy on home selection preference, the authors use a standard between-subjects experimental design. Each buyer is presented with side-by-side property listings. Each listing has a photo, property description, and price. The home is offered using either just below or rounded pricing. A just-below price is exemplified by $199,900, whereas rounded means $200,000. The homebuyer then selects between the price choices. Between subjects, the photo, property description, price, and listing order are randomized. This is a standard design technique to remove unintended influences on the homebuyer's selection preference. By effectively altering only the pricing strategy between trials, homebuyer selection preference is attributable to this single variable.

The second experiment relates to the perceived differential ability to negotiate on homes offered with different psychological listing price techniques. Buyers more heavily negotiate on homes that employ just-below prices as compared to either rounded or precise. This study represents one of many examples where the research question on negotiating power cannot be addressed using transactions data alone. By merging transactions data with a controlled experiment, researchers can isolate specific theories while holding everything else constant.

Transactions data give market participants a chance to express their net financial opinions. The disadvantage is that in the real world the presence of so many moving parts makes holding everything else constant impossible. Instead, researchers use a large sample size in the hope of effectively holding everything else constant.

Bloomfield and Anderson (2010) discuss how hedonic models suffer from endogeneity. An alternative approach is to collect experimental data. An experiment allows a specific theory to be tested in isolation under controlled conditions, everything else equal. The disadvantage is that one always wonders if what held inside the lab will hold in the real world.

DO RESEARCHERS ALREADY HAVE DATA ON EVERYTHING THEY WANT TO STUDY?

Even if transactions-based data were strictly preferred over all behavioral approaches, sometimes these are unavailable. Seiler, Madhavan, and Liechty (2012a, 2012b) study how buyers search for homes on the Internet. In a controlled environment, all the homes within their search engine are similarly presented. Each property listing contains a photo along with quantitative characteristics and qualitative agent open remarks, where the agent describes the property using marketing efforts found in actual listings.

Ocular tracking technology is used to measure exactly where homebuyers look when searching for homes on the Internet. By learning where homebuyers look within the web page and how long they concentrate on each component of the page, recommendations can be made to listing agents in terms of where to focus their marketing efforts.

In a related study, Arndt, Harrison, Lane, Seiler, and Seiler (2013) revisit the seminal work of Haag, Rutherford, and Thomson (2000) to examine the ability of the listing agent's open-ended remarks to affect selling prices and TOM. Agent comments are divided between those that are (1) factually verifiable such as being recently painted, new roof, located on or near a lake, and (2) statements of opinion such as "good buy," "motivated seller," "good location," or "well-maintained." Three of the four variables relating to the agents' statements of opinion are statistically significant in explaining selling prices. Interestingly, the negative coefficients indicate that the homes sold for less, not more. Consistent with the pricing result, homes took significantly longer to sell based on the inclusion of three of the four groups of opinion-based agent comments.

The significance implies that agent comments provide valuable information about the home. Concerning the negative signs on significant variables, the authors suggest that agents might include the positive words in their property description to create interest and increase the pool of potential buyers. Alternatively, buyers discount extensive hype regarding a property.

Arndt, Harrison, Lane, Seiler, and Seiler (2013) argue that Haag, Rutherford, and Thomson (2000) find weak and inconsistent results because of the difficulty of holding everything else constant and isolating the impact of agent comments. Moreover, agent comments are difficult to quantify and classify.

An alternative approach to understanding the impact of agent remarks is to conduct an experiment, which can account for information provided to homebuyers. To this end, a virtual tour of a single property is created. An audio-visual tour of the home is recorded using a female voice that incorporates hyperbolic rhetoric. *Hyperbolic rhetoric* describes the use of superlative words and other phrases to promote a property with the intent of creating an opinion of greater market value for the home. Then, the hyperbolic rhetoric phrases are removed to provide a property description conveying the facts of the home. This results in a hyperbolic and non-hyperbolic rhetoric recording otherwise perfectly identical.

In an attempt to hold these variants constant across gender lines, a voice-altering software program converted each female recording into a male equivalent. Finally, since voice and physical appearance are unrelated, the resulting recordings are mapped onto four real estate agent photographs to examine the influence of attractiveness. To isolate agent attractiveness, extreme makeover before-and-after photos of both a man and a woman are used.

What results is an ability to isolate the impact of three variables—agent attractiveness, gender, and hyperbolic rhetoric—to determine which is most important in changing the home value opinions of potential homebuyers. Only the attractive female agent is successful when employing hyperbolic rhetoric. For other agents, the use of hyperbolic rhetoric can actually work against increasing the opinion of the home's value.

Examples of Behavioral Real Estate Applications

Behavioral research techniques have been used in different research contexts. This section discusses several examples of behavioral applications to real estate research.

TESTING SPECIFIC BEHAVIORAL CONCEPTS

In Kahneman and Tversky (1979) and Tversky and Kahneman (1991), prospect theory's loss aversion describes how people treat losses and gains asymmetrically in their value functions. A realized loss results in twice as much disutility as an equivalently sized gain adds to utility. Extensive studies use loss aversion theory to help explain anomalous results across various disciplines. In residential real estate, Genesove and Mayer (2001) examine seller behavior in the Boston market during the 1990s. Suppose the expected market price is lower than the seller's reservation value. Under loss aversion, the seller will list at an above-market price, attain a higher selling price, experience a greater time on the market, and exhibit a lower probability of sale. The positive price-volume relationship is also attributable to loss aversion.

Sun and Seiler (2013) argue that a conceptual mismatch occurs between the theoretical definition of loss aversion in Kahneman and Tversky (1979) and what is empirically tested in Genesove and Mayer (2001). Specifically, asymmetry in the value function is not necessary to achieve the same results. As such, loss aversion only potentially explains seller behavior. An inter-temporal choice problem can potentially drive loss aversion as well. Evidence shows that consumers possess present-biased preferences (Laibson 1997; O'Donoghue and Rabin 1999). Their preferences are dynamically inconsistent in the way choices are made between two payoffs in the future. This feature, known as *hyperbolic discounting*, describes how consumers discount short horizon payoffs with higher rates than those with a longer horizon. Sun and Seiler show that people may exhibit what appears to be loss aversion behavior even when they treat losses and gains in a symmetric manner within their value functions.

Additional behavioral concepts such as false reference points, regret aversion, familiarity bias, and mental accounting have all been applied to real estate. *False reference points* refer to the irrelevant figures people anchor on when making decisions about the future. In a residential real estate setting, false reference points might include the purchase price of a home and how that influences a homeowner's willingness to sell (Genesove and Mayer 2001; Seiler, Seiler, Traub, and Harrison 2008a). The purchase price of the home is an irrelevant sunk cost that should have no bearing on the current willingness to sell. Homeowners seek to minimize their regret or realized loss aversion by holding onto a property even though they may receive an above current market price today. Lane, Seiler, and Seiler (2011) discuss this concept as it relates to behavioral explanations for the real estate shadow market.

People want to sell their homes but do not have the property listed for sale. Based on traditional measures of utility, the preference for minimizing regret over the willingness to make less than wealth-maximizing decisions is deemed strictly irrational. The conclusion of irrationality is a function of how one defines utility. The human brain is hardwired to protect oneself against harm—the experience of both physical and emotional pain. Can holding onto assets longer than is financially beneficial to avoid feeling regret be rational? The research community needs to be more open-minded in its definition of utility.

Familiarity bias refers to being overly familiar with an environment resulting in either the underestimation of risk or the overestimation of return. In the context of residential real estate, Seiler, Seiler, Traub, and Harrison (2008b) and Seiler, Seiler, Harrison, and Lane (2013) find that homeowners consistently believe their home is more recession-proof than others around them. This effect is true for homes located right across the street and becomes increasingly powerful when comparing homes across the state and country. As the circle of reference increases, homeowners feel more justified in their opinion that other homes are more likely to decrease in value over a future 12-month period.

The *endowment effect* describes the observation that people require more compensation to give up an asset that they already possess than to obtain a similar one. *Mental accounting* is when an investor's willingness to sell differs when considering the asset in isolation versus as part of an overall portfolio. Seiler, Seiler, and Lane (2012) demonstrate that investors are statistically significantly more willing to sell their real estate asset when it is held as part of a larger portfolio that has gone up in value. The aggregate shape of the disposition curve is similar to their real estate in isolation trials, but is significantly higher at all points along the curve when considered in a portfolio context. Seiler and Seiler (2010) further demonstrate that after real estate investors experience a loss, their unwillingness to sell to avoid regret results in a greater eventual loss in the future. Avoiding a small loss now results in larger regret later.

STOCK MARKET APPLICATIONS

Mankert and Seiler (2011, 2012) discuss an alternative approach to Markowitz (1952, 1991) portfolio management in their adaptation of the behaviorally based Black and Litterman (1992) model. Luchtenberg and Seiler (2014), who consider the impact of financial skewness on asset selection preference, provide further expansion of the expected mean, variance, and standard deviation framework. When operating in the loss domain, investors are more willing to take long-shot bets with high levels of skewness. Their hope is to return to at least the price they paid for the asset, a false reference point. When operating in the gains domain, investors sell investments that might result in a price below what they originally paid. No matter how small the probability, the authors clearly demonstrate the consistent preference to remain in the gains domain or get out of the loss domain.

EMINENT DOMAIN STUDIES

Eminent domain describes where a condemning authority such as a governmental entity is allowed to take private property for the greater public good. In return, the condemnor is required to pay the property owner just compensation. When the condemnor does not need all of the property owner's land, it is known as a *partial take*. The task then becomes valuing the remaining parcel of land. This remainder interest can become difficult to value because it may involve the taking of land or easement access rights. The value of the remainder property depends on what the government builds (Seiler 2012a). The government project may either enhance or detract from value. For example, the installation of power lines next to a home detracts from value, whereas the widening of a road may help drive additional customers to a strip mall.

Seiler (2014b) uses an experimental design to measure the impact on residential home values resulting from a partial take of land by the federal government for the installation of a public bike trail. While the condemning authority did not take the actual land, it did take easement rights. Along this 50-foot deep area, the clearing of trees and underbrush resulted in additional proximity damage due to noise and a loss of privacy.

Appraisers first used a comparable sales approach in a traditional attempt to arrive at the value of the affected properties. As this was a new development, the appraiser felt no valid "comps" were available anywhere close to the area. The appraiser had little to go on in terms of establishing fair market value in its pre-take condition, much less establish an accurate value in its after-take condition. In this case, traditional methods were not applicable, and the courts needed to learn value impaction using a different method.

Seiler (2012b) describes a commercial real estate eminent domain case that benefitted from an experimental approach. A Red Roof Inn is located adjacent to Interstate 77 in Statesville, North Carolina. The North Carolina Department of Transportation decided to widen the interstate to allow for increased traffic. As a result, the Red Roof Inn must move its sign further away from the interstate. The problem is that when driving northbound, the interstate curves around a hill, obscuring the Red Roof Inn sign in its new location. By surveying current guests, nearly 60 percent relied on seeing the sign on the interstate before pulling over. For southbound travelers, the number was closer to 80 percent. The sign in its new location would be further from the interstate, outside the natural line of sight for drivers. Clearly, no data exist to estimate the impact that moving a sign has on future occupancy rates. Seiler (2012b) combined the percentage of guests who rely on the sign in its pre-take position with the percentage of guests who would likely see the sign in its post-take position to arrive at an estimate of diminution in value.

Traditional theoretical models relating to eminent domain can be constructed as in Turnbull (2012). However, the testing of such models is another example of where experimental design can be useful. Read, Seiler, and Zillante (2014) examine the holdout problem in commercial real estate development where a developer needs to acquire several parcels of land in order to complete a large-scale property, such as a shopping mall. To acquire enough land, the developer must convince a sufficient number of adjacent landowners to sell.

The problem is that a developer unable to secure a sufficient block of land does not want to own any of it. Obtaining actual transactions data to understand the holdout problem is unrealistic. The holdout problem centers on the inability to buy land, not an actual transaction. Instead, examining various theories relating to collusion among current land owners, analysis of the linchpin parcel, negotiation power amongst various landowners, understanding how power shifts once one or more landowners agree to sell, are only possible in a controlled experimental setting where all other factors are held constant. If researchers insist on using only case studies to understand these complex issues, results will be marred by small sample sizes, incomplete information revelation, a lack of transaction data, and virtually no control over exogenous factors considered by each landowner.

APPLY BEHAVIORAL CONCEPTS TO STRATEGIC MORTGAGE DEFAULT

Since the beginning of the financial crisis in 2008, new research questions have emerged. Possibly the most influential emerging line of research relates to the burgeoning concept of strategic mortgage default. An *economic default* describes a situation where a borrower no longer pays on a mortgage, lacking the financial means to do so. Alternatively, a *strategic mortgage default* describes where a borrower has the financial ability to continue making payments, but for other reasons decides not to do so. Wyman (2010) and Guiso, Sapienza, and Zingales (2013) establish that the percentage of all defaults that are strategic in nature is on the rise, between 17 percent and 26 percent.

The downturn in the economy understandably resulted in an uptick in economic defaults. An unemployment rate increase means more people have lost their jobs and can no longer make mortgage payments. However, negative equity drives strategic mortgage default. People can still afford to make their mortgage payments, but decide against doing so when faced with being substantially underwater (i.e., have negative equity) on their mortgage.

Other factors contribute to strategic default such as borrowers expecting home prices to continue to fall. Also, borrowers are frustrated with their lender for being unwilling to entertain loan modification even after the biggest government bailout in U.S. history (Seiler 2014a). This situation helps to explain why borrowers are willing to alter their moral stance on the controversial issue of walking away from their mortgage.

White (2010), Seiler, Seiler, Lane, and Harrison (2012), and Guiso, Sapienza, and Zingales (2013) use various behavioral approaches when establishing the emotional considerations by borrowers contemplating strategic mortgage default. Gangel, Seiler, and Collins (2013a) then add these behavioral considerations to the traditional economic factors. They use a technology from modeling and simulation called agent-based modeling (ABM). The purpose of conducting research inside the ABM framework is to allow specific factors to change. The authors then measure the impact that each variable has on overall home price levels within the system. Of particular interest is a list of variables that might cause an eventual market collapse.

The agents in the ABM are 2,500 homes. Each has a mortgage similar to the historical make-up of the local markets. This type of testing can only be safely performed within the confines of a controlled, artificial environment as opposed to unleashing an untested solution to the financial crisis in an actual housing market. The number of displaced homeowners, wasted taxpayer dollars, and irrevocable damage such a live field experiment might cause is unacceptable to policymakers.

Within the safe ABM environment, Gangel, Seiler, and Collins (2013a) find that due to foreclosure contagion or spillover, disposition time is the most significant contributory variable to market collapse. *Disposition time* is the number of months between when a lender decides to foreclose and title is transferred to a new buyer. Laws surrounding the foreclosure process vary by state, which directly affects disposition times.

A disadvantage to using a transaction-based approach is that the results are specific to a particular time and place. When measuring the effect that a single foreclosure has on the market value of a neighboring property, Immergluck and Smith (2006), Harding, Rosenblatt, and Yao (2009), Lin, Rosenblatt, and Yao (2009), and Rogers and Winter (2009) arrive at disparate estimates. Spillover effects range from less than 1 percent to almost 9 percent. Gangel, Seiler, and Collins (2013b) use the entire range of estimates for their ABM examination.

A generally accepted notion in psychology is that mimetic or observational learning is a natural developmental growth tool possessed in humans. *Mimetics* refers to how children learn mannerisms by observing those of their parents. They emulate facial expressions before they understand what they convey. Children pick up on dialects from listening to others around them. Seiler, Lane, and Harrison (2014) and Luchtenberg and Seiler (2013) use mimetic theory to test the concept of financial herding in the context of strategic mortgage default. Herding describes how individual investors abandon private information in favor of the collective set. Herding can be rational if the individual believes the market possess a more complete information set. By following the herd quickly, the investor forgoes understanding the drivers behind the price shift in favor of achieving safety in numbers. Herding is different from an information cascade as described in Bikhchandani, Hirshleifer, and Welch (1992, 1998) and Seiler (2014b).

Seiler, Lane and Harrison (2013) and Luchtenberg and Seiler (2013) examine strategic mortgage default in the absence of outside influencers as well as in the presence of a maven or real estate knowledge leader. Many advocate strategic default action despite the severe negative penalties it imposes. Borrowers are constantly being bombarded with advice from people they trust who argue that walking away from their mortgage is in their best interest. Other mavens, or real estate experts, speak out against the burgeoning action taken by frustrated and struggling homeowner borrowers. That is, some mavens within the model seek to spread the disease of strategic default, while others work to spread the cure. This is a standard approach to measuring the outbreak of disease and the steps needed to introduce an antidote or vaccination.

A maven's ability to influence the behavior of others is a function of not only the subject matter expertise but also access to borrowers. Seiler, Collins, and Fefferman (2013) include an additional variable in their foreclosure contagion model for social connectivity. Instead of modeling foreclosure spillover effects as a purely economic phenomenon, borrowers incorporate behavioral factors. A maven may possess a greater ability to persuade a borrower to change a stance on strategic mortgage default. However, if the maven never comes in contact with borrowers, a change in the belief system cannot occur. The spread of strategic default belief adoption or contagion occurs in a manner consistent with how epidemiologists examine disease contagion.

One key difference between how a disease versus a social contagion spreads is that the former requires physical contact. Alternatively, a social contagion can spread through physical exchanges such as talking to a neighbor, but can also jump space such as by watching a TV show or talking on the phone. As a result, a social contagion can spread much more quickly than a traditional disease. With the increasingly popular use of social media, not much time or effort is needed for an idea to go viral—hence the reference to disease modeling.

Being a maven means the strategic default signal being sent out will be stronger than that of a non-maven. What about the receiver of that signal? Seiler, Collins, and Fefferman (2013) describe susceptibility to normative influence (SNI), a measure of the probability of changing the behavior of a person when new ideas are communicated. SNI is context specific. For example, convincing someone to change a brand of toothpaste is easier than convincing them to default on a mortgage. Seiler and Harrison (2011) conduct a separate study with the specific intent of capturing a variable that relates to strategic mortgage default.

Seiler, Collins, and Fefferman (2013) conclude that within the social network variables, in a fragile real estate market, mavens more easily influence borrowers to strategically default. The result is a potential collapse of residential home prices. Conversely, when mavens advocate continued payment of a mortgage even though the borrower is underwater (i.e., owes more on the mortgage than their home is worth), they are less able to save a market teetering on the brink of collapse. This asymmetric finding sounds a warning to policymakers. Having mavens trumpet positive news about the housing market has limited benefit. By contrast, having experts encourage walking away is an idea people are far more willing to adopt.

Mortgage Modifications

In the current environment of increased strategic mortgage defaults, Seiler, Seiler, Lane, and Harrison (2012) identify borrower frustration with their lender as a significant contributory factor in the decision to strategically default. Seiler (2014a) uses inequity aversion, a theory describing how people are willing to give up wealth in order to penalize those whose actions they view as unfair. Borrowers are much more likely to default on lenders who they deem to have engaged in egregious behavior such as taking government bailout funds or originating sub-prime loans. Moreover, borrowers are less likely to default on a local bank as opposed to a lender they find on-line.

Perhaps most disturbing, Seiler (2014a) finds that borrowers have no idea that the entity servicing their loan and the mortgage investor are likely to be different. As a result, borrowers attempt to punish the wrong entity. Additionally, the average homeowner believes far more banks engage in these types of egregious behaviors than they actually do resulting in an unjustified number of strategic mortgage defaults currently in the marketplace.

Seiler (2014a) finds that if a lender offers even a modest modification, such as $100 on a $1,600 monthly payment, the borrower's desire to retaliate through strategic mortgage default goes away entirely. Borrowers are willing to forgive past lender practices if they perceive the lender as sending a signal of cooperation moving forward. The study makes several policy recommendations to mitigate this burgeoning retaliatory practice.

The question then becomes, "Why are there so few loans being modified today?" Edmans (2012) suggests that securitization may offer a powerful explanation. Alternatively, Collins, Harrison, and Seiler (2014) use a game theoretic approach to examine the incentives of the lender to modify the loan and the borrower to strategically default. Besides economic incentives, reasons include behavioral considerations such as reputational capital, reduced Fair, Isaac & Company (FICO) score, and the probability of the lender pursuing recourse. Interestingly, the mathematical results demonstrate that only a narrow band of conditions exist where modifying a loan makes sense for the lender. Although not addressed, one has to wonder how wide this band would become in the absence of behavioral considerations. This would explain the apparent discrepancy between lender behavior and what many perceive to be a stubborn unwillingness to resolve the current crisis.

fMRI Studies

In a continual search to understand the complexity of the strategic mortgage default decision, two studies borrow from the field of neuroscience to unlock what goes on inside the mind of a strategic defaulter. Building off of Seiler (2014a), Seiler and Walden (2014a) use functional magnetic resonance imaging (fMRI) to understand how homeowners process non-financial information when considering strategic mortgage default. Borrowers initially attempt to inhibit their tendency to retaliate against a lender who has engaged in egregious lending practices when compared to a financially conservative lender. When defaults are rare, borrowers are less likely to default because violating the social norm results in feelings of disgust. When a lender refuses a loan modification, the borrower seeks retribution. Consistent with Seiler (2014a), the study confirms that granting even a modest loan modification removes the desire of homeowners to seek retribution toward their lender no matter the borrower's impression of the lender's character.

Based on the mimetic herding work of Seiler, Lane, and Harrison (2014), the second study using fMRI technology by Seiler and Walden (2014b) investigates the substrates, or regions of the brain, that activate when making various strategic default choices. The left interior parietal lobe is linked to herding in participants who observe the default behavior of a maven or real estate expert. Homeowners only significantly follow the herd when mavens advocate strategic default, not when they recommend against it. In trials where the homeowner is severely underwater, the motor cortex and anterior cingulate cortex show significantly more activation. This brain region is particularly sensitive to situations where behavior may produce errors. When faced with loan parameters that entice homeowners to strategically default, subjects show significant activation of their left lingual gyrus and motor cortex suggesting a greater level of self-reflection. Even with these two groundbreaking studies, much work remains to understand the true nature of strategic mortgage default.

Experimental Study Datasets

There are two primary sources of contention when collecting data through an experiment. The first is whether the sample will consist of students or actual decision-makers. In fields such as psychology, a widely accepted notion is that students represent an acceptable pool from which to pull participants. In economics, the practice is less standard. Experimental design studies such as Yavas, Miceli, and Sirmans (2001), Seiler, Seiler, Traub, and Harrison (2008a), Seiler and Seiler (2010), Ikromov and Yavas (2012a, 2012b) use student subjects while Seiler (2014a), Seiler et al. (2012a, b), Seiler, Seiler, Harrison, and Lane (2013), and Seiler, Seiler, Lane, and Harrison (2012) use actual decision-makers. When the economic decision to be made involves a wealth maximization problem, students are qualified to participate in the experiment. However, on strategic mortgage default, the preference is to use as participants only those who can experience the full range of complex emotions surrounding the decision within the confines of the experimental design.

The second most heavily debated experimental design component relates to whether or not participants need to be compensated based on their performance within the experiment. Yavas et al. (2001) and Ikromov and Yavas (2012a, 2012b) reward their student participants with money based on the payoff realized within their experimental design. This approach makes sense because their experiment revolves around the buying and selling of an asset. However, not all experiments relate to right versus wrong or rational versus irrational choices. When considering the strategic mortgage default line of research, there is definitely not a "right" or "wrong" course of action. Instead, both options carry severe potential advantages and disadvantages that in many cases will not be felt for years to come. Moreover, even after several years and with complete hindsight, the preferred course of action could conceivably remain unclear. As such, decisions relating to strategic mortgage default should not necessarily be directly linked to a particular payoff within the experiment. Doing so would incorrectly assume a correct answer to the problem.

Summary and Conclusions

Behavioral real estate is becoming increasingly accepted as a standard approach to answering common questions in the field. While many problems within real estate need not be addressed using behavioral considerations, others are more amenable to these procedures.

Difficulty in obtaining full and accurate information is one reason to implement a behavioral approach. Within a controlled experiment, researchers can control and take into account other relevant variables. They can also analyze the influence of information in isolation. Experimental data are replicable. Because experimental data are generated under controlled laboratory conditions, reproducing results is easier in other markets and over time. In sum, behavioral and experimental techniques are some of the many tools researchers can use to resolve real estate research questions.

Discussion Questions

1. Identify several misconceptions about behavioral real estate.
2. When would someone want to use a behavioral real estate concept instead of purely traditional transactions data?
3. Provide several examples of how behavioral real estate has been used to answer real estate research questions.
4. List several technologies being used in behavioral real estate research.
5. Identify fields from which behavioral real estate has borrowed ideas.

References

Allen, Marcus T., and William Dare. 2004. "The Effects of Charm Listing Prices on House Transaction Prices." *Real Estate Economics* 32:4, 695–713.

Allen, Marcus T., and William Dare. 2006. "Charm Pricing as a Signal of Listing Price Precision." *Journal of Housing Research* 15:2, 113–127.

Arndt, Aaron D., David M. Harrison, Mark A. Lane, Michael J. Seiler, and Vicky L. Seiler. 2013. "Can Agents Influence Property Perceptions Through Their Appearance and Use of Pathos?" *Housing Studies* 28:8, 1105–1116.

Benefield, Justin, and William G. Hardin, III. 2013. "Time-on-Market Issues in the Literature." Working Paper, Florida International University.

Beracha, Eli, and Michael J. Seiler. 2014. "The Effect of Listing Price Strategy on Transaction Selling Prices." *Journal of Real Estate Finance and Economics*, forthcoming.

Bikhchandani, Sushil, David Hirshleifer, and Ivo Welch. 1992. "A Theory of Fads, Fashion, Custom, and Cultural Change as Informational Cascades." *Journal of Political Economy* 100:5, 992–1026.

Bikhchandani, Sushil, David Hirshleifer, and Ivo Welch. 1998. "Learning from the Behavior of Others: Conformity, Fads, and Informational Cascades." *Journal of Economic Perspectives* 12:3, 151–170.

Black, Fisher, and Robert Litterman. 1992. "Global Portfolio Optimization." *Financial Analysts Journal* 48:5, 28–43.

Bloomfield, Robert, and Alyssa Anderson. 2010. "Experimental Finance." Working Paper, Cornell University.

Collins, Andrew J., David M. Harrison, and Michael J. Seiler. 2014. "Mortgage Modification and the Decision to Strategically Default: A Game Theoretic Approach." Working Paper, The College of William & Mary.

Edmans, Alex. 2012. "The Responsible Homeowner Reward: An Incentive–Based Solution to Strategic Mortgage Default." Working Paper, Wharton.

Fama, Eugene. 1970. "Efficient Capital Markets: A Review of Theory and Empirical Work." *Journal of Finance* 25:2, 383–417.

Gangel, Marshall, Michael J. Seiler, and Andrew J. Collins. 2013a. "Exploring the Foreclosure Contagion Effect Using Agent-Based Modeling." *Journal of Real Estate Finance and Economics* 46:2, 339–354.

Gangel, Marshall, Michael J. Seiler, and Andrew J. Collins. 2013b. "Latin Hypercube Sampling and the Identification of the Foreclosure Contagion Threshold." *Journal of Behavioral Finance* 14:2, 149–159.

Genesove, David, and Christopher Mayer. 2001. "Loss Aversion and Seller Behavior: Evidence from the Housing Market." *Quarterly Journal of Economics* 116:4, 1233–1260.

Guiso, Luigi, Paola Sapienza, and Luigi Zingales. 2013. "The Determinants of Attitudes towards Strategic Default on Mortgages." *Journal of Finance* 68:4, 1473–1515.

Haag, Jerry T., Ronald C. Rutherford, and Thomas A. Thomson. 2000. "Real Estate Agent Remarks: Help or Hype?" *Journal of Real Estate Research* 20:1/2, 205–215.

Harding, John P., Eric Rosenblatt, and Vincent W. Yao. 2009. "The Contagion Effect of Foreclosed Properties." *Journal of Urban Economics* 66:3, 164–178.

Ikromov, Nuriddin, and Abdullah Yavas. 2012a. "Asset Characteristics and the Boom and Bust Periods: An Experimental Study." *Real Estate Economics* 40:3, 603–636.

Ikromov, Nuriddin, and Abdullah Yavas. 2012b. "Cash Flow Volatility, Prices and Price Volatility: An Experimental Study." *Journal of Real Estate Finance and Economics* 44:1/2, 203–229.

Immergluck, Dan, and Geoff Smith. 2006. "The External Costs of Foreclosures: The Impact of Single-Family Mortgage Foreclosures on Property Values." *Housing Policy Debate* 17:1, 57–79.

Kahneman, Daniel, and Amos Tversky. 1979. "Prospect Theory: An Analysis of Decision under Risk." *Econometrica* 47:2, 263–291.

Laibson, David. 1997. "Golden Eggs and Hyperbolic Discounting." *Quarterly Journal of Economics* 112:2, 443–477.

Lane, Mark A., Michael J. Seiler, and Vicky L. Seiler. 2011. "Identifying Behavioral Explanations for a Subset of the Real Estate Shadow Market." *Journal of Housing Research* 20:2, 191–210.

Lin, Zhenguo, Eric Rosenblatt, and Vincent Yao. 2009. "Spillover Effects of Foreclosures on Neighborhood Property Values." *Journal of Real Estate Finance and Economics* 38:4, 387–407.

Luchtenberg, Kimberly F., and Michael J. Seiler. 2014. "Do Institutional and Individual Investors Differ in Their Preference for Financial Skewness?" *Journal of Behavioral Finance*, forthcoming.

Luchtenberg, Kimberly F., and Michael J. Seiler. 2013. "The Effect of Exogenous Information Signal Strength on Herding." *Review of Behavioral Finance* 5:2, 153–174.

Mankert, Charlotta, and Michael J. Seiler. 2011. "Mathematical Derivations and Practical Implications for the Use of the Black–Litterman Model." *Journal of Real Estate Portfolio Management* 17:2, 139–159.

Mankert, Charlotta, and Michael J. Seiler. 2012. "Behavioral Finance and Its Implication in the Use of the Black–Litterman Model." *Journal of Real Estate Portfolio Management* 18:1, 99–121.

Markowitz, Harry. 1952. "Portfolio Selection." *Journal of Finance* 7:1, 77–91.

Markowitz, Harry. 1991. *Portfolio Selection*. Oxford: Blackwell.

O'Donoghue, Ted, and Matthew Rabin. 1999. "Doing It Now or Later." *American Economic Review* 89:1, 103–124.

Palmon, Oded, Barton A. Smith, and Ben J. Sopranzetti. 2004. "Clustering in Real Estate Prices: Determinants and Consequences." *Journal of Real Estate Research* 26:2, 115–136.

Read, Dustin, Michael J. Seiler, and Arthur Zillante. 2014. "Eminent Domain, Lynchpin Properties, and the Holdout Problem." Working Paper, The College of William & Mary.

Rogers, William, and William Winter. 2009. "The Impact of Foreclosures on Neighboring Housing Sales." *Journal of Real Estate Research* 31:4, 455–479.

Seiler, Michael J. 2012a. "Forward and Falsely Induced Reverse Information Cascades." *Journal of Behavioral Finance* 13:3, 226–240

Seiler, Michael J. 2012b. "Understanding the Impact of Eminent Domain on Retail Space: An Alternative Approach to Measuring Value Diminution to Shopping Centers." *Retail Property Insights* 19:2, 33–36.

Seiler, Michael J. 2014a. "The Effect of Perceived Lender Characteristics and Market Conditions on Strategic Mortgage Defaults." *Journal of Real Estate Finance and Economics* 48:2, 256–270.

Seiler, Michael J. 2014b. "Measuring the Impact of Eminent Domain Partial Takings: A Behavioral Approach." *International Real Estate Review*, forthcoming.

Seiler, Michael J., and David M. Harrison. 2011. "Perceived Versus Actual Susceptibility to Normative Influence in the Presence of Defaulting Landlords." *Review of Behavioral Finance* 3:2, 55–77.

Seiler, Michael J., and Vicky L. Seiler. 2010. "Mitigating Investor Risk-Seeking Behavior in a Down Real Estate Market." *Journal of Behavioral Finance* 11:3, 161–167.

Seiler, Michael J., and Eric Walden. 2014a. "Lender Characteristics and the Neurological Reasons for Strategic Mortgage Default." *Journal of Real Estate Research*, forthcoming.

Seiler, Michael J., and Eric Walden. 2014b. "Strategic Mortgage Default and the Decision to Follow the Herd: A Neurological Explanation." Working Paper, The College of William & Mary.

Seiler, Michael J., Poornima Madhavan, and Molly Liechty. 2012a. "Toward an Understanding of Real Estate Homebuyer Internet Search Behavior: An Application of Ocular Tracking Technology." *Journal of Real Estate Research* 34:2, 211–241.

Seiler, Michael J., Poornima Madhavan, and Molly Liechty. 2012b. "Ocular Tracking and the Behavioral Effects of Negative Externalities on Market Prices and Opinion." *Journal of Housing Research* 21:2, 123–137.

Seiler, Michael J., Vicky L. Seiler, and Mark A. Lane. 2012. "Mental Accounting and False Reference Points in Real Estate Investment Decision Making." *Journal of Behavioral Finance* 13:1, 17–26.

Seiler, Michael J., Andrew J. Collins, and Nina H. Fefferman. 2013. "Strategic Mortgage Default in the Context of a Social Network." *Journal of Real Estate Research* 35:4, 445–475.

Seiler, Michael J., Mark A. Lane, and David M. Harrison. 2014. "Mimetic Herding Behavior and the Decision to Strategically Default." *Journal of Real Estate Finance and Economics*, forthcoming.

Seiler, Michael J., Vicky L. Seiler, Stefan Traub, and David M. Harrison. 2008a. "Regret Aversion and False Reference Points in Residential Real Estate." *Journal of Real Estate Research* 30:4, 461–474.

Seiler, Michael J., Vicky L. Seiler, Stefan Traub, and David M. Harrison. 2008b. "Familiarity Bias and the Status Quo Alternative." *Journal of Housing Research* 17:2, 139–154.

Seiler, Michael J., Vicky L. Seiler, Mark A. Lane, and David M. Harrison. 2012. "Fear, Shame, and Guilt: Economic and Behavioral Motivations for Strategic Default." *Real Estate Economics* 40:S1, 199–233.

Seiler, Michael J., Vicky L. Seiler, David M. Harrison, and Mark A. Lane. 2013. "Familiarity Bias and Perceived Future Home Price Movements." *Journal of Behavioral Finance* 14:1, 9–24.

Sun, Hua, and Michael J. Seiler. 2013. "Hyperbolic Discounting, Reference Dependence and Its Implications for the Housing Market." *Journal of Real Estate Research* 35:1, 1–23.

Turnbull, Geoffrey K. 2012. "Delegating Eminent Domain Powers to Private Firms: Land Use and Efficiency Implications." *Journal of Real Estate Finance and Economics* 45:2, 305–325.

Tversky, Amos, and Daniel Kahneman. 1991. "Loss Aversion in Riskless Choice: A Reference Dependent Model." *Quarterly Journal of Economics* 106:4, 1039–1061.

White, Brent T. 2010. "Underwater and Not Walking Away: Shame, Fear, and the Social Management of the Housing Crisis." *Wake Forest Law Review* 45, 971–1023.

Wyman, Oliver. 2010. "Experian/Oliver Wyman Market Intelligence Report: Understanding Strategic Default in Mortgages: Q2 2010 Update." http://www.experian.com/assets/decision-analytics/reports/strategic-default-report-2-2010.pdf.

Yavas, Abdullah, and C. F. Sirmans. 2005. "Real Options: Experimental Evidence." *Journal of Real Estate Finance and Economics* 31:1, 27–52.

Yavas, Abdullah, Thomas J. Miceli, and C. F. Sirmans. 2001. "An Experimental Analysis of the Impact of Intermediaries on the Outcome of Bargaining Games." *Real Estate Economics* 29:2, 251–276.

Part Two

PRIVATE ASSETS AND PROPERTIES

5

Multifamily Investment

WILLIAM G. HARDIN III
Director of The Hollo School of Real Estate and The Jerome Bain Real Estate Institute
Professor of Real Estate and Finance, Florida International University

Introduction

Multifamily housing is the subdivision of a single building or group of buildings into multiple space units allowing for individual unit use, occupancy, and possibly ownership. This definition obviates segmentation of this property type. Primary delineations are on whether units are owned or controlled by a single person or legal entity and whether the units are owner-occupied or rented.

In 2007 there were 138 million individual tax returns filed in the United States (Internal Revenue Service 2013) and 17 million included Schedule E for Rental Income and Expenses. Nearly 15 percent of taxpayers are reporting publicly to the IRS that they own rental real estate directly, nearly all of it residential in apartments, duplexes, and houses. This is apart from those investing in real estate through entities or securities.

When a property has a single owner, control and management is straightforward. With multiple unit owners, control and management is based on condominium regulations. Recognition of the differences in ownership structure is essential to understanding the broad asset class. Organization of a property into a condominium structure places limitations on the role of individual owners and restricts the initial developer's actions. Concurrently, ownership of a multi-unit property by a single entity or ownership group is the typical way a property held for investment is structured, especially for an institutional investor. Outside of markets with large scale, functioning capital markets, the condominium may be a more prevalent property structure even for investment-oriented units. Without the ability to aggregate capital at the project level, the financing of the overall project is more dependent on retail rather than wholesale sources of capital.

The multifamily investment market is a broad sector that includes some of the largest institutional investors. The sector includes real estate investment trusts (REITs) and other large-scale property owners as well as small individual unit owners buying property as an investment. The present focus is on ownership of and investment in multi-unit properties that generate a return, composed of both operating cash flows and potential capital gains on sales. These properties may be as small as duplex units or encompass properties that span many acres with thousands of units. The units may be in high and midrise buildings or garden-style apartments. The link across all these iterations is an end-user paying rent to occupy space. The rental rate is re-priced to the market level over a relatively short period of time. Special cases of multifamily include rent-controlled units and situations where the typical lease term may be greater than 12 months.

The multifamily product draws investors with access to public markets. It is also a focus for investors making both large and small direct investments in real estate. Debt for the property type is generally widely available. Debt includes bank related short- and intermediate-term loans. In the United States, it includes Fannie Mae and Freddie Mac loans, conduit loans, and government-sponsored lending programs run through the Federal Housing Administration (FHA). Debt tends to be more available for this property type because multifamily is classified as residential. It is also arguably the most transparent property type. Markets rents are more readily known with less uncertainty on expenses and tenant improvement related costs. Multifamily generates a cash flow that is typically more stable over time because any one individual tenant or lease has less impact on overall valuation. Hence, the attractiveness of multifamily is related to transparency of operations, the recurring mark-to-market of rents, the potential substantial diversification of tenants and resulting stability in revenues, access to debt markets, and reduction in legal risk associated with tenant–landlord conflicts.

The residential lease is one of the least complex of real estate contracts. Standard leases are the norm and the lease duration is short. This makes rent negotiations less important and simplifies the relationship between the tenant and the owner. An apartment property does not have value restricted by long-term leases at below-market rents. Concurrently, barring rent control, lease terms are unlikely to deviate markedly across tenants positively or negatively.

Multifamily real estate has a downside. That downside is the need for management. Properties have tenants that need to be served and leases that need renewal. Space is continuously on the market at larger properties as tenants turn over, with space being made available for rent. This management can be costly. Poor management leads to lower effective rents, effective gross income, and operating income. This requirement for property-level management is important and affects actual and prospective investment returns. While Genesove (2003) notes the stability of rents, stickiness in rental rate adjustment has been linked to landlords not effectively managing tenant relations. Management is also related to investment strategy and associated investor clienteles.

Investment Returns

As with other property types, the returns to apartment investments come from operating cash flows and reversionary or exit strategy related cash at disposition. With this being the case, related questions on tenants and landlords need to be addressed. What drives the tenant demand for space? Who are the tenants and what can they pay? What will landlords pay for this cash flow? The latter analysis can take the form of capitalization (cap) rates and market driven required discount rates. While firms such as REIS, Korpacz, IRR, and CoStar provide data on rents and cap rates, the present focus is on the fundamentals that determine market rents and cap rates. The demand analysis overlays with supply analysis since markets and submarkets can be constrained or unconstrained. Demand differs between the tenant and the landlord. The tenant is seeking a place to live in the market for space. The landlord offers the space. In a second market, the landlord holds an asset for investment.

Understanding multifamily investment starts with the rental market and operating cash flows. Typical or natural occupancy and vacancy rates within in a market or submarket along with property characteristics and economic drivers must be assessed. The rental determinants and resultant cash flows are then valued or priced by the investment community. Positive and negative rental market attributes flow to asset valuation, ultimate returns, and return attributions. Zietz (2003) provides a comprehensive overview of much of the research for multifamily real estate.

OPERATING RETURNS

A market's rental rate varies based on the interaction of supply and demand at the lowest market and unit levels. While an inherent interaction exists, the tenant operates at a submarket level. That is, a tenant is looking to rent an apartment within a defined geographical location. Each market and submarket has a natural vacancy rate. The *natural vacancy rate* is that rate where rent increases are zero. Rent growth is negative or falling when vacancy is above the natural rate. Alternative definitions of the natural vacancy rate are where rent increases are expected to be or are equal to the rate of inflation. Consequently, understanding the natural vacancy rate as applied to multifamily properties is necessary because it will impact stabilized cash flows that will then serve as the basis for asset price and value.

Rosen and Smith (1983) and Hendershott and Haurin (1988) assess the endogenous relationship between vacancy rates and rents in rental housing. Eubanks and Sirmans (1979) find that the vacancy coefficient is zero in the rent growth equation. Rent growth is constant, except for shifts in other variables. Gabriel and Nothaft (1988) find natural vacancy rates for apartments to vary between 3.9 and 10.0 percent during 1981–1985 across U.S. cities. Later, Gabriel and Nothaft (2001) find natural apartment vacancy rates of 4.0–4.5 percent for 29 cities over 1987–1996, or low variation.

The natural vacancy rate for multifamily rental varies across geographic markets and even submarkets. Hagen and Hansen (2010) provide an evaluation of natural vacancy rates for rental apartments at the submarket level using data from Seattle. Natural vacancy is not unit type dependent, but is influenced by geographic submarket. Advances in technology have lowered the natural vacancy rate because of a reduction in search and matching costs. Miceli and Sirmans (2013) suggest that increased vacancy spurs investment in maintenance to reduce this conditional vacancy and improve property cash flows.

The existing studies on the natural vacancy rate of multifamily properties highlight that unit rentals are dependent on geographical markets with an emphasis on submarket characteristics. No national or regional market is available for housing rentals. The interaction of supply and demand at the unit level is submarket dependent. From an investment standpoint, this implies a need to address and understand local rental markets. These issues include regulatory limitations on supply, identification of existing and prospective competition, and recognition of economic and demographic trends.

Multifamily Rents

Extensive research shows that multifamily rents are related to demographics. As Carn, Rabianski, Racster, and Seldin (1988) point out in their real estate market analysis, rental unit demand and subsequent rents are related to population, density, and income. Confirmation includes Ogur (1973), Rosen (1989), Rosen (1996), Jud, Benjamin, and Sirmans (1996), and Wilson and Frew (2007). Bible and Hsieh (1996) add neighborhood effects and show the importance of submarkets. Hanink, Cromley, and Ebenstein (2012) show the links in demographics, income, and rents in China supporting a robust underlying theory on housing rents. Common practice is to relate rents to demographics, although this is often on a default basis by segmenting larger markets into submarkets. Demographics change the demand for hedonic characteristics. As Valente, Wu, Gelfand, and Sirmans (2005) note, these relations further suggest that economic base is important. Well-defined location attributes are also considered.

Hedonic or physical characteristics affect rent. Jud et al. (1996) provide an overview of studies related to property hedonics. Marks (1984), Guntermann and Norrbin (1987), Sirmans, Sirmans, and Benjamin (1989), Sirmans and Benjamin (1991), and McDonald (2001) carry out hedonic pricing analyses. Unit size, unit type, project size, and a host of amenity-related variables increase rents and are standard modeling variables. Additional studies confirm that the number of units in a complex, the size of the individual unit, whether a building is garden-style or high-rise and the number of bedrooms in a unit are factors affecting rent. Wolverton, Hardin, and Cheng (1999) show the presence of separate markets by unit type such as one-bedroom, one-bath and two-bedrooms, two-baths.

Location within a building, within a city, and within a submarket is important. Benjamin and Sirmans (1996) show that location in proximity to transit matters. Gatzlaff and Smith (1993) investigate rail transit access and unit rents. Locations with negative externalities suffer reduced rents. As Boes and Nuesch (2011) show, airport noise negatively affects rents. Baranzini and Ramirez (2005) find a value associated with silence. Amenities and micro location matter and are priced in the rental equation and in unit prices. Asabere and Huffman (1996) show that property rents decline with distance from major thoroughfares and transportation corridors.

Jud and Frew (1990) find that atypical properties suffer a rental discount and have higher natural vacancy rates. Benjamin, Sirmans, and Zietz (1997) investigate security issues in high-rise buildings in Washington, DC. Characteristics associated with security including on-site management, restricted access, and 24-hour security increase rents. Hardin and Cheng (2003) look at garden-style apartments and find that communities with gated access generate a premium. Differences in the benefits of security occur across unit types. While limited, research associated with security implies a benefit to multifamily properties that incorporate appropriate security into their amenity packages.

Restrictions or services associated with use and lifestyle effects are also important in rent determination. Evidence by Benjamin, Jud, and Winkler (2001) shows that smoking restrictions can affect rents. Hardin and Cheng (2003) find that allowing pets increases rents and Lin, Allen, and Carter (2013) show permitting pets has a positive impact on condominium unit prices. Benjamin, Lusht, and Shilling (1998) examine the trade-off between requiring a higher security deposit on signing a lease versus a lower rent. This is a moral hazard, captured by higher rents for lower deposits. Renters with less liquidity or a lower willingness to allocate cash at the time of signing the rental contract pay higher rents.

Another condition of a lease is rent concessions. The tenant receives free rent for the initial or other months, or reduced rent in exchange for signing a lease of a longer term. Sirmans, Sirmans, and Benjamin (1994) show that effective rent and occupancy are related to concessions. Existing literature studies either asking rents or rents before concessions. From a practical point of view, when investigating properties for investment, the role of concessions needs assessment.

Apartment management plays a role in rent generation. Sirmans and Sirmans (1991b) look at professional designations as a signal of management ability. Managers with designations are associated with higher rents. Benjamin and Lusht (1993) contend that apartment management with scale reduces tenant search costs with a benefit to operators with better and larger scale management.

Sirmans, Sirmans, and Turnbull (1999) maintain that owner-managed apartments have higher rents than third-party managed firms for apartment buildings in Tallahassee, Florida. Using a larger set of data for Atlanta, Benjamin, Chinloy, and Hardin (2007) show that local players with scale generate higher rents. Hardin, Hill and Hopper (2009) show larger scale operators including REITs benefit from higher effective rents as suggested by Sirmans et al. (1999). Pagliari and Webb (1996) show a benefit to quality of management. The literature supports a benefit to professional management including self-management and scale of operations.

A few dominant factors determine rent. These include the location in neighborhood or submarket, unit size, and physical quality often proxied by property age along with differentials, both positive and negative, from the amenities of direct competition. Identifying direct property-level competition within a submarket is possible as is identifying variability in amenities and accessibility across properties. Investors at the property level have the ability to obtain substantive data on actual competing property rents, concessions, and occupancy. The unit or space market is transparent to the tenant. While it appears in the apartment unit market that the product is homogeneous, Benjamin, Chinloy, and Hardin (2006) show that operators can brand their product to signal quality. Scale operators benefit by generating higher gross and effective rents.

Investors also have the ability to monitor new supply. While investors in other property types such as commercial or nonresidential real estate also monitor new supply, the apartment sector is a commodity market at the construction and submarket level. Only when construction is completed is the space customized to create product differentiation. Multifamily investors deal with short-term leases. They are close to the market with tenants and prospective tenants continuously providing value or rent feedback. Limitations in development do affect rents, but this is more systematic over the long term (Wilson and Frew 2007).

From an investment standpoint, identifying market rents and occupancy levels is possible as is comparing existing property performance with these benchmarks. This makes the investment analysis for top line revenue more accurate. In turn, this leads to better projections of gross potential income, vacancy rates, and effective gross income.

Concurrently, professional management affects operating results with at least some evidence that owner managers are more effective. These two broad attributes are major reasons that the asset class appeals to both small scale and institutional investors.

MULTIFAMILY EXPENSES AND NET CASH FLOW

Less transparency occurs on the expense side of the property analysis. The range of properties that make up the multifamily property is extensive, and includes many smaller properties. If the apartment sector includes individually owned and leased units in multifamily buildings, the variance in actual and reported expenses is even more important. Smaller investors and properties create the most ambiguity. The assignment of management and leasing costs is often the problem.

For large properties, expenses are better quantified. At the large property, institutional level, comparisons are available. Goodman (2004) highlights that expenses can be estimated and documents the relations between property age and operating expenses. Because age is a proxy for depreciation and perhaps deferred maintenance, older properties post higher operating expense ratios. Springer and Waller (1996) show that smaller properties have higher per square foot expenses. They find that tenant turnover increases expenses and older properties have higher expenses. Additionally, higher quality product with more amenities and services has greater expenses.

Benchmarking can be done for external expenses such as property taxes. On an overall basis the common measure is the operating expense ratio. The *operating expense ratio* is operating expenses including property-level management as a percentage of effective gross income. *Effective gross income* is the rent roll when all units are occupied, less vacancy and concessions, plus other income such as from laundry, late fees, and parking. This metric is driven by the amenities offered by a property, the age of the property as a proxy for physical obsolescence, and managerial skill.

Many small investors do not fully consider cost management. For example, if small investors carry out repairs themselves or provide management without direct pay, they are not making cash charges against the rent revenue and net operating income (NOI) appears higher. *Net operating income* is effective gross income less operating expenses for repairs, utilities, property management, insurance, and property taxes. That leaves the issue of where to place capital expenses such as roof and structure and appliances. A management strategy of putting capital expenses above the line before computing NOI apparently understates performance. Self-management often leads to understating expenses and overstating returns to investment.

Research identifies quantified differences in expense management and operational efficiencies starting with the generation of effective gross income. As Benjamin et al. (2007) show, being a scale operator with local knowledge enhances performance with higher effective income. Location, especially when substantial changes in land values occur within a market, affects expenses. Property taxes are an example where location, especially when concurrent with an underutilized property, can be high due to a prospective change in highest and best use. This is also the case for insurance, especially for properties in high-risk areas related to flooding and hurricanes. The moral hazard of bailouts by government agencies in areas that are prone to hurricane and wind risk provides an incentive for apartment owners to go without insurance. However, because lenders require insurance coverage, the moral hazard comes when the property is unencumbered and has no mortgage. The added risk of not carrying hazard insurance is positively correlated with the ratio of land value to total value and whether the property has its highest and best use. Excluding property insurance reduces operating expenses and raises apparent returns.

Given that apartments typically use a gross lease, charging tenants rent before expenses, cost management is important. Rents must increase over time to pay for increasing expenses. Common indexes relate to changes in rent, but no such measures are found for expenses. Investors need to match rent and expense growth expectations and should not be complacent with a sole focus on rents. Expenses related to debt service can affect rents. Sirmans and Sirmans (1991a) show that below market financing is associated with lower rents, but has a positive effect on price.

Required capital expenditures are more transparent for apartments. A cost exists to turn units when one tenant leaves and is replaced by another. These turn costs include painting, floor repair, and cleaning. A cost is associated with a change in tenancy, but the cost is low compared to actual tenant improvement dollars in other properties. This cost can be absorbed within the expense category or at least standardized. Unlike office and retail and other property types, minimal tenant improvement dollars are available or expended. Landlords do not customize the space to meet the requests of apartment tenants, as is the case in the commercial market. In some cases deferred maintenance can occur, but it is usually reflected in rents and ultimately in property restructuring as noted by Chinloy, Hardin, and Wu (2013a).

Overall, multifamily properties have less ambiguity in assessing and projecting cash flows than in non-residential commercial real estate. Investors in larger multi-unit properties receive cash flow generated from multiple tenants. The property's operating performance is not linked to that of an individual tenant. With extensive information on market rents and occupancy, initial risk for the property class is mitigated. Investors buying multifamily assets should have an historic operating statement that allows assessment of cash flows and benchmarking, reducing risk. The reduced risk also allows yields and returns to be forecasted with greater accuracy.

The ability to mark rents to market makes the asset class appealing to both investors and lenders. Given that calculating NOI is both straightforward and meaningful, loan-to-value (LTV) ratios are often higher for this group. Required debt service coverage ratios (DSCR) of NOI to debt service are lower. While Archer, Elmer, Harrison, and Ling (2002) identify low initial NOI or cash flow as a primary determinant of mortgage default, the added benefit associated with additional leveraged returns makes the property type appealing. The relatively stable cash flows allow for meaningful initial yield and cap rate comparisons.

Multifamily Cap Rates, Price, and Per Unit Prices

A primary return assessment and valuation technique used in the multifamily property class is the capitalization rate or cap rate methodology. While this technique is applied to other property types, it is perhaps best suited for multifamily properties due to the marking of rents to market and a lower requirement for tenant improvement investments. The *cap rate* is the NOI of a property divided by the property's imputed value or price. It is an unleveraged yield calculation and used in practice to estimate value. Cap rates from property sales are used as a denominator with existing property NOI as the numerator in estimating value. The research on cap rates includes Ambrose and Nourse (1993), Jud and Winkler (1995), Chen, Hudson-Wilson, and Nordby (2004), and Hendershott and MacGregor (2005a, b).

Chichernea, Miller, Fisher, White, and Sklarz (2008) examine the basic constructs associated with the cap rate in the multifamily property market. The focus is on the determinants of cap rates with an emphasis on the Gordon growth model. When applied to real estate cap rates, it allows for testing the relationship between discount rates and NOI growth rates. For a given nominal discount rate, properties with better prospects for growth in NOI will sell at lower cap rates. Unfortunately, the empirical results do not support the Gordon growth model. No strong relationship between economic growth and cap rates is found at the metropolitan statistical area (MSA) level. Yet, Plazzi, Torous, and Valkanov (2010) show a positive link between returns and growth rates in rents.

Part of the ambiguity in results may stem from a limited data set at the MSA versus the submarket level. Chervachidze and Wheaton (2013) propose that compression in cap rate spreads is due to changes in macroeconomic conditions. That suggests a marginal contribution to cap determination from solely real estate oriented factors. Although specific differences may exist between properties, capital markets and other economic forces strongly influence the real estate asset market. Initial yield, when measured using cap rates, is determined by capital market returns.

Submarket effects on cap rates are based primarily on local economic performance along with local regulatory conditions that affect supply. Malpezzi, Chun, and Green (1998) and Schuetz (2008) point out that regulatory and other conditions create supply constraints. Clayton, Ling, and Naranjo (2009) suggest that investor sentiment affects cap rates at the national level. Using data from the Atlanta MSA, Wheaton and Nechayev (2005) show that the theoretical rent growth and yield relation holds when modeled at the submarket level. Local factors associated with supply constraints and market participant behavior affect cap rates on the margin.

A common practice is to price or value multifamily assets with hedonic and spatial attributes. Frew and Jud (2003) estimate multifamily properties in Portland, Oregon, and find that size, number of units, location, and neighborhood factors influence price. Multifamily properties are also valued on a per unit basis. Although this valuation metric does not generate an investment yield, it does tie together property characteristics, submarkets, price, and value. Hedonic characteristics, participant characteristics, and submarket effects are stressed. The models appear to be efficient with high adjusted R^2 outcomes.

Various researchers investigate per unit multifamily prices. The factors affecting value as consistent price determinants include submarket, age, size, number of units, overall land size, and property quality. Debate remains as to the importance of the location of apartment investors. Lambson, McQueen, and Slade (2004) postulate that out-of-towners pay more. Chinloy, Hardin, and Wu (2013a) contend that local experience is the determinant. A very small cohort of active investors obtains discounts, with out-of-towners getting the typical transaction prices. It is not out-of-towners paying a premium, but the small group of active local players that get a discount. Benjamin, Chinloy, Hardin, and Wu (2008) further show that participant type can impact price. Condo converters paid premiums during the housing boom era.

Apartment properties are valued or priced based on a combination of economic, demographic, hedonic, and market participant factors, along with yields derived from the capital markets. Wheaton and Nechayev (2005) highlight the tie in with capital markets and show that cap rates can be empirically associated with capital market returns when models properly address submarket conditions. Investors can identify submarkets where rent growth is aligned with cap rates. The modeling of cap rates, however, remains difficult. At the asset or per unit level submarket conditions matter, related to demographics and economics. Hedonic characteristics including age, unit size, overall size, and quality along with amenities and clientele effects of market participants have effects on price and cap rates.

Returns, Diversification, and Disposition

Studies of actual returns for multifamily are limited because income returns are not readily available even as transaction data are public. Data from the National Council of Real Estate Investment Fiduciaries (NCREIF) showing that the majority of returns to the apartment class over the long term come from income highlight the attraction. Rosen (1996) maintains that multifamily is a good long-term investment due to positive demographics and limits in supply. The results bear out this projection. Fiorilla, Liang, and Nitschke (2012) provide a relatively positive outlook with a large build up in the core renter cohort, offset by high relative rents and the affordability of home purchases.

Anderson, McLemore, Conner, and Liang (2003) provide a foundation for apartment investments within an institutional portfolio context. Empirical results show limited rental market or income volatility and high risk-adjusted returns. Garden-style apartments have high risk-adjusted returns and the asset class is becoming more accepted by institutional investors. Multifamily is also shown to be defensive during weak economic times. These results follow an earlier study by Abrahams (1996) that highlights the cash flow characteristics associated with apartments. Plazzi, Torous, and Valkanov (2008) highlight the range of dispersion in rental growth and returns, which seems to suggest that submarket delineation is a requirement in projecting returns to a heterogeneous asset class. As Huang (2008) shows, apartments are optimal for a mixed asset portfolio that includes real estate. Huang and Hudson-Wilson (2007) suggest that apartments are also long-term inflation hedges, providing an additional investment benefit.

Plazzi et al. (2010) suggest that cap rates capture expected returns in apartments. Growth rates in rents do not appear to add much expected returns. The implications are that apartment investors are price or yield takers and are at the mercy of changes in capital market yields in generating returns. Expected real capital gains are zero. This is a likely outcome looking at the cash flow or income returns for apartments provided by NCREIF and comparing them with the appreciation returns. Over 1984–2012 apartments had an annual total return of 9.3 percent, above the 7.8 percent for all commercial real estate. The premium is concentrated in two post-recession periods of 1992–1994 and from 2009 to 2012. Apartments account for 25 percent of the NCREIF coverage universe (National Multi Housing Council 2013). The former return series is rising with minimal variability while the latter has substantial volatility around a zero mean in real terms. Hence, total returns are dependent both on long-term cap rates and disturbances in capital market fluctuations but shift with changes in market participant characteristics.

Certain cohorts of investors affect transaction prices. Out-of-towners, tax deferred exchangers, condominium converters, REITs, institutional investors providing additional capital, value-added investors, owners of foreclosed properties, and other clienteles pay different transaction prices. The first four groups—out-of-towners, tax deferred exchangers, condominium converters, and REITs—appear to pay higher prices at acquisition. As these market participants enter and exit the market, prices will deviate from fundamental values.

Using data from the Phoenix market, Lambson et al. (2004) postulate that out-of-state buyers pay an acquisition premium of about 4 percent. Classifying properties with a binary variable to differentiate buyer location, they show a premium paid by out-of-state buyers. Other studies show a similar result. Nonetheless, Chinloy et al. (2013a) contend that a very small group of experienced investors obtains this purchase discount. A value exists to being local with experience, current market transactions, and having a reputation for closing. When the pricing model is thus specified and controls for submarkets are imposed, out-of-market buyers are not shown to pay a premium. The benefit is to locality on the buy side.

Ling and Petrova (2008) show that market participants completing a tax-deferred exchange pay 9 percent higher prices. These prices are in excess of the tax deferral. This is especially important given the increase in tax-deferred transactions evidenced by the growth in tenant in common investments. These apartment buyers, especially those in the lower end of the market by price, pay a premium.

A similar circumstance occurs in the case of condominium converters during housing booms. Benjamin et al. (2008) provide evidence that condo converters pay premiums in the South Florida market. Investors converting rental units to single owner units pay a premium of at least 6 percent over investors buying properties based on cash flow generation. The converters lead the market and concurrently pay premiums.

Evidence shows that REITs also pay acquisition premiums for apartments. Hardin and Wolverton (1999) show that REITs paid premiums in some markets at the beginning of the modern REIT era. Hardin and Wu (2008) argue that the premiums were confined to a specific time period and further assessments are needed. Wiley (2013) shows that apartments sold by REITs classified as opportunistic obtain sales prices above fundamental value.

Research also shows that capital flows affect price. Although early work on syndicators by Beaton and Sirmans (1986) using a small dataset shows an impact related to capital flows and source, more recent research finds different results. Fisher, Ling, and Naranjo (2009) provide empirical evidence that capital flows predict returns in the apartment market. They provide additional evidence that market participants can affect the apartment market. Chinloy et al. (2013b) contend that value-added investors affect prices. Transaction prices are dependent on where on the repositioning sequence the transaction takes place. Value-added investors buy properties needing repositioning and dispose when the apartments are performing at market. Two consecutive or repeat transactions for the same property are actually representative of two qualities of property with differing return potentials. Distressed property with foreclosure status transact at discounts (Hardin and Wolverton 1996).

Apartment investment returns are characterized by quantifiable cash flows with lower levels of income volatility than found in other property types. The asset class has high risk- adjusted returns as compared with other real estate assets. Long-term results are dependent on general investment conditions that impact cap rates. Market participants also affect prices. This is based on differing investment strategies by investor cohort and ownership position.

A separate issue is leveraged investments in apartments and the potential to hedge interest rate risk with long-term debt. Bradley, Cutts, and Follain (2001) provide a descriptive analysis of mortgage lending and Huang and Hudson-Wilson (2007) look at inflation hedges. This is a major limitation in the existing research in the area, especially given the widespread acceptance of lending on this property type. Studies of actual returns with leverage have been limited given that private data are required, inclusive of debt service and financing terms.

Controls, Seniors, and Condominiums

Other areas relate to the multifamily property class. Because housing has major public policy implications, the impact of regulation on apartment operations and returns is required. Smith and Tomlinson (1981) find a negative relationship between rental controls and value using data from Ontario. Shulman (1981) provides a similar study and outcome. Rents decline, but so do values, which will limit new supply (Holm 1983). Rent controls cause a reduction in supply and high rents for non-controlled units while reducing real rents for controlled units.

Glaeser, Gyorko, and Saks (2005) maintain that the reason real estate is so expensive in Manhattan is that regulations drive prices above production costs. The idea is one that permeates the apartment investment market. Properties located in areas with more restrictive land use have higher rents and sell for lower cap rates.

Another way to specifically look at regulatory impacts is with senior housing markets. Guntermann and Thomas (2004) and Allen (1997) contend that imposing minimum age restrictions such as 55 years old are value enhancing. In the United States, the Fair Housing Act of 1968 and the Housing for Older Persons Act of 1995 allow such restrictions without being considered discriminatory. Other studies are less positive. Carter, Lin, Allen, and Haloupek (2013) find a large discount during the global financial crisis for individual units of senior housing. For institutional investment in senior housing, Worzala, Karofsky, and Davis (2009) provide survey data and Laposa and Singer (1999) preliminary data on the sector's potential and scale.

Finally, there is the market of individual investors buying single-family homes and condominiums or apartments for rental. Return attributions have not been studied and the role of small investors in the provision of rental housing has been minimal.

Summary and Conclusions

The multifamily or apartment property class invites small-scale and large-scale investors. Its appeal is based on the ability to obtain debt, often with government protection and the wide range of price points.

Apartments have several important attributes. They offer a greater level of transparency in rents when compared to other commercial property. The property type has short-term leases that are quickly re-priced to market. Market rents are readily available. Rents and growth in rents tie to economic and demographic characteristics. Amenities and locational attributes are reflected in rents and prices. The greatest operating ambiguity is related to actual property expenses. These expenses can be misstated, especially when management costs are not fully assigned to a property.

In the asset market for apartments, a link exists between cap rates and income growth. This link varies across submarkets and is inconsistent across national, regional, and broad metro areas. What is evident is the yield or prospective yield at purchase. With value or price of the apartment asset on a per unit basis, the models can address hedonic conditions. In all cases, the apartment buildings can be well modeled and the characteristics that determine price defined. These characteristics will include those of the market participants as well as the properties.

The ability to generate cash flows is important when evaluating overall returns. In a portfolio context, multifamily property has a lower volatility in cash flows and strong risk-adjusted returns. Institutional and non-institutional lenders value these attributes as do investors. Given the asset type's prominence and ubiquity, knowing returns at all levels of investment, including small duplex properties, is desirable. The 17 million small residential real estate investors have a rung on the property ladder and are likely more numerous than any other type of small business owner. These small investors should understand depreciation as well as operating and capital expenses. Few studies, however, address the characteristics and actual returns of the smaller investor.

While scale institutional investment in large properties with multiple rental units is common in the United States, investment in single units by small investors is also prevalent, as it is globally. Why certain global markets lack large-scale investment in rental properties needs investigation. Although benefits of scale in management exist, such benefits can accrue only when capital markets are sufficiently developed. That scale does not restrict millions of investors from entering multifamily investment.

Discussion Questions

1. Explain why multifamily property may be a preferred investment for both institutional and small investors.
2. Identify the primary determinants of cap rates in the multifamily sector and indicate whether these rates are more or less known with certainty.
3. Discuss the role of the natural vacancy rate in multifamily investment.
4. Explain what shifts rental rates, expenses, and returns.
5. Identify the factors that affect per unit prices in multifamily.

References

Abrahams, Jesse. 1996. "On the Use of a Cash-Flow Time-Series to Measure Property Performance." *Journal of Real Estate Research* 11:3, 291–308.

Allen, Marcus. 1997. "Measuring the Effects of 'Adults Only' Age Restrictions on Condominium Prices." *Journal of Real Estate Research* 14:3, 339–346.

Ambrose, Brent W., and Hugh O. Nourse. 1993. "Factors Influencing Capitalization Rates." *Journal of Real Estate Research* 8:2, 221–237.

Anderson, Randy I., Richard McLemore, Phillip Conner, and Youguo Liang. 2003. "Portfolio Implications of Apartment Investing." *Journal of Real Estate Research* 25:2, 113–131.

Archer, Wayne, Peter Elmer, David Harrison, and David Ling. 2002. "Determinants of Multifamily Mortgage Default." *Real Estate Economics* 30:3, 445–473.

Asabere, Paul, and Forrest Huffman. 1996. "Thoroughfares and Apartment Values." *Journal of Real Estate Research* 12:1, 9–16.

Baranzini, Andrea, and Jose Ramirez. 2005. "Paying for Quietness: The Impact of Noise on Geneva Rents." *Urban Studies* 42:4, 633–646.

Beaton, William, and C. F. Sirmans. 1986. "Do Syndicators Pay More for Real Estate?" *Real Estate Economics* 14:2, 206–215.

Benjamin, John, and Kenneth Lusht. 1993. "Search Cost and Apartment Rents." *Journal of Real Estate Finance and Economics* 6:3; 189–197.

Benjamin, John, and Stacy Sirmans. 1996. "Mass Transportation, Apartment Rent and Property Values." *Journal of Real Estate Research* 8:1, 1–8.

Benjamin, John, Stacy Sirmans, and Emily Zietz. 1997. "Security Measures and the Apartment Market." *Journal of Real Estate Research* 14:3, 347–358.

Benjamin, John, Kenneth Lusht, and James Shilling. 1998. "What Do Rental Contracts Reveal about Adverse Selection and Moral Hazard in Rental Housing Markets?" *Real Estate Economics* 26:2, 309–329.

Benjamin, John, Donald Jud, and Daniel Winkler. 2001. "The Value of Smoking Prohibitions in Vacation Rental Properties." *Journal of Real Estate Finance and Economics* 22:1, 117–128.

Benjamin, John, Peter Chinloy, and William Hardin III. 2006. "Local Presence, Scale and Vertical Integration: Brands and Signals." *Journal of Real Estate Finance and Economics* 33:4, 389–402.

Benjamin, John, Peter Chinloy, and William Hardin III. 2007. "Institutional–Grade Properties: Performance and Ownership." *Journal of Real Estate Research* 29:3, 219–240.

Benjamin, John, Peter Chinloy, William Hardin III, and Zhonghua Wu. 2008. "Clientele Effects and Condo Conversions." *Real Estate Economics* 36:4, 611–634.

Bible, Douglas, and Cheng-Ho Hsieh. 1996. "Applications of Geographic Information Systems for the Analysis of Apartment Rents." *Journal of Real Estate Research* 12:1, 79–88.

Boes, Stefan, and Stephan Nuesch. 2011. "Quasi-Experimental Evidence on the Effect of Aircraft Noise on Apartment Rents." *Journal of Urban Economics* 69:2, 196–204.

Bradley, Donald, Amy Crews Cutts, and James Follain. 2001. "An Examination of Mortgage Debt Characteristics and Financial Risk among Multifamily Properties." *Journal of Housing Economics* 10:4, 482–506.

Carn, Neil, Joseph Rabianski, Ronald Racster, and Maury Seldin. 1988. *Real Estate Market Analysis: Techniques and Applications*. Englewood Cliffs, NJ: Prentice-Hall.

Carter, Charles, Zhenguo Lin, Marcus Allen, and William Haloupek. 2013. "Another Look at Effects of 'Adults-Only' Age Restrictions on Housing Prices." *Journal of Real Estate Finance and Economics* 46:1, 115–130.

Chen, Jun, Susan Hudson-Wilson, and Hans Nordby. 2004. "Real Estate Pricing: Spreads and Sensibilities: Why Real Estate Pricing is Rational." *Journal of Real Estate Portfolio Management* 10:1, 1–22.

Chervachidze, Serguei, and William Wheaton. 2013. "What Determined the Great Cap Rate Compression of 2000–2007, and the Dramatic Reversal during the 2008–2009 Financial Crisis?" *Journal of Real Estate Finance and Economics* 46:2, 208–231.

Chichernea, Doina, Norman Miller, Jeffrey Fisher, Bob White, and Michael Sklarz. 2008. "A Cross-Sectional Analysis of Cap Rates by MSA." *Journal of Real Estate Research* 30:3, 249–292.

Chinloy, Peter, William Hardin III, and Zhonghua Wu. 2013. "Price, Place, People and Local Experience." *Journal of Real Estate Research* 35:4, 477–505 .

Chinloy, Peter, William Hardin III, and Zhonghua Wu. 20134 "Transaction Frequency and Commercial Property." *Journal of Real Estate Finance and Economics* 47:4, 640–658.

Clayton, James, David Ling, and Andy Naranjo. 2009. "Commercial Real Estate Valuation: Fundamentals versus Investor Sentiment." *Journal of Real Estate Finance and Economics* 38:1, 5–37.

Eubanks, Arthur, Jr., and C. F. Sirmans. 1979. "The Price Adjustment Mechanism for Rental Housing in the United States." *Quarterly Journal of Economics* 93:1,163–183.

Fiorilla, Paul, Youguo Liang, and Frank Nitschke. 2012. "From Bullish to Balanced: A Changing View of the U.S. Apartment Market." *Journal of Real Estate Portfolio Management* 18:2, 239–246.

Fisher, Jeffrey, David Ling, and Andy Naranjo. 2009. "Institutional Capital Flows and Return Dynamics in Private Commercial Real Estate Markets." *Real Estate Economics* 37:1, 85–116.

Frew, James, and G. Donald Jud. 2003. "Estimating the Value of Apartment Buildings." *Journal of Real Estate Research* 25:1, 77–86.

Gabriel, Stuart, and Frank Nothaft. 1988. "Rental Housing Markets and the Natural Vacancy Rate." *Real Estate Economics* 16:4, 419–429.

Gabriel, Stuart, and Frank Nothaft. 2001. "Rental Housing Markets, the Incidence and Duration of Vacancy, and the Natural Vacancy Rate." *Journal of Urban Economics* 49:1, 121–149.

Gatzlaff, Dean, and Marc Smith. 1993. "The Impact of the Miami Metrorail on the Value of Residences near Rail Stations." *Land Economics* 69:1, 54–66.

Genesove, David. 2003. "The Nominal Rigidity of Apartment Rents." *Review of Economics and Statistics* 85:4, 844–853.

Glaeser, Edward, Joseph Gyourko, and Raven Saks. 2005. "Why Is Manhattan So Expensive? Regulation and the Rise in Housing Prices." *Journal of Law and Economics* 48:2, 331–369.

Goodman, Jack. 2004. "Determinants of Operating Costs of Multifamily Rental Housing." *Journal of Housing Economics* 13:3, 226–244.

Guntermann, Karl, and Stefan Norrbin. 1987. "Explaining the Variability in Apartment Rents." *Real Estate Economics* 15:4, 321–340.

Guntermann, Karl, and Gareth Thomas. 2004. "Loss of Age-Restricted Status and Property Values: Youngtown Arizona." *Journal of Real Estate Research* 26:3, 255–275.

Hagen, Daniel, and Julia Hansen. 2010. "Rental Housing and the Natural Vacancy Rate." *Journal of Real Estate Research* 32:4, 413–433.

Hanink, Dean, Robert Cromley, and Avraham Ebenstein. 2012. "Spatial Variation in the Determinants of House Prices and Apartment Rents in China." *Journal of Real Estate Finance and Economics* 45:2, 347–363.

Hardin, William, III, and Ping Cheng. 2003. "Apartment Security: A Note on Gated Access and Rental Rates." *Journal of Real Estate Research* 25:2, 145–157.

Hardin, William, III, and Marvin Wolverton. 1996. "The Relationship between Foreclosure Status and Apartment Price." Journal of Real Estate Research 12:1, 101–109.

Hardin, William, III, and Marvin Wolverton. 1999. "Equity REIT Property Acquisitions: Do Apartments REITs Pay a Premium?" *Journal of Real Estate Research* 17:1, 113–126.

Hardin, William, III, and Zhonghua Wu. 2008. "Clientele Effects, REITs, and Acquisition Premiums." *Journal of Real Estate Portfolio Management* 14:4, 375–384.

Hardin, William, III, Matt Hill, and James Hopper. 2009. "Ownership Structure, Property Performance, Multifamily Properties and REITs." *Journal of Real Estate Research* 31:3, 285–306.

Hendershott, Patric, and Donald Haurin. 1988. "Adjustments in the Real Estate Markets." *Real Estate Economics* 16:4, 343–353.

Hendershott, Patric, and Bryan MacGregor. 2005a. "Investor Rationality: An Analysis of the NCREIF Commercial Property Data." *Journal of Real Estate Research* 27:4, 345–375.

Hendershott, Patric, and Bryan MacGregor. 2005b. "Investor Rationality: Evidence from UK Capitalization Rates." *Real Estate Economics* 33:2, 299–322.

Holm, Charles. 1983. "The Reaction of Landlords to Rent Control." *Real Estate Economics* 11:4, 504–520.

Huang, Haibo, and Susan Hudson-Wilson. 2007. "Private Commercial Real Estate Equity Returns and Inflation: New News on Hedging Power." *Journal of Portfolio Management* 33:5, 63–73.

Huang, Shuyun. 2008. "Mixed Asset Portfolio Analysis with Different Real Estate Sectors in the U.S." *Economic and Financial Modeling* 15:2, 53–98.

Internal Revenue Service. 2013. *Tax Statistics, 2007*. http://www.irs.gov/taxstats/.

Jud, Donald, and James Frew. 1990. "Atypicality and the Natural Vacancy Rate Hypothesis." *Real Estate Economics* 18:3, 294–301.

Jud, Donald, and Daniel Winkler. 1995. "The Capitalization Rate of Commercial Properties and Market Returns." *Journal of Real Estate Research* 10:5, 509–518.

Jud, Donald, John Benjamin, and G. Stacy Sirmans. 1996. "What Do We Know about Apartments and Their Markets?" *Journal of Real Estate Research* 11:3, 243–258.

Lambson, Val, Grant McQueen, and Barrett Slade. 2004. "Do Out-of-State Buyers Pay More for Real Estate?" *Real Estate Economics* 32:1, 85–126.

Laposa, Steven, and Harvey Singer. 1999. "Size, Scope and Performance of the Seniors' Housing and Care Industry." *Journal of Real Estate Portfolio Management* 5:3, 211–224.

Lin, Zhenguo, Marcus Allen, and Charles Carter. 2013. "Pet Policies and Housing Prices: Evidence from the Condominium Market." *Journal of Real Estate Finance and Economics* 47:1,109–122.

Ling, David, and Milena Petrova. 2008. "Avoiding Taxes at Any Cost: The Economics of Tax-Deferred Real Estate Exchanges." *Journal of Real Estate Finance and Economics* 36:3, 367–404.

Malpezzi, Stephen, Gregory Chun, and Richard Green. 1998. "New Place-to-Place Housing Price Indexes for U.S. Metropolitan Areas, and Their Determinants: An Application of Urban Indicators." *Real Estate Economics* 26:2, 235–274.

Marks, David. 1984. "The Effect of Rent Control on the Price of Rental Housing: An Hedonic Approach." *Land Economics* 60:1, 81–94.

McDonald, John. 2001. "Cost-Benefit Analysis of Local Land Use Allocation Decisions." *Journal of Regional Science* 41:2, 277–299.

Miceli, Thomas, and C. F. Sirmans. 2013. "Efficiency Rents: A New Theory of the Natural Vacancy Rate for Rental Housing." *Journal of Housing Economics* 22:1, 20–24.

National Multi Housing Council. 2013. "Quick Facts: Investment Returns on Apartments." http://www.nmhc.org.

Ogur, Jonathan. 1973. "Higher Education and Housing: The Impact of Colleges and Universities on Local Rental Housing Markets." *American Journal of Economics and Sociology* 32:4, 387–394.

Pagliari, James, Jr., and James Webb. 1996. "On Setting Apartment Rental Rates: A Regression-Based Approach." *Journal of Real Estate Research* 12:1, 37–61.

Plazzi, Alberto, Walter Torous, and Rossen Valkanov. 2008. "The Cross Sectional Dispersion of Commercial Real Estate Returns and Rent Growth: Time Variation and Economic Fluctuations." *Real Estate Eco*nomics 36:3, 403–439.

Plazzi, Alberto, Walter Torous, and Rossen Valkanov. 2010. "Expected Returns and Expected Growth in Rents in Commercial Real Estate." *Review of Financial Studies* 23:9, 3469–3519.

Rosen, Kenneth. 1989. "The Apartment Market—Changing Demographics and Economic Environment." *Housing Finance* 8:1, 63–80.

Rosen, Kenneth. 1996. "The Economics of the Apartment Market in the 1990s." *Journal of Real Estate Research* 11:3, 215–241.

Rosen, Kenneth, and Lawrence Smith. 1983. "The Price-Adjustment Process for Rental Housing and the Natural Vacancy Rate." *American Economic Review* 73:4, 779–785.

Schuetz, Jenny. 2008. "Guarding the Town Walls: Mechanisms and Motives for Restricting Multifamily Housing in Massachusetts." *Real Estate Economics* 36:3, 555–586.

Shulman, David. 1981. "Real Estate Valuation under Rent Controls: The Case of Santa Monica." *Real Estate Economics* 9:1, 38–53.

Sirmans, Stacy, and John Benjamin. 1991. "Determinants of Market Rent." *Journal of Real Estate Research* 6:3, 357–380.

Sirmans, Stacy, and C. F. Sirmans. 1991a. "Rents, Selling Prices and Financing Premiums." *Urban Studies* 28:2, 267–276.

Sirmans, Stacy, and C. F. Sirmans. 1991b. "Property Manager Designations and Apartment Rent." *Journal of Real Estate Research* 7:1, 91–98.

Sirmans, Stacy, C. F. Sirmans, and John Benjamin. 1989. "Determining Apartment Rent: The Value of Amenities, Services, and External Factors." *Journal of Real Estate Research* 3:1, 33–43.

Sirmans, Stacy, C. F. Sirmans, and John Benjamin. 1994. "Apartment Rent, Concessions and Occupancy Rates." *Journal of Real Estate Research* 9:3, 299–312.

Sirmans, Stacy, C. F. Sirmans, and Geoffrey Turnbull. 1999. "Prices, Incentives and Choice of Management Form." *Regional Science and Urban Economics* 29:2, 173–195.

Smith, Lawrence, and Peter Tomlinson. 1981. "Rent Controls in Ontario: Roofs or Ceilings." *Real Estate Economics* 9:2, 93–114.

Springer, Thomas, and Neil Waller. 1996. "Maintenance of Residential Rental Property: An Empirical Analysis." *Journal of Real Estate Research* 12:1, 89–100.

Valente, James, ShanShan Wu, Alan Gelfand, and C. F. Sirmans. 2005. "Apartment Rent Predictions Using Spatial Modeling." *Journal of Real Estate Research* 27:1, 105–136.

Wheaton, William, and Gleb Nechayev. 2005. "Does Location Matter? Do Property Fundamentals Vary Within Markets, and Is This Reflected in Pricing?" *Journal of Portfolio Management*, Special Issue, 100–108.

Wiley, Jonathan. 2013. "REIT Asset Sales: Opportunistic Versus Liquidation." *Real Estate Economics* 41:3, 1–47.

Wilson, Beth, and James Frew. 2007. "Apartment Rents and Location in Portland, Oregon: 1992–2002." *Journal of Real Estate Research* 29:2, 2001–2017.

Wolverton, Marvin, William Hardin III, and Ping Cheng. 1999. "The Relationship between Unit Mix and Apartment Property Performance." *Journal of Real Estate Finance and Economics* 19:3, 113–126.

Worzala, Elaine, Judith Karofsky, and Jeffrey Davis. 2009. "The Senior Living Property Sector: How Is It Perceived by the Institutional Investor?" *Journal of Real Estate Portfolio Management* 15:2, 141–156.

Zietz, Emily. 2003. "Multifamily Housing: A Review of Theory and Evidence." *Journal of Real Estate Research* 25:2, 185–244.

6

Retail Real Estate

FRANÇOIS DES ROSIERS
Professor, Department of Finance, Insurance and Real Estate, Laval University

MARIUS THÉRIAULT
Professor, Graduate School of Land Use Planning and Regional Development, Laval University

Introduction

Retail real estate encompasses a wide range of property goods and services categories, each following its own market dynamics. Technological and demographic changes have reshaped retail activities in developed economies over the past century. The private car revolution that occurred in the 1920s and which, following World War II, allowed the suburban way of life to flourish throughout the United States and Canada has triggered the shopping center culture that still prevails.

Strip malls are open-air shopping centers with stores arranged in a row and made accessible through a front sidewalk. Since the late 1960s, strip malls evolved into larger, self-contained, and enclosed establishments often offering multiple entertainment facilities. In the mid-1980s, the retail sector saw the emergence of *big-box* stores (also called big boxes) selling either general merchandise or specialty goods and offering direct parking facilities. The concept spread throughout North American and European cities. *Power centers* consist of a group of three or more big-box retailers complemented by smaller stores usually located in strip plazas, all sharing parking. The fierce competition that big-box stores and power centers exert on traditional shopping malls has forced the latter to revisit their retail mix strategy and to capitalize on newcomers' proximity so as to attract a targeted clientele.

Shopping mall development is at a standstill and even big-box and power center development approaches its maturity stage, at least in most North American cities. The cause is electronic commerce, or e-commerce, thriving around the world and grasping an ever-growing share of retail sales. As of 2010, the United Kingdom had the biggest e-commerce market in the world when measured by the amount spent per capita (Boston Consulting Group 2010). During 2013, e-commerce sales worldwide are expected to reach $1.3 trillion, up from $1 trillion in 2012. North America is expected to have a world market share of 31.5 percent, down from 33.5 percent in 2012. Among emerging economies, Asia-Pacific countries display the highest growth. Their share of worldwide e-commerce sales, which stood at 27.9 percent in 2011, is expected to reach

33.4 percent by the end of 2013 (Emarketer 2013). As with financial services and industrial production, retail activities are being delocalized and globalized, which unavoidably affects in-store marketing strategies at the local level.

This chapter examines two topics in a Canadian context. The first topic addresses spatial competition between big-box stores, traditional shopping centers, and commercial streets in Quebec City using an extensive Origin-Destination (OD) phone survey providing detailed information on households' socioeconomic and demographic profiles as well as daily shopping trip patterns. The second focuses on the rent determination process in Montreal and Quebec City regional and super-regional shopping centers. Using a database of 1,499 leases running over 2000–2003, unit base rents are regressed on selected descriptors. Although several issues are discussed, emphasis is placed on the influence of retail concentration on rent.

Spatial Competition among Big-Box Stores, Shopping Centers, and Commercial Streets

Macroeconomic studies investigate the emergence of large retail formats. The microeconomic literature focuses on consumer behavior, with special emphasis on utility functions as well as on tenant mix (Yuo, Crosby, Lizieri, and McCann 2003, 2004). Other issues are brand choice attributes and their effects on firm strategies (Fotheringham 1988a; Jones and Doucet 2000). Marketing and urban economics studies look at consumer behavior in the context of competing shopping alternatives and locations (Thill and Timmermans 1992), while transportation research inquires into travel mode choice (Limanond and Niemeier 2004), departure time, route choice, trip chaining and duration (Bhat 1998).

Urban geography largely investigated the spatial structure of retail markets. Researchers developed various models to address issues related to store location, split of market shares, consumer behavior, and their impacts on the urban form (Parr 1995; Des Rosiers, Thériault, and Ménétrier 2005). Market area analysis emphasizes customer catchment areas of stores considering their positioning in the city (Fotheringham 1988b) using radial approaches (Hyson and Hyson 1950), gravitational models (Reilly 1931; Lösch 1940) or time geography concepts such as the spatio-temporal prism (Hägerstrand 1970; Kim and Kwan 2003). The basic assumption of equal sale prices and attractiveness is unrealistic. Utility theory improves the modeling of preferences (Nakanishi and Cooper 1974). Geographical information systems (GIS) refine spatial description of individual choices and access to facilities.

Utility approaches enhance understanding of consumer spatial behavior (Timmermans 1982; Hansen and Solgaard 2004). In a random utility function (Manski 1977), the consumer chooses one option from a set of alternatives under the assumption of utility maximization. The heterogeneity of preferences and the omission or weak estimation of attributes introduces an uncertainty dimension in the utility function, impeding accurate prediction of a consumer's choice.

Thus, the utility function (U_{in}) of alternative i for individual n (Equation 6.1) includes deterministic (V_{in}) and stochastic (ε_{in}) components (Biba and Villeneuve 2011). The deterministic part (Equation 6.2) uses a set of k independent variables describing each alternative and the attributes of the individual (X_{ink}) making a choice. The marginal effects of the variables on the utility function are provided by regression coefficients (β_{ik}).

$$U_{in} = V_{in} + \varepsilon_{in} \tag{6.1}$$

$$V_{in} = \sum_{k-1}^{K} \beta_{ik} X_{ink} = \beta_i^{'} X_{in} \tag{6.2}$$

The error term (ε_{in}) results from random effects for which distribution assumptions must be formulated. In destination models, the dependent variable is generally discrete with mutually exclusive choices. The most widely used assumption is of identical and independently distributed errors leading to a logistic regression (McFadden 1981; Ben-Akiva and Lerman 1985). This type of discrete choice modeling is widely used in spatial, transportation, and marketing analyses. It allows estimating the probabilities. Choosing between two includes a binomial logit. Choosing between several includes multinomial logit or MNL. These consider individual profiles of consumer and environmental attributes including socioeconomic and spatial of *J* possible alternatives (Louviere, Hensher, Swait, and Adamowicz 2000). Equation 6.3 shows the multinomial logit, the general form of the binomial logit where *J* equals 2. Thus, the utility ratio of the alternative *i* for an individual *n* ($\beta_i^{'} X_{in}$) could lead to the probability of making this choice when it is divided by the sum of the utilities offered by all alternatives available in C_n. The expression μ is a parameter inversely related to the variance of the error terms (the stochastic utilities). Maximum likelihood estimates are of the probability of the choice made by consumers (Louviere et al. 2000).

$$P_n(i) = \frac{e^{\mu(\beta_i^{'} X_{in})}}{\sum_{J=1}^{J} e^{\mu(\beta_i^{'} X_{in})}}, i \in C_n, J \in C_n \tag{6.3}$$

MNL is criticized because it assumes independence of irrelevant alternatives (IIA) and equally weighted alternatives. Under IIA, choices between any two shopping locations do not depend on whether a third is available. A new alternative modifies the market, but not relative shares when alternatives are in pairs (Biba and Villeneuve 2011). Nevertheless, the IIA assumption remains plausible, and empirical evidence has shown MNL robustness (Hausman and McFadden 1984). This supports using this model for choices among types of stores and retail agglomerations. Moreover, discrete choice modeling provides predictive performance and flexibility in comparing stated and revealed preferences (Adamowicz, Louviere, and Williams 1994).

With Christaller's (1966) central place theory in the background, spatial interaction models mostly minimizing distance are widely used for retail competition analysis (Mejia and Benjamin 2002; Biba, Des Rosiers, Thériault, and Villeneuve 2006). Spatial interaction combines with random utility concepts MNL models. Examples are the distance between shoppers' home and retail facilities (Arentze, Borgers, and Timmermans 1993), the distribution of workplaces, and geographical and socioeconomic attributes of residential neighborhoods (Gober, McHugh, and Leclerc 1993; Des Rosiers et al. 2005).

CONSUMER CHOICE AND COMPETITION BETWEEN SHOPPING AGGLOMERATIONS

Biba et al. (2006) and Biba, Thériault, Villeneuve, and Des Rosiers (2008) summarize this combined approach to study competition between types of shops and retail agglomerations. First, the location of 6,571 retail and leisure enterprises in Quebec City is set into a GIS providing location of businesses within buildings. Second, the authors classify shops and facilities by type of goods and services to identify retail agglomerations using classification rules in Table 6.1. This allows for distinguishing commercial streets, shopping centers of various sizes, and big boxes usually agglomerating within power centers. Third, the authors extract all individual shopping trips including going to stores, groceries, restaurants, or leisure facilities from an origin-destination (OD) survey.

The survey by the transit authority Société de Transport de la Communauté Urbaine de Québec (STCUQ) (2001) describes 14,627 consumer trips from Monday to Friday. Details include purpose, departure place, destination place, departure time, transportation mode, and distance. Finally, the authors managed all this information through the GIS to build a database combining destination types, as well as trip (e.g., transportation mode and departure place), consumer (e.g., gender and age), household (e.g., family with children and lone parent family), and environmental (e.g., home neighborhood) attributes.

Table 6.2 presents aggregate consumer profiles on shops and retail agglomerations as defined in Table 6.1. Regional and super-regional shopping centers are not attractive for grocery (about 4.1 percent of trips), leaving this activity to commercial streets (32.9 percent), isolated stores (29.2 percent), community centers (19.5 percent), and power centers (14.3 percent).

While informative, these figures have a major drawback: the effect of each variable is considered independently, which prevents measuring its marginal contribution to destination choice. In fact, such raw outcomes do not distinguish direct from indirect effects. For example, women choose regional and super-regional centers in larger proportions than men (19.9 percent versus 15.4 percent). Men patronize big boxes and power centers (9.0 percent versus 7.7 percent). But women use public transit more than men, and regional and super-regional centers are more accessible by bus than power centers (33.0 percent versus 1.4 percent of trips). Is this gender difference only attributable to transit access? Answering this question implies controlling for simultaneous multiple effects, which is what logistic regression does.

Table 6.3 presents results from a binary logistic regression model comparing big boxes and power centers with regional and super-regional shopping centers. It is based on a subset of 6,426 trips from the OD survey (4,390 to regional and super-regional centers; 2,036 to big boxes). The model considers a mix of shopping purposes, trip attributes and socioeconomic profiles of consumers, providing net effects for categories of each variable. When using discrete variables, coefficients measure deviations from a reference category. The reference for the dependent variable is shopping centers. Each coefficient expresses the premium for big boxes over shopping centers for each variable. Similarly, shopping purposes are compared with a reference (buying any product that is not grocery). The positive b coefficient of 2.386 for grocery means that big boxes are

Table 6.1 **Typology of Retail Agglomerations**

Retail Structure	*Floor Area (m^2)*	*Number of Stores*	*Specific Characteristics of the Supply*	*Market Area*
Isolated store	< 4,600	Isolated building with one store	According to type of business	According to type of goods
Commercial street	According to store	Density ≥ 10 stores/per km (Mean = 32 stores/km)	Variety of businesses and services; different transportation means to shop	Neighborhood and visiting clientele—large percentage of foot traffic
Shopping Centers				
Neighborhood	< 14,000	5–14 (with a large grocery store or pharmacy)	Daily use products and services	Neighborhood clientele—commutes on foot or by car
Community	14,000–50,000	15–99 (at least one large, national chain store)	Regular needs such as clothing and shoes.	Neighborhood clientele or from surrounding areas–served by public transportation
Regional	50,000–80,000	100–199 (at least two large, national chain stores)	Large diversity of products	Regional clientele–accessible by car and public transportation
Super-regional	> 80,000	> 200 (several large, national chain stores)	Very large diversity of products and services	Clientele exceeding the metropolitan area limits
Department stores				
Big-box store	> 4,600	Main store that may rent custom boutique space	Wide range of mixed or specialized merchandise	Local and regional clientele (according to the size and specialty of stores)—mostly accessible by car
Power center	> 25,000	Several neighboring big-box stores	Conglomeration of big-box stores with some smaller, similar-style businesses	Regional and possibly super-regional—accessible by highway

Table 6.2 **Consumers' Profiles and Travel Attributes**

		Types of Shop or Agglomeration					*Total*
		Isolated Store (%)	*Commercial Street/ Neighborhood Center (%)*	*Community Center (%)*	*Regional/Super-regional Center (%)*	*Big-Box/Power Center (%)*	
Shopping purpose	Grocery	29.2	32.9	19.5	4.1	14.3	21.4
	Leisure	68.4	20.0	6.5	3.5	1.5	26.9
	Restaurant	50.0	32.5	7.3	9.1	1.1	12.0
	Any other product	21.5	15.5	13.4	37.8	11.8	39.7
Consumer and household socioeconomic profile							
Gender	Woman	36.5	22.7	13.1	19.9	7.7	55.8
	Man	42.5	22.1	10.9	15.4	9.0	44.2
Age	< 25 years	53.4	20.9	5.7	15.3	4.6	13.2
	25–64 year	38.8	23.0	11.6	17.2	9.4	67.1
	≥ 65 years	30.9	21.8	18.2	22.1	7.0	19.7
Occupation	Worker	40.7	23.2	10.4	16.6	9.2	29.9
	Professional	44.3	24.2	9.8	14.1	7.6	14.1
	Student	53.2	21.1	5.7	15.2	4.7	11.2
	Retired	32.5	20.7	16.6	21.6	8.6	32.4
	Others	34.5	24.6	13.2	18.5	9.2	12.4

Table 6.2 **continued**

		Types of Shop or Agglomeration					*Total*
		Isolated Store (%)	*Commercial Street/ Neighborhood Center (%)*	*Community Center (%)*	*Regional/Super-regional Center (%)*	*Big-Box/Power Center (%)*	
Household Type	Lone person	33.9	29.1	14.1	17.5	5.4	16.3
	Childless household	36.6	21.7	13.6	19.3	8.9	51.0
	Family with children	46.3	19.8	8.8	16.0	9.1	29.2
	Single-parent family	42.5	25.2	9.3	16.5	6.5	3.5
Car Ownership	Without car or driver	28.2	38.0	14.0	17.5	2.3	8.1
	Less than one car/driver	40.0	20.8	11.9	18.5	8.8	36.6
	One car per driver	40.0	21.1	12.1	17.8	8.9	52.6
	More than one car/driver	44.5	24.7	9.8	13.5	7.6	2.6
Trip attributes							
Transportation mode	Car (driver or passenger)	39.9	19.6	12.3	18.7	9.4	85.0
	Bus	28.9	25.5	11.3	33.0	1.4	4.1
	Foot	35.6	45.3	11.3	5.9	1.9	9.8
	Other	49.8	26.3	10.0	11.1	2.8	1.2
Day of week	Monday to Wednesday	41.1	22.8	11.5	16.2	8.4	48.2
	Thursday or Friday	37.4	22.2	12.8	19.5	8.2	51.8
Departure time	8 a.m. to 6 p.m.	34.3	22.0	13.6	21.0	9.1	69.8
	After 6 p.m.	50.4	23.7	8.7	10.8	6.5	30.2

continued

Table 6.2 **continued**

		Types of Shop or Agglomeration					*Total*
		Isolated Store (%)	*Commercial Street/ Neighborhood Center (%)*	*Community Center (%)*	*Regional/Super-regional Center (%)*	*Big-Box/Power Center (%)*	
Departure place	Home	40.0	22.1	12.3	18.2	7.4	69.1
	Work/school	41.1	23.0	9.9	19.7	6.3	9.0
	Other (making a tour)	35.8	23.4	12.4	16.5	12.0	21.9
Distance	0–2.5 km	35.9	34.4	14.6	10.3	4.8	34.4
	2.5–5 km	35.7	20.6	14.8	19.0	9.8	19.9
	5–10 km	43.0	14.4	10.2	20.9	11.4	25.8
	10–20 km	40.7	14.9	7.9	27.8	8.7	15.5
	> 20 km	53.4	11.3	6.4	20.0	8.9	4.3
Proportion of trips (by type of shop or agglomeration)		39.2	22.5	12.1	17.9	8.3	100.0

Source: Biba et al. 2008.

Table 6.3 **Binary Logistic Model**

Variables	*Frequency*	*% of Trips*	*β*	*S.E.*	*Wald Statistics*	*Sig.*	*Odds Ratio*
Shopping purpose (Ref. Any others products)	4,830	75.2			295.130	0.000	
Grocery	965	15.0	2.386	0.143	280.168	0.000	10.865
Leisure	330	5.1	0.888	0.264	11.288	0.001	2.429
Restaurant	301	4.7	−0.752	0.347	4.701	0.030	0.472
Trip attributes							
Transportation mode (Ref. Car)	5,857	91.1			29.152	0.000	
Bus	342	5.3	−2.402	0.472	25.865	0.000	0.091
Foot	187	2.9	−0.640	0.296	4.659	0.031	0.527
Other	40	0.6	−0.520	0.560	0.863	0.353	0.594
Day of week (Ref. Thursday or Friday)	3,516	54.7					
Monday to Wednesday	2,910	45.3	0.373	0.064	33.877	0.000	1.452
Departure time (ref. 8 a.m. to 6 p.m.)	5,152	80.2					
After 6 p.m.	1,274	19.8	0.337	0.083	16.466	0.000	1.400
Departure place (Ref. Home)	4,325	67.3			89.766	0.000	
Work/School	573	8.9	−0.094	0.132	0.509	0.476	0.910
Other (making a tour)	1,528	23.8	0.655	0.072	82.670	0.000	1.926
Distance (Ref. 0–5 km)	2,684	41.8			34.597	0.000	
5–10 km	2,047	31.9	−0.254	0.083	9.382	0.002	1.290
10–15 km	953	14.8	0.349	0.114	9.313	0.002	0.705
15–20 km	438	6.8	−0.247	0.147	2.808	0.094	0.782
>20 km	304	4.7	−0.049	0.171	0.083	0.773	0.952

continued

Table 6.3 **continued**

Variables	*Frequency*	*% of Trips*	*β*	*S.E.*	*Wald Statistics*	*Sig.*	*Odds Ratio*
Socioeconomic profile							
Gender (Ref. Woman)	3,776	58.8					
Man	2,650	41.2	0.653	0.072	82.814	0.000	1.922
Age (Ref. 25–64 years)	4,370	68.0			43.274	0.000	
< 25 years	645	10.0	−0.413	0.118	12.352	0.000	0.661
≥ 65 years	1,411	22.0	−0.510	0.089	32.880	0.000	0.600
Household type (Ref. 2 adults or more at work)	1,735	27.0			10.718	0.013	
2 adults or more without workers	3,578	55.7	−0.219	0.078	7.871	0.005	0.804
Lone-person or single-parent family with work	482	7.5	−0.229	0.136	2.848	0.091	0.795
Lone-person or single-parent family without work	631	9.8	−0.376	0.144	6.780	0.009	0.687
Car ownership (Ref. One car/driver)	3,447	53.6			12.409	0.006	
Without car or driver	393	6.1	−0.315	0.0207	2.308	0.129	0.730
< one car/driver	2,450	38.1	0.143	0.083	2.960	0.085	1.153
> one car/driver	136	2.1	0.236	0.080	8.627	0.003	1.266

Note: The binary logistic model estimates the probability to shop at big boxes and power centers as opposed to regional and super-regional shopping centers used as the reference category. It is based on 6,426 shopping trips from the 2001 OD survey.

Source: Biba et al. 2006.

more attractive for grocery purposes than shopping centers are. Odds ratios express this difference in probabilistic terms (Equation 6.4):

$$Odds_i = e^{\beta_i} = \frac{P(i)}{1-P(i)} \tag{6.4}$$

The odds of choosing a big box for grocery are 10.8 against 1.0 (e^0) for a regional or super-regional shopping center. The question about gender and bus riding can now be answered. Men are twice as likely (odds ratio of 1.922 versus 1; $P_{(i)} = 0.658$) to patronize big boxes as women are. A complementary effect also exists because people traveling by bus target big boxes far less than car users do (with an odds ratio of 0.091 versus 1; $P(i) = 0.083$). Big boxes are highly competitive for grocery and leisure, when accessed by car, from Monday to Wednesday, on multipurpose trips, within a distance range of 5–10 kilometers from home. They target men and are particularly attractive to households with more than one car per driver. Big-box stores are less attractive to restaurants, bus riders, and pedestrians, and beyond 10 kilometers of home. Women, people younger than 25 or older than 65 and jobless households are less attracted by big boxes.

Multinomial logistic regression enables simultaneous comparison of mutually exclusive alternatives. Table 6.4 shows odds ratios for competition among four types of retail shopping: commercial streets including neighborhood centers; community shopping centers; regional and super-regional centers (the reference); and big boxes including power centers. For each independent variable, odds ratios compare each shopping type to regional and super-regional centers and each category to the reference.

For grocery, consumers are 15.8 times more likely to attend commercial streets than regional shopping centers. The odds ratio is 11.2 for big boxes, which is close to the result in Table 6.3. The odds ratio can be compared between types, so the odds ratio for commercial streets as opposed to big boxes is 1.418 = 15.846/11.174. Both commercial streets and community centers are advantaged by pedestrian accessibility, while this factor is twice as important for commercial streets. Regional and super-regional shopping centers benefit from proximity to workplaces. Commercial streets and big boxes generate multipurpose trips, which involve going to several places in one tour. Visiting a regional shopping center involves mostly home-based trips.

While powerful for specific effects, these models often display limited efficiency for forecasting individual outcomes. This can be observed from both the low McFadden and Nagelkerke R^2, leaving ample room for the stochastic component in Equation 6.1, and for the uniqueness of individual behavior.

Setting Shopping Center Rents

Theories of urban spatial structure (Hotelling 1929; Lösch 1940; Christaller 1966) have grounded shopping center research. Agglomeration economies explain anchor or lead tenants' bargaining power in negotiating rents with landlords (Mejia and Benjamin 2002). Research has examined the rent-setting process in shopping centers (Benjamin, Boyle, and Sirmans 1990; Tay, Lau, and Leung 1999; Hardin and Wolverton 2000, 2001; Hardin and Carr 2005; DeLisle 2005).

Table 6.4 **Multinomial Logistic Model**

Variables		***Commercial Streets and Neighborhood Centers***		
Shopping Purpose (Ref. Any other product)		*Grocery*	*Community Centers*	*Big Boxes and Power Centers*
Shopping purpose (Ref. Any other product) Trip Attributes				
Leisure		15.846***	10.795***	11.174***
Restaurant		15.085***	6.402***	1.326**
Transportation mode (Ref. Car)		9.086***	2.336***	0.349***
Trip Attributes Socioeconomic profile				
	Bus	–	0.756*	0.186***
	Foot	4.296***	2.138***	–
Day of week (Ref. Monday to Wednesday)	Other	–	–	–
Departure time (Ref. 9 a.m. to 6 p.m.)	Thursday or Friday	0.680***	0.796***	0.668***
Departure place (Ref. Home)	After 6 PM	1.475***	1.172*	1.265**
	Work/School	0.579***	0.674***	0.671**
Distance (Ref. 2.5–5 km)	Other (making a tour)	1.388***	–	1.649***
	0–2.5 km	1.808***	1.180*	0.623***
	5–10 km	0.484***	0.486***	0.856**
	10–15 km	0.352***	0.282***	0.459***
	15–20 km	0.290***	0.244***	0.447***
Gender (Ref. man)	> 20 km	0.360***	0.321***	0.668**

Table 6.4 **continued**

Variables		*Commercial Streets and Neighborhood Centers*		
Shopping Purpose (Ref. Any other product)		*Grocery*	*Community Centers*	*Big Boxes and Power Centers*
Socioeconomic profile				
Age (Ref. 25–64 years)	Woman	0.684***	0.795***	0.529***
	< 25 years	0.749**	0.504***	0.656***
Household type (Other)	≥ 65 years	0.621***	–	0.503***
Car ownership (Ref. With cars)	Family with children	0.879**	0.780***	1.133*
Urbanization period at home (Ref. Before 1961)	Carless	–	–	0.680*
	1961–1978	0.892***	1.139**	–
	1978–2000	0.697***	–	–

Note: This table shows odds ratios of choosing among retail shopping agglomerations as opposed to regional and super-regional shopping centers, which is the reference category. It is based on 14,626 shopping trips from the 2001 OD survey. Results are reported as odds ratios.

Significance thresholds: Non-significant ($p > 0.10$); * $p \leq 0.10$; ** $p \leq 0.05$; *** $p \leq 0.01$N = 14,627 trips; Likelihood ratio chi-square = 8628; $P = 0.0000$; McFadden's adjusted $R^2 = 0.213$; Nagelkerke $R^2 = 0.426$

Source: Biba et al. 2008.

RETAIL CONCENTRATION AS A DETERMINANT OF SHOPPING CENTER RENTS

The following case study focuses on the role retail concentration plays in rent setting within regional and super-regional shopping centers and summarizes findings by Des Rosiers, Thériault, and Lavoie (2009). It follows Yuo et al. (2003, 2004) and Des Rosiers and Thériault (2004) in considering retail concentration and its impact on retail rents. Yuo et al. (2003) find that the higher the agglomeration economies, the greater the rents charged to tenants. Notable store types are fashion, special goods, information technology, and health products categories.

A comparative analysis raises two questions. First, do fewer but larger tenants holding greater control over category or subcategory sales command higher base rents? Alternatively, are rents lower as a consequence of bargaining power? Second, is the effect on rents uniform or varying with the type of product?

A retail rent model is developed based on 11 regional and super-regional shopping malls located in Montreal (6) and Quebec City (5), totaling 1,499 non-anchor stores and nearly 5.4 million square feet of gross leasable area (GLA), excluding storage space. The Montreal subsample includes 653 retail units (2.3 million square feet) while Quebec City has 846 (3.0 million square feet). Base rents are for 1,499 leases initiated or renewed and still running over the 2000–2003 period.

Base rent is the net rent to the landlord excluding any expense or additional charge transferable to the tenant. Where applicable, base rent also reflects escalator clauses or rental steps or bumps in the initial lease. Mean unit base rent is $57.18 per square foot, with $67.46 per square foot in Montreal and $49.25 per square foot in Quebec City. *Percentage rent* is an additional payment to the landlord when annual sales per square foot exceed a given threshold. For leases with percentage rent, the mean is 4.2 percent of yearly sales while the maximum rate is 15 percent.

Rent determinants include percentage rent rate, store size or GLA, in square feet, lease duration in years since the first landlord-tenant negotiation and shopping center age. Age is weighted to account for expansions and modifications to the building (Eppli and Tu 2005). A time variable (time elapsed since January 1971, in years) captures rent inflation.

Mean GLA per store is 3,579 square feet while tenants have been in operation at the location for roughly nine years of lease duration. Mean shopping center age is 26 years. Additionally, 31 retail categories are identified based on the North American Industry Classification System (NAICS), with women's clothing and fast food being dominant with 245 and 182 stores, respectively.

The level of retail concentration is measured using the Herfindahl index (AmosWeb 2003; Des Rosiers and Thériault 2004), expressed as the sum of the squares of each firm's market share. It is computed for each retail category and shopping center on the basis of the individual retail units' GLA. The index may stand anywhere between 0 (absence of a store in a given retail category) and 1 (all retail activity is concentrated in the hands of a single tenant). The Herfindahl index for retail concentration gives more weight to larger, dominant tenants who may exert control over retail categories and sales. The concentration index for any given retail category in a given shopping center is:

$$\mathbf{CONCINDX}_{ij} = \sum_{k=1}^{n} [GLA_{ij}^{k} / GLA_{ij}]^2 \quad (6.5)$$

Here $\boldsymbol{i}$ is the retail category or subcategory; $\boldsymbol{j}$ the shopping center; $\boldsymbol{k}$ the store within category or subcategory i in shopping center j; $\boldsymbol{n}$ i is the number of stores within category or subcategory i in shopping center j; $\boldsymbol{GLA_{ij}^{k}}$ is the gross leasable area of any k store belonging to category or subcategory i and located in shopping center j; and $\boldsymbol{GLA_{ij}}$ is the gross leasable area of all premises belonging to category or subcategory i in shopping center j.

Here "BaseRent" is defined as base rent per square foot while "Percent," "Size," "Age," "Duration," "Time," "Mix," and "Conc," are the percentage rent rate, store size, shopping center age, lease duration, inflation, retail categories, and concentration index, respectively. Considering that the statistical distribution of unit base rents is highly skewed to the right, regressions are calibrated using a log-linear functional form. Similarly, a logarithmic transformation is applied to the store size (GLA) variable, whose regression parameter is therefore expressed as the size-elasticity of unit rent. Thus,

$$\begin{aligned} \text{LnBaseRent} = {} & B_0 + B_1\text{Percent} + B_2\text{LnSize} + B_3\text{Age} \\ & + B_4\text{Duration} + B_5\text{Time} + B_6\text{Mix} + B_7\text{Conc} + e \end{aligned} \quad (6.6)$$

The standard multiple linear regression procedure is used, with only nonzero base rent and GLA values as well as non-storage retail. The analysis includes only cases with full information. Models discussed below exclude extreme residuals with a standard error of estimate (SEE) in excess of +/–3. Montreal is the reference for location variables (Table 6.6, model 2) while men's clothing is the reference for retail categories (Table 6.5, model 1). Once filtered and excluding extreme residuals, the overall sample size stands at 1,474 valid cases, with the Montreal and Quebec City subsamples including 639 and 835 cases.

Table 6.5 and 6.6 present two regression models. Model 1 shown in Table 6.5 uses two location-specific concentration indexes to test for differences between Montreal and Quebec City. Model 2 (Table 6.6) substitutes interactive terms combining retail mix attributes with category-specific concentration indexes for basic retail categories to test whether goods and services categories behave differently with respect to retail concentration. Nearly 62 percent of the LnBaseRent variance is explained. The F-value is 65 despite a relatively large SEE (0.454), which is the norm for retail rent models.

Several conclusions emerge from these findings.

- The percentage rent rate coefficient is highly significant and displays a positive sign, suggesting it acts as a substitute for, rather than as a complement to, base rent. Such findings are in line with Wheaton (2000) and corroborate Cho and Shilling (2007) where percentage rent compensates for tenant default risk.
- A negative and highly significant relationship exists between unit base rent and store size. A 10 percent increase in GLA results in a unit rent reduction of 4 percent. Store size is the most prominent determinant of shopping center rents, with a standardized coefficient of –0.659.

Table 6.5 **Model 1 Retail Rent Model with Location-Specific Concentration Indexes**

Variable	*B*	*S.E.*	*Beta*	*t-Value*	*p-Value*	*VIF*
(Constant)	6.469	0.157		41.223	0.000	
Percentage rent rate	2.696	0.440	0.117	6.123	0.000	1.406
Ln_gross leaseable area	−0.395	0.014	−0.661	−28.089	0.000	2.138
Shopping center weighted age taking into account expansions and additions	−0.018	0.002	−0.214	−11.378	0.000	1.369
Time elapsed since January 1971, in years	0.008	0.004	0.055	1.911	0.056	3.146
Lease duration in years	0.015	0.004	0.107	3.564	0.000	3.454
Camera and photographic supplies	0.271	0.111	0.043	2.432	0.015	1.186
Beer, wine, and liquor	0.803	0.194	0.070	4.139	0.000	1.090
Optical goods	0.366	0.101	0.064	3.607	0.000	1.225
Women's clothing	0.105	0.059	0.053	1.787	0.074	3.365
Children's and infants' clothing	0.009	0.101	0.002	0.086	0.931	1.212
Family clothing	0.247	0.082	0.057	2.998	0.003	1.403
Clothing accessories	0.342	0.096	0.066	3.578	0.000	1.304
Other (unisex) clothing	0.202	0.066	0.068	3.041	0.002	1.957
Shoe	0.144	0.067	0.049	2.161	0.031	1.980
Luggage and leather goods	0.223	0.098	0.041	2.266	0.024	1.243
Sporting goods	0.083	0.102	0.015	0.813	0.416	1.242
Hobby, toy, and game	−0.080	0.117	−0.012	−0.682	0.495	1.176
Sewing, needlework, and piece goods	−0.565	0.136	−0.072	−4.165	0.000	1.147
Gambling industries	0.565	0.139	0.075	4.060	0.000	1.302
Full-service restaurants	−0.012	0.145	−0.001	−0.080	0.936	1.111
Limited-service restaurants (fast food)	0.135	0.062	0.060	2.188	0.029	2.918

Table 6.5 **continued**

Variable	*B*	*S.E.*	*Beta*	*t-Value*	*p-Value*	*VIF*
Furniture and home furnishings—1	−0.050	0.072	−0.014	−0.702	0.483	1.595
Electronics and house appliance—2	0.011	0.089	0.002	0.124	0.901	1.288
Specialty food—3	0.084	0.086	0.019	0.979	0.328	1.424
Drug, health, and personal care—4	0.066	0.073	0.018	0.893	0.372	1.527
Grocery—5	0.324	0.119	0.048	2.736	0.006	1.210
Jewelry and luggage—6	0.225	0.072	0.068	3.144	0.002	1.790
Music and book—7	0.235	0.097	0.044	2.417	0.016	1.252
Department and discount department—8	−0.077	0.095	−0.017	−0.812	0.417	1.615
Office supplies, stationery, and gift—9	0.292	0.119	0.042	2.443	0.015	1.159
Telecommunications—10	0.489	0.094	0.097	5.189	0.000	1.348
Banking, finance, insurance, and real estate–11	0.411	0.095	0.080	4.317	0.000	1.331
Hair, nail, and skin care services—12	−0.232	0.105	−0.039	−2.213	0.027	1.210
Travel Agencies—13	−0.023	0.131	−0.003	−0.173	0.863	1.147
Dry cleaning and footwear repair—14	−0.545	0.128	−0.074	−4.246	0.000	1.184
Concentration Index based on GLA for Quebec City centers	−0.182	0.078	−0.059	−2.340	0.019	2.461
Concentration index based on GLA for Montreal centers	−0.273	0.073	−0.089	−3.743	0.000	2.189
Dependent variable: Ln_base rent ($/sq. ft)						

Note: This table shows that intra-category retail concentration, as measured by the Herfindahl index, significantly affects shopping center rents downward. The higher the retail concentration index, the lower the base rent. Store-type variables are the Herfindahl concentration index and numbers are for store codes. The last column has the variance inflation factor (VIF) as a test for multicollinearity, present at a standard level if exceeding 20.

Adjusted $R^2 = 0.617$; standard error of the estimate (S.E.) = 0.454; *F*-value = 65.307; significance = 0.0.000.

Source: Des Rosiers, Thériault, and Lavoie 2009.

Table 6.6 **Model 2 Retail Rent Model with Category-Specific Concentration Indexes**

Variable	*B*	*S.E.*	*Beta*	*t-Value*	*p-value*	*VIF*
(Constant)	6.515	0.150		43.436	0.000	
Percentage rent rate	3.078	0.461	−0.134	6.676	0.000	1.494
Ln_gross leaseable area	−0.401	0.013	−0.672	−30.472	0.000	1.817
Shopping center weighted age taking into account expansions and additions	−0.020	0.002	−0.245	−12.197	0.000	1.511
Time elapsed since January 1971, years	0.009	0.004	0.063	2.132	0.033	3.214
Lease duration, years	0.016	0.004	0.116	3.821	0.000	3.418
Shopping center is located in Quebec City	0.102	0.032	0.069	3.228	0.001	1.696
Camera	0.157	0.185	0.014	0.847	0.397	1.043
Liquor store	0.585	0.220	0.044	2.666	0.008	1.031
Optical	0.324	0.174	0.031	1.864	0.063	1.050
Men's clothing	−0.237	0.245	−0.017	−0.969	0.333	1.120
Women's clothing	0.151	0.573	0.005	0.264	0.792	1.392
Children's and infant's clothing	−0.228	0.197	−0.019	−1.157	0.248	1.054
Family clothing	0.275	0.181	0.026	1.518	0.129	1.100
Clothing accessories	0.328	0.204	0.027	1.606	0.108	1.069
Unisex clothing	0.484	0.300	0.028	1.611	0.107	1.166
Shoe stores	0.144	0.325	0.008	0.444	0.657	1.171
Luggage and leather goods	0.056	0.197	0.005	0.283	0.777	1.050
Sporting goods	−0.091	0.176	−0.009	−0.520	0.603	1.094
Hobby, toy, and game	−0.356	0.158	−0.038	−2.261	0.024	1.041
Sewing, needlework, and piece goods	−0.939	0.171	−0.091	−5.478	0.000	1.025

Table 6.6 **continued**

Variable	*B*	*S.E.*	*Beta*	*t-Value*	*p-value*	*VIF*
Gambling industries	0.506	0.193	0.046	2.618	0.009	1.141
Full-service restaurants	−0.167	0.194	−0.014	−0.858	0.391	1.028
Fast food	0.667	0.301	−0.042	2.214	0.027	1.356
Furniture and home furnishings	−0.322	0.187	0.030	−1.719	0.086	1.110
Electronics and house appliance	−0.300	0.165	−0.031	−1.819	0.069	1.069
Specialty food	−0.161	0.174	−0.016	−0.924	0.356	1.089
Drug, health, and personal care	0.214	0.156	−0.024	−1.372	0.170	1.119
Grocery	0.089	0.135	0.011	0.658	0.510	1.036
Jewelry and luggage	0.594	0.269	0.039	2.209	0.027	1.138
Music and book stores	0.260	0.170	0.026	1.533	0.126	1.083
Department and discount department stores	−0.531	0.211	−0.046	−2.521	0.012	1.217
Office supplies, confectionery and gift stores	0.214	0.189	0.019	1.136	0.256	1.036
Telecommunications	0.681	0.171	0.069	3.988	0.000	1.107
Banking, finance, insurance, and real estate	0.431	0.169	0.044	2.549	0.011	1.101
Hair, nail, and skin care services	−0.764	0.180	−0.071	−4.244	0.000	1.054
Travel agencies	−0.309	0.204	−0.025	−1.521	0.129	1.047
Dry cleaning and footwear repair	−0.841	0.163	−0.086	−5.172	0.000	1.042
Dependent variable: Ln_base rent ($/sq. ft)						

Note: This table shows that the influence of retail concentration of each store type on unit base rent, where significant, varies markedly among categories. A higher level of retail concentration yields substantial rent premiums for higher order goods stores. The reverse occurs for lower order goods stores that are assigned rent discounts. The last column has the variance inflation factor (VIF) as a test for multicollinearity, present at a standard level if exceeding 20.

Adjusted $R^2 = 0.605$; standard error of the estimate (S.E.) = 0.462; *F*-value = 62.027; significance = 0.0000.

Source: Des Rosiers, Thériault, and Lavoie 2009.

- The age of a shopping center reduces rents. This stresses the importance of renovation and image enhancing strategies for shopping center investors (Sirmans and Guidry 1993; Gatzlaff, Sirmans, and Diskin 1994).
- The time coefficient is positive suggesting that retail rents and real estate are inflation hedges. The vast majority of leases used have been negotiated since 1990. In Quebec, a decade of very slow economic growth followed a property crash in the early 1990s, which explains why the overall annual rent inflation rate is slightly below 1 percent.
- Lease duration positively affects rents. Each additional year in lease duration translates into a 1.5 percent rise in unit base rent. Fisher and Lentz (1990) regard shopping center landlords as being able to capture through higher rents part of the business enterprise value generated by successful, long established tenants.
- Most retail categories generate highly significant coefficients. Related unit base rents differ from men's clothing stores used as the reference, either positively or negatively. Most significant and positively signed categories fit the description that Yuo et al. (2004) give for core retail categories. The two highest positive coefficients are for liquor stores and gambling outlets. These stores are regulated or operated by the government, indicating that economic rents are being shared with landlords. Significant and negatively signed categories are in hobbies, sewing, and discount stores, which sell lower order goods and services.
- Intra-category retail concentration, as measured by the Herfindahl index, significantly affects shopping center rents and its impact is negative. This applies to both markets although the magnitude of the location-specific concentration index parameter is larger for Montreal shopping centers (–0.273) than for Quebec City's (–0.182). Such findings give rise to an interpretation similar to the one developed by Yuo et al. (2004) based on product brand. Despite higher agglomeration economies accruing from the presence of fewer but larger stores, the enhanced bargaining power such retailers exert on a given goods and services category drives rents down. The higher the retail concentration index the lower the base rent.

Findings from model 2 (Table 6.6), which looks at the rent impact of category-specific concentration indexes using interactive variables, bring some nuance to the latter statement. They suggest that retail concentration significantly affects several goods and services categories, although base rent is unaffected in a majority of cases. The influence of retail concentration on unit base rent, where significant, varies in sign and magnitude among goods and services categories. A higher level of retail concentration yields premiums for tenants already paying above-average rents, for instance in regulated liquor and gambling. It is the reverse for hobby and sewing stores with no barriers to entry that receive added rent discounts.

A rationale for such a discrepancy is that competition exists for the best locations for a store type with restricted outlets and high barriers to entry. These restrictions offer almost a guarantee for higher sales volumes and profits. These effects outweigh the bargaining power effect where a higher level of retail concentration results in higher base rents. For stores with no barriers to entry and targeting customer with low values of time, less benefit accrues from agglomeration economies.

Summary and Conclusions

This chapter on retail real estate develops two different topics, both in a Canadian context. The first case study addresses the issue of spatial competition between big-box stores and traditional shopping centers in Quebec City. The second case study focuses on the rent determination process in Montreal and Quebec City regional and super-regional shopping centers and investigates the impact of retail concentration on unit base rent.

Regarding spatial competition among shopping agglomerations, commercial streets, and community centers are only competitive at the very local scale where shoppers live within a mile radius. Big-box stores have a smaller market area when compared to regional and super-regional shopping centers. However, big-box stores configured as groceries compete with community centers. On the other side, commercial streets remain highly efficient for attracting trips for grocery, restaurant, and leisure activities. They perform better than regional centers, especially after 6 p.m.

Strong differences are linked to gender, age, and car ownership. Women prefer large shopping centers, especially to big-box stores. Younger and older people are going to regional centers more often. Car ownership allows access to large commercial agglomerations, especially power centers. Finally, the attractiveness of commercial streets is progressively decreasing with distance to traditional urban core areas built before 1961.

In order to investigate the influence of retail concentration on rents, a retail rent model is developed based on detailed information on 11 regional and super-regional shopping malls. Log-transformed unit base rents are regressed on a series of rent determinants including the percentage rent rate, store size, lease duration, shopping center weighted age, a time variable as well as 31 retail category dummies. Retail concentration is measured for each retail category using the Herfindahl index. A first model is run using location-specific concentration indexes. In a second model, category-specific indexes are substituted for the latter.

Results obtained from the first model show that retail concentration significantly affects shopping center unit base rents. The effect is negative as a result of the bargaining power enjoyed by dominant tenants. In the second model, retail concentration varies markedly, in sign and magnitude, among goods and services categories. For stores in categories with high barriers to entry and competing for scarce prime locations, agglomeration economies outweigh bargaining power, with a higher level of retail concentration resulting in higher base rents. This is not the case for stores with low barriers to entry and offering at-home leisure activities competing with the Internet. These stores receive rent discounts as retail concentration increases.

Discussion Questions

1. The OD survey used to model shopping destination choices includes only weekdays (Monday to Friday) but stores are also open on weekends. What is the effect of such a data bias on the model reliability and how could it be handled?

2. For the same independent variables, odds ratios between big-box stores versus regional shopping centers can differ. How can these differences be explained and how do they relate to the IIA issue?
3. What is the key concept underlying the existence and development of shopping centers and how does this concept apply to them?
4. Why was the Herfindahl index initially developed and how is it operationally defined here for measuring retail concentration in shopping centers?
5. What do regression findings from this case study suggest about the influence of retail concentration on shopping center unit base rents?

References

Adamowicz, Wiktor, Jordan Louviere, and Michael Williams. 1994. "Combining Revealed and Stated Preference Methods for Valuing Environmental Amenities." *Journal of Environmental Economics and Management* 26:3, 271–292.

AmosWeb. 2003. "Herfindahl Index." http://www.amosweb.com/.

Arentze, Theo, Aloys Borgers, and Harry Timmermans. 1993. "A Model of Multi–Purpose Trip Behavior." *Regional Science* 72:3, 239–256.

Ben-Akiva, Moshe, and Steven R. Lerman. 1985. *Discrete Choice Analysis: Theory and Application to Travel Demand*. Cambridge, MA: MIT Press.

Benjamin, John D., Glenn W. Boyle, and C. F. Sirmans. 1990. "Retail Leasing: Determinants of Shopping Center Rents." *Journal of the American Real Estate and Urban Economics Association* 18:3, 302–312.

Bhat, Chandra R. 1998. "Analysis of Travel Mode and Departure Time Choice for Urban Shopping Trips." *Transportation Research Part B* 32:6, 361–371.

Biba, Gjin, and Paul Villeneuve. 2011. "Spatiotemporal Modeling of Destination Choices for Consumption Purposes: Market Areas Delineation and Market Share Estimation." In Marius Thériault and François Des Rosiers, eds., *Modeling Urban Dynamics*, 57–81. London: ISTE-Wiley.

Biba, Gjin, François Des Rosiers, Marius Thériault, and Paul Villeneuve. 2006. "Big Boxes versus Traditional Shopping Centers: Looking at Households' Shopping Trip Patterns." *Journal of Real Estate Literature* 14:2, 177–204.

Biba, Gjin, Marius Thériault, Paul Villeneuve, and François Des Rosiers. 2008. "Aires de Marché et Choix des Destinations de Consommation Pour les Achats Réalisés au Cours de la Semaine: Le Cas de la Région de Québec." *Le Géographe Canadien* 52:1, 39–64.

Boston Consulting Group. 2010. *How the Internet Is Transforming the U.K. Economy*. London: Boston Consulting Group.

Cho, Hoon, and James D. Shilling. 2007. "Valuing Retail Shopping Center Lease Contracts." *Real Estate Economics* 35:4, 623–649.

Christaller, Walter. 1966. *Central Places in Southern Germany* [Die Zentralen Orte in Suddeutschland]. Translated by Charlisle W. Baskin. Englewood Cliffs, NJ: Prentice-Hall.

DeLisle, James R. 2005. "The Evolution of Shopping Center Research: A 12-Year Retrospective." *Journal of Shopping Center Research* 12:2, 1–83.

Des Rosiers, François, and Marius Thériault. 2004. "Agglomeration Economies and Retail Concentration as Determinants of Shopping Center Rent." Working Paper, Faculty of Business Administration, Laval University.

Des Rosiers, François, Marius Thériault, and Catherine Lavoie. 2009. "Retail Concentration and Shopping Center Rent: A Comparison of Two Cities." *Journal of Real Estate Research* 31:2, 165–207.

Des Rosiers, François, Marius Thériault, and Laurent Ménétrier. 2005. "Spatial Versus Non-Spatial Determinants of Shopping Center Rents: Modeling Location and Neighborhood-Related Factors." *Journal of Real Estate Research*, 27:3, 293–319.

Emarketer. 2013. http://www.emarketer.com/Article/Ecommerce-Sales-Topped-1-Trillion-First-Time-2012/100969.

Eppli, Mark J., and Charles C. Tu. 2005. "An Event Study Analysis of Mall Renovation and Expansion." *Journal of Shopping Center Research* 12:2, 117–130.

Fisher, Jeffrey D., and George H. Lentz.1990. "Business Enterprise Value in Shopping Malls: An Empirical Test." *Journal of Real Estate Research* 5:1, 167–175.

Fotheringham, A. Stewart. 1988a. "Consumer Store Choice and Choice Set Definition." *Marketing Science* 7:3, 299–310.

Fotheringham, A. Stewart. 1988b. "Market Share Analysis Techniques: A Review and Illustration of Current U.S. Practice." In Neil Wrigley, ed., *Store Choice, Store Location and Market Analysis*, 120–159. London: Routledge.

Gatzlaff, Dean H., G. Stacy Sirmans, and Barry A. Diskin. 1994. "The Effect of Anchor Tenant Loss on Shopping Center Rents." *Journal of Real Estate Research* 9:1, 99–110.

Gober, Patricia, Kevin E. McHugh, and Denis Leclerc. 1993. "Job-Rich but Housing-Poor: The Dilemma of a Western Amenity Town." *The Professional Geographer* 45:1, 12–20.

Hägerstrand, R. Torsten. 1970. "What about People in Regional Science?" *Papers of the Regional Science Association* 4:1, 7–21.

Hansen, Torben, and Hans Stubbe Solgaard. 2004. *New Perspectives on Retailing and Store Patronage Behavior*. Boston: Kluwer Academic.

Hardin, William G., III, and Jon Carr. 2005. "Disaggregating Neighborhood and Community Center Property Types." *Journal of Shopping Centre Research* 12:1, 77–101.

Hardin, William G., III, and Martin L. Wolverton. 2000. "Micro-Market Determinants of Neighborhood Center Rental Rates." *Journal of Real Estate Research* 20:3, 299–322.

Hardin, William G., III, and Martin L. Wolverton. 2001. "Neighborhood Center Image and Rents." *Journal of Real Estate Finance and Economics* 23:1, 31–46.

Hardin, William G., III, Martin L. Wolverton, and Jon Carr. 2002. "An Empirical Analysis of Community Center Rents." *Journal of Real Estate Research* 23:1–2, 163–178.

Hausman, Jerry, and Daniel McFadden. 1984. "A Specification Test for the Multinomial Logit Model." *Econometrica* 52:5, 1219–1240.

Hotelling, Harold. 1929. "Stability in Competition." *Economic Journal* 39:1, 41–57.

Hyson, C. D., and W. P. Hyson. 1950. "The Economic Law of Market Areas." *Quarterly Journal of Economics* 64:2, 319–327.

Jones, Ken, and Michael Doucet. 2000. "Big-Box Retailing and the Urban Retail Structure: The Case of the Toronto Area." *Journal of Retailing and Consumer Services* 7:2, 233–247.

Kim, Hyun-Mi, and Mei-Po Kwan. 2003. "Space-Time Accessibility Measures: A Geo-computational Algorithm with a Focus on the Feasible Opportunity Set and Possible Activity Duration." *Journal of Geographical Systems* 5:1, 71–91.

Limanond, Thirayoot, and Debbie A. Niemeier. 2004. "Effect of Land Use on Decisions of a Shopping Tour Generation: A Case Study of Three Traditional Neighborhoods." *Transportation* 31:2, 153–181.

Lösch, August. [1940] 1954. *The Economics of Location*. Translated by William H. Woglom and Wolfgang F. Stolper. New Haven: Yale University Press.

Louviere, Jordan J., David A. Hensher, Joffre D. Swait, and Wiktor Adamowicz. 2000. *Stated Choice Methods: Analysis and Application*. Cambridge: Cambridge University Press.

Manski, Charles F. 1977. "The Structure of Random Utility Models." *Theory and Decision* 8:2, 229–254.

McFadden, Daniel. 1981. "Econometric Models of Probabilistic Choice." In Charles F. Manski and Daniel McFadden, eds., *Structural Analysis of Discrete Data*, 198–272. Cambridge, MA: MIT Press.

Mejia, Luis C., and John D. Benjamin. 2002. "What Do We Know about the Determinants of Shopping Center Sales? Spatial Versus Non-Spatial Factors." *Journal of Real Estate Literature* 10:1, 3–26.

Nakanishi, Masao, and Lee G. Cooper. 1974. "Parameter Estimation for a Multiplicative Competitive Interaction Model—Least Squares Approach." *Journal of Marketing Research* 11:3, 303–311.

Parr, John B. 1995. "Alternative Approaches to Market-Area Structure in the Urban System." *Urban Studies* 32:8, 1317–1329.

Reilly, William J. 1931. *The Law of Retail Gravitation.* New York: Pillsbury Publishers.

Sirmans, C. F., and Krisandra A. Guidry. 1993. "The Determinants of Shopping Centre Rents." *Journal of Real Estate Research* 8:1, 107–115.

Société de Transport de la Communauté Urbaine de Québec (STCUQ). 2001. *Enquête Origine-Destination.* Québec: Réseau de transport de la Capitale.

Tay, Richard S., Clement K. Lau, and Marie S. Leung. 1999. "The Determination of Rent in Shopping Centers: Some Evidence from Hong Kong." *Journal of Real Estate Literature* 7:2, 183–196.

Thill, Jean-Claude, and Harry J. P. Timmermans. 1992. "Analyse des décisions spatiales et du processus de choix des consommateurs: Théorie, méthodes et exemples d'applications." *L'Espace Géographique* 2:1, 143–166.

Timmermans, Harry J. P. 1982. "Consumer Choice of Shopping Centre: An Information Integration Approach." *Regional Studies* 16:3, 171–182.

Wheaton, William C. 2000. "Percentage Rent in Retail Leasing: The Alignment of Landlord–Tenant Interests." *Real Estate Economics* 28:2, 185–204.

Yuo, Tony Shun-Te, Neil Crosby, Colin Lizieri, and Philip McCann. 2003. "The Management of Positive Inter-Store Externalities in Shopping Centres: Some Empirical Evidence." Working Paper in Real Estate and Planning, University of Reading Business School.

Yuo, Tony Shun-Te, Neil Crosby, Colin Lizieri, and Philip McCann. 2004. "Tenant Mix Variety in Regional Shopping Centres: Some U.K. Empirical Analyses." Working Paper in Real Estate and Planning, University of Reading Business School.

7

Healthcare Facilities

ISAAC F. MEGBOLUGBE
Associate Professor, Carey Business School, Johns Hopkins University

DOUGLAS HOUGH
Associate Scientist, Bloomberg School of Public Health, Johns Hopkins University

Introduction

The healthcare system has two types of real estate. Hospitals are short-stay and nursing homes are long-stay facilities. Hospitals in the United States have every incentive to respond to price and revenue signals because nongovernmental entities own more than three-quarters of them.

According to the American Hospital Association (2013), the United States had 5,724 registered hospitals in 2012. Of these, 4,973 were community hospitals available to admit general patients. Non-community hospitals such as psychiatric or military have a restricted patient clientele. Of the community hospitals, 2,903 were non-government, nonprofits focused on revenue. For-profit operators owned another 1,025. This for-profit number increased from 823 in 2004 despite a decline in the total number of hospitals.

Although hospitals are motivated to generate profit or at least revenue, they act as price takers. Private insurers negotiate prices for procedures or diagnosis related groups. Government programs for Medicare and Medicaid, which pay two-fifths of all U.S. healthcare spending, operate with preset prices. With prices predetermined and operators motivated for revenue, hospitals should suffer the classic conditions of a rent-controlled market. Excess demand occurs with waiting lines and times for elective procedures.

Hospitals have another vacancy-related issue related to peak-load demand. A lack of differential pricing for doctors and professionals exists, and no time-sensitive or dynamic pricing is available. The system is aware that demand is seasonal. Vacancy is higher on weekends and during the summer, particularly in July (Weissman 2005). Because of low demand, teaching hospitals use July as the month for the shift change when interns and residents replace the existing group, causing a risk of lower quality care to patients during this period. During these low-demand periods, care is of lower quality.

Another seasonal phenomenon is a day-of-the week effect. Occupancy of hospital beds is high during the week and falls on weekends. Vacancy falls below 10 percent in suburban areas on Monday to Thursday nights. Outside these peak hours and during the summer months the hospital vacancy rate can exceed 50 percent. This situation almost parallels the hotel industry in the business sector. Given the magnitudes involved for healthcare spending, any explanation for this paradox of falling availability, rising excess capacity, and regulated prices has substantial cost implications.

This chapter examines real estate in its pivotal role as an expense in the delivery of medical services, a topic often ignored by the literature. The rest of the chapter is organized as follows. The next section deals with healthcare choices. Hospitals and nursing homes are then addressed as separate investable assets. The next section discusses how real estate facilities are part of healthcare spending. Construction costs are the next issue on the supply side. Agency and incentive issues are examined as motivators of the demand side. Users do not pay the full price and rely on recommendations from professionals. The final section presents a summary and conclusions.

Healthcare Choices

Beds have a rate tied to insurer reimbursement procedures. Occupancy has a separate price of waiting for a bed. If regulated hospital bed rates and waiting time prices rise faster than incomes and costs of non-healthcare items, patient care declines. The patient must accept a lower level of both beds and occupancy.

In the U.S. healthcare system, bed counts fall while vacancy rises even though prices and provider rates are controlled. As room rates rise, vacancy rates rise. Depending on expectations and the structure, a relatively large increase in vacancy is needed to dampen rising rate increases. In the capital asset market for hospitals and their beds, the rising rates create incentives for new construction, which is regulated and restricted. According to the National Council of State Legislatures (2013), 36 states and the District of Columbia restricted construction in 2010. These agencies require certificates of need to justify new construction. If that regulated initial bed supply exceeds the number that patients want to occupy, the rising prices and rates force falling capacity and rising vacancy.

The analogy of rent control of apartments predicts that excess demand occurs with regulated prices. With healthcare prices similarly regulated, waiting lists will exist for hospital beds, elective surgical procedures in operating rooms, and technology including magnetic resonance imaging (MRI). Depending on whether the regulated rates are rising relative to income, these restrictions will lead to excess supply and rising vacancy, not excess demand.

Americans face regulated prices for healthcare despite no waiting lists at hospitals. In the U.S. multi-payer insurance market, prices rise faster than incomes and restrictions remain on usage and supply. More rigid demand restrictions on networks and construction certificates of need increase the vacancy rate. The United Kingdom, Korea, and Canada are cases of single-payer markets likely to impose price regulation. When healthcare rates rise more slowly than income, patients occupy beds more intensively and no or minimal vacancy exists. Patients wait longer and pay a price for delays not counted in healthcare costs, even though more beds per capita are available than in a multi-payer market.

In healthcare, fixed costs dominate relative to variable costs. Demand fluctuates, but providers must meet peak-load capacity. Users pay a fraction of the total price and do not negotiate directly. Gatekeepers including insurers and employers negotiate price and quality rather than patient users directly. Public insurers set rates for procedures. Private insurers negotiate with employers on premium payments and with providers for fees. In exchange, users accept a constrained set of providers within quality or price limits.

Medical services can be delivered across a spectrum of locations ranging from a hospital outpatient clinic to a doctor's office. Nursing services can be delivered at a hospital, rehabilitation (rehab) center, senior housing, or even within-home care. Which location is least costly and most efficient for treatment delivery depends on the disease, provider, and treatment protocol. Medical treatments are performed at the location with the lowest rental price. Rental price analysis leads to an optimum location for treatment. Without a rental-pricing framework, facilities such as hospitals can paradoxically be favored over low-cost alternatives such as at home or in senior housing.

Full rental pricing addresses the excess capacity plaguing the hospital industry. The proportion of licensed hospital beds not occupied has been rising. This has occurred even as the total number of beds and hospitals has been declining. The vacancy rate of assisted-living facilities has been rising even as capacity in that senior housing sector has been increasing. Vacancy rates indicate rising real estate excess capacity even as the healthcare system imposes price and quantity regulations normally associated with excess demand.

For hospitals, regulations include mandated, preset rates for specific treatments and stay limits set by public providers including Medicare and Medicaid and by other third-party payers. Medicare provides healthcare for the elderly and disabled and Medicaid for the poor. Public policy in the United States requires open access to emergency rooms for all comers regardless of the ability to pay. Unlike other real estate facilities, intermediaries including public and private insurers, not users, control hospital admission.

Location shifts of households to the suburbs and of service provision have led to the growth of specialty hospitals, including those that are physician owned. These hospitals exist in the minority of states not requiring certificates of need for new construction. These unrestricted states allow a hospital not to have an emergency room to treat all-comers. The federal government has placed restrictions on specialty hospitals while subsidizing teaching, low-income, and rural hospitals. Determining whether such policy measures are efficient occurs only when estimated rental prices for healthcare locations are available. Then the price paid to subsidize activities, such as preserving a hospital in a rural area, can be made explicit.

Estimating rental prices for healthcare would potentially facilitate the further emergence of alternative, horizontally bundled providers in addition to the vertically integrated existing system that serves a variety of illnesses. The vertical entities include general hospitals, insurers, and health maintenance organizations. A horizontal, unbundled delivery of medical services specializing in specific diseases produces the rental price of facilities in each treatment. A full rental system prices provider services such as those of doctors, medical staff including nurses, hospital workers, drugs and supplies, equipment, and real estate. Once these rental prices are obtained, the services can be repackaged, including being offered by horizontal, disease-focused entities.

One explanation for the rising cost of health is that medical care quality is rising and patients and their insurers are willing to pay for it. Healthcare costs, which already account for one-sixth of gross domestic product (GDP) in the United States, are projected to rise to as much as one-third of output by 2050. Cutler (2004) contends that healthcare investments have benefit-cost ratios as high as 6 to 1, a rationale for the rising share. This argument is tempered by the use of $100,000 as the benefit of an added year of life expectancy.

A second explanation is that patients have incentives for excess demand and overuse because of insurance provisions. Patients have deductibles and co-payments that are a fraction of the bill, with public or private insurers paying the rest. Patients as users have a moral hazard incentive to overuse the healthcare system. The response by public and private insurers is to negotiate rates and payments by outcome or coding, such as the Current Procedural Terminology (CPT) used in the United States, and to determine which treatments are covered.

A third explanation is that while the healthcare market in the United States is nominally competitive having a large number of providers and users, its incentives act against cost-saving innovation. Insurers place limits on the time that doctors spend with patients, leading to risks of incorrect diagnoses and of subsequent expensive treatment. Technology raises healthcare costs because the low-deductible system gives patients little incentive to seek low-cost treatment. At the user level, only limited competition exists among providers. Doctors use referrals instead of pricing and hospitals have pre-negotiated prices.

These are not necessarily mutually exclusive reasons for the rising cost of healthcare. The relatively low deductibles and co-payments to patients, coupled with preset prices negotiated by insurers, should create excess demand. The price is below what patients would pay on their own, encouraging them to increase their demand for healthcare. Raising the price to patients reduces these disincentives. An example is medical savings accounts for small bills with high-deductible health insurance policies for catastrophic coverage.

Hospitals and Nursing Homes

These three explanations of demand for quality, subsidies, and incentives to avoid low-cost treatment derive from incentives built into the U.S. healthcare system. These conditions are symptoms of excess demand. Prices are regulated while usage is constrained. Herzlinger and McPherson (1997) discuss these issues.

Yet, the United States is not facing excess demand for healthcare facilities. According to the American Hospital Association (2013), the number of registered beds at all hospitals was 1.47 million in 1975. The number of registered beds had declined to 987,000 by 2001, 944,000 in 2009, and to 924,333 by 2012. A decrease of more than one-third of the hospital bed capacity in the United States occurred during a quarter century. For general-access community hospitals, the bed count declined but less severely. In 2001, community hospitals had 925,000 beds but by 2012 the number of beds had fallen to 797,403. Less-invasive procedures are shifting to surgery centers and other outpatient facilities that do not require overnight beds.

Even as overall beds available fell, that decline was insufficient to curb excess capacity. Vacancy rates at hospital beds rose sharply until the late 1990s and then began to plateau.

The occupancy rate of beds fell despite a cut of one-third in total capacity. The occupancy rate of hospital beds was 76.7 percent in 1975. The rate fell to 69.5 percent in 1990 and then to 65.7 percent in 1995. It was at 66.1 percent in 2000, 68.2 percent in 2008, and 67.8 percent in 2009. Although the number of hospitals has been falling and the population rising, the occupancy of beds has remained at about two-thirds. On average, 250,000 hospital beds in the United States are empty (American Hospital Association 2013).

Private or for-profit ownership of hospitals is not reducing the vacancy. In fact, the opposite occurs. Private hospitals are holding even more excess capacity than at non-profit or state and local counterparts. The bed vacancy rates at private, for-profit hospitals exceed 40 percent. If private ownership is more efficient, what can be accounting for a higher vacancy rate there than at public facilities? The answer must lie in the public valuing excess capacity and availability. The demand for excess capacity is leading for-profit hospitals to provide more excess capacity as a convenience for potential patients. The introduction of the private sector to hospital ownership has not necessarily curbed excess capacity.

Another possibility is that hospitals have become places where medical intervention is performed and not places for long-term care. Long-term care is delivered in specialized housing such as nursing homes. The excess capacity in hospitals could partly be attributable to long-term care patients being shifted to nursing homes.

According to the National Nursing Home Survey (NNHS) of the United States National Center for Health Statistics of the Centers for Disease Control (2013), 1.624 million nursing home beds were available in 1985 including 1.491 million occupied beds. That represents an occupancy rate of 91.8 percent, or a bed vacancy rate of 8.2 percent. In 1999, the year reported in the 2003 NNHS, there were 1.879 million nursing home beds of which 1.628 million were occupied, or an occupancy rate of 86.6 percent. The vacancy rate of nursing home beds rose from 8.2 percent in 1985 to 13.4 percent in 1999. The number of occupants began to level off. In 2004, nursing homes had 1.73 million beds with 1.49 million occupied. This represents an occupancy rate of 86.1 percent or a vacancy rate of 13.9 percent. This is the most recent NNHS survey, but it confirms the data for hospitals. The vacancy rate of nursing home beds has been rising over time, reaching 13.9 percent, a five-percentage point increase over 20 years.

The number of nursing home beds is declining, which is a pattern followed at hospitals. This trend is an ongoing paradox. The United States is an aging society with an ongoing and rising demand for healthcare. Yet, healthcare occupancy at hospitals and nursing homes has been declining. The healthcare system has been delivering services that do not require patients to be hospitalized or in long-term treatment at real estate facilities.

The result is that the number of people in institutional healthcare in hospitals and nursing homes is falling in absolute numbers, even as the population increases and ages. In 1985, community hospitals had 1.07 million beds with 65 percent occupancy or 695,000 in-patients (American Hospital Association 2013). Adding that to the 1.491 million in nursing homes (United States Centers for Disease Control 2013) results in

2.2 million people in health institutions. By 2000, the number of people in health institutions had declined to 2.1 million. In 2012, fewer than 2 million people occupied a hospital or nursing home bed on a given night. These data do not indicate excess demand or patients rushing to occupy hospital beds because of low co-pays or deductibles or even nursing homes, where Medicaid is a principal payer. All of these data are occurring as the population rises and ages.

An objective of this chapter is to explain why this excess supply coexists with apparent excess demand from underpricing at health insurers. The analysis takes a different approach in analyzing the rising cost of healthcare by considering the facilities or supply side. The rising excess capacity is the result of a standby option for well people to gain access to health facilities. Because hospitals can only charge those admitted, sick people pay for well people, exactly the opposite of insurance or public policy principles.

Until 1992, Medicare reimbursed hospitals and other facilities on a cost-plus basis, which provided incentives to build expensive facilities. Since then, the incentives have changed to reimbursement based on cash operating costs.

Cash operating costs are relatively high for older, more obsolete facilities located in rural or inner-city areas but are low for expensive, newer facilities located in suburban areas. A rental price for a hospital bed per night reflects the cost of capital invested and needed to maintain the facility. With reimbursements fixed in price based on outcome or code, such as Current Procedural Terminology (CPT) inner city hospitals have lower margins than suburban counterparts because their operating costs are higher. Their response is to cut back on care, leading to reduced quality in inner-city hospitals. The low quality of healthcare in the inner city and the poor health outcomes of minorities do not result solely from poor environment or even discrimination. Instead, poor outcomes are from a set of misplaced incentives in the healthcare system.

The sick are paying for the well. The poor are paying for the affluent. Inner-city hospitals are rationally forced to cut the quality of their services, leading to poorer outcomes. All these actions are consistent, but result from perverse incentives. The focus is on the supply or delivery of healthcare in the United States. A supply side approach contrasts with a focus on the demand side of medical services with emphasis on patient and treatment costs. The next section further defines the real estate aspects of healthcare.

Real Estate and Healthcare

An inherent linkage exists between real estate and healthcare. Real estate has a traditional division into five sectors: apartment, office, retail, industrial, and hotel. Healthcare adds a sixth. The debt side includes mortgages of privately operated healthcare facilities including nursing homes, hospitals, biotech and lab space, and doctors' offices. These mortgages along with the other five types in commercial loans are combined to construct mortgage-backed securities (MBS). Other investable assets are direct commercial mortgages and derivative securities.

On the equity side, all property types including healthcare have publicly traded real estate investment trusts (REITs). Healthcare REITs offer tax-preferred investments in a portfolio of medical facilities. Healthcare Property Investors (HCP) is a REIT that invests in office buildings and other facilities that deliver healthcare. A healthcare REIT

(HCN) owns and finances nursing homes and specialty hospitals. Omega Healthcare Investors (OHI) offers sale and leaseback provisions for medical offices, testing facilities, and specialty hospitals. A separate industry has emerged that owns and manages assisted-living facilities.

Healthcare offers unique real estate features. Partly because healthcare intervention is expensive, patients are not paying the full price of the treatment. Third-party providers, including governmental entities, health insurance companies, and managed care providers make payments. These providers use regulations and administrative guidelines including preset payment rates rather than market prices to manage demand. On the demand side, prices facing patients are below equilibrium because most costs are shifted to employers and tax benefits exist. In exchange, the insurers impose restrictions on usage and selection and impose price controls. All this would normally lead to excess demand.

Legislation controls both demand and supply of healthcare facilities. These regulatory features include the Affordable Care Act of 2010. Hospitals are required to treat all-comers in their emergency rooms. Treatment cannot be denied to patients without insurance, leading to hospitals having uncompensated care. Under the Affordable Care Act, the intention is to reduce the proportion of people without insurance from an estimated 47 million to less than 30 million. Increasing the number of the insured lowers the pressure on emergency rooms.

Another development is hospitals forming networks and buying doctor practices. Over 60 percent of doctors worked for hospitals as opposed to having private practices by 2010. Insurance and reimbursement rules restrict facility fees from being charged for doctors' offices. Hospitals have nevertheless been submitting reimbursement for facility fees in doctors' offices.

Within private ownership of healthcare facilities, issues of agency, self-referral, and organization occur. Referral is one of the important factors affecting the competitive position of a hospital. Doctors make referrals and the number and quality of medical doctors that are affiliated with a hospital becomes important. A case of hyper-competition, or "cherry picking" of patients, exists in certain hospital markets.

The federal government is already the dominant payer for medical services. Medicare alone is the dominant provider of hospital revenues through its client base of those over 65 years of age. According to the *Health Forum* from the American Hospital Association (2013), in 2010 Medicare provided 39 percent of all hospital revenues, with Medicaid 12 percent and other government 4 percent. Thus, 55 percent of hospital revenues are from government programs. Third-party insurers paid 38 percent and self-pay 6 percent, with the remaining 1 percent in other categories.

Treatment prices set by Medicare and Medicaid are less than a hospital's costs for the services provided. State governments administer Medicaid and have flexibility in setting reimbursement rates and coverage. Direct payment from individual patients is a small part of revenues, and collection of amounts due from individuals is typically more difficult than from governmental or third party payers.

Hospital operators generally grant discounts from normal rates to certain group purchasers of healthcare services such as Blue Cross-Blue Shield, other private health insurance companies, employers, health maintenance organizations (HMOs), preferred provider organizations (PPOs), and other managed care plans. These discount programs restrict a hospital's ability to increase billing rates and revenues due to increasing costs. Although users are receiving healthcare, insurers are paying the bills. Because these entities are not directly making the payments to manage the system, they resort to rationing devices for medical care, including maximum prices and limits on procedures and on demand such as hospital stay length.

Setting prices and rules at levels below equilibrium would result in excess demand and waiting times for hospital admission. Although waiting times exist, particularly in public hospitals, the industry is characterized by excess supply and vacancy rather than excess demand. This is a paradoxical result because pricing is apparently below the levels that some patients might pay while hospital beds go empty. The vacancy rate for hospital beds has been rising, even as the number of beds has fallen. What appears to explain the phenomenon is pressure by hospital managers to increase capacity even as demand is subsidized. That pressure to add expensive capacity outweighs the low pricing on demand and leads to greater excess capacity.

Factors accounting for an occupancy decline are an increasing tendency to perform surgery on an outpatient rather than an inpatient basis. Elderly patients who had previously viewed hospitals as long-stay locations have become patients in assisted-living facilities. The average length of stay for most illnesses decreased with rehabilitation and recovery shifted to specialty hospitals and nursing homes.

Pauly and Redisch (1973) view hospitals as managed by a physician's cooperative, dependent on admitting privileges. If admitting privileges are tight and restrictive, the physicians have more control over the facility. The incentive exists to limit the number of doctors and to expand the size of the hospital so as to expand the capital-labor ratio. Added bed capacity provides convenience, but more doctors leads to increased competition for patients. Because doctors are not charged for carrying the real estate cost, excess capacity occurs. This physician control model is turned upside down by hospital purchases of medical practices.

Another part of the pressure to create and add to facilities comes from a dispersion of households across metro and other areas. This sequence leads to a demand for healthcare services including hospitals in suburban locations. When facilities are located near suburban residents, they avoid having indigent patients in the emergency rooms. This paradox is made more acute if the hospitals and facilities are publicly funded but the payment is from private insurers.

An opposite problem is occurring for rural hospitals where the population is aging and typically declining. Private sector nursing and assisted-living providers are not attracted to rural areas because of low population density and an absence of urban amenities. Local governments are strapped, with elderly residents resisting tax increases to support hospitals even as they consume the services. The result is political pressure on Medicare to provide subsidies for rural hospitals. These subsidies prevent hospital consolidation and restrict the unbundling of services for more efficient delivery.

Consolidation in the hospital industry is being pushed from several sources. Economies of scale exist in information technology, increasingly mandated by insurers and by the Affordable Care Act. Some nonprofits are undercapitalized. These factors may accelerate the consolidation of the hospital industry toward privately operated hospitals. The well-capitalized investor-owned hospital operators should benefit from these changes. Increases in Medicare and Medicaid reimbursement rates forestall consolidation.

Real estate markets deal extensively with the financial benefits returned to owners. Vacancy and pricing vacant space become important financial issues. The owner of a facility with vacancy consciously holds it as an option for future use and prices for holding it. Space held involuntarily must take a reduction in rent to obtain a user. Any building's owner may deliberately choose to hold excess capacity. Similarly, a hospital holds unused licensed beds to handle unforeseen demand such as a tragic emergency. The hospital retains a staff to manage this unforeseen demand. The patients hold options on the staff and the hospital to use healthcare without waiting.

Choosing that option to hold excess capacity necessitates adjustments included in the overall price charged to each patient. Where the hospital holds involuntary excess capacity for other reasons such as from overbuilding, that excess should be priced as a separate cost. Otherwise, patients would be charged for mistakes in overbuilding.

Relevant for a real estate analysis is that Medicare allows hospitals to charge for capital costs. Medicare reimburses hospitals for depreciation, interest, taxes, and insurance. These are soft costs for services that are incorporated into annual budgets. Medicare's capital cost portion is 5 percent of hospital revenues. Medicare spends one-eighth of its allocation to hospitals for capital expenses on existing facilities. That spending does not include the hard costs of new construction. Medicare rules and regulations are uniform across hospitals. Medicare provides added subsidies for providers who have a low-income caseload under its Disproportionate Share Hospital (DSH) program, along with teaching and rural hospitals.

Commercial real estate mortgages and rental payments from leases with cash flows have been extensively securitized. One possibility would be to sell a securitized stream of Medicare receipts to investors in order to raise funds for the hospital. The type and use for real estate will distinguish the different types of cash received. Those streams received from the federal government are valued more highly to investors and require a lower rate of discount that increases the value of the cash flows.

Construction Costs

Part of this analysis centers on why hospitals and other delivery systems cost so much as compared with other types of real estate. These procedures include the pricing of the facility and other assets, the rental price of the rooms, equipment and services, and the appropriate ownership. The funding system for healthcare, where capital budgets are separate from operating budgets, can lead to a misallocation of resources. In a hospital, even if privately operated, one entity manages and operates the facility. Another entity, frequently a public sector body, is responsible for permitting the construction decision.

Several public policy factors are at play in the decision process to construct medical facilities. If construction is paid directly or through municipal bonds and if those taxpayers are diffuse, an agency incentive exists to promote new construction and not to manage costs. A majority of states have limitations on a hospital's ability to make capital expenditures by requiring certificates of need (CON), even for adding to an existing bed count. Hospital construction falls under restrictive rules for contracting, which leads to a small but restricted supply from local contractors to manage and promote construction. Even with guaranteed maximum price construction procedures, incentives for cost overruns and additional expensive facilities exist.

If existing hospitals are not closed, these new facilities compete for scarce staffing, notably in nursing, lab technicians, and radiology. Such hospital-related jobs are in relatively tight supply and are tied to the number of beds in service.

Focusing on the real estate side, other reasons help to explain why for-profit hospitals have higher expenses. These reasons include more expensive land and building use costs. The real estate issue is not whether the hospital is owned privately or publicly, but who the decision-maker is and whether a market-driven charge is made for a service.

In a real estate approach to pricing, established rental markets are available for buildings and facilities. The owners of facilities use market determined rental rates in setting prices and allocation. A rental price or user cost links current services to a capital stock of real estate, connecting the income statement with the balance sheet.

The owner receives a return on holding the land and building, and the delivery of medical services is separately priced. This economic rental structure already applies in many private practitioners' offices. The extension is to analyze the costs of real estate for hospitals and other large medical facilities. It deals with the private versus public ownership issue, but in all cases determining rental prices for facilities is appropriate.

Agency Issues

The demand for healthcare facilities comes from referrals by skilled and informed professionals including doctors. When this demand is for labs and blood and other testing and if doctors own the testing and treatment facilities, an incentive exists to refer. Some medical plans and rules restrict doctors from having ownership in lab and testing facilities. Other restrictions occur regarding doctors owning hospitals. If doctors own the hospitals, the tendency to over-refer causes overuse of the facility.

For the healthcare industry, reimbursement rates and usage limits for procedures are set by federal guidelines in Medicare and Medicaid. In this restrictive pricing environment, treatments have higher built-in margins than others due to lower costs.

Market driven healthcare along the lines of Herzlinger and McPherson (1997) offers insightful analogies in a quest for efficient real estate use. Two areas of particular concern are cost reduction in the emergency room and in specialized procedures. The emergency room must treat all-comers regardless of the ability to pay. Besides reducing operating costs by having current technology and equipment, the for-profit provider can locate in a suburban area that has fewer low-income or uninsured patients. Other ways are available to reduce emergency room expenses. These procedures include the provider reducing capacity in the emergency room, increasing wait times, and creating incentives for the indigent to go to nonprofit hospitals. Another action is to charge an up-front fee to patients at the emergency room deemed to be using it as a substitute for a regular doctor office visit. The tendency for tax-exempt and nonprofit teaching hospitals to locate in central cities for historical and complex case reasons only increases the problem.

General hospitals have criticized specialty hospitals that do not have an emergency room to treat the indigent. Specialty hospitals that focus on diseases such as cancer and cardiology with high reimbursement rates are particularly profitable. Even if cream skimming or adverse selection is occurring, that is not necessarily inefficient from a real estate or economic perspective. The indigent or low-income patients receive a subsidy or alternatives to the emergency room.

These explanations of rising quality, subsidized demand, and imperfect competition derive from incentives into the healthcare system as symptoms of excess demand. Prices are regulated and usage is constrained. Despite this situation, the United States is not facing excess demand for hospitals and health facilities. Rather, excess supply exists despite price regulation.

Anderson, Hussey, Frogner, and Waters (2005) find that despite the lack of waiting lists at hospitals, relatively less capacity is available in the United States than in other developed countries in the Organization for Economic Co-operation and Development (OECD). The authors note that in 2002, the United States had 2.9 hospital beds per 1,000 people, with the OECD median being 3.7. The number of hospital beds per thousand people places the United States in the bottom quartile among developed countries, despite a cut of more than one-third of capacity in 20 years. Although one-third of U.S. hospital beds are vacant on a given night, Europeans and Canadians who have more beds per capita have waiting lists for up to six months for elective surgeries.

The system has rising rates and higher costs of hospital beds and gross asset values with increased vacancies and falling numbers of beds. Even as the bed count declines, the vacancy of those beds rises in a U.S.-style multi-payer system. Healthcare costs rise faster than income and construction is throttled. The expenditure on the hospital as a real estate entity rises even as the number of beds falls and the vacancy rises.

Dranove, Shanley, and Simon (1992) examine two alternative explanations of facility supply. Their *arms-race hypothesis* is that the addition of facilities causes a welfare loss by leading to costly duplication of specialized services. Free entry can lead to social inefficiency. When new products are substitutes for existing products, the business stolen from incumbents places a wedge between private and social benefits of entry. The *alternative extent-of-market hypothesis* is that added facilities increase choice.

Lynk (1995) compares the performance of for-profit, nonprofit, and government hospitals. The author regresses the weighted average price of patient care received on market share and a concentration index used to simulate mergers of two like hospitals. A merger of two for-profit hospitals increases the average price for a procedure.

The price is that paid for in-patient admission for acute care by a patient with private insurance. That price is not a complete measure of revenue because Medicare accounts for 40 percent of patient days in hospitals. The concentration uses a Herfindahl-Hirschman index based on county or metropolitan area. The case mix of the hospitals is adjusted by the diagnostic related group treatment.

Watt, Derson, Renn, Schramm, Hahn, and Pillari (1986) compare 80 matched pairs of data for for-profit and nonprofit hospitals. They adjust all data for case and patient mix. Prices and revenues are higher in the for-profit hospitals largely because of ancillary charges. Costs related to patient care are similar. Although for-profit hospitals have higher overhead, they are more profitable. Both managers and shareholders come out ahead, but largely because of added charges to insurers and not lower operating costs. The profitability of for-profit hospitals comes from price aggressiveness rather than operating efficiency. For-profit hospitals have adjusted prices 3–11 percent higher than nonprofit hospitals.

On the demand side, Gruber (1994) examines price-comparison shopping among hospitals for those with uncompensated care. Net income for nonprofit California hospitals grows more slowly in less concentrated markets. Uncompensated care by nonprofits in less concentrated markets falls relative to more concentrated markets. From these two results, nonprofits in less concentrated markets provide less uncompensated care. Increased price competition decreases the market power and net income.

One theory of nonprofits is that administrators seek to maximize the quantity or patients served. A larger number served increases the support for publicfunds. Newhouse (1970) develops a theory where nonprofits maximize quantity and quality. If the nonprofit has market power, it will offer some high-priced services to subsidize indigent and uncompensated care. Nonprofit hospitals offer healthcare until profits are driven to zero. Neighboring hospitals affect the nonprofit's choice of how to maximize output.

According to Pauly and Redisch (1973), employees capture nonprofit hospitals, operating them to benefit physician cartels by maximizing doctors' incomes. Nonprofit hospitals have ratios of equipment, facilities, infrastructure, and staff that are higher than for profit hospitals. The rationale is that the doctors have additional capacity with which to work, thus raising incomes.

Using American Hospital Association *Annual Survey of Hospitals* data between 1988 and 2005, Horwitz and Nichol (2007) conclude that the data support the output maximization theory. Nonprofit hospitals in markets with a high concentration of for-profit hospitals are more likely to offer profitable services such as MRI than those in low for-profit concentration markets. Nonprofit hospitals are less likely to provide unprofitable services such as for AIDS in high for-profit penetration markets.

Nursing home revenues are not based on treatment. Instead, the billing is on a per day basis. Patients are billed one charge for room, board, and care while in a long-term facility. More than half of all nursing home revenues come from Medicaid, the federal-state program for the poor. A nursing home resident must exhaust other assets before being placed on Medicaid.

For-profit nursing homes have lower expenditures on care, with similar revenue or billing rates relative to other nursing homes. For-profit nursing homes have higher expenditures on facilities than nonprofits (Pauly and Redisch 1973).

As medical training has become more expensive and price regulation controls costs, doctors have reduced bargaining power. After four years of medical school, itself a graduate degree with two years of clinical rotations, a doctor cannot obtain licensing without carrying out a residency in a specialization. That residency involves working 80 hours a week at a hospital at relatively low pay and for an additional four years or more.

A resident with a Medicare-funded fellowship is paid $50,000 annually to work those 80-hour weeks. Residency itself takes at least four years and six years in surgical specialties such as plastic surgery. Federal student loans under the Title IV program allow medical students to borrow up to $245,000, and private loans are commonly used. With this type of debt load, medical graduates are in no position to buy their way into a private practice. They are overwhelmingly choosing to work for a hospital or related chain, where 80 percent of newly licensed doctors are going. That makes doctors employees of a hospital. The hospital controls the doctors, rather than the other way around. From the 2008 *Health Tracking Physician Survey*, Boukus, Cassil, and O'Malley (2009) report that 44 percent of doctors are on salary with a performance-based bonus and another 25 percent are on fixed salary. More than two-thirds of doctors are employees, usually of hospital systems.

For-profit hospitals are not only growing within a shrinking industry but also tend to be located in urban rather than rural areas. The for-profit hospitals that reduce costs are those managing the physician cooperative effect. On the revenue side, for-profits are more successful in searching for revenue benefits through loopholes in Medicare and Medicaid reimbursements. These reimbursement rates are higher for hospitals with a high rural or low-income population or for teaching facilities for clinical and resident medical students.

The structure includes the rate, stay, and in-network limits with mandated, preset prices for specific treatments set by public providers and by private third-party payers. Apart from certificates of need, states impose restrictions on capital expenditures. Hospitals face other operating regulations. Federally mandated capital expenses exist for bar coding of pharmaceuticals. Public policy requires open access of emergency rooms to all-comers regardless of ability to pay. Specialty hospitals lack emergency rooms and claim to limit their caseload. These hospitals would not be permitted to operate in states with certificates of need, but are restricted by federal regulation.

Hospital Statistics cover all registered hospitals, whether members of the American Hospital Association or not (American Hospital Association 2013). A registered hospital must meet a series of criteria. Governance requires an identifiable authority to which a chief executive reports. The hospital has a licensed medical staff. Admittance is only after privileges with licensed doctors. As exceptions, medical staff other than a doctor can make an admission in an emergency, but subsequent doctor certification is necessary. Record keeping is required on each patient and must be available on demand. Pharmacy services are delivered at the hospital and are supervised by a licensed pharmacist. The hospital provides food service to meet dietary guidelines for medical conditions, including special diets if requested. The number of in-patient beds available for 24 hour a day service must be at least six.

The hospital system is carrying the standby capacity, but does not send insurers a bill for all potential users. The system sends a bill to actual patients and their insurers. So to carry the excess capacity, the hospitals must bill the sick, even though those who are well are deriving utility from the capacity. Well people never receive a hospital bill for standby capacity.

In the United States, healthcare is not rationed by delays for procedures. Waiting occurs in countries where a single-payer, government-controlled entity exists. Although the federal government is the dominant payer through Medicare and Medicaid, patients can choose their doctors, and hospitals are subject to insurer in-network constraints. The hospitals by their governance structures must manage costs and provide facilities to attract patients. In a single-payer system, the opposite occurs. Hospitals ration by waiting and excess demand. Prices cannot adjust and perpetual excess demand occurs. In the United States, insurers negotiate prices in advance with hospitals and other providers. Although providers criticize prices as being too low, the hospital system in the United States is not in excess demand. Instead, hospitals offer ongoing excess supply.

If doctors agreed to admission privileges at more hospitals, they and their patients could search for capacity, convenience, and price. Gruber (1994) examines price shopping at hospitals. With a shift of healthcare cost from third-party insurers and employers to self-payment, those incentives might change.

Hotels operate with relatively high vacancy rates of between 25 percent and 35 percent to absorb peak-load capacity. Business hotels have high occupancy during the week and from September through June. Business hotel occupancy is low on weekends and during the summer, exactly the weekend and July effects observed at hospitals. Hotels have been offering this perishable off-peak capacity on-line.

Hospitals have similar occupancy patterns if doctors want to schedule elective surgery during the week and not during school vacations. The hospital must have capacity to meet a peak load, but is not charging off-peak pricing. With off-peak pricing hospitals induce doctors to work on weekends or during the summer, as they once did as interns and residents. Any ability to manage the capacity more efficiently across the peak load times has substantial implications for reducing healthcare costs.

Hospitals share an economic structure with other industries such as utilities, hotels, airlines, and other types of transportation. For these industries, fixed costs are substantial relative to variable or marginal costs. Healthcare services cannot be stored for peak demand. Demand fluctuates daily, weekly, monthly, and seasonally. Dynamic peak pricing responds efficiently to demand fluctuations.

The hospital industry has engaged in static price discrimination along its demand curve, but less on predictable, dynamic adjustment. The Virginia Hospital Center in Arlington, Virginia, offers an executive physical for $3,300 with round-trip limousine service. The Cleveland Clinic has a subsidiary in Miami targeting full-pay, direct-billed treatment. Matching its fellow top-five ranked hospital, the Mayo Clinic in Scottsdale, Arizona operates a similar facility. These static adjustments indicate that hospitals are capable of making flexible pricing decisions.

Even with the relatively high average vacancy rates, some facilities may have tight access from the rigid and pre-negotiated prices. This is one of the paradoxes of healthcare in the United States: regulated prices and excess supply.

Summary and Conclusions

Healthcare is delivered in facilities including hospitals. These hospitals are real estate facilities with extensive equipment installed. They have occupancy issues and are subject to seasonality. Low occupancy occurs during the summer and the weekend. In this sense, healthcare facilities are similar to other real estate that generates revenue at the source, including retail stores and hotels. Hospitals have vacancy, which could be available to meet surge capacity in the event of a catastrophe.

Nursing homes are another type of healthcare real estate. They offer long-term convalescent facilities. Nursing homes are similar to apartments, other than offering room and board as additional services. Rehab facilities and doctors' offices are other types of healthcare real estate.

The healthcare facility sector paradoxically has chronic excess capacity. Although the total number of hospital beds has declined since 1983, the average occupancy rate in percentage terms has also declined. At assisted-living facilities, the rate of occupancy has fallen even as the number of rooms available has increased.

Discussion Questions

1. Discuss whether hospital and nursing home beds are rising or falling in the United States.
2. In the presence of price controls and regulation, discuss whether excess demand or supply for healthcare facilities would exist.
3. Identify the major issues regarding demand and pricing for healthcare facilities.
4. Identify the methods for managing the construction of hospitals and beds.

Acknowledgments

The authors are grateful to Mike Anikeeff, Peter Chinloy, Darrell Gaskin, and Bobby Lipnick for valuable comments and suggestions

References

American Hospital Association. 2013. *Hospital Statistics*. Chicago: American Hospital Association. http://www.aha.org.

Anderson, Gerard F., Peter S. Hussey, Bianca K. Frogner, and Hugh R. Waters. 2005. "Health Spending in the United States and the Rest of the Industrialized World." *Health Affairs* 24:4, 903–914.

Boukus, Ellyn R., Alwyn Cassil, and Ann O'Malley. 2009. "A Snapshot of U.S. Physicians: Key Findings from the 2008 *Health Tracking Physician Survey*." Data Bulletin 35. Washington, DC: Center for Health System Change.

Cutler, David M. 2004. *Your Money or Your Life: Strong Medicine for America's Health*. New York: Oxford University Press.

Dranove, David, Mark Shanley, and Carol Simon. 1992. "Is Hospital Competition Wasteful?" *Rand Journal of Economics* 23:2, 247–262.

Gruber, Jonathan. 1994. "The Effect of Competitive Pressure on Charity: Hospital Responses to Price Shopping in California." *Journal of Health Economics* 13:2, 183–212.

Herzlinger, Regina E., and Nancy McPherson. 1997. *Market-Driven Healthcare: Who Wins, Who Loses in the Transformation of America's Largest Service Industry*. New York: Basic Books.

Horwitz, Jill, and Austin Nichols. 2007. "What Do Nonprofits Maximize? Nonprofit Hospital Service Provision and Market Ownership Mix." Working Paper 13246, National Bureau of Economic Research.

Lynk, William J. 1995. "The Creation of Economic Efficiencies in Hospital Mergers." *Journal of Health Economics* 14:5, 507–530.

Newhouse, Joseph P. 1970. "Toward a Theory of Nonprofit Institutions: An Economic Model of a Hospital." *American Economic Review* 60:1, 64–73.

Pauly, Mark V., and Michael Redisch. 1973. "The Not-For-Profit Hospital as a Physician's Cooperative." *American Economic Review* 63:1, 87–99.

United States Centers for Disease Control, National Center for Health Statistics. 2013. *National Nursing Home Survey*. http://www.cdc.gov/nchs/nnhs/nnhs_products.htm.

Watt, Michael J., Robert A. Derzon, Steven C. Renn, Carl J. Schramm, Jin S. Hahn, and George D. Pillari. 1986. "The Comparative Economic Performance of Investor-Owned Chain and Not-For-Profit Hospitals." *New England Journal of Medicine* 314:2, 89–96.

Weissman, Joel. 2005. "Weekend Effects and the July Phenomenon in Patient Safety." Working Paper, Massachusetts General Hospital, Agency for Healthcare Quality and Research.

8

Healthcare Providers

DOUGLAS HOUGH
Associate Scientist, Bloomberg School of Public Health, Johns Hopkins University

ISAAC F. MEGBOLUGBE
Associate Professor, Carey Business School, Johns Hopkins University

Introduction

The healthcare delivery system in the United States is a very peculiar industry. Those who control the allocation of resources within hospitals—the physicians—are usually not owners and not always employees of the hospital. Those who consume healthcare services—the patients—rarely pay the full price of these services. Those that do pay most of the price—the insurers and the government—do not consume the services. Those advising patients on which services to consume—the physicians—often provide those same services. The most capital-intensive parts of the delivery system—the hospitals—are usually not-for-profit organizations and are "owned" by community or religious organizations. The providers of care are paid largely based on volume of services; higher quality physicians and hospitals are paid no more than lower quality providers.

This all makes little sense. If a restaurant operated like a hospital, it would have multiple chefs, one of whom might cook Italian style, while another specialized in Middle Eastern food on the same night. The waiters would provide different menus to each diner, who would have to get permission from the company that would be paying for the meal before the diner could order. At the end of the meal, the restaurant would send a bill to the diner or paying company, and the chef (and any sous chefs) would bill the diner or the company separately for services. If lucky, the restaurant would be paid its bill (but perhaps not the full amount) in 30–60 days. All restaurants would be paid the same amount for the same dish. An upscale restaurant in New York City would be paid the same price for its hamburger as McDonald's.

This chapter explores the structure of the healthcare delivery system, with an emphasis on those elements most relevant to the real estate industry. It describes how the healthcare delivery system got to its current state. It then examines the structure of the system: the services (outpatient, inpatient, post-acute, and prevention and wellness); healthcare organizations (hospitals, physician practices, and ambulatory care facilities); and the role of technology. Next it considers the payment structure for healthcare services and how payment affects incentives, performance, structure, and relationships among providers. Finally, the chapter examines the primary drivers of change in the U.S. healthcare delivery system—changing incentive structures; the trend toward paying for quality and outcomes; and the organizational tension between increasing intensity of services and highly distributed services. The ultimate goal of this chapter is to create a context for understanding how real estate fits into the fabric of this industry.

A Brief History of the U.S. Healthcare Delivery System

Healthcare delivery in the United States started as a cottage industry and has only adopted a more commercial model in the past two decades. Physicians in the eighteenth and nineteenth centuries practiced almost exclusively as sole practitioners, often working out of their houses or visiting patients in house calls. Further, until the mid-nineteenth century, many of these physicians did not earn a medical degree, but learned their craft through apprenticeships (Raffel and Barsukiewicz 2002).

In terms of hospitals, Goldsteen and Goldsteen (2012) note that before the twentieth century, hospitals (often called "pest houses") were where people went to die. The first nongovernmental charity hospital was Pennsylvania Hospital, founded by Benjamin Franklin in 1751. Other prominent hospitals followed, such as Massachusetts General Hospital in 1811 and the Johns Hopkins Hospital in 1877. What held back the development of hospitals and physician practices was the fact that a hospital or physician could offer the sick little other than comfort and support. This changed dramatically when healthcare began to be based on true science. In 1846, ether was first used in an operation at Massachusetts General Hospital. Ignaz Semmelweis in 1847 determined that the unclean hands of physicians caused childbed fever of new mothers. In 1865 Joseph Lister reduced surgical infections by using carbolic acid. The real breakthrough, when hospitals became places to go to recover health, was when Robert Koch established the germ theory of disease in 1876. With these innovations, hospitals could begin to control the environment that their patients faced (Raffel and Barsukiewicz 2002).

This foundation enabled modern technology, such as pathology laboratories and x-ray machines, to be developed and introduced into medical care. Once physicians and hospitals could change the course of illness, they did so. One consequence of having more tools to use and procedures to perform was that the costs of care began to rise. Eighty years ago, the Committee on the Costs of Medical Care (1932, 41–42) came to the following conclusion: "The problem of providing satisfactory medical service to all the people of the United States at costs that they can meet is a pressing one. . . . We have the economic resources, the organizing ability, and the technical experience to solve this problem." One method for assuaging the financial stress of the costs of healthcare was health insurance. Health insurance has been sold in the United States since the mid-nineteenth century, when it was used primarily to compensate for lost wages. In the 1920s modern health insurance began to be offered. In 1929 Justin Ford Kimball created a hospital insurance plan at Baylor University Hospital for teachers in Dallas (Raffel and Barsukiewicz 2002). This innovation was followed by other single-hospital insurance plans. The Blue Cross Association was established in the 1930s to sponsor the development of nonprofit, community-based hospital insurance plans (American Hospital Association 2013) The California Medical Association led a similar effort for physician insurance plans, known as Blue Shield. Blue Cross and Blue Shield plans dominated the market for decades, until for-profit companies such as Aetna, United Healthcare, and Cigna entered the market. The health insurance market grew as a result of the tax exemption of employment-based health insurance, which enabled employers to attract and retain employees through benefits as well as salary.

Table 8.1 shows the consequences of the increase in the capacity and capabilities of health care providers in the United States. In 1940 spending on healthcare was under $4 billion. By 2011 that had grown 675 times to $2.7 trillion. From 1940 to 1990, national health expenditures tripled every decade and have slowed to doubling every decade since. In 1940 spending on health was about $30 per person; in 2011 it was $8,680. Healthcare costs are outstripping the nation's growth in economic wealth; whereas healthcare costs consumed 4 percent of gross domestic product (GDP) in 1940, it took 18 percent in 2011.

This share of national income would be understandable if the American people were receiving substantial value for their investment. Unfortunately, by most measures the United States is lagging other countries in return on investment in healthcare. Table 8.2 shows the performance of the United States and nine other countries in terms of health expenditures and some standard measures of performance. Only Luxembourg spends close to the United States in per capita expenditures on health, with major developed countries (Canada, Germany, France, and the United Kingdom) spending dramatically less and receiving comparable or better value in terms of life expectancy, infant mortality rate, and adult obesity rate. Ironically, Cuba spends the equivalent of $583 per capita on healthcare—just 7 percent of what the United States spends—yet achieves health outcomes equivalent of the United States. Some contend that the high utilization of healthcare in the United States reflects social and not true health pathologies, butvidence suggests that the United States is not unique in this regard (Marmot and Wilkinson 2006).

Not surprisingly, there have been continual calls for healthcare reform. In the late 1960s the Nixon administration and Congressional Democrats debated the shape of national health insurance, with the expectation that such a program was inevitable. In the 1990s the efforts of Bill and Hillary Clinton renewed the interest in health reform. However, their 1,343-page bill never even came up for a vote in either house of Congress. Although controversial, the Affordable Care Act of 2010 stands to fundamentally change the structure of healthcare delivery and financing in the United States.

STRUCTURE OF THE U.S. HEALTHCARE DELIVERY SYSTEM

Healthcare services fall into five major categories.

- *Primary care.* Episodic and relatively simple services that address non-life-threatening health issues, are routine, and require little practitioner time or effort.
- *Secondary care.* More complex services that involve more intensive and time-consuming care.
- *Tertiary care.* Very complex services that require highly skilled practitioners, technology, and facilities; often life-threatening situations.

Table 8.1 **U.S. National Health Expenditures: 1960–2011**

National Health Expenditures	*1940*	*1950*	*1960*	*1970*	*1980*	*1990*	*2000*	*2005*	*2010*	*2011*
Total (in $bn)	$3.9	$12.0	$27.4	$74.9	$255.8	$724.3	$1,377.2	$2,030.5	$2,600.0	$2,700.7
Per capita	$30	$78	$147	$356	$1,110	$2,854	$4,878	$6,875	$8,417	$8,680
Percentage of GDP	4.1	4.5	5.2	7.2	9.2	12.5	13.8	16.1	17.9	17.9

Note: The table shows that total expenditures on healthcare in the United States, in per capita terms and as a percentage of GDP, have risen exponentially over the past 70 years.

Source: Centers for Medicare and Medicaid Services 2013.

Table 8.2 **National Health Expenditures for Selected Countries in 2011**

Country	*Per Capita Expenditures on Health (in US$)*	*Healthcare Expenditures (percent GDP)*	*Life Expectancy at Birth*	*Infant Mortality Rate (per 1,000 births)*	*Percentage of Obese Adults*
United States	8,233	17.6	79	6	33.2
Luxembourg	8,193	7.9	82	2	22.2
Canada	5,257	11.4	82	5	23.9
Germany	4,654	11.5	81	3	19.2
France	4,618	11.7	82	3	14.6
United Kingdom	3,495	9.6	80	4	25.2
United Arab Emirates	1,467	3.7	76	6	43.0
South Africa	631	8.7	58	35	42.8
Cuba	583	10.2	78	5	27.5
Afghanistan	44	10.4	60	73	3.3

Note: The table shows that the United States has the highest per capita health spending, but not the best outcomes.

Source: World Health Organization 2013.

- *Post-acute care.* Less complex services that occur after secondary or tertiary care and usually occur over an extended period and require moderate practitioner skill.
- *Prevention/wellness.* Services intended to preserve and maintain an individual's health status over an extended period.

As Table 8.3 shows, the structure of healthcare organizations follows the structure of healthcare services. Although hospitals provide a small amount of primary care and post-acute care, the bulk of their services are devoted to secondary and tertiary care, which often require large and expensive technologies such as magnetic resonance imaging (MRI) machines and operating rooms as well as services provided across multiple days. Physicians, on the other hand, provide services across the continuum of care, although they are only moderately involved in post-acute care, prevention, and wellness. As Table 8.3 also shows, other major healthcare providers and organizations are much more specialized: ambulatory medical centers address largely secondary care, which involve more technologies than primary care but less than tertiary care; short-term rehabilitation facilities, long-term care facilities, and home care agencies focus almost exclusively on post-acute care.

Table 8.3 **Healthcare Services and Providers/Organizations**

		Healthcare Providers					
		Hospitals	*Physicians*	*Ambulatory Medical Centers*	*Short-term/ rehabilitation facilities*	*Long-term Care Facilities*	*Home Care Agencies*
Healthcare Services	Primary Care						
	Secondary Care						
	Tertiary Care						
	Post-acute						
	Prevention/ Wellness						

Note: As this table indicates, each healthcare provider emphasizes a particular level of care, but provides other levels as well.

Legend:

Major *Degree of Emphasis* *Minor*

HOSPITALS

In 2010 the United States had 4,985 nonfederal, short-term hospitals of which 2,941 were part of a health system and 2,044 were stand-alone facilities. The number of hospitals has stayed relatively stable over the past 20 years. However, the number of beds has dropped by 13 percent, from 926,436 in 1990 to 804,943 in 2010. At the same time, the number of inpatient admissions has increased 13 percent, from 31,181,000 in 1990 to 35,149,000 in 2010. What has made this possible is that the average length of stay of a hospital admission has fallen by 25 percent, from 7.2 days to 5.4 days, driven both by technology and reimbursement. Additionally, hospitals have seen an explosion of outpatient care during this period. The number of outpatient visits in hospitals more than doubled in the past two decades, from 301 million in 1990 to 651 million in 2010; outpatient surgeries surged during this same period, from 11.1 million to 17.4 million. Outpatient surgeries now outnumber inpatient surgeries in hospitals by almost two-to-one (American Hospital Association 2013).

Ownership of short-term hospitals in the United States primarily falls into three categories: (1) nongovernmental, not-for-profit (of which there were 2,903 in 2011), (2) investor-owned/for-profit (1,025), and (3) state and local governmental (1,045). Although a distinct minority form of hospital ownership, for-profit hospitals have been in operation for decades. They were growing modestly until about 1995, when a combination of acquisition of not-for-profits and new construction increased their numbers by over 35 percent. Usually part of a system such as HCA and Tenet, these hospitals tend to be smaller than other short-term hospitals and sometimes focus on a single-specialty service such as cardiac or orthopedics. For the past two decades the number of single-specialty hospitals grew substantially. These so-called "focused factories" (Herzlinger 1997) can be more efficient and more profitable than general hospitals by concentrating on a small set of clinical conditions and procedures for which they have expertise. This trend has stalled, as the vaunted efficiencies have not been realized.

Mission or scope is another way to categorize hospitals. Community hospitals, which provide the bulk of hospital care in the United States, are organized almost exclusively to provide direct patient care services. On the other hand, academic medical centers, also called teaching hospitals, have a more complicated mission of patient care, education of health professionals, and basic and applied research. The scope and size of teaching hospitals varies widely. Of the approximately 1,100 teaching hospitals in the United States, fewer than 400 carry out the tripartite mission. These are the most famous U.S. hospitals–Johns Hopkins Health System, Cleveland Clinic, Mayo Clinic, Massachusetts General Hospital, and University of California at San Francisco Medical Center—that usually rank as the best hospitals in the country.

The final item to note about the structure of American hospitals is the increasing importance of the emergency department (ED). Once called the emergency room (ER), the ED in most hospitals is often the most frequent site of care provided and can be the chief source of inpatient admissions. In 2010 there were 128,843,000 visits to a hospital ED; only 16 percent arrived by ambulance; only 11.3 percent of visits were defined as "immediate" or "emergent," and 43.4 percent were defined as "urgent" triage status (National Center for Health Statistics 2013). Of all the visits, 16.2 percent resulted in admission to the same or different hospital, representing almost 60 percent of total admissions to the hospital. The median ED saw 20,000 visits per year, with 800 EDs experiencing over 50,000 visits per year (Emergency Medical Network 2013). Thus, the ED represents a major source of activity and revenue for many hospitals.

PHYSICIANS

Unlike hospitals, the number of physicians in the United States has grown substantially over the past several decades. In fact, this number has doubled since 1980, with now more than 1 million in the United States. Although the U.S. population has grown over that period, the number of physicians in patient care per 100,000 people has grown from 163 in 1980 to 246 in 2011. The bulk of the growth of the physician population has been in office-based physicians, including both primary care physicians and specialists. This trend suggests an increase in access of patients to medical care. On the other hand, the growth of specialists has far outstripped that of primary care physicians (which include family physicians, general internists, pediatricians, and obstetricians/gynecologists), so that the proportion of physicians in primary care has actually fallen, from 36.5 percent in 1980 to 30.8 percent in 2011. This trend has concerned many policymakers, as the likely surge in demand brought on by the Affordable Care Act may not be met with increased capacity. Table 8.4 presents data about physicians in the United States and selected specialties.

Another worrisome trend is the aging of the physician population in the United States. The medical profession expanded dramatically in the 1960s and 1970s, generated by the growth in the number and size of medical schools plus the growth of offshore medical schools and the maturation of the baby boomer generation into the workforce. More than two of every five physicians is 55 years or age or older, and one out of five is over 65 years of age. One would expect these physicians to begin slowing down, by not accepting new patients and even closing their practices. At the same time,

Table 8.4 **Number of Physicians in the United States by Selected Specialties and Years, 1980–2010**

Type of Physician	*1980*	*1990*	*2000*	*2011*
All physicians	467,679	615,421	813,770	1,004,635
All patient-care physicians	376,512	503,870	647,430	767,782
Office-based	272,000	360,995	490,398	575,641
Hospital-based	104,512	142,875	157,032	192,141
Percentage, primary care	36.5	34.7	33.8	30.8
Percentage 55 +	28.3	29.1	32.3	41.9
Percentage 65 +	13.7	15.5	17.8	21.5
Physicians/100,000 people	163	200	229	246

Note: As this table shows, the number of office and hospital-based doctors has virtually doubled from 1980 to 2011, with a substantial rise in the number of physicians available per population.

Source: Smart 2004, 2013.

anecdotal evidence suggests that younger physicians are seeking a better work/life balance and are not interested in working the kinds of hours and seeing as many patients as their predecessors. All of these trends do not bode well for access to care.

The stereotypical image of a physician practice is a solo practitioner. The reality is not that far from that image, as physicians still largely operate as a cottage industry. According to the American Medical Association (AMA) (Smart 2004), only 10 percent of physicians were in group practice in 1965; by 1986 that percentage had increased to 31.9 percent. (The AMA defines a group practice as three or more physicians formally organized as a legal entity sharing business, clinical, and administrative facilities.) At that time, group practice was becoming the predominant mode of practice. However, this trend appeared to stall out after 1986, with only 30.2 percent of physicians in group practices in 2003 (Kocher and Sahni 2011). Data from this report also reveal that group practices are still relatively small, with 69 percent of group practices in 1994–1995 and 65 percent of group practices in 2003 having three to six full-time-equivalent physicians.

In a more recent AMA study, Kane (2009) reports that 24.6 percent of physicians in clinical practice and 32.5 percent of physicians in office-based practices were in solo practice in 2007–2008. Also 21.4 percent were in practices of two to four physicians, suggesting a decline in solo practice over the decade. This study finds that those physicians who were organized in group practices far favored single-specialty groups (72 percent) to multispecialty groups (28 percent).

Another related trend is the acquisition of physician practices by hospitals and health systems. This is the second time that hospitals have sought to purchase physician practices. The first was in the 1990s, when managed care was growing and hospitals wanted to secure their distribution networks of primary care physicians, who admit their patients to the hospital. This earlier relationship did not work out well for three reasons: Many physicians chose not to work as hard when they were employees; most hospitals did not know how to manage the business; and the specter of managed care faded due to patient resistance.

The current trend seems more sustainable, as health reform through the Affordable Care Act is likely to prevail and hospitals have probably learned a few lessons about the proper ways to acquire and manage physician practices. The Medical Group Management Association (2012), through its annual Physician Compensation and Production survey, indicates that in 2002, physicians owned 70 percent of physician practices and hospitals owned only 22 percent. Those proportions had changed to 39 percent physician-owned and 55 percent hospital-owned by 2012.

AMBULATORY MEDICAL CENTERS

Besides hospitals and physician practices, patient care is provided in ambulatory medical centers. These centers are often freestanding facilities and can be owned by hospitals, physicians, or independent investors. The level of care provided can range from basic primary care (e.g., vaccinations and treatment of simple conditions) to urgent care (e.g., broken limbs, sprains, and wounds) to surgical procedures. These facilities have become popular in the past decade. The Urgent Care Association of America reports that the number of urgent care facilities has grown from 8,000 in 2008 to 9,300 in 2012 (Galewitz 2012). The Medicare Payment Advisory Commission (2012) reports that the number of Medicare-certified ambulatory surgical centers has surged by 33 percent from 2004 (4,033 centers) to 2011 (5,344 centers), almost all of which are for-profit.

The popularity of ambulatory medical centers has stemmed from both demand and supply forces. First, patients like the convenience of these centers. The centers often are open seven days a week with operating hours late in the evenings unlike most physician practices. Often, they offer one-stop care, with imaging, laboratory, and pharmacy services within the same facility. The centers are attractive to providers for their convenience and efficiency. In addition, these centers generate substantial revenue for physicians who are owners, with payments for direct care and ancillary services. As a result, ambulatory medical centers are likely to continue to grow.

Payment for Healthcare Services

As noted earlier in this chapter, the system for paying for healthcare services has evolved over time. Figure 8.1 displays this evolution over the past 50 years. In 1960 patients paid out-of-pocket for a little over half of healthcare expenditures; in 2010 patients directly paid for only 12 percent of healthcare expenditures.

Private insurance, largely sponsored through employers as an employee benefit, has grown at a 10 percent annual rate since 1960, so that it now pays about 35 percent of healthcare expenditures. The biggest change in the source of funds for healthcare services has been the enactment of Medicare and Medicaid in 1965. Medicare is the primary source of funding for healthcare to the elderly, with the federal government acting as the insurer. Medicaid is the primary funding source for healthcare to the poor, with the federal government and state governments sharing financial responsibility. The Medicare program now pays for 21 percent of the total healthcare bill, and the Medicaid program pays for 16 percent.

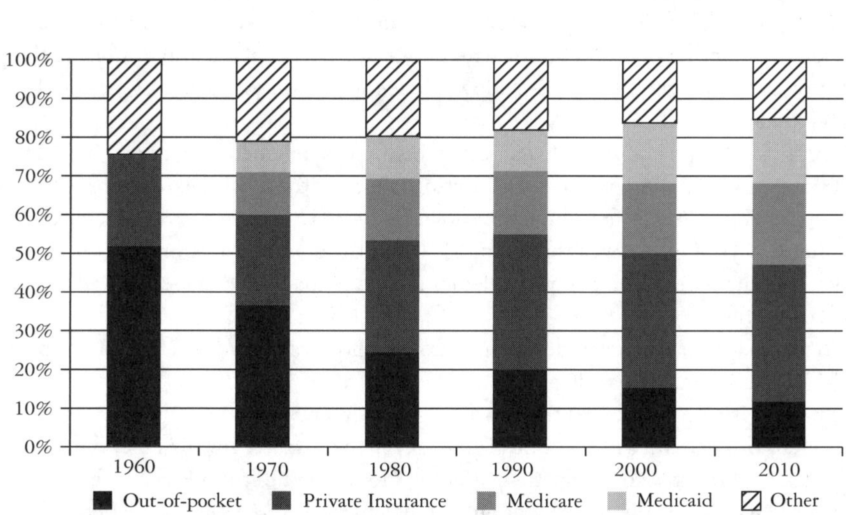

Figure 8.1 Percentage of U.S. Health Consumption Expenditures by Sources of Funds: 1960–2010. *Source*: Centers for Medicaid and Medicare Services 2013.

Pricing: Driven by Real Estate

In an odd sense, real estate drives the pricing of healthcare in the United States. A provider can submit two different prices to an insurer for essentially the same service. A higher price is allowed for a service provided at a facility such as a hospital or related center or clinic. A lower price for the same service would be required for the same service provided in a doctor's office, deemed a non-facility by the system. This section examines how the demand side and pricing of healthcare services works in the United States and how real estate is at the center of it.

CURRENT PROCEDURAL TERMINOLOGY (CPT)

The prices of medical services in the United States are based on Current Procedural Terminology (CPT) codes, which are assigned to every task and service. The AMA, which develops, maintains, and has copyrighted CPT codes, receives considerable licensing fees. The codes are uniform and standardized across the healthcare system. For instance, CPT code 99213 (the most frequently used code) is for a medium-intensity office visit with an established patient. CPT 99397 is for a preventive exam for a person aged over 65; 90658 is for administration of a flu shot; 44950 is for a traditional open appendectomy; and 44970 is for a laparoscopic appendectomy.

Some insurers have their own coding system which complement the CPT system. For instance, Medicare uses a Medicare Physician Fee Schedule (MPFS) and a related Healthcare Common Procedure Coding System. This latter is analogous to the CPT. Using Medicare as an example, a provider might agree to be what is called a "participating provider." A participating provider agrees to accept the Medicare allowable fee as payment in full (known as "assignment"). Medicare will pay 80 percent of the allowable amount of the MPFS and the patient pays a 20 percent co-payment (either out-of-pocket or with a Medicare supplemental insurance policy). Non-participating providers decide on an individual claim basis whether or not to accept assignment or bill the patient on an unassigned basis. The allowable fee for a non-participating provider is reduced by 5 percent.

Suppose the allowable fee for an office with an established patient (CPT 99213) is $100 for a participating provider. In addition, suppose that basic lab tests are performed at the physician's office, for which the allowable fee is $50, leading to a total fee of $150. Medicare pays 80 percent of this fee or $120 and the patient is responsible for a $30 co-payment. The patient can carry supplemental health insurance that covers all or part of the co-payment.

A non-participating provider would have an allowable fee of $142.50, or 95 percent of $150. Medicare will pay 80 percent of the $142.50 or $114. If assignment is accepted, the patient is responsible for the remaining 20 percent or $28.50. If assignment is not accepted, the patient will pay out-of-pocket for the service. In this case, the most the provider is permitted to charge the patient is 115 percent of the allowable fee. Since the allowable fee is $95, the most a patient can be charged is $163.88, or 15 percent above the MPFS fee. A provider opting out of all insurance and never agreeing to any restrictions has no limit on billing to the patient.

RELATIVE VALUE UNITS (RVU)

In the past Medicare and private insurers established their allowable fee based on what was "usual, customary, and reasonable" in the community. This system led to substantial variation in payment for the same service, differences that were not supported by differences in providers' costs. As a result, the Centers for Medicare and Medicaid Services (CMS), which administer Medicare, created a Resource-Based Relative Value Scale (RBRVS), which assigned Relative Value Units (RVUs) to each CPT code. When multiplied by a conversion factor (CF) and a geographical adjustment (GPCI), the RVU sets the compensation level for a particular service.

RVUs have three separate components for the provider's work, practice expense, and malpractice expense. The physician work RVU measures the relative level of time, skill, training, and intensity to provide a given service. Each CPT code is reviewed at least every five years to determine the work RVU for a particular service. Code prices can increase or decrease if the components of service have changed during the preceding years. A code with a higher work RVU, or wRVU, takes more time or more intensity. CPT codes apply for all medical procedures, including those where no doctors are directly involved, such as for equipment.

The practice expense RVU addresses the costs of maintaining a practice including rent, equipment, supplies, and staff. Practice expense RVU includes direct or variable and indirect or fixed costs. The practice expense RVU starts with the direct costs of providing a service. *Direct costs* are those that can be assigned to a specific service; a direct cost would be the actual supplies, equipment, and staff time used for a given CPT code. These costs include staff time, supplies, equipment, and rent. *Indirect costs,* which are equivalent to common area maintenance (CAM) charges in real estate, are then allocated. These overhead or indirect costs include the waiting room, overhead in real estate at the facility, or charges by a hospital that may own the practice.

Real estate is typically a fixed cost or indirect charge for practice expense purposes. A CPT code will be assigned for a practice expense RVU at a facility including hospitals. A separate practice expense RVU for a given CPT code is assigned for a non-facility setting, such as an outpatient center, ambulatory care location, or doctor's office.

The malpractice RVU represents payment for professional liability expenses and is the smallest component of the three RVU values.

From the RVUs for each CPT code, CMS makes two adjustments. One is for geographical differentials in cost. This adjustment uses a geographic practice cost index (GPCI). A GPCI is constructed for each of the three RVU components for physician work, practice expense, and malpractice. The other adjustment is a conversion factor (CF). The conversion factor is similar to an exchange rate. It converts the relative value units into dollars.

The conversion factor adjusted for budget neutrality in 2013 was $34.023.

The formulas that reflect the above components and result in the scheduled payment amount for each CPT code of:

$$\begin{aligned}\text{Non-facility payment} = {} & [(\text{Work RVU})\,(\text{Work GPCI}) \\ & + (\text{Non-facility expense RVU})\,(\text{Expense GPCI}) \\ & + (\text{MP RVU})\,(\text{MP GPCI})] \\ & \quad (\text{Conversion factor adjusted for budget neutrality})\end{aligned} \tag{8.1}$$

$$\begin{aligned}\text{Facility payment} = {} & [(\text{Work RVU})\ (\text{Work GPCI}) + (\text{Facility expense RVU}) \\ & (\text{Expense GPCI}) + (\text{Malpractice RVU})\ (\text{Malpractice GPCI})] \\ & (\text{Conversion factor adjusted for budget neutrality})\end{aligned} \quad (8.2)$$

From Equations 8.1 and 8.2, the reimbursement for a given procedure differs depending on whether it was done in a facility or not. A facility includes inpatients at hospitals or in a hospital outpatient clinic. The facility expense RVU and geographic price adjustments exceed those outside a facility. This system has created an incentive for hospitals to buy practices. Non-facility services are generally provided in a freestanding physician office. The hospital as owner submits claims for doctors' offices being facilities and then subject to higher reimbursement. A patient is affected only through the copayments. The premium that a hospital or other more expensive real estate facility earns is:

$$\begin{aligned}\text{Facility premium} = {} & [(\text{Facility expense RVU} - \text{Non-facility expense RVU}) \\ & (\text{Expense GPCI})\ (\text{Conversion factor})]\end{aligned} \quad (8.3)$$

Thus, differential reimbursement depends on where services are provided. In effect, real estate drives healthcare costs.

COMPENSATION

One outcome of the system, apart from the healthcare delivered, is the compensation received by physicians. Paradoxical results occur here. Even though the geographical adjustments are to compensate for high-cost areas such as on the East and West Coasts, average actual doctor incomes are highest in the middle of the country. The Medical Group Management Association (2012) conducts an annual survey of medical practice performance. For 2011 by specialty, the median compensation in internal medicine rose from $205,379 to $215,689, a 5.0 percent increase over 2010. In radiology the median compensation rose from $440,000 to $486,764, or by 10.6 percent. Anesthesiology saw a rise from $404,996 to $423,753 or 4.6 percent. In obstetrics and gynecology compensation increased from $271,747 to $278,300, a 2.4 percent increase. Incomes in pediatrics increased from $164,813 to $182,048, a 10.5 percent increase. Incomes for hospitalists went from $220,000 to $225,000, a 2.3 percent increase.

Compensation per unit of work is obtained by dividing total compensation by work RVUs billed. This is a measure of pure price increase. In neurology, this ratio went from $51.56 to $52.64, a 2.1 percent increase between 2010 and 2011. In occupational medicine the compensation per work RVU increased from $57.92 to $59.14. In radiology it went from $56.48 to $54.34 or a 3.8 percent decrease. Given the RVU compensation system, no guarantee exists that the payment per unit of work increases. That depends on the formulas and how they incorporate technological change. Put alternatively, for the doctors to have compensation increases requires seeing more patients, or more work RVUs.

MGMA estimates median compensation for specialists to be:

- Region 1: Connecticut, Maine, Massachusetts, New Hampshire, Rhode Island, and Vermont ($331,510);
- Region 2: New Jersey and New York ($418,106);
- Region 3: Delaware, District of Columbia, Maryland, Pennsylvania, Virginia, and West Virginia ($337,000);
- Region 4: Alabama, Florida, Georgia, Kentucky, Mississippi, North Carolina, South Carolina, and Tennessee ($415,382);
- Region 5: Illinois, Indiana, Michigan, Minnesota, Ohio, and Wisconsin ($379,370);
- Region 6: Arkansas, Louisiana, New Mexico, Oklahoma, and Texas ($387,000);
- Region 7: Iowa, Kansas, Missouri, and Nebraska ($453,579);
- Region 8: Colorado, Montana, North Dakota, South Dakota, Utah, and Wyoming ($402,737);
- Region 9: Arizona, California, Hawaii, and Nevada ($379,576); and
- Region 10: Alaska, Idaho, Oregon, and Washington ($360,293).

The lowest median compensation for specialists is in Regions 1 and 3 (the Northeast and Mid-Atlantic, respectively), whereas the highest is in Region 7 (the Plains states).

Patients and Providers: Action and Regret Bias

The next section examines decision-making in healthcare from both the patient and provider perspective. Demand comes from patients who are almost always less informed about healthcare than are physicians. Providers are dealing with a real estate-intensive system. Both patients and providers are responding to a complex pricing mechanism. Because the health insurance company pays for most of their care, patients are disconnected from the real costs. Doctors are healers who are motivated by a complex set of goals and not just their fiscal bottom line. Patients do not act like calculating machines to make sound decisions about their health. As a result of these factors, standard economic ideas cannot be readily applied to the nation's complex healthcare situation.

Given these circumstances, one theory of patient decision-making is the "idiot patient" who is unable to make smart healthcare decisions. This idea has formed the basis of laws banishing cigarette ads from television and trans fats from restaurant fare. Another theory is of a "physician conspiracy." Doctors collude with each other as well as pharmaceutical companies to stifle competition. Regulatory responses lead to bans on doctor-owned hospitals and on ordering tests performed by the prescribing doctor.

Standard economics assumes that people are rational and make mistakes in a random way. Behavioral economics says they sometimes act non-rationally in predictable ways. Imperfect people make imperfect decisions. Standard economics posits that self-interest drives people to act rationally in the marketplace. The situation changes when that marketplace is a hospital or doctor's office. Patients demand useless tests, ignore treatment regimens, and act irrationally amid their aches and pains. Behavioral economics draws on the perspectives, hypotheses, and studies of behavioral psychologists to explain marketplace behaviors. People are not always rational, but their irrationality at least happens in predictable ways. Two aspects of patient and provider decision-making illustrate this situation: action bias and regret bias.

ACTION BIAS

Action bias is reflected by the statement "don't just stand there, do something." When patients visit a physician, they expect a physician to do something. These actions include making a diagnosis, creating a treatment plan, writing a prescription, ordering an MRI, or admitting the patient to a hospital. The physician often knows that no action is needed, because many illnesses resolve themselves without clinical intervention. Yet, patients want action by the physician. That action bias creates a demand for sometimes unnecessary healthcare and unnecessary facilities.

Patients who demand pills or tests when symptoms send them to the doctor do so because of action bias. People are predisposed to the idea that doing something is better than doing nothing, even though watchful waiting might be the most rational and cost-effective course. Patients with virus-based illnesses end up with prescriptions for antibiotics that do nothing against viruses.

However, as Hough (2013) notes, patients never fill one quarter of new prescriptions. Patients are asking for something to be done, yet for 25 percent of the orders, they do not fill their prescriptions. Why? Standard economic reasons could explain this phenomenon. The price could be too high or getting the prescription could be too time-consuming. Where behavioral economics enters is that when the presenting problem starts to subside, it is no longer as salient to the patient, and the patient decides on his own that the prescription is no longer necessary.

It is well-known that patients often do not adhere to a treatment regimen. Adherence to treatment regimens increases a few days before seeing a physician and a few days after seeing a physician. If a physician is concerned about a patient adhering to a treatment regimen, the doctor might simply recommend that the patient come back within a week.

REGRET BIAS

People love choice. Nevertheless, they often perform better when they have fewer choices. Most economists think that more choice is better. What behavioral psychologists and behavioral economists have discovered is that more choice is not necessarily better. The problem is *regret bias*, which refers to the inability of an individual to choose because of a fear that the decision will be incorrect.

If a physician presents five healthcare options and asks a patient to choose among them, patients can probably choose well. But if patients are offered 25 or 50 choices, they end up not choosing at all. This is what happened at the beginning of the Medicare Part D program introduced in 2005, when patients were given a large number of prescription drug plan choices. Many elderly individuals were unable to make that choice, in part because they were afraid that they would pick the wrong plan.

Another problem is in choosing among the options and who makes them. Suppose that an expert identifies the 10 best choices. That expert might not have the right set of preferences for an individual. One way to do this is to offer an individual five different choices randomly chosen from the 50 different health plans. If the patient rejects all, then another five plans are selected. These choices come from a restricted set because too many choices lead to confusion.

In other healthcare systems (such as in France), patients often pay for the entire service and get reimbursed later by the insurer. This system is much like business travel reimbursement programs by employers. The insured bears the cost and has an incentive to seek lower cost treatment. Standard economics says raising the price from effectively zero for an insured individual to a positive price incentivizes careful use of services. The behavioral economics argument is that raising the price affects behavior even when patients will be reimbursed for that payment within a short period. Thus, having patients "front the money" could be an effective way of controlling unnecessary utilization of healthcare services.

Hough (2013) considers a series of paradoxical behaviors. Why do tens of thousands of patients die each year from hospital-acquired infections when a simple five-step checklist used by physicians and nurses could reduce that number by two-thirds? The checklist in Gawande (2009) offers opportunities to reduce healthcare costs substantially with relatively limited intervention. Errors often result from ignorance and ineptitude. Errors of ignorance are from a lack of information. Errors of ineptitude are from failure to use existing information. Failure is concentrated in the second of these errors of ineptitude, particularly in healthcare. Failures come from missing a step, forgetting to ask a key question, or failing to plan properly for every eventuality. The same issues occur with real estate construction. The solution is to prepare checklists for repetitive procedures.

The five-step checklist process developed in 2001 by Peter Pronovost at Johns Hopkins Hospital was for inserting intravenous lines in patients. The five steps to reduce risks are: (1) wash hands with soap; (2) clean the patient's skin with chlorhexidine antiseptic; (3) cover the patient's entire body with sterile drapes; (4) wear a mask, hat, sterile gown, and gloves; and (5) put a sterile dressing over the insertion site after inserting the line. Doctors' resistance to checklists has a tangle of psychological roots. Chief among them is that many physicians see checklists as a loss of power and authority, and behavioral economists have found that *loss aversion*—the fact that people hate losses much more than they like gains—is an extraordinarily powerful force.

Summary and Conclusions

The Affordable Care Act of 2010 dealt primarily with improving access to healthcare, especially the 50 million Americans without health insurance. The act did little to address the inexorable rise in healthcare costs. Directing healthcare dollars provides incentives for physicians and other healthcare professionals to address wellness as well as sickness (i.e., pay physicians when they keep their patients well, rather than paying them on the volume of their sickness services). Individuals should be encouraged to take more responsibility financially and conceptually over their health and healthcare. Most illnesses will resolve themselves without major intervention. Serious consequences result from making bad lifestyle choices such as overeating, overdrinking, and overmedicating.

Even if the government were not involved in the market for healthcare, people are not effective consumers. One of the major findings of behavioral economics is that people make different decisions when they are in a cold dispassionate state than in a hot, immediate-response one. They do not appreciate the differences. In healthcare, an individual can make considered, rational decisions about the demand for healthcare services when they are well in a cold state. Those decisions disappear when an illness event occurs and the individual and family demand that everything be done, regardless of the cost. Health insurance facilitates this hot-state demand because the individual pays relatively little of the "everything be done" costs.

The usual concerns arise about supplier-induced demand, in which physicians have the ability to influence how much healthcare is demanded by patients. Further, some behavioral economics phenomena influence physicians in ways that limit the effectiveness of a market for healthcare. For instance, physicians in different communities practice differently. Physicians learn the basics of medicine in medical school, but they learn how to practice medicine when they are in residency and fellowship, and more importantly when they are finally on their own. The community exerts a powerful influence over the medical decisions that a physician makes: when to order a test, refer a patient, and perform a procedure. This community has more influence over the behavior of physicians than market pressures.

The Affordable Care Act increases access of millions of the insured. It secures those currently with health insurance, with assurance that they will not lose coverage. It offers support for some quality initiatives. The act pays little attention to controlling or managing cost, other than competition among insurers through exchanges where individuals can buy health insurance. The Centers for Disease Control estimate that 75 percent of healthcare costs are from chronic diseases from cancer, heart, liver, and lungs. Much of these costs can be controlled, but until then healthcare costs and demand will remain real estate-focused.

Discussion Questions

1. Identify two behavioral issues leading to increased demand for healthcare.
2. Discuss how the U.S. healthcare system rewards facilities.
3. Explain how patients and physicians inflate the demand for real estate in healthcare in the United States.
4. Discuss the locational differences in healthcare costs.

References

American Hospital Association. 2013. *TrendWatch Chartbook*. Washington, DC: American Hospital Association.

Centers for Medicare and Medicaid Services. 2013. *National Health Expenditures*. http://www.cms.gov/Research-Statistics-Data-and-Systems/Statistics-Trends-and-Reports/NationalHealthExpendData/Downloads/tables.pdf.

Committee on the Costs of Medical Care. 1932. *Medical Care for the American People*, Report 28. Chicago: University of Chicago Press.

Emergency Medical Network. 2013. *2011 National ED Inventory—USA*. http://www.emnet-usa.org/nedi/USA.htm.

Galewitz, Phil. 2012. "Urgent Care Centers are Booming, which Worries Some Doctors." *Kaiser Health News*, September 17.

Gawande, Atul. 2009. *The Checklist Manifesto*. New York: Macmillan.

Goldsteen, Raymond L., and Karen Goldsteen. 2012. *Jonas: Introduction to the U.S. Health Care System*. 7th edn. New York: Springer Publishing Company.

Herzlinger, Regina E. 1997. *Market-Driven Health Care: Who Wins, Who Loses in the Transformation of America's Largest Service Industry*. Reading, MA: Addison-Wesley.
Hough, Douglas. 2013. *Irrationality in Health Care: What Behavioral Economics Reveals about What We Do and Why*. Palo Alto, CA: Stanford University Press.
Kane, Carol K. 2009. "The Practice Arrangements of Patient Care Physicians, 2007–2008: An Analysis by Age Cohort and Gender". Policy Research Perspectives Working Paper. Washington, DC: American Medical Association.
Kocher, Robert, and Nikhil R. Sahni. 2011. "Hospitals' Race to Employ Physicians—the Logic behind a Money-Losing Proposition". *New England Journal of Medicine* 364:19, 1790–1793.
Marmot, Michael G., and Richard G. Wilkinson. 2006. *Social Determinants of Health*. 2nd edn. Oxford: Oxford University Press.
Medical Group Management Association (MGMA) and Center for Research in Ambulatory Health Care Administration. 2012. *Physician Compensation and Production Survey*. Englewood, CO: MGMA.
Medicare Payment Advisory Commission. 2012. *Health Care Spending and the Medicare Program: A Data Book*. Washington, DC: Medicare Payment Advisory Commission. http://www.medpac.gov/documents/Jun12DataBookEntireReport.pdf.
National Center for Health Statistics. 2013. *National Hospital Ambulatory Medical Care Survey: 2010 Emergency Department Summary Tables*. http://www.nchs.gov.
Raffel, Marshall W., and Camille K. Barsukiewicz. 2002. *The U.S. Health System: Origins and Functions*. 5th edn. Albany, NY: Delmar Thomson Learning.
Smart, Derek R. 2004. *Medical Group Practices in the US, 2004 Edition*. Chicago: American Medical Association.
Smart, Derek R. 2013. *Physician Characteristics and Distribution in the U.S.* Chicago: American Medical Association.
World Health Organization. 2013. *World Health Statistics 2013*. http://www.who.int/gho/publications/world_health_statistics/EN_WHS2013_Full.pdf.

9

Corporate Real Estate

PETER LINNEMAN
Professor of Real Estate, Finance, and Public Policy, Emeritus, Wharton School, University of Pennsylvania
Chief Executive Officer of the American Land Funds, KL Realty, and Linneman Associates

Introduction

Most firms currently base their decision to lease space on whether the present value of future rent is less than the present value of the cost of self-ownership, net of depreciation benefits and expected property appreciation that is only the differential costs of the alternatives. However, this treats capital as having no opportunity cost. The correct model for the own-versus-lease decision must compare the present value of total profits the firm expects if it leases with the present value of expected total profits if it decides to own, as the freed-up capital also changes revenues.

In an era of industrial and manufacturing companies, a high proportion of corporate real estate facilities were idiosyncratic properties such as factories, workshops, and industrial plants. There was generally no competitive rental market for the bulk of their properties, so companies set up sizable corporate real estate departments.

Since product life cycles were long and relatively little merger and acquisition (M&A) activity occurred, the long-term nature of corporate real estate ownership provided a reasonable match to both product and corporate life cycles. Further, unsophisticated capital markets forgave operating companies that misused their capital. In addition, senior executives were loath to return capital to shareholders, even when they lacked value-enhancing investment opportunities. Instead, they frequently chose to build corporate facilities as architectural monuments to themselves using shareholder money, rather than to lease more modest general-purpose space.

Both product and corporate life cycles have been greatly reduced by rapidly changing consumer preferences, new technologies, global competition, M&A activity, and greater capital market sophistication. As a result, the ownership of corporate real estate is now generally detrimental to shareholder value. The emergence of the service sector and the explosion of professional jobs, even at industrial firms, have shifted the nature of corporate real estate usage dramatically toward general-purpose buildings, which are available in increasingly competitive leasing markets.

Capital markets increasingly reward firms that create shareholder value by focusing their capital on the areas of company core competence. Highly incentivized executives are beginning to realize that disposing of their corporate real estate creates shareholder value by freeing up capital that is more profitably deployed elsewhere.

Today's large real estate companies, including real estate investment trusts (REITs) focus on the efficient operation of existing assets rather than the development of new assets. These real estate companies have created a highly competitive group of well-capitalized real estate companies capable of providing leasing services for both regional and national bases required by operating companies. Although the evolution of the real estate industry is still in its infancy, corporate real estate owners can sell their properties efficiently and select their desired lease duration at competitive rental rates.

As the real estate industry has joined the global capital markets, major real estate owner-operators efficiently raise large amounts of debt and equity. These entities have strong balance sheets, investment-grade debt, and are closely followed by stock analysts. This allows these major real estate companies to attract large pools of capital at a cost competitive with that of corporate users. Hence, operating companies no longer have a capital-raising advantage in terms of owning their properties.

As larger and more transparent real estate companies evolve, more corporate real estate portfolios should be sold. Future sales of corporate real estate will not be mere sale-leaseback financing transactions by financially challenged companies, but rather sales of general-purpose real estate by strong operating companies to strong real estate companies. This has already taken place in the retail mall industry, with many retailers selling their properties to large property companies.

For most operating companies, a positive arbitrage opportunity exists between the expected return on core investment alternatives and the returns they can realistically expect on their corporate real estate through reduced rental expenses and expected appreciation. This is particularly true for high-growth operating companies, who have much higher return expectations than the 7–12 percent annual returns they can expect to realize on their general-purpose real estate. Every dollar invested in corporate real estate represents the destruction of shareholder value equal to at least the difference between a firm's weighted average cost of capital (WACC) and the expected return on comparably levered real estate. For example, consider a company with a 13 percent WACC and a $1 billion corporate real estate portfolio. This negative arbitrage opportunity means foregone income of $20 million a year, assuming an expected real estate total return of 11 percent annually. At a value multiple of 20 on $1 billion of assets, this represents a loss of shareholder value of $400 million.

Even when the arbitrage opportunity associated with the sale of real estate is minimal, a loss of shareholder value occurs from deploying capital and management energy on corporate real estate. Consider an electronics company that raises $1 billion in an initial public offering (IPO) at a WACC of 10 percent. The company's IPO prospectus describes in great detail the business plans, areas of core competence, competitive dynamics, and the operating expense and backgrounds of the management team. Because of its operating risk, this firm's WACC of 10 percent is less than the expected 11 percent from owning real estate. At first blush this might seem that the firm can generate shareholder value by merely investing in real estate and reaping a percentage point higher annual return. However, this is not the case. If the firm spends its $1 billion on buildings its stock price would crash, as shareholders were not seeking to invest in a real estate business. Investors desiring to invest in real estate will give their money to real estate companies.

Many corporate real estate officers resist efforts to sell their company's properties. In part, this reflects a natural inclination to protect vested interests. It also reflects the fact that there had been a shortage of real estate companies capable of providing competitive rental rates and uniform service quality for leased properties. Most executives do not understand that while a sale of their corporate real estate raises rental expenditures, it increases the company's bottom line by freeing capital that generates greater returns in core operations.

Money tied up in real estate does not disappear when the property is sold. However, increased company returns derived from the freed-up real estate capital are not credited to the real estate department, but rather to the company's operating divisions. This creates a dilemma for many corporate real estate officers, whose performance metric is occupancy cost. Senior management must structure incentives that reward corporate real estate officers for freeing up capital that can be employed more profitably elsewhere.

Senior executives often state that they do not know what they would do with the additional capital. This attitude is symptomatic of the larger problem of not returning capital to shareholders, either through a share buyback or dividends, when a company believes it cannot find value-enhancing investments. Stockpiling the company's assets in corporate real estate because of an absence of good investment opportunities in core operations merely deprives shareholders of the opportunity to create value by giving their money to companies that offer value-adding investment opportunities.

An additional advantage associated with selling corporate real estate is that it allows leases to be structured in a manner consistent with corporate and product life cycles, and saves the considerable expense associated with the disposition of surplus properties. A better choice is to leave the property recycling to professionals with a broader set of real estate skills and an investor base seeking such risks.

Various issues face operating companies that decide to sell corporate real estate. Should they sell in bulk or one at a time? If they own a large, high-quality property portfolio they will generally realize superior value by a sale to a single buyer that can provide a uniform quality of service across these properties. Such buyers place a value on being able to enlarge it via a single, large transaction. Aggressive real estate companies exist that are large enough to purchase multi-city portfolios of quality, general-use properties from corporate users.

If the company attaches little value to homogeneity of landlord service, or the properties are of lesser quality, or only a few and disparate properties are available, individual sales will generate the greatest value. Alternatively, particularly for the owner of a large portfolio of lower quality properties, the owner could spin out the portfolio to its existing shareholders as a new real estate company. In some cases the spinout can be structured as a tax-free spinoff. The operating company can maintain a minority ownership position in the new real estate company in order to provide a strategic alignment of interests between the property owner and the user. The primary difficulties with the spinouts are satisfying the restrictions associated with a tax-free spinoff, and that the management team may not achieve effective pricing. The new real estate company's lack of tenant diversification will also depress its pricing relative to real estate companies with a more diversified base.

Another alternative is to sell the corporate real estate for ownership interests in the purchaser. Accepting ownership reduces the fees in raising capital. This option is particularly attractive for large corporations for which the equity is a small portion of the overall cash position. The sale of shares over time maximizes shareholder value.

Another issue is to select the lease durations for the properties being sold. The first inclination of most selling companies is to make very long leases, as this will maximize sale value. But while long leases generate the highest value for real estate holdings, they do not necessarily maximize shareholder value. This is because long leases reduce the seller's ability to realize operating benefits derived from the flexibility of short leases. Long leases with a common expiration date burden the purchaser with a lumpy lease rollover exposure, reducing attractiveness to real estate investors.

As the real estate industry integrates with global capital markets, a shift will continue from corporate ownership of real estate to leasing. This will be the potential source for $100–200 billion of added annual growth in the ownership of public real estate companies. Corporate real estate owners should take advantage of periods of strong property and capital markets to implement the sales.

Rodriguez and Sirmans (1996) indicate that real estate constitutes between 25 and 40 percent of assets held by corporations on their balance sheets. Nourse and Roulac (1993) also note that real estate is at least 25 percent of corporate assets. Firms typically do not have a consistent strategy for holding or acquiring real estate. Where it exists, the strategy can be in conflict with corporate goals. Tuzel (2010) provides a rationale for why firms hold real estate. Real estate is long-lived, depreciates slowly, and is indivisible. It is more risky and part of the value premium, allowing firms to obtain a return. During booms, firms holding real estate have the capacity to increase output at lower marginal cost. During slumps, they have higher fixed costs.

The European Context: A German Case Study

Linneman and Pfirsching (2008) examine why corporations have been slow to realize that real estate assets contribute to their financial performance. They conclude that flawed analysis leads companies to own far more corporate real estate than is economically justified. This is clearly true in Germany, where Linneman and Pfirshing note that corporate users own as much as 75 percent of commercial real estate, as well as in the United States, where corporate users own 40 percent.

The correct model for the own-versus-lease decision compares the present value of total profits the corporation expects if it leases against the present value of expected total profits if it decides to own its real estate. The key insight provided by this corrected approach is that the own-versus-lease decision revolves around the comparison of the reduced revenues associated with moving corporate capital from core operations to real estate, versus the differential costs achieved by real estate owners. This decision affects both revenues and costs. Hence, the focus on cost differences alone provides a flawed analytic tool for such decision-making.

Capital freed up from real estate ownership enhances the company's core business rate of return, that is, it raises revenues. Because most companies have higher expected rates of return in their core business than are achievable through real estate ownership, this decision model indicates that the vast majority of corporate real estate should be leased. The intuition of this result is simply that by moving capital from low-yielding real estate to high-yielding core operations, companies increase profits.

Linneman and Pfirsching (2008) show that Germany, the third-largest economy in the world, is relatively inefficient in terms of capital allocation and managing corporate capital. Some 75 percent of corporate real estate is owned, one of the highest proportions in the developed world. Major German companies have taken some tentative steps to reduce their ownership of corporate real estate. However, these efforts have typically followed the general pattern of disposing of corporate real estate only when no alternative for raising capital is available, or as a gimmick to remove the ownership from the company's balance sheet even though ownership remains.

Germany's largest retailer, Metro, transferred all of its 357 real estate assets, which included department stores, supermarkets, and hardware stores, into a joint venture. Metro retained a 49 percent ownership, with a major mortgage bank owning 49.5 percent and a large insurance company owning the remaining 1.5 percent. The transaction was worth €2.7 billion, yielding approximately €1.3 billion in cash for Metro.

Metro systematically shed non-core businesses through its subsidiary Divaco, initially Divag. The banished businesses included 813 Vobis computer stores, 143 Kaufhalle, and 25 unprofitable Kaufhof department stores, fashion, and shoe stores, Tip discount stores, and Kaufhalle's real estate business. Trying to raise cash for expansion, Metro disposed of additional assets by selling and leasing back its retail real estate. In a joint venture with Westdeutsche Landesbank, Metro sold the ground under 290 retail outlets in Germany, Turkey, Greece, Hungary, and Luxembourg.

These transactions resulted in Metro leasing these properties on a long-term basis from the joint venture and successfully moved the assets from Metro's balance sheet. In 2002 and 2003, Metro attempted to sell the entire joint venture (JV) to third-party investors. But after two failed attempts with buyer consortia, Metro abandoned the attempt. Metro ultimately repurchased the ownership shares, resulting in a reconsolidation of the real estate onto Metro's balance sheet, largely purging the cash raised in the original sale.

State-owned Deutsche Bahn spun off all of its land and development properties into a JV. This transaction raised €1.1 billion for Deutsche Bahn and was structured almost identically to the Metro transaction. Like Metro's transaction, this transaction was also reversed when Deutsche Bahn subsequently repurchased the shares of the JV investors. Deutsche Bahn sold the real estate assets in September 2007 to a JV of the German construction company Hochtief and investor Redwood Grove International LP for €1.64 billion.

The German engineering conglomerate Siemens entered into an agreement transferring 18 properties to a newly established open-end German real estate fund. Siemens received €750 million for these properties from the fund and immediately contributed these proceeds to its corporate pension fund to cover outstanding liabilities. This resulted in the transfer of the real estate as well as its pension liabilities to off-balance-sheet status. A management company wholly owned by Siemens provided the management of the open-ended fund. This fund subsequently acquired more real estate, bringing in additional shareholders beyond Siemens' pension trust. Siemens sold the fund management company to a third party.

In a similar transaction, Dresdner Bank transferred a portfolio of 300 bank buildings to a newly established open-ended real estate fund managed by its wholly owned subsidiary. In this case, shares in the open-ended fund were never offered to other investors, as Dresdner Bank sold this fund to Eurocastle. There have also been other smaller transactions where companies sold one or more properties to third-party purchasers in sale-lease back transactions. For the most part, however, German corporate owners continue to retain their corporate real estate.

In an effort to identify why German corporations have failed in their real estate monetization efforts and are so predisposed to corporate real estate ownership, Pfirsching (2007) conducted detailed research documenting that the problems are both technical and strategic in nature. Among key technical problems are: insufficient data quality and poor data management; unprofessional management of the transaction; the seller's lack of knowledge of the value of its assets; and demands by investors for re-trades. The key strategic problems are: lack of seller commitment to the sale; unrealistic valuations, often based on book value; the seller changing the portfolio of assets available for sale during the sale process; and changing space requirements of the seller throughout the sale process.

Additional studies identify other reasons for the failure of sale and monetization efforts of corporate real estate. These reasons include the seller's unwillingness to take book value losses; the seller's desire for complete control over all real estate assets; concern about image and reputation damage to the seller; preservation of social peace in the company; fear of losing key properties and sites to competitors; the lack of off-balance sheet treatment if the seller retains long-term control of the asset; poor data quality; and higher perceived long-term occupancy costs.

As in any business effort, a clear strategy is essential when disposing of corporate real estate. A lack of such clarity inevitably leads to an inefficient and ineffective process. Moreover, many corporate real estate executives appear to conduct faulty analysis of the benefits of leasing rather than owning their real estate.

Owning Versus Leasing

Jensen (1986) argues that interests and incentives of managers and shareholders conflict over such issues as the optimal size of the firm and the payment of cash to shareholders. These conflicts are especially severe in firms with large free cash flows or more cash than profitable investment opportunities. In this context, debt reduces agency costs of free cash flows and substitutes for dividends. Diversification generates losses greater than takeovers or expansion in the same line of business, and corporate real estate ownership is just a non-core line of business.

Table 9.1 provides a numerical example of a firm not in the real estate business deciding to own or lease. The firm uses a hurdle rate for its cost of capital of 10 percent annually on an after-tax basis. A commercial property has a current value of $1,000,000, of which 17 percent is land and the remaining 83 percent is depreciable improvements. The building rents for a 7 percent cap rate full service or for $70,000 annually. Full service implies that the outside landlord pays the operating expenses. These operating expenses are half the initial rent. The lease provides for no bumps or rent increases, but operating expenses rise by 3 percent annually. Although the net rent is declining, appreciation in the local market is expected to be 16 percent cumulatively over a five-year hold.

Table 9.1 **Renting versus Owning Corporate Real Estate**

Decisions	*0*	*1*	*2*	*3*	*4*	*5*
Purchase price	($1,003,000)					
Loan	$750,000					
Operating expense		$35,000	$36,050	$37,132	$38,245	$39,393
Depreciation		$2,043	$21,282	$21,282	$21,282	$21,282
Interest		$70,685	$69,374	$67,933	$66,349	$64,608
Expenses		$107,728	$126,706	$126,347	$125,877	$125,283
Tax rate		35%	35%	35%	35%	35%
Tax shield		$37,705	$44,347	$44,221	$44,057	$43,849
Operating expense		$35,000	$36,050	$37,132	$38,245	$39,393
Interest		$70,685	$69,374	$67,933	$66,349	$64,608
Principal		$13,207	$14,518	$15,959	$17,543	$19,284
Tax shield		($37,705)	($44,347)	($44,221)	($44,057)	($43,849)
After-tax cost		$81,187	$75,595	$76,802	$78,080	$79,436
Resale cash flow						
Sales price						$1,160,000
Loan payoff						($669,490)
Capital gain						$157,000
Depreciation						$87,171
Cash events	***0***	***1***	***2***	***3***	***4***	***5***
Equity	($253,000)					
After-tax cost		($81,187)	($75,595)	($76,802)	($78,080)	($79,436)
Sales proceeds						$490,510
Taxes, capital gain and recapture						($53,193)
	($253,000)	($81,187)	($75,595)	($76,802)	($78,080)	$357,881
PV factor		0.9091	0.8264	0.7513	0.6830	0.6209
Present value	($253,000)	($73,806)	($62,475)	($57,702)	($53,330)	$222,216
Net present value	($278,098)					
Rent		($70,000)	($70,000)	($70,000)	($70,000)	($70,000)
PV factor		0.9091	0.8264	0.7513	0.6830	0.6209
Present value	($265,355)	($63,636)	($57,851)	($52,592)	($47,811)	($43,464)

Note: This table gives an example of a firm not in the real estate business deciding to own or lease. The chapter sets forth the assumptions underlying this example.

The firm has the opportunity to borrow funds for a mortgage with a loan-to-value (LTV) ratio of 75 percent with $3,000 in closing costs, at a 9.5 percent annual rate paid monthly over 20 years and fully amortizing. While fully amortizing, a balloon payment of the outstanding principal is due at the end of the five-year holding period.

These conditions apply to a firm in any country, though tax institutions vary. The application is for 2013 institutions in the United States. Depreciation is on a straight-line basis for 39 years of useful life. The depreciation expense for accounting purposes is then $830,000 divided by 39 annually. The rate of corporate income tax is 35 percent. Capital gains are taxed at a rate of 20 percent and depreciation expenses taken are cumulatively taxed at a rate of 25 percent on sale.

The table does not show the firm's first choice because it is straightforward. The firm immediately sells its property for $1,000,000 and invests those funds in its business at the rate of 10 percent annually, for $100,000 a year. Its rent payment is $70,000 a year, so it can engage in a sale-and-leaseback transaction with a cash flow gain of at least $30,000 annually. The calculations exclude any administrative cost saving from having to operate the property.

The next choice is to hold the property for the next five years. Even though the firm benefits from the appreciation on the property and the various tax benefits of depreciation, the net present value (NPV) of all cash outflows at the 10 percent rate is $278,098 from ownership. From renting, the same five-year lease costs $265,355 as a NPV. Because both cases involve outflows given that real estate costs are an expense, the best strategy is to lease.

Holding real estate for a firm not in this business is a form of diversification that dissipates free cash flow. Holding real estate also ties up cash, particularly when the LTV ratio is relatively low as is often the case with corporate real estate.

The typical own versus lease analysis evaluates only the differential operating costs associated with owning versus leasing, net of the depreciation tax advantages and expected appreciation on the corporate real estate, not differential profits. That is, differential expected revenues and costs—not just costs—must be considered.

Hartmann, Linneman, Pfnur, and Siperstein (2009) and Hartmann, Linneman, Pfnur, Moy, and Siperstein (2010) examine the trade-offs involved in corporate real estate analysis. The structure is based on comparing the costs of owning versus leasing and taking into account the distraction and opportunity cost of diversification strategies, of which owning real estate is one.

The present value of the after-tax profits associated with owning corporate real estate is equal to the present value of after-tax profits from core operations, ignoring the incremental costs of owning corporate real estate costs minus the present value of the after-tax incremental costs associated with real estate ownership. To this is added the present value of the tax savings associated with the depreciation allowance provided to owners of corporate real estate plus the present value of the expected after-tax appreciation on the corporate real estate. This relationship is:

$$\text{Net profit} = \text{After-tax operating margin} + \text{Depreciation benefits} + \text{Capital gains} \tag{9.1}$$

The present value of core operations profitability ignoring incremental real estate ownership costs is equal to the rate of return the firm achieves on capital invested in core operations, times the capital it invests in core operations times the company's cash flow valuation multiple:

$$\text{Cash flow} = (\text{Target return})(\text{Cash flow multiple})(\text{Capital invested}) \tag{9.2}$$

That is, core cash flow is the product of a target return and a cash flow multiple, both of which are selected parameters, multiplied by the capital invested in additional core operations. The capital is at work in the core business, and cash flows are translated into value via the firm's cash flow multiple.

By owning real estate the firm becomes a landlord. Landlord profits are equal to the expected rate of return on real estate, times the cash flow multiple and the capital invested in real estate. The cash stream is converted to present value via the real estate's cash flow multiple. The condition is exactly the same as for the firm's cash flow, except that real estate may have different, and potentially lower, target returns and cash flow multiples on its real estate investments. The return for a corporate user is:

$$\text{Real estate return (user)} = (\text{Target return})(\text{Cash flow multiple})(\text{Capital invested}) \tag{9.3}$$

When the firm is using target returns and cash flow multiples on real estate that are lower than on core operations, it is not deploying its capital as efficiently as in core operations.

This condition is for the return to holding real estate, with the target return being the expected sum of the yield and expected capital gains. Any real estate investor has a return that is the sum of the present value of rental payments plus the value of the depreciation tax shield by owning the property plus the present value after-tax capital gains, minus real estate operating costs. So the real estate return for a specialized real estate investor is:

$$\begin{aligned}\text{Real estate return (specialist)} = {} & (\text{Rent} + \text{Depreciation shield} + \text{Capital gains} \\ & - \text{Operating and capital costs})(\text{Cash flow multiple})\end{aligned} \tag{9.4}$$

The inverse of the cash flow multiple for real estate is the capitalization (cap) rate. The inverse of the cash flow multiple times target return of the firm's funds is its hurdle rate. If the hurdle rate exceeds the cap rate, then the firm is better off selling real estate and deploying capital in core operations.

The user is not in the real estate business while the specialist is. These are dollar returns, and the capital structure is implicitly viewed as being identical. A separate issue is that the corporate user is likely to use a low LTV ratio as a cash dissipation method, following Jensen (1986). Here the present value of the cash flows is over the planned period of ownership. Note that for a fixed or given level of return, rents decline with the tax benefits of depreciation and expected property appreciation. The depreciation and capital gain components are the same irrespective of whether the property is owned by a corporate user or a third party landlord up to differences in effective tax rates. The landlord could potentially be more efficient in deriving higher capital gains. Owners have different marginal tax rates to take advantage of both depreciation and capital gains.

The landlord may be a more efficient provider of real estate from the perspective of operating costs. A landlord may achieve lower operating costs via scale economies, and detailed operating expertise derived from greater experience or specialization. Further, the corporate owner may lack knowledge of real estate and make mistakes that a professional landlord can avoid.

The corporate owner's present value of incremental real estate costs, should it choose to own, can be expressed as the proportional costs relative to property value times the owner's cash flow multiple, which converts annual operating costs to value. The corporate owner's after-tax present value of profits if it leases its corporate real estate, and redeploys its real estate capital in core operations, is the after-tax present value difference between core profits and rental payments. The present value of core profits if the corporation leases is the core business rate of return times capital employed in core operations converted to value by the corporation's cash flow multiple.

Core profits are higher because the firm invests additional dollars in core operations rather than real estate. Turning to the present value of rental payments, analyzing the present value of the landlord's profits is instructive. Rents must be sufficiently high for the landlord to achieve an expected required return. The real estate may be so unique and idiosyncratic that the corporate owner has lower operating costs than a landlord. The presence of operating cost efficiency is captured by expressing the present value of the landlord's real estate costs as lower (higher) than those of the corporate owner.

When no cost difference exists, landlords and corporate owners have the same operating costs. Alternatively, landlords may have lower operating costs, or the property may be so idiosyncratic that operating costs are lower if self-provided by the user. The presence of landlord operating cost efficiencies lowers rents for any given landlord rate of return, meaning lower landlord operating costs could translate into lower rents. The landlord can pass the benefits of its operating cost efficiencies to tenants in the form of lower rents.

The nature of the relevant property market will determine the rate of return that the landlord expects to earn given operating costs, depreciation, and appreciation benefits. In a highly competitive market, competitive pressures reduce rents, resulting in a lower landlord expected rate of return. In contrast, if the property is such that there is little landlord competition, rents will be higher, allowing landlords to achieve a super competitive rate of return. This is the case for less developed property and geographic markets, as well as for highly idiosyncratic properties for which landlords require a high rate of return. The rent established in the marketplace is such that the landlord receives a rate of return on operating costs, after realizing the return benefits of depreciation and property appreciation.

The difference is the after-tax value of deploying dollars of capital in core operations rather than real estate ownership. If the capital is employed in core operations, it generates a rate of return that is converted to present value by the core operation valuation multiple. This core return derives both directly from the rate of return earned on core capital, plus any additional capital that is freed by arbitraging landlord operating cost efficiencies or inefficiencies that exist.

If the company invests the same dollars of capital in corporate real estate, they generate a rate of return that is converted to present value by the real estate's cash flow multiple. Finally, set against this are the tax benefits of depreciation and capital gains achieved by self-ownership times the corporate tax rate. This latter effect reflects the fact that since rents are lower due to depreciation and property appreciation benefits, only a fraction of these benefits differentially flow to self-ownership.

This differential profit expression indicates that a firm should own when renting generates greater after-tax present value profitability. Leasing is more profitable in cases when: core returns are high; landlord efficiencies exist; the core cash flow multiple is high; real estate returns are low; real estate's cash flow multiple is low; the corporate tax rate is low; depreciation benefits are low; and capital gains expectations for the real estate are low.

Firms with high core returns such as in financial services and technology are growing rapidly. Others are located in highly competitive metro areas where land is a large component of property costs, such as in New York, Tokyo, and London. Yet others are in macroeconomic environments where inflation is low. In all these cases, firms should rent their real estate.

At the other extreme, firms using highly idiosyncratic space in non-competitive markets should own their real estate. Cases include specialized manufacturing facilities in developing countries and corporate headquarters in small markets. Some metro markets are not core and are thus less attractive to real estate investors. In other cases the firm is slow growing, while real estate appreciation is high. Each firm and property will have a unique combination of these factors. Further, what is optimal will change over time as capital and real estate markets change.

A key element of the ownership decision is the value arbitrage associated with draining capital from core operations. If core operations generate a relatively low rate of return (as is the case in many old-line businesses), while real estate returns are high (as may be the case for expanding operations into non-competitive property markets), ownership makes economic sense. But since core returns are typically higher than real estate returns, renting tends to be more profitable.

Another way to describe the return arbitrage associated with renting is that taking capital from assets generating 7–10 percent returns (corporate real estate) and transferring the capital to core operations that generate 10–15 percent returns yields substantial value gains. Hence, by converting dollars from earnings before interest, taxes, depreciation, and amortization (EBITDA) into rent, the firm can create value, as rent generates a higher multiple than EBITDA for most companies. This entails designing a lease that allows sufficient operating control for the company to achieve the core return on its capital. If core operating ability is compromised by an imperfect lease, than the core return would reflect this lack of control. However, in markets with sophisticated legal systems, this should rarely be a problem, except with the most idiosyncratic operating facilities.

A key insight is that the more competitive the real estate market is, the greater is the incentive to rent, as competition reduces rents. Thus, as more corporate real estate is sold to landlords, a virtuous cycle is created. If all corporations own their real estate, a competitive landlord market is unlikely to evolve. As landlords buy property from corporate owners, a deeper and more competitive rental market evolves. This condition reduces landlord returns, causing lower rents and encouraging less corporate real estate ownership.

More developed capital markets and more competitive property markets, such as those found in major U.S. cities, should have greater corporate leasing due to greater competition and landlord operating cost efficiency. It also suggests that as the markets become more globally integrated and real estate returns are reduced by greater competition, liquidity, and transparency, the ownership of corporate real estate should decline.

A case example demonstrates the own versus lease decision. First, consider the case of a typical firm. It has 35 percent corporate tax rate, a 12 percent core return, and a 13 cash flow multiple. The property return is 9 percent and has a 13 cash flow multiple. Landlords have 10 percent lower operating costs than corporate owners due to the commodity nature of the real estate and depth of the property market, while self-provided operating costs are 3 percent of value. The property is expected to appreciate 3 percent annually, the effective capital gains tax is 20 percent, 2.5 percent of non-land is depreciable annually, and land accounts for 30 percent of real estate value. For this company/property/market combination, leasing generates a present value greater profit equal to 24 percent of the value of the real estate. That is, every $100 million deployed in corporate real estate destroys a staggering $24 million in corporate value.

Corporate Real Estate Management

Research recognizes the sizable value of real estate to non-real estate firms. But in spite of this recognition, corporations continue to under-manage real estate assets and resources. In part, this is because corporate real estate management departments lack prominence in most companies. As a result, this valuable part of corporate balance sheets goes largely unnoticed and undermanaged.

Maximizing the value of real estate has become an increasingly important competitive factor in the ongoing globalization process. More than 25 percent of corporate assets are invested in real estate and total occupancy costs of corporate real estate represent 5–8 percent of total pre-tax gross sales, or 40–50 percent of net income (Veale 1989). The conclusions are based on a survey of 284 U.S. corporations conducted by MIT. Despite this dominant position, real estate is undermanaged at the firm. Competition is forcing companies to examine all their assets, especially corporate real estate.

What role do corporate real estate decision-makers play within their companies? A broad survey of organizations reveals that corporate real estate management, while becoming increasingly sophisticated, remains a corporate backwater. However, the role that corporate real estate officers and their departments play within the organizations varies widely. Organizations placing more importance on corporate real estate report that it plays a more central role in decision-making, is better staffed and equipped, has clearer objectives, and has a more focused and effective approach to corporate real estate management, at both an asset level and a property management level.

To establish the importance of corporate real estate requires defining the role of corporate real estate management in a company. The objective should be the creation of a return from real estate without distracting the focus from the firm's core business. Furthermore, corporate real estate management should make a contribution toward the strength and competitiveness of a company by ensuring that company-owned resources are used effectively. In short, the objective should be to increase profitability of the company from both core and non-core operations.

Hartmann et al. (2009) survey corporate real estate executives of European and U.S. non-property companies in the banking, energy, telecommunication, and transportation and logistics industries to assess how they manage their real estate holdings. The primary focus was on companies with a large number of leased and/or owned properties. The authors show that corporate real estate has always been a valuable asset on corporate balance sheets, even if many companies do not realize this is the case.

Brounen and Eichholtz (2005) examine corporate real estate ownership internationally. They confirm that idiosyncratic and notably industry-specific reasons exist for corporations owning real estate. A sample of 4,636 companies from 18 industries and 9 countries shows different patterns and trends in the corporate ownership level of real estate. Real estate ownership differs by industry rather than nation. The proportion of real estate assets in a sector under corporate ownership ranges from 13 percent in business services to 0.63 percent in mining. Real estate ownership is decreasing over time, attributable to the increasing popularity of lease alternatives.

Regarding stock performance, Brounen and Eichholtz (2005) find a negative relationship between real estate ownership and a firm's systematic risk. Real estate ownership is trending downwards. Idiosyncratic risk bears no significant relationship with real estate ownership. Returns are lowest among firms with the highest real estate ownership levels in each industry. After controlling for the variation in risks, the remaining return patterns differ strongly across industries. Even when a firm owns its real estate, how it holds ownership and title leads to different performance. Owning real estate directly inside the corporation leads to other types of dissipation. That suggests internal restructurings of corporate real estate when for idiosyncratic, security or other reasons a firm wants to retain ownership.

Individual owners of a business should purchase the property through a single-asset entity such as a limited liability company (LLC) in the United States, rather than in the corporation itself. Limited liability company ownership is preferable to corporate ownership because the losses that often occur in the early years of real estate ownership can provide a tax benefit directly to the individual owners of the limited liability company.

Ownership through an LLC can provide an element of asset protection. From a corporate perspective, future separation of corporate owned realty is possible when the firm is sold but the real estate is retained. When a corporation makes a distribution of appreciated property, it must recognize a gain and pay tax on the appreciated value. For a C corporation, this gain is taxed at the same tax rates as ordinary corporate income. The shareholder receiving the property distribution from a C Corporation may be required to recognize a taxable dividend. Ownership through an LLC facilitates like-kind exchanges to defer taxation more easily than through a corporation. Ownership with the corporation exposes its assets in the event of litigation.

Although distributing the realty from the corporation can be costly, maintaining it in the same corporation as the operating business can have negative consequences particularly if the goal of the owner is to sell the business. Potential acquirers may not desire the real estate. If the real estate is beyond the basic needs of the business, then potential acquirers may view it as an unnecessary additional investment. In the case of a pre-defined group of potential buyers, such as employees or current minority owners, the increase in sales price due to the realty can make the sale more difficult because of additional funds needed. Moreover, the combined value of the separated realty and operating business will generally be greater than the value of a corporation holding all of the assets.

Summary and Conclusions

High-multiple firms with high core rates of return, particularly if they are looking for real estate that is readily available in a competitive real estate environment, should lease. Idiosyncratic properties in less competitive property markets and companies with low rates of return in their core business will gain by owning their real estate, particularly if the rental market is very inefficient.

The structure can be applied to every property to determine if the firm should own or lease the property. A critical insight is that shifting dollars from EBITDA to rent can enhance corporate value. The capital is allocated to higher return core businesses, generating greater bang on the firm's limited capital bucks, by freeing capital from relatively low-yielding real estate to high-yielding corporate operations. This decision also allows corporate management to focus its energies on its core competencies.

The traditional decision analysis currently used by most corporations to decide whether to own or lease their operating real estate is fundamentally flawed, resulting in much more corporate-owned commercial property than is economically justified. Most firms currently lease space if the present value of future rent is less than the present value of the cost of self-ownership, net of depreciation benefits and expected property appreciation. The correct model for the own-versus-lease decision reflects the fact that revenue rises when the company leases and compares the present value of profits the corporation expects from leasing with the present value of expected profits from owning real estate.

Space is one of the largest expenses within an organization. Also, land and buildings are considerable items on corporate balance sheets. The average return on a corporate real estate investment portfolio is 7–10 percent annually, which is lower than the typical corporate hurdle rates of 10–15 percent. Much capital is consequently locked-up in corporate real estate assets.

Most real estate managers, investors, and consultants still focus on cost (as opposed to profits) and operational issues unless a corporation is in financial distress. Linking real estate and corporate finance, on an ongoing basis, is essential in determining the overall performance and success of managing corporate real estate.

In the past, operating companies that owned their real estate were not at a major competitive disadvantage. A high proportion of corporate real estate facilities were idiosyncratic properties such as factories, workshops, and industrial plants. Because of a lack of a competitive rental market for the bulk of their properties, companies set up sizable corporate real estate departments. While corporate users primarily focused on efficiently operating their existing facilities, real estate companies mainly focused on developing new properties. However, these real estate developers were too small to realize major scale economies in terms of either operating or capital costs. Large-scale corporate owners were often more efficient property operators, even of general-purpose buildings, and had better access to capital than small developers and owners. Thus, corporate real estate departments expanded their influence in the absence of efficient real estate companies by acquiring and operating general use properties.

Since product life cycles were long, and relatively little M&A activity occurred, the long-term nature of corporate real estate ownership provided a reasonable match with respect to duration for both product and corporate life cycles. Capital markets forgave operating companies that misused their capital. Further, many senior executives were loath to return capital to shareholders, even when they lacked value-enhancing investment opportunities.

Rapidly changing consumer preferences, new technologies, global competition, and M&A activity have greatly reduced product and corporate life cycles. As a result, the ownership of corporate real estate has become a detriment to shareholder value. The emergence of the service sector and the explosion of professional jobs, even at industrial firms, have shifted the nature of corporate real estate usage dramatically toward general-purpose buildings, which are available in increasingly competitive leasing markets.

Another issue is to select the lease durations for the properties being sold. The first inclination of most selling companies is to make very long leases, as this will maximize sale value. Long leases generate the highest value for real estate holdings, but do not necessarily generate maximum shareholder value. That is because long leases reduce the seller's ability to realize the operating benefits associated with the flexibility of short leases. Long leases may burden the purchaser with a lumpy lease rollover exposure and little leasing upside, detracting from attractiveness to real estate investors.

As the real estate industry enters global capital markets, a shift will occur from corporate to real estate company ownership. This will be the source for $100–200 billion of added growth in the ownership of public real estate companies. Corporate real estate owners should take advantage of the strong property and capital markets available to implement the sales.

Discussion Questions

1. How do firms not in real estate make their decisions to buy property and why are these decisions flawed?
2. Why did firms not in the real estate business own property?
3. Why has the rationale for operating businesses owning real estate changed?
4. What alternatives exist for selling off real estate?

Acknowledgments

Isaac Megbolugbe made constructive contributions to this chapter.

References

Brounen, Dirk, and Piet M. A. Eichholtz. 2005. "Corporate Real Estate Ownership and Firm Performance: International Evidence." *Journal of Real Estate Finance and Economics* 30:4, 429–445.

Hartmann, Steffen, Peter Linneman, Andreas Pfnur, and Boris Siperstein. 2009. "Realizing the Value of Corporate Real Estate Management." *Wharton Real Estate Review* 13:1, 21–33.

Hartmann, Steffen, Peter Linneman, Andreas Pfnur, Denis Moy, and Boris Siperstein. 2010. "Responsibility for and Performance of Corporate Real Estate Functions." *Journal of Corporate Real Estate* 12:1, 7–25.

Jensen, Michael. 1986. "Agency Costs of Free Cash Flow, Corporate Finance and Takeovers." *American Economic Review* 76:2, 323–329.

Linneman, Peter, and Frank Pfirsching. 2008. "Evaluating the Decision to Own Corporate Real Estate." *Wharton Real Estate Review* 12:1, 74–83.

Nourse, Hugh O., and Stephen Roulac. 1993. "Linking Real Estate Decisions to Corporate Strategy." *Journal of Real Estate Research* 8:4, 475–494.

Pfirsching, Frank. 2007. *Portfoliotransaktionen von Selbstnutzern: Eine immobilienwirtschaftliche Analyse*. Frankfurt: DUV.

Rodriguez, Mauricio, and C. F. Sirmans. 1996. "Managing Corporate Real Estate: Evidence from the Capital Markets." *Journal of Real Estate Literature* 4:1, 13–33.

Tuzel, Selale. 2010. "Corporate Real Estate Holdings and the Cross-Section of Stock Returns." *Review of Financial Studies* 23:6, 2268–2302.

Veale, Peter R. 1989. "Managing Corporate Real Estate Assets: Current Executive Attitudes and Prospects for an Emergent Management Discipline." *Journal of Real Estate Research* 4:3, 1–22.

10

Mineral Rights

JOHN S. BAEN
Professor of Real Estate, College of Business, University of North Texas
Founder and Chairman, Baen and Company

MING KAI LOW
Chief Information Officer, Baen and Company

Introduction

The purpose of the chapter is to introduce an alternative type of real estate investment. This investment is real estate given that it is part of a property. But the investment lies below the surface, including rights to minerals, oil, and gas. These rights can be retained when the surface estate is sold, assigned, transferred, or moved to different owners other than the surface estate owner.

The chapter is organized as follows. It starts with an introduction to mineral rights, and how hydraulic fracturing and horizontal drilling have unlocked otherwise dormant and "hidden" asset value. The chapter notes that the fundamental reason for the energy boom in the United States is the property holder's ownership of subsurface mineral rights. The owner rather than the government holds the right to drill, leaving powerful local interests in favor of oil and gas exploration. The next section deals with the bundle of rights of U.S. landowners. This bundle includes the surface rights to build on or use the land but also to retain or sell interests below the surface. Due diligence, risks, and ownership issues are part of the discussion. Pricing of royalty income converts the mineral rights into realizable and quantifiable asset values, analogous to how a capitalization (cap) rate converts net operating income into improved cash flowing surface property value.

Mineral Rights

Initially, mineral rights valuation focused on sand, stone, and gravel from excavation (Grossman 1935). As the development of automobile transportation continued, oil and gas became the dominant driver of mineral rights. Parks (1972) summarizes the features of oil and gas mineral rights valuation using a Hoskold procedure. In a Hoskold procedure, two discount rates are used to value the rights. The first is applied to the present values of cash flows and the second is assigned to reserves set aside to cover depletion. These reserves are assumed invested at a safe, lower rate of return. Since that time there has been several additional oil and gas appraisal methodologies used (Baen 1988, 1996, 2004).

The purposeful or accidental investment returns from oil and gas rights have produced high returns for mineral right owners in various parts of the United States. These returns have accelerated, particularly since the introduction of hydraulic fracturing or fracking and horizontal drilling after 2005. Drilling booms in areas that never have previously had substantial oil and gas activity have ignited the value and speculative value of mineral rights. These booms have led to an increase in the demand for information on the topic of mineral rights by investors and owners. Previously, some considered mineral rights as a low valued economic option. This option on minerals under the ground as compared with the surface rights to build and develop, or to farm, had little to no value. The more valuable options were tied to the surface rights, which property owners typically and accidentally sold. They were not retained in deeds when selling.

Farmers in New York, Ohio, North Dakota, North Texas, and Pennsylvania have realized that they accidentally invested in mineral rights when they acquired their farms. These mineral rights, both present value and future value became more valuable than the surface estate value for farming. Later they discovered that by simply signing an oil and gas lease, they often got a signing bonus of $5,000 per acre. That bonus was often followed by wealth creation or cash flow having a present value of $25,000 per acre.

Mineral rights are valued similar to those for the surface. *Net revenue interest* (NRI) is equivalent to net operating income (NOI) in traditional real estate investments. Royalty NOI is often bought and sold by discounting the income stream. The discount rate, which is analogous to the income cap rate, is typically 10 percent annually. Consider a NRI of $1,000 annually paid to the owner by the mining or oil and gas company firm annually. Using the 10 percent equivalent cap rate and viewing the payment to be for the oil and gas royalty after wells are drilled and producing, the value of the mineral rights is $10,000 per acre.

This situation has all become possible because of the new horizontal drilling technology and revolutionary well completion techniques called *hydraulic fracturing*. These techniques are not unique to the United States. As of 2013, the United States has about 1,825 drilling rigs working (Baker Hughes 2013). These rigs will drill about 54,750 new oil and gas wells a year.

Mineral rights ownership refers to the party who owns the rights or leasing rights to extract oil, gas, gold, coal, and other metals and minerals. In virtually all countries around the world, the owner of the surface land for a house, building, or farmland has no rights to mineral ownership. The central government owns such rights. In the United States, the owner of the surface land generally also has the rights to extract minerals from underneath that land. Consequently, private owners of the surface land often own much of the mineral rights across the United States, as opposed to governments, unless those rights were previously sold, transferred, or retained by historic previous deeds.

As an example, the U.S. process involves a natural gas company contacting the owner of the mineral rights directly to negotiate a contract. These leasing terms comprise a cash bonus payment paid on completion of the mineral lease agreement and a royalty share of natural gas extracted. The lease agreement has a primary term during which the company is required to drill a well, generally 3–10 years. The cash bonus payment can vary from $50 to several thousand dollars per acre, depending on geology and drilling activity. Quite often, the bonus can reach $5,000 an acre in proven oil and gas areas. The royalty share typically varies from 15 to 25 percent and varies on several factors that include but are not limited to many factors: sophistication of the owner, size of bonus versus royalty share, mineral or majority of mineral ownership, and size of tract of land. A *royalty* is a share of any oil and gas extracted from the land, which is paid in cash, on a monthly basis and before any operating expenses.

In other countries, governments own mineral rights. Firms then negotiate with governments directly for granting of the rights. Governments often give preference to their own nationally owned oil companies such as PetroChina and more liberal due diligence and have less political risks. In the United States, smaller firms bear these front-end and wildcat exploratory risks. Larger mineral firms only enter when a smaller independent drilling program is successful. In the United States, an opportunity exists to acquire privately owned mineral rights. These mineral rights (MR) include royalty rights (RR), overriding royalty rights interests (ORRI), or individual shares of individual wells and their costs of drilling and operations as investments or working interests (WI).

The last category is known as *working interest*. The working interest is ownership of both the income and expenses. The owner with a 50 percent working interest must pay half the bills that are due for that lease. A percentage of the income is net revenue interest (NRI). The NRI is the income share of the 100 percent of all income; while working interest of expenses are greater due to the free ride of the royalty mineral owner in regards to expenses. As an example, a landowner owns the mineral rights and signs a lease with a 20 percent royalty. The oil company drills and finds oil and produces it. The landowner owns 20 percent of the gross revenue interest, receiving 20 percent of the revenues. The oil company owns 100 percent of the working interest, and pays for 100 percent of all expenses. However, the oil company only has 80 percent of the net revenue interest due to the 20 percent carried interest of the royalty and mineral owner. In other countries, governments own the mineral rights and benefits and pay no income stream or royalty directly to the property or surface owner. In the United States, a surface owner generally gets surface damages paid for a drill site regardless of whether there are owned minerals or not. The surface is legally a separate estate.

According to the United States Energy Information Agency (USEIA 2013), oil production surged since 2008 almost entirely because of onshore development of shale and fracking. Oil production in the United States had been declining since 1986. In 2008 U.S. oil production was 5 million barrels a day. By 2013 production had increased to nearly 8 million barrels a day.

Figure 10.1 shows the major oil and gas fields in the United States as of 2011 (United States Energy Information Agency 2011). The Barnett Shale near Dallas-Fort Worth has estimated natural gas reserves of as much as 252 trillion cubic feet. The largest field known and proven to be economic in area is the Marcellus and Utica Shale, stretching between Ohio, Pennsylvania, and West Virginia, and including Maryland and New York. Maryland and New York have politically imposed drilling moratoriums, which significantly reduce the value of mineral rights in these areas.

Figure 10.2 shows the U.S. shale gas plays, or fields in production, from the USEIA. The concentration occurs in fields from the Rocky Mountain to Texas, across the South,

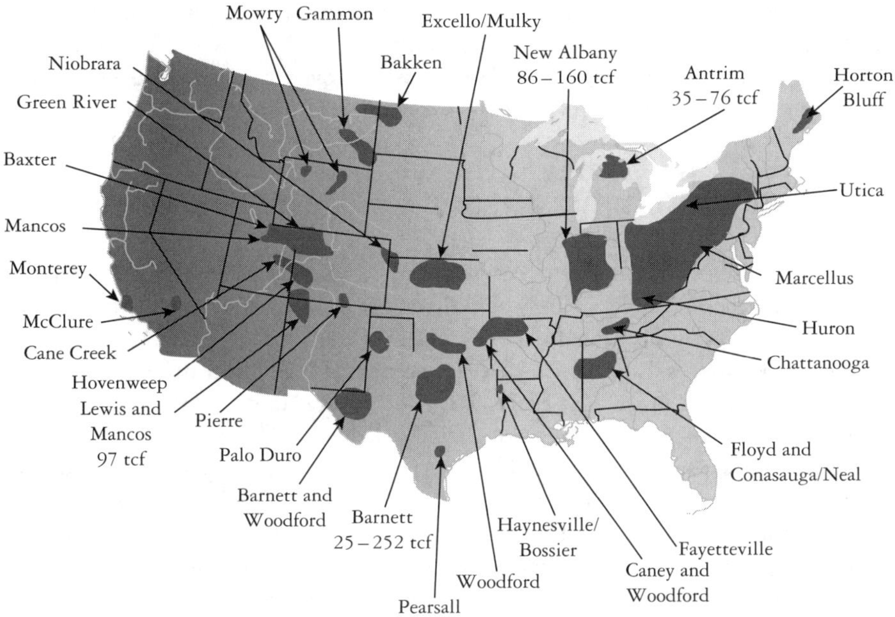

Figure 10.1 Major Named New Oil and Gas Fields in the United States. Source: Energy Information Administration.

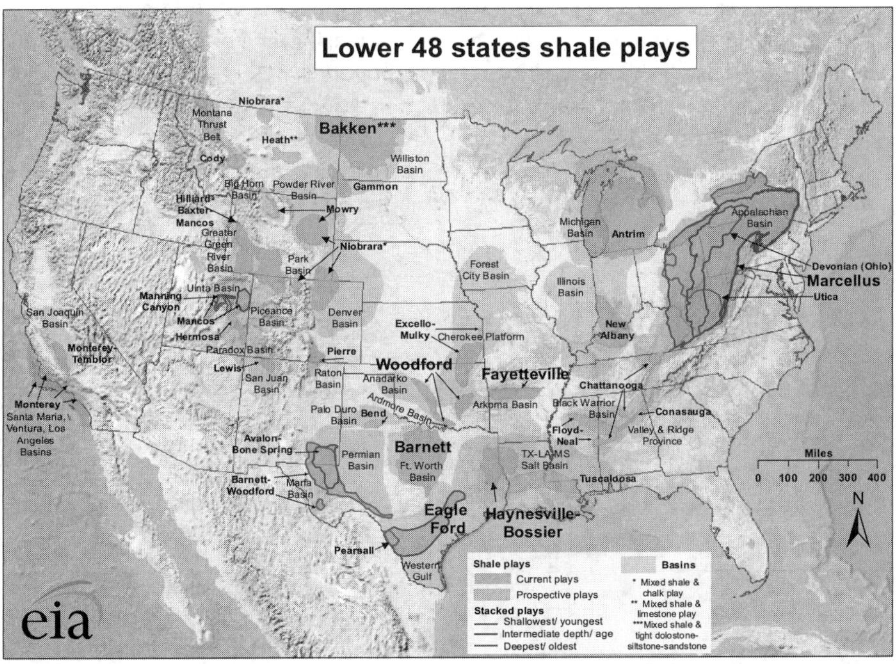

Figure 10.2 United States Shale Gas Plays. *Source*: Energy Information Administration based on data from various published studies. Updated May 9, 2011.

and in the Marcellus and Utica Shale. The U.S. government retains many of the mineral rights under large ranches in the Rocky Mountain areas that have caused tension and conflicts between oil companies leasing from the U.S. government and land owners who have no mineral rights or oil and gas activity benefits.

The Bundle of Rights Theory

To make, retain, or sell mineral rights investments requires understanding aspects of mineral rights that can be collectively or individually acquired, sold, or retained. Assume that various types of investments in mineral rights are associated with rural farmland for the balance of this discussion. However, all concepts carry over to larger or smaller urban tracts in locations such as Dallas/Fort Worth, Houston, Los Angeles, and many cities in the Northeast and Midwestern United States.

Figure 10.3 shows the farmland bundle of rights. On the left side are the surface rights that a farmland holder has and the various rights and uses of farm and ranch lands. On the right are surface rights that support mineral or energy activity. These include geothermal, wind rights, and access as well as surface fracking ponds that support oil and gas exploration. On the right side are the subsurface rights that are separate but held by the property owner. These subsurface rights are virtually unique in the U.S. context. At the top is the right to allow pipelines, either on or below the surface, regardless of whether the subject property has minerals. The mineral rights include for oil and gas and metals access, water, and the payment of royalties and overriding royalties.

These rights accrue to the owner and can be sold. On the left side of Figure 10.3, the owner has the right to farm, to use the land for grazing, and to offer hunting rights. The owner also has royalty and overriding royalty rights as well as geothermal and wind rights. The farmland owner has the ability to grant easements for pipelines, oil and gas access roads and drilling pad-sites, injection wells, subsurface water rights, and fracking ponds. Fee simple ownership includes the surface and subsurface rights. All these rights and access rights have economic value to the land/mineral owners.

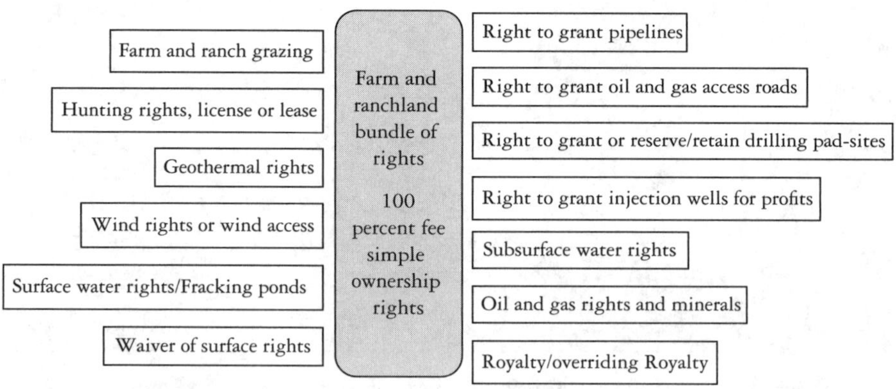

Figure 10.3 Farm and Ranchland Bundle of Rights Theory.

Mineral Rights Ownership and Investment

Table 10.1 shows three types of mineral ownership rights: (1) private fee owned/surface and mineral, (2) private fee owned/no mineral rights, and (3) publicly/government owned minerals. With private fee simple ownership of both surface and mineral rights, an oil and gas company is responsible for damages through negotiations directly with the owner.

This chapter considers only direct and individual ownership of minerals or fractions of the mineral estate. The investment in public company drilling and oil and gas stocks is another form of investment but is not considered here. What are considered are direct ownership investments into mineral rights.

The long-term benefits of mineral rights investments in land include cash flow and liquidity. Regarding cash flow, an up-front lease-signing bonus takes place. The cash return is the actual royalty and potential speculative cash flow from oil and gas leases, and a share of income from all future wells.

Mineral rights are highly liquid and marketable in areas having oil and gas potential. Royalty income streams are very marketable and generally sell for a present value based on a representative 10 percent discount rate. The procedure is to take the series of projected cash flows and discount it using 10 percent annually. Another approach is to multiply one month's cash flow by a multiplier, adjusted down by the remaining term on the lease. That multiplier is between 36 and 60 for one month of gross income.

Mineral rights have low management costs. Dormant or unleased mineral rights require no management until a gas or oil lease is offered. After the royalty is established

Table 10.1 **Types of Mineral Ownership Rights**

Variable Types of Ownership	*Oil and Gas Lease Negotiations Royalty*	*Surface Estate Damages (1–5 acres)*
1. Private fee owned/surface and mineral. Estates are intact and have not been partitioned	Surface owner and company private negotiation	Negotiable if part of written lease or by separate agreement before, during, or after drilling activities
2. Private fee owned/no mineral rights (retained by previous owners, deeded out to other investor owned entities, or purchased by other private parties)	Mineral owner and oil company. No surface owner input and little damages paid	Outside of lease/Subservient surface owner
3. Publicly/government owned minerals (surface owned for grazing to third party)	U.S. government agency or state and oil company. No agricultural tenant or owner input and very little damages paid	Varies by agricultural lease document but generally none

by the drilling of a well or wells, little management is required. The only costs are for accounting and monitoring the monthly royalty income and matching the production posted with the actual production reported to the state.

Mineral rights offer tax benefits and planning potential. Although few opportunities exist to shelter royalty income from taxation, many tax-planning opportunities are available for the mineral rights themselves. Mineral rights are counted as real estate and can be placed in a 1031 tax deferred exchange. Capital gains taxation is deferred by trading for other types of real estate. If held for more than one year, mineral rights qualify for long-term capital gains rates on the resale profits over the basis if rights are sold. Long-term capital gains are taxed at lower preferential rates. Many estate-planning opportunities are available to reduce federal and state inheritance taxes.

Mineral rights are forever and do not depreciate like bricks and mortar real estate. They have multiple depths of ownership and royalty potential to the center of the earth. Investors acquire direct mineral and royalty investments in several ways, such as by buying surface land or property. Buying surface property often includes receiving the mineral and oil and gas rights if the mineral rights have not previously been sold or retained by previous owners. These mineral rights come as a part of the bundle of rights being purchased with the property. Investors can also buy stand-alone speculative, never drilled mineral rights as an investment vehicle without buying the surface estate. They can also buy or sell mineral rights that are leased but not drilled.

Another method of acquiring direct mineral and royalty rights is by deeding and transferring various interests in land by unbundling the rights and retaining the mineral rights before or at the time of the surface estate/use sale. Investors buy or sell producing mineral rights and royalty rights that include all future mineral potential as well as current cash flow from existing wells (royalty). They also buy or sell producing royalty rights or cash flows from existing individual well bores but not the mineral rights or potential income from additional wells drilled.

Investors trade an option-like contract on mineral rights. The overriding royalty interests (ORRI) are not minerals or a mineral right. Instead they are a percentage or decimal interest of 100 percent of all income from a well or mineral lease. ORRI includes carried interest in a well awarded to a landowner, oil and gas professional, or anyone as a bonus. This payment includes compensation for performance based leasing, research, or compensation for those who work for ORRI instead of a salary, hourly, or day rate in the oil, gas, or other minerals business. Oil and gas leasing agents, title attorneys, and executives often receive ORRI and sell these interests before or after well completion or drilling.

Due Diligence

Mineral rights as special real estate investments are unique. They require extensive analysis, title work and research before assigning any value to the purchase or valuation decision. Although most land does not have an oil and gas well drilled, this does not mean that the mineral estate has no economic value. Market data on comparable sales are nearly impossible to obtain. These data are often inaccurate regarding the minerals. Appraisals and comparable sales rarely detail the mineral status or percentage of the mineral estate included in their analysis. Any mineral rights, however, have some implied value or option value. These mineral rights are extremely long-term investments. That is, mineral rights are forever. Those retained or acquired decades ago are just now becoming economic due to new drilling and completion technologies. Before obtaining a prospective investment, investors should consider the following due diligence matters before funding.

The first due diligence issue involves title or ownership on whether the seller has a good and merchantable title to the land and specifically the minerals. Because separate parties can hold the surface and mineral rights. Also, the title opinion includes whether any liens, loans, or taxes are due on the mineral estate.

Three primary ways are available to confirm good title. The first method of confirming a good title is to obtain a title opinion from a title company, title attorney, abstract office, or independent professional. A second confirmation method is that the seller is already receiving royalty checks from an oil and gas company. These companies generally do their own title opinion before leasing and the first payment of a royalty is paid. The company issues a division order indicating the owner's name and ownership fraction. Copies of current and historical checks and check stubs are indications of good title and also include income and expense details. The third way to confirm good title is that the royalty or mineral deed should provide warranty language similar to a warranty deed.

A second due diligence issue is whether an area has any oil and gas potential. This involves research on known prospective oil and gas zones in the area of subject property. Oil and gas maps include historical and present oil and gas wells drilled. Fourteen states have leasing and oil shale drilling booms gains due to new drilling and completion technologies that did not exist before 1998. Future technological advances could make currently speculative minerals valuable in the future.

A third due diligence matter is to investigate whether any wells have been drilled in the area. Potential investors should research historic wells drilled in the state, region, county, or township from public information sources. Various state oil and gas commission and regulators differ by quality, quantity, and reliability of available information. Internet searches of news articles are another source for determining local drilling activity. Another source is libraries offering historic and contemporary oil and gas information. Searches include geological studies and U.S. federal publications on potential oil and gas productive areas, available since the 1930s. Other sources include oil and gas journals for research on the production of individual wells and determining the economic potential and natural production decline curves for the area. Hiring a local geologist to write a report of the mineral potential is another source. An initial very basic report costs $1,000–1,500.

Figure 10.4 shows an example of a listing of mineral rights for sale. The lease includes a held by production (HBP) provision. Under HBP, in an oil or natural gas property lease the lessee, generally an energy company, continues drilling activities on the property as long as it is producing a minimum paying amount of oil or gas. The HBP provision extends the lessee's right to operate the property beyond the initial lease term and often for decades. This provision is also a feature of most mineral property leases. Economic production extends and rolls over the lease. The production is in barrels of oil per day (BOPD) and the royalty interest is RI and net revenue income.

Eagleford Minerals Frio County, TX: For sale is 12.585 net mineral acres that are HBPs by a well making 5 – 6 BOPD. This interest has 0.006411 RI in the 327.27 acres. It currently generates about $50 – 60+ per month. $4,000.00 per NMA.
Barnett Shale Producing Royalty Ellis County, TX: Seller divesting only a portion of its interest in the Orr Unit operated by EOG. This 324.27 acres unit has four-seasoned Barnett Shale wells all drilled in 2009 on a very flat decline. The unit has been configured to hold two more Hz PUDs. Seller divesting a 0.008368 NRI. The 6-month revenue to this interest has been $989 per month and the 3-month average has been $1,142 per month with higher gas prices. Make offer.

HBP = Held by production; lease renews as long as production continues
BOPD = Barrels of oil per day of production
NMA = Net mineral acres
Hz PUD = Horizontal proven undeveloped reserves
RI = Royalty income
NRI = Net revenue interest

Figure 10.4 Mineral Rights Listing. Source: List Mineral Rights 2013.

The seller is listing in Frio County, Texas, 12.585 net mineral acres that are HBP with 5–6 BOPD. The lease generates $50–60 per month. Using $50, the annual lease income is $600, with an ask price of $4,000 per net mineral acre (NMA). The implied yield rate equivalent to a cap rate is 8 percent with a seven (7) year payback if prices and production stay constant.

Sellers and Buyers of Mineral Rights

This section addresses the market for mineral rights. Sellers can transact the subsurface mineral rights without selling surface rights or vice versa. The motivation is to remove small parcels or as part of portfolio consolidation. Buyers are looking to increase their size and to exploit potential information differentials on the quality of reserves.

Sellers of mineral and royalty rights sell for various reasons. Although many people, farmers, in particular, say "Never sell your mineral rights," doing so is often prudent or required due to financial hardship. Owners accidentally sell most mineral rights as a part of any sale of the surface estate. In these sales, mineral rights are not specifically retained in the deed. Many contemporary land sales involve an acquisition at market value. This market value, particularly in farmland areas, does not necessarily have to do with the surface farming, building, or construction. Instead, hidden mineral rights are the primary motivation of the buyers. Ignorance, oversight, or poor professional advice or practices by real estate agents are the most common reasons this occurs.

Other transfers occur under distress. A court ordered sale due to bankruptcy, divorce, or any type of litigation involving the settling of an estate, judgment, or collection of a debt can transfer the mineral rights. Many wills state that all properties will be sold to settle the estate and proceeds distributed to heirs. This would include mineral rights and royalty. Baen (2011, 2012) offers suggestions on estate planning in regards to protecting mineral rights and reducing federal estate taxes. The seller may need to sell due to financial hardship and debts such as hospital bills.

Sophisticated sellers buy mineral or royalty rights when commodity prices are low and sell when oil and gas cycles reach a high. They make a rational business decision to maximize their yield on investment and realize their capital gains by selling at the peak of a cycle of activity. For example, oil and gas prices, leasing activity, or other market indicators generally occur in cycles.

On the other side of the transaction are the buyers of mineral rights. The liquidity or conversion rights to cash for speculative mineral rights can be very high in known areas of mineral activity. Royalty rights having an existing income stream can be easily sold and are pursued by many investors. Buyers include but are not limited to the following types.

Individual investors are buying by private treaty or contract, not necessarily planning to drill themselves. Oil companies operating the wells or potential wells often make offers to buy mineral rights that they already have leased. These purchases increase their rate of return on existing wells. Royalty trusts that often are publicly traded and listed firms are players in the purchase of mineral rights. Middlemen or wholesale buyers are resellers to publicly traded royalty trustees. Wholesale buyers often acquire the entire mineral estate. They then strip off the royalty income stream of existing wells and retain the speculative Deep Rights. A pricing standard is for a 16 percent yield on a 60-month payback on a subsequent set of royalties. These cash flows are pooled, packaged, and then resold to retail investors. Offered pricing is an 8 percent annual yield to a pool of passive investors at twice the acquisition price. What is not widely known is that wholesale buyers retain a residual tranche. This equity or non-cash tranche contains the balance of the mineral estate. These include future well income, deep rights as very long-term investments. Bank trust departments have various trusts and individuals who acquire mineral rights for very long-term investments.

Risk Factors

Mineral rights investment factors extend beyond individual well performance that could reduce potential income. The due diligence should but does not always detect an inability to develop the mineral estate due to local zoning or permitting ordinances.

A risk comes from a drop in commodity prices below the current long-term market trend lines. This comes from reduced economic activity in the United States and elsewhere and therefore a loss of demand. Associated economic risks are overdevelopment and new finds of natural gas or oil with lower production costs. A risk of overproduction exists due to supply and new gas fields in states such as Louisiana and Pennsylvania. A lack or loss of available drilling capital can exist due to higher rates of return on other alternative investments.

Another risk is anticipated changes in federal and state rules and regulations regarding after tax benefits or costs to oil and gas operators and investors. Proposed changes in governmental environmental rules and regulations involving various technologies pose additional risk. These technologies include hydro-fracking, water disposal, noise, and air pollution of rigs that could limit or shut down drilling. Individual companies can opt to shut in or not complete drilled wells until prices increase in the future.

The holder faces risks of the company not performing on the contract. One risk is operator bankruptcy and crooked operators, including "fly-by-night" speculators. The company may not pay the agreed-on royalty, or make claims such as difficulty of extraction that it should be reduced. Other risks include financial shenanigans, theft, and other forms of business fraud.

Another risk is of a challenge to the title of mineral rights owned. Such risk rarely occurs after proper due diligence. Mineral rights pass through many generations and are often lost or watered down by diffusion as the number of heirs grows over time. Mineral rights should be placed in trust to protect the title and ease the job of oil companies finding the owner of record.

Calculating or Auditing the Net Royalty Interest

This section examines the collection and payment procedures for royalties and uses the various terms and procedures in leases. Oil companies confirm income and the rights to that income before paying any royalty. The payment is confirmed by detailed title opinions, based on leases being signed and an official *division order* (DO) being issued. A DO details the net decimal interest of 100 percent of the gross production value each month.

As an example, if an oil well's total production is 100 barrels (BBLs) per day for 30 days based on an investor owning 100 percent of the minerals or royalty, the following calculation indicates the mineral rights owner's share. This share is the net revenue interest (NRI) before local property taxes and before federal or state income taxes. Suppose oil is priced at $110 a barrel. The reference price is usually West Texas Intermediate (WTI). Then NRI is (100 barrels per day) ($110 per barrel) (30 days) 20 percent Royalty (NRI = $66,000 per month to the mineral owner.

Some states charge all owners a severance tax on each barrel of oil and all gas produced. No operating expenses of the well are generally charged to the mineral owner other than pipeline and compressor chargers for the sale of natural gas. Often the investor or owners do not own 100 percent of the minerals. In this case, the investor owns a fractional interest or small tracts of land or minerals that are part of a *drilling unit* (DU).

For example, if the same owner as above owns 100 acres of minerals that are part of a 640 acre drilling unit, the calculation becomes: [100 acres owned/640 acres (DU)] [(100 barrels per day) ($110per barrel) (30 days) (0.2)] = $10,312 per month to the fractional mineral owner. This amounts to a watering down effect of the income stream, but allows investors to diversify across holdings.

The upfront lease signing bonus, royalty amount, maximum size of the drilling unit, and depth limitations are matters to consider when negotiating oil and gas leases. Baen (2012) offers structures for negotiating oil and gas leases. Oil companies use professionals to represent them. Mineral owners generally use a local attorney who is licensed to practice law, but not necessarily a specialist in oil and gas leases or negotiations. Each oil and gas lease and terms is individually unique.

The "standard" or "producer 88 lease" is a boilerplate document that transfers most favorable terms to the oil or gas firm. Instead, a lease should have some core provisions on term, royalty, bonus, and shut-in. The lease is a conveyance of the mineral rights for a length of time or term. The owner has only a royalty interest in the mineral rights. The primary term is a fixed number of years. The secondary term is after the primary term and is extended if production occurs and continues. Production is not required during the primary term.

The royalty is an interest paid without deducting the costs of production, expressed as a fraction or percentage, usually between 1/8 (12.5 percent) and 1/4 (25 percent). The bonus is the up-front payment on execution of the lease. The bonus is based on net mineral acres, the number of acres in the property times the interest in the minerals owned by the property owner or holder of mineral rights as the lessor. For a one-half mineral interest in a tract of 100 acres, the lessor owns 50 net mineral acres.

A lease may provide for the payment of delay rental during the primary term. The delay rental is paid at the end of each lease year during the primary term if no production has been established on the lease, in order to keep the lease in effect during the primary term. If a lease is paid up, it remains in effect during the entire primary term with no further payments to the lessor unless and until actual production of oil or gas is established.

In general, the owner wants the highest bonus, delay rental and royalty fraction, and the shortest primary term. There should be an outside professional to balance the negotiation process and terms of a lease. The standard producer 88 lease can have hidden terms and clauses favorable to the minerals company.

Valuation of Mineral and Royalty Rights Investments

The quality and quantity of mineral rights is a cash flow stream. That stream is not constant over time and is volatile due to eventual declines in the productivity of wells as the resource is depleted. The stabilized, flatter, decline curve of mature producing wells generally has a market value of 36–42 months of royalty income. Many less reputable firms offer 12–24 months net income in blanket offers to purchase via mail outs to royalty owners. These offers understate the value of the mineral rights. Many of those offers border on fraud.

Many variables extend beyond the terms, conditions, and uniqueness of oil and gas leases including, but are not limited to:

- age of the well or wells; volume of water as a ratio of oil or gas produced, which has economic implications to the operator and longevity of production; quality of the operator and long-term staying power and performance; pipeline contract if a line is present for oil and gas produced; and the effect of the pipeline expenses and net revenue received by royalty mineral owner;
- pressure of pipeline and availability of compressors;
- quality of gas, in British thermal units (BTU), and the quantity of liquids found in wet or dry gas;
- quality of oil produced (American Petroleum Institute API gravity);
- type of well (vertical or horizontal);
- prospects for re-drilling or refracking;
- sophistication and tenacity of mineral owner to enforce lease provisions and obtain releases or partial releases, when wells become uneconomic;
- type and quality of the completion or *frac* of the well;

- length of lateral, the horizontal drilling bore length through the productive zone 4000–7000 feet laterally;
- size of unit [(number of mineral acres owned) / (total of mineral acres in unit times)] (oil and gas lease);
- for wells, the density of spacing and performance of wells on adjoining or nearby properties;
- individual characteristics of various areas and individual wells; and
- geology of the rock.

Of concern to the oil and gas mineral appraiser is the net revenue (income) or royalty percentage found on the oil and gas royalty or potential oil and gas revenue checks.

Table 10.2 provides different methods for valuing mineral rights. The residual value of minerals establishes a price for the fee simple interest or entire property, including surface rights and the value of actual or potential buildings or improvements above ground. From this price the surface land and improvement values are subtracted, leaving the mineral rights as a residual. The *comparable sales approach* compares the subject property's mineral rights with recent transactions. The number of months of royalties used ranges between 36 and 60.

The *direct sale approach* calculates the royalty directly from the sale price of the oil or gas, expected output, and royalty rate. The *income approach* takes the actual royalties paid and discounts them, often using a 10 percent annual rate. The appraisal district rate uses the valuation of the local tax assessor. In Texas, statute requires using a 15 percent annual discount rate. Another method of valuation uses entirely the up-front or bonus payments times a multiplier. That multiplier ranges between three and five times the up-front. Another method is using the replacement cost.

Recommendations

Individual professional analysis leads to recommendations to those leasing owned mineral rights to oil or gas companies. The recommendations aim to maximize the return on minerals while considering protections to land provisions. If unleased mineral rights lead to an inquiry by an oil company or their representative or land man to lease rights, investors should respond in a similar way. The response should be a request to put the offer in the form of a lease, together with a letter that includes the amount of signing bonus money to be paid per acre. Often mineral owners either discuss verbally or sign an option agreement that is both nebulous and dangerous.

A written lease offer on the standard 88 oil and gas lease form has risks. Nothing is standard about these leases and they are complicated and binding legal documents. That legal document affects the owner's title through the initial term or time period and as long as oil and gas is produced. Baen (2012) discusses some issues involved in negotiating such leases, terms and specific recommendations. The following are four main recommendations.

- *Obtain qualified help.* This help should be obtained in negotiation of leases, lease bonus and signing bonus royalty amounts, and surface damages. Oil and gas companies, inde-

Table 10.2 **Correlation of Various Approaches to Value/Mineral Estate for Investment or Divest Time**

	Mineral Acres
Residual/extracted value of minerals (assumes signing a bonus at $6,000 paid at lease signing and $24,000 per acre present value of CF/Royalty income discounted @ 10 percent)	$30,000/acre
Comparable sales of mineral and royalty rights (36–60 months NOI or royalty production) and data collected from market sales	$30,000/acre
Sale/purchase of mineral reserves (Example: Barnett shale field)	$25,210/acre[a] (PV of Reserves)
2.4 BCF/well × 2.00 wells/119 ± acres × $2.50/MCF × 25 percent "Royalty" = $3,000,000/119 ± acres = $25,210/acre Income approach to value/discount cash flow = $24,000/mineral acre + 6,000 bonuses paid initially	$24,000/acre
Appraisal district indicated value of producing royalty (varies by state if taxable Texas used by statute 15 percent discount based on production value)	$12,000–15,000/acre at 15 percent discount rate[b]
Based on prevailing bonuses being paid July 1, 2008, at $6,000/acre times (3x–5x) or 300–500 percent = $18,000–30,000/acre	$25,000/acre
Replacement cost and carried interest (royalty) in $4 million well on 90 acres of minerals with 25 percent royalty × 200 percent	$25,000/acre
Conclusion: Market value of the minerals	$25,000/acre (plus other bonuses)

Note: This table summarizes the conditions for valuation of a mineral estate lease over time. Buying reserves is speculative and requires wells to be drilled to have value. Based on several assumptions and seven indications of value shown, the mineral value of this subject property is $30,000 per mineral acre as of July 1, 2008.

[a]Assumes sold based on reserves only and no bonuses paid, or bonuses already paid.

[b]Based on known market factors, gas prices, market bonuses being paid at the time, and fully developed mineral lease with one best practices wells drilled on 80 acres or the equivalent number of wells drilled on any unit formed based on one well per 80 acres.

Source: Baen 2011.

pendent land men, leasing agents, and most oil and gas attorneys focus only on bonus and royalty amounts. However, many other economic factors should be considered.

- *Address damage compensation or mitigations.* This topic should be specifically addressed in each lease if the mineral owner also owns the rights above the surface. Compensation is based on unique features and potential for the land's highest and best use. Damages for drill sites, roads, and pipelines should be specific at market prices and fair to all parties. Fairness is based on the total impact to land, not on specific acreage damaged.

- *Prepare a long-term or eventual highest and best use land plan for the surface estate without oil and gas wells.* This should become a base map for identifying locations for potential well sites and access roads/right-of-ways. The plan should identify valuable parts of the property to be avoided, such as road frontage, wetlands, mature forest areas, and high visibility locations including the top of a plateau in northwest New Mexico. Whether the wells are drilled first or the surface estate is developed into urban or suburban uses, the land plans or plat should clearly identify potential drill sites for buyers, tenants, and public officials. This identification allows all to be informed during long-term regional planning, annexations, platting, and subdivision.
- *Provide lease provisions that allow for drill sites, pipelines, and acres to be agreed on before any soil disruption.* Release of surface rights by oil and gas companies should be agreed on before any soil disruption. Release of surface rights by oil and gas companies should include all precisely defined land not designated or held by production. This allows for residential land, mortgages, and title policies to be obtained that are not subject to oil and gas surface disruption.

As an example, consider the following cash flow analysis of an oil and gas well in Texas. Oil quantity is measured as barrels of condensate per day (BCPD). Gas is measured in thousand cubic feet per day (MCF). The area has surface property taxes ad valorem of 2.4 percent annually. Oil has a severance tax of 4.61 percent and natural gas 7.5 percent. One well is drilled, which has operating expenses of $1,000 per month. The well has capital expenses (capex) of $750,000. The well produces 577 MCF. Natural gas sells for between $2.50 and $15.00 per thousand cubic feet. There is no oil production.

The royalty rate is 25 percent. The owner receives that royalty, multiplied by the price of natural gas and the production in each year of the lease. From this royalty revenue, operating expenses and ad valorem property taxes are subtracted, leaving net royalty income. Production from the well declines over time, and prices shift upwards and downwards with the market. The royalty net income cash flows are discounted to a net present value (NPV) using a 10 percent annual rate in order to determine the value of the mineral rights lease. The producer collects its share or 75 percent of the income, less its operating expenses and the capital expense of $750,000 for the well. Each party carries out a NPV calculation to determine whether to sign the lease.

Summary and Conclusions

Sophisticated property owners should be aware of the long-term potential value of mineral rights. These mineral rights lie beneath all classes of land and land uses. Investors often consider the probability that the mineral rights may be economic and add value to a long-term real estate investment unimportant. These mineral rights have real potential. Mineral rights always have an option value greater than zero. Real estate is a long-term investment. Mineral rights are a longer-term investment that often realizes income on value greater than the ownership of the surface estate.

In virtually all countries, the owner of the surface land for a house, building, or farmland has no rights to mineral ownership. The central government owns such rights. In the United States, the owner of the surface land often has the rights to extract minerals from underneath that land. Consequently, private holders of the surface land or previous landowners own much of the mineral rights across the United States, as opposed to governments. The surface owner has the right to farm and to use the land for grazing, and to offer hunting rights. The mineral owner also has royalty and overriding royalty rights and geothermal and wind rights. The farmland owner has the ability to grant easements for pipelines, oil and gas access roads and drilling pad-sites, injection wells, subsurface water rights, and fracking ponds. Fee simple ownership includes the surface and subsurface rights.

Due diligence should but does not always detect an inability to develop the mineral estate due to local zoning or permitting ordinances. A risk comes from a drop in commodity prices below the current long-term market trend lines. Associated economic risks are overdevelopment and new finds of new natural gas that is economical to produce. Another risk is anticipated changes in federal and state taxing rules and regulations. Proposed changes in governmental environmental rules and regulations involving technologies pose additional risk. These technologies include hydro-fracking, water disposal, noise, and air pollution of rigs that could limit or shut down drilling. The mineral owner faces risks in the company performing on the contract. One risk is operator bankruptcy and crooked operators, including fly-by-night operators. The company may not pay the agreed-on royalty, or make claims such as difficulty of extraction that it should be reduced. Other risks include financial shenanigans, theft, and other forms of business fraud. Another risk is of a challenge to the title of mineral rights owned.

Discussion Questions

1. What is different about mineral rights ownership in the United States versus other countries?
2. Discuss the bundle of rights that a U.S. farmland holder has.
3. How is net revenue interest used to value the mineral rights in land?
4. Identify some specific risk factors in mineral rights.

References

Baen, John S. 1988. "Oil and Gas Mineral Rights in Land Appraisal." *The Appraisal Journal* 56:2, 205–216.

Baen, John S. 1996. "The Impact and Implications of Mineral Rights, Oil and Gas Activities on Agricultural Land Values—A Reduction in the Property's Ultimate Highest and Best Use and Possible Environmental Exposure." *The Appraisal Journal* 64:1, 67–75.

Baen, John S. 2004. "Urban and Public Lands (BLM) Oil and Gas Site Planning, Drilling, Construction, and Production—Techniques to Reduce or Eliminate Surface Estate Value Impacts and Environmental Damages". Presented at the American Real Estate Society, Captain Island, Florida.

Baen, John S. 2011. "Contemporary Land, Oil and Gas Valuations, Estate Planning Opportunities, and Possible Strategies in the New Estate and Tax Environment". Presented at the American Real Estate Society, Seattle, Washington.

Baen, John S. 2012. "Standard Producers 88 Oil and Gas Lease in America". Presented at the American Real Estate Society, St. Petersburg, Florida.

Baker Hughes. 2013. "Rig Count." *Oil and Gas Journal* 111, 7–10. http://www.ogj.com/articles/2013/07/us-drilling-rig-count-climbs-9-units-to-1-757.html.

Brian Wolf. 2013. "Oil & Gas Properties Mineral Rights Marketing." http://www.BWOGP.com.

List Mineral Rights (2013). Accessed at www.listmineralrights.com

Grossman, Philip. 1935. "The Valuation of Land with Underlying Natural Resources". *Appraisal Journal* 3:4, 236–241.

Parks, Roland. 1972. "Valuation of Mineral Property". *Real Estate Appraiser*, May–June, 37–38.

United States Energy Information Agency (USEIA). 2011. *Annual Energy Review*. Washington, DC: USEIA. http// www.eia.doe.gov/multifuel/038409.pdf.

United States Energy Information Agency (USEIA). 2013. *Annual Energy Outlook*. Washington, DC: USEIA. http://www.eia.gov/forecasts/aeo/pdf/0383 (2013).pdf.

11

Infrastructure

HSU WEN PENG
Assistant Professor, National Taipei University

GRAEME NEWELL
Professor, University of Western Sydney

Introduction

Considerable yield compression has occurred in many international bond and fixed-asset markets in recent years, resulting in large capital flows into property. With the increased level of investment capital available, pension funds and institutional investors have considered a range of alternative investments including infrastructure to enhance the performance and provide diversification benefits in their portfolios.

Infrastructure involves the physical structures and networks that provide the essential services for a community's economic and social needs (RREEF 2005; McCarthy 2006). Infrastructure is fundamental to a country's economy. Effective infrastructure is essential for economic growth and competitiveness. The size and quality of infrastructure is highly correlated with the size of a country's economy (Hobbs 2007; Newell and Peng 2008a, b). In a Chinese study, infrastructure quality highly correlates ($r = 0.92$) with global competitiveness (Newell, Chau, and Wong 2009). Table 11.1 presents the rank of infrastructure quality and global competitiveness for the leading international economies. As Table 11.1 shows, Hong Kong and Singapore rank first and second in infrastructure quality. Switzerland and Singapore hold the top two rankings in global competitiveness. An interrelationship and correspondence exist between infrastructure quality and global competitiveness.

Infrastructure has recently emerged as a separate asset class for institutional capital. The infrastructure asset class has distinctive characteristics and attractive features, notably inelastic demand and long duration (Rakowski 2003, 2004; RREEF 2005; McCarthy 2006; UBS 2006a). These benefits occur in a climate of reduced government spending on infrastructure in most developed countries. Governments seek alternative funding options for infrastructure development and maintenance.

National, regional, and local governments have typically provided infrastructure. The government finances, builds, owns, and operates the infrastructure. Yet, government budgetary constraints have recently reduced involvement in providing infrastructure in

Table 11.1 **The Ranking of Infrastructure Quality and Global Competitiveness for Leading International Economies**

Country	*Infrastructure Quality*	*Global Competitiveness*
Hong Kong	1	9
Singapore	2	2
Germany	3	6
France	4	21
Switzerland	5	1
United Kingdom	6	8
Netherlands	7	5
United Arab Emirates	8	24
Korea	9	19
Spain	10	36
Japan	11	10
Luxembourg	12	22
Canada	13	14
United States	14	7
Austria	18	16
China	48	29
India	84	29

Note: This table shows the correlations between infrastructure quality and global competitiveness for leading international economies. Countries with higher quality infrastructure present stronger competitiveness.

Source: Authors' compilation from WEF 2012.

most developed countries. That reduction comes with a demand for high levels of infrastructure commitment in developing countries such as in Asia.

Developed countries are currently only allocating an average of 2.2 percent of gross domestic product (GDP) to infrastructure, which is a substantial decrease from previous levels (OECD 2006). In the 1970s, infrastructure spending by governments in selected OECD countries was still in double digits as a proportion of GDP. Nevertheless, the expenses on infrastructure decreased to below 6 percent of GDP by 2002 (Mercer 2005).

A World Bank (2006) study suggests that developing countries invest 7 percent of GDP to new infrastructure and maintenance of existing facilities. This is double the spending after 2010 of 3–4 percent of GDP. A large investment gap exists for developed and developing countries, which suggests a need for alternative private investment sources for infrastructure development (Rakowski 2003, 2004; RREEF 2005; Macquarie 2006).

To put this investment gap in perspective, more than $30 trillion will be needed for global infrastructure development and maintenance up to 2030 (World Bank 2006).

These investments offer private infrastructure opportunities in both developed and developing countries. Given these supply constraints, the demand drivers for infrastructure growth are increasing population growth and improving standards of living in developing countries such as China and India, large capital inflows from pension funds, acceptance of infrastructure as a unique and separate asset class, and the size of the global infrastructure markets (RREEF 2005; UBS 2006b).

Context of Infrastructure

In terms of infrastructure asset type, investable assets can be broadly classified into two categories: economic and social. *Economic infrastructure* usually describes an asset with a large investment scale and a high ratio of fixed to variable cost including transport, utilities, and communications. Privatized economic infrastructure is offered to the public on a user pay basis such as toll roads, rail, airports, and utilities.

Social infrastructure typically consists of facilities where the government provides the services while the private sector builds and maintains the assets. These facilities include healthcare and correctional facilities (DB RREEF 2005; Russell Investment Management 2007). The healthcare system can operate on a user pay basis depending on personal and insurer charges on delivery. Table 11.2 provides the types of infrastructure assets, which are classified into economic and social categories. From the investment point of view, infrastructure assets can be classified by their stage of the life cycle or maturity. As maturity increases, the infrastructure investment risk is reduced. Reduced

Table 11.2 **Types of Infrastructure Assets**

	Economic Infrastructure		***Social Infrastructure***
Transport	***Utility***	***Communications***	
Toll roads	Gas pipeline and storage facilities	Cable networks	Healthcare facilities
Bridges	Electricity grid and power plants	Satellite systems	Education facilities
Tunnels	Water and waste-water networks, sewerage facilities, and desalination plants	Broadcast facilities	Housing
Seaports	Renewable energy		Prisons
Airports			Courts
Rail			Police stations
Ferries			
Car parks			

Source: Authors' compilation from DB RREEF 2005; ING 2008; and Russell Investment Management 2007.

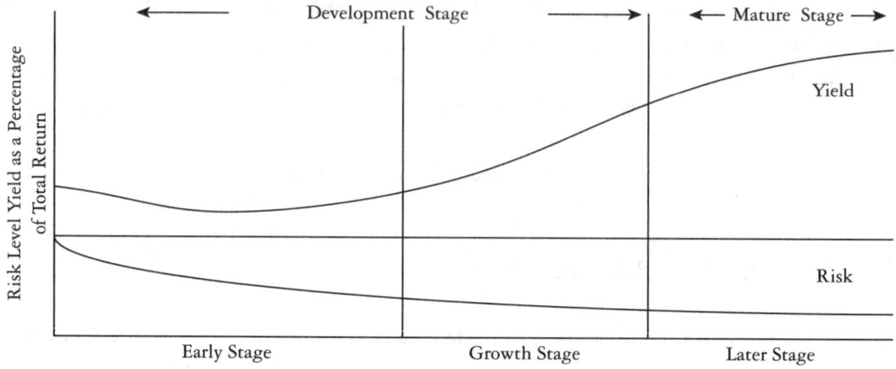

Figure 11.1 Life Cycle of Infrastructure Assets.

investment risk results in lower required returns, reflecting an enhanced infrastructure asset price (Russell Investment Management 2007).

Infrastructure life cycles broadly consist of two stages: development and mature. As an alternative, Figure 11.1 shows three stages: early, growth, and mature. Infrastructure under construction or newly built is classified into the early stage, which is characterized by high risk due to unproven demand. This unproven demand has seen the Cross City Tunnel in Sydney that opened in 2005 never reach the levels forecast for its traffic target. In December 2006, the toll way was insolvent with debts of more than A$500 million. However, early stage infrastructure also has the most potential for capital gains. The second stage is growth, which is characterized by decreasing investment risk as well as increasing yield. This stage includes expansion and potential infrastructure projects. The last stage of the infrastructure asset life cycle is the mature stage. In this stage, established usage drives stable risk and predictable income. This stage includes established transportation facilities, utilities, and regulated infrastructure assets.

Economic and political risks vary from region to region. The geographic dimension is one of the most important criteria for selecting infrastructure assets. Infrastructure assets can be classified by the maturity of the market. The maturity of infrastructure markets is divided into three levels: emerging, maturing, and mature. The classification is by terms of legal regime for private ownership of infrastructure and the number and value of deals (RREEF 2006a). Australia is the most mature infrastructure market, followed by the United Kingdom and the United States. These three countries represent mature infrastructure investment markets. Almost all remaining developed countries are classified into maturing infrastructure markets. The majority of developing countries including most of Asia except Japan, Latin America, and some countries of the European Union (EU) are classified as emerging infrastructure markets.

Characteristics of Infrastructure Investment

Infrastructure investments have many characteristics (RREEF 2005; UBS 2006a; Hopkins 2007), including:

- high entry barriers;
- monopoly characteristics;
- long duration on operating concessions (up to 99-year leases);
- large investment scale;
- inelastic demand;
- stable, tax effective and predictable cash flows via government regulation and long-term contracts; normally inflation-indexed;
- low volatility of cash flows;
- low correlation with major asset classes;
- low operating cost relative to fixed cost;
- attractive returns via long-term income streams and capital growth;
- high degree of regulatory control;
- track record of public-private partnership performance;
- hybrid performance regarding income and capital returns; and
- support for the community.

These infrastructure characteristics effectively match the long-term liabilities of pension funds (Rakowski 2003; RREEF 2005). Many consider up to 10 percent exposure to infrastructure in a balanced fund as appropriate (Liem and Timotijevic 2005; Blundell 2005, 2006; Macquarie 2006).

Infrastructure includes the following investment risk factors (Liem and Timotijevic 2005; RREEF 2005; McCarthy 2006; Hopkins 2007):

- complex and highly geared structures (up to 90 percent loan-to-value ratio);
- impact of increasing interest rates on debt servicing;
- high management fees;
- increasing investor competition;
- over-valuation of assets;
- mature versus developing infrastructure assets;
- potential misalignment of interests via some integrated investment platforms;
- uncertainty of patronage estimates (e.g., toll roads); and
- changing regulatory, legal, and environmental context.

Institutional investors such as pension funds should consider these risk factors when investing in infrastructure.

Investing in Infrastructure

The investment options for infrastructure investing include direct investment, an unlisted infrastructure fund, a listed infrastructure company or fund, and an unlisted infrastructure securities fund. The term "private infrastructure" is also popular and often used interchangeably with direct investments or unlisted investments. Infrastructure bonds are another choice for the investor. The vehicle is through public private partnership (PPP) or private finance initiative (PFI) bonds.

Direct infrastructure investment has distinctive features as compared with indirect investment (Russell 2012). For example, direct infrastructure investment provides institutional investors a potential for constructing a portfolio that better matches the assets and liability structure, accessing a board seat, and adding to control and influence over investment. On the other hand, the disadvantages of direct infrastructure include requiring appropriate government structures, having a large allocation, experiencing single asset risk, handling the substantial demands of managing direct investment, and possibility of negative publicity associated with the investment. Typically, pension funds use unlisted infrastructure funds to obtain exposure to a range of local and global projects. Retail investors tend to use listed infrastructure companies or funds (RREEF 2005; Liem and Timotijevic 2005; McCarthy 2006).

Infrastructure Versus Property

Given infrastructure's enhanced investment stature, the key issue is whether infrastructure is considered as a separate asset class or treated as a subsector within a property portfolio. The consensus industry view is that infrastructure should be treated as a separate asset class with its own allocation in a portfolio (Larsen 2005; RREEF 2005; Blundell 2005, 2006; Hopkins 2007). Generally, property and infrastructure are classified into two separate asset groups, but some sectors such as senior housing, education facilities, correctional facilities, and parking lots are characterized both as property and infrastructure (Newell and Peng 2006; ING 2008). Figure 11.2 positions infrastructure relative to the risk and return characteristics of the other major asset classes including property (RREEF 2005; Colonial First State Asset Management 2007; Inderst 2010; J. P. Morgan Asset Management 2010).

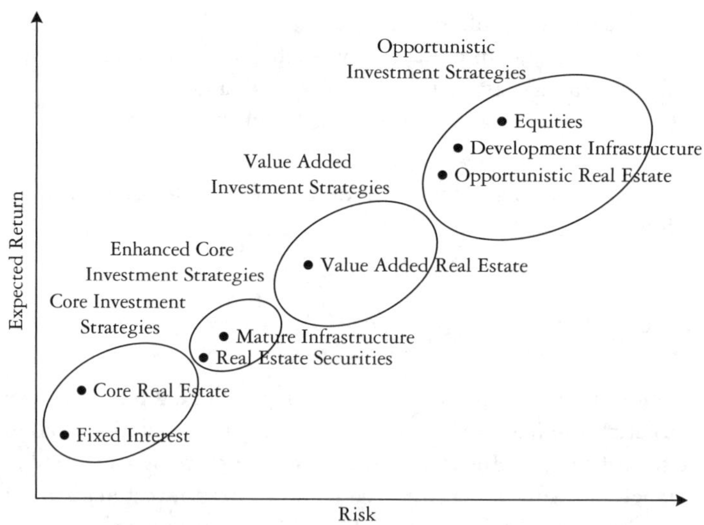

Figure 11.2 Risk and Return Characteristics of the Major Asset Classes.

The similarities between infrastructure and property include predictable cash flows, high yields, competition for quality assets, limited liquidity, and valuation-based performance. Yet, the differences between infrastructure and property are considerable. They include different structures and investment packaging, ownership of the property asset versus the right to operate the infrastructure asset, and the larger investment scale for infrastructure. As Table 11.3 shows, RREEF (2005) summarizes the similar and different factors of infrastructure investment.

Infrastructure and property are also expected to behave differently, bringing potential diversification benefits to a mixed-asset portfolio. In particular, Peng and Newell

Table 11.3 **A Comparison of Infrastructure and Property Investment**

Characteristic	*Institutional Property*	*Infrastructure Investments*
Typical investment size	> \$50 million per asset	> \$200 million per asset
Nature of asset	Physical property	Typically an operating company with right to provide service
Competition	High for quality assets	High for quality assets
Asset availability	Moderate to deep volumes in most markets	Asset scarcity, many in unique, monopoly situations
Acquisition dynamic	Competitive tenders, environmental and social issues common	Competitive tenders, regulatory, environmental, social, and political issues
Liquidity	Moderate in most sectors	Low
Income	Mixture of fixed and variable; interest rate and sector dependent	Once assets mature, very stable, inflation/GDP growth relative. Higher than bonds and core real estate
Growth	Dependent upon asset characteristics; modest to high	Dependent upon asset life stage: modest (mature) to high (development)
Volatility	Moderate (value added) to low (core)	Moderate (development) to low (mature)
Total return	Core: ≈ 7–9 percent	Mature portfolio: ≈ 7–10 percent
expectation	Value added: ≈ 12–18 percent Opportunity: 18 + percent	Development portfolio: ≈ 10–15 percent

Note: This table summarizes the similar and different factors between institutional property investment and infrastructure investment. Infrastructure investment is characterized by larger investment scale and different business models compared to property investment.

Source: Authors' compilation from RREEF 2005.

(2007) find unlisted infrastructure in Australia over 1995–2006 performed strongly with an annual return of 14.1 percent as compared to property at 10.9 percent annually. Infrastructure has a higher risk, with a standard deviation of 5.83 percent annually compared with 1.46 percent for property. Their evidence shows unlisted infrastructure as the second-best performing asset on a risk-adjusted basis over this 11-year period. Unlisted infrastructure is not significantly correlated with direct property ($r = 0.26$), stocks ($r = 0.06$), Australian REITs ($r = 0.24$), or bonds ($r = 0.17$). The correlation coefficient between listed and unlisted infrastructure is 0.36. Listed infrastructure is also not significantly correlated with stocks ($r = 0.21$). This reinforces the performance differences and portfolio diversification benefits of infrastructure with property and in a mixed-asset portfolio.

Importance of Infrastructure

Previous sections have discussed the investment characteristics and vehicles of infrastructure investment. This section presents the infrastructure market for Australia, the United States, and Europe and reviews the development of private investment.

SIGNIFICANCE OF AUSTRALIAN INFRASTRUCTURE

Table 11.4 gives a general social, economic, and financial profile of Australia in 2012. Analysts estimate that 89 percent of the Australian population lives in major urban

Table 11.4 **Infrastructure Profile: Australia, 2012**

Infrastructure competitiveness: #18 globally (Hong Kong #1, Singapore #2, and Germany #3)
Quality of overall infrastructure: #36
Quality of roads: #36
Quality of railroads: #28
Quality of air transport: #29
Quality of ports: #38
Quality of electricity systems: #27
Quality of telecommunication systems: #17
Roadways: 823,217 km
Railways: 38,445 km
Waterways: 2,000 km
Ports: 60
Communications networks: 10.6 million phones and 24.5 million mobile phones
Pipelines: gas (27,900 km), oil (3257 km), LPG (240 km)

Sources: Authors' compilation from Central Intelligence Agency 2013 and World Economic Forum 2012.

areas. The population is projected to increase by 64 percent to 35 million by 2030. Effective infrastructure is essential to facilitate this development and population growth. Nevertheless, Australia faced a shortage of infrastructure investment in the 1980s and 1990s. Since the 2000s, the Australian government increased public spending on infrastructure to deal with the strong demand generated by population and economic growth (OECD 2011).

Effective infrastructure is also an important ingredient for the commercial property markets in Australia. Jones Lang LaSalle, a real estate brokerage firm, produces the Global Real Estate Transparency Index (GRETI). The index weights information flows, fair and consistent application of real estate laws, and debt regulation. In 2012 Australia ranked third, behind only the United States and the United Kingdom. Australia provides major financial services centers at a regional, Asia-Pacific, and international level including at Sydney. Staying globally competitive has seen the development of a strategic blueprint for Australia's future infrastructure needs (Infrastructure Australia 2010).

Australia has a long track record of investment covering both listed and unlisted infrastructure. Currently, the Australian Securities Exchange lists 15 infrastructure funds, accounting for more than $38 billion in market capitalization (cap). Unlisted infrastructure investment has seen involvement across the various subsectors. Major institutional investors in Australia include AMP, Macquarie, Colonial First State, and Hastings. The subsectors in these unlisted infrastructure fund portfolios include airports, toll roads, railways, seaports, telecommunications, water, and electricity and gas transmission and generation. These diversified portfolios include local infrastructure investments. They also include overseas investments in mature markets in the United States and Europe and in emerging markets such as India and Africa.

Key motivating factors for investing in infrastructure are long duration, asset and liability matching, and predictable and stable cash flows. Risk factors in infrastructure investment include uncertainty of government policy, overvaluation, lack of quality assets, uncertainty of patronage estimates, and competition for investments (Newell and Peng 2008c).

Defined benefit accounts in Australia had more than $1.5 trillion in total assets in December 2012 (Australian Prudential Regulatory Authority (APRA) 2013). Various superannuation funds have major exposure to infrastructure in their portfolios through listed, unlisted, and co-investment vehicles. In terms of total assets and infrastructure, respectively, these funds include: AustralianSuper (A$26 billion, 14 percent); UniSuper (A$36 billion, 4 percent); Telstra (A$12 billion, 5 percent); MTAA (A$6 billion, 16 percent); REST (A$22 billion, 5 percent (balanced fund)), and HESTA (A$20 billion, 13 percent (balanced fund)).

Infrastructure is typically given a separate asset allocation as distinct from property (Newell 2008) and classified as an alternative asset class along with private equity.

INFRASTRUCTURE IN THE UNITED STATES

Compared to Europe and Australia, the United States does not have a strong history of infrastructure privatization. The United States currently allocates less than 4 percent of GDP to infrastructure, as compared with 8 percent in 1970 (OECD 2006). Ongoing budgetary constraints exist at all levels of the U.S. government. The historic

Table 11.5 **Infrastructure Profile: United States, 2012**

Infrastructure competitiveness: #14 globally
Quality of overall infrastructure: #25
Quality of roads: #20
Quality of railroads: #18
Quality of air transport: #30
Quality of ports: #19
Quality of electricity systems: #33
Quality of telecommunication systems: #15
Roadways: 6,506,204 km
Railways: 224,792 km
Waterways: 41,009 km
Ports: 393
Communications networks: 146 million phones and 290.3 million mobile phones
Pipelines: gas (548,665 km), oil (244,620 km)

Sources: Authors' compilation from Central Intelligence Agency 2013 and World Economic Federation 2012.

under-investment in infrastructure at national and regional levels results in a large investment gap, with $3.6 trillion needed to bring U.S. infrastructure to acceptable levels (American Society of Civil Engineers 2013). As Table 11.5 shows, the United States ranks in a global context as only the fourteenth best in terms of infrastructure quality (World Economic Forum 2012).

Many view toll roads as the most likely infrastructure sector for privatization (RREEF 2006b; UBS 2006c). The United States has more than 120 existing toll roads. Successful examples of toll road privatization include the Chicago Skyway, Indiana Tollway, SH130, South Bay Expressway, Pocahontas Parkway, and Dulles Greenway, valued at more than $8.8 billion in total. These toll road privatizations involve global infrastructure investors such as Macquarie Infrastructure Group, Cintra, and Transurban. Investors often receive 99-year lease terms. These global toll road investors have experience in countries with a history of privatization including Spain, France, Germany, Italy, and Australia. Municipal bonds are the traditional source of toll road funding in the United States. Potential toll road extensions including high occupancy toll (HOT) lanes provide potential opportunities for as much $225 billion in private toll road infrastructure funding. Such projects include the Garden State Turnpike, New Jersey Turnpike, New York State Thruway, Ohio Turnpike, and LBJ Freeway. The privatization of such infrastructure has constraints. Only 25 states have the necessary transportation legislative authority to offer public-private partnerships (PPPs) including Florida, Texas, and Virginia (OECD 2011).

The following are major listed infrastructure companies and funds in the United States.

- American Tower: own, lease, and manage over 45,000 communication sites and towers in the United States and internationally.
- Crown Castle International: own, lease, and manage over 30,000 communication towers in the United States including Puerto Rico, Australia; typically 5–10 year leases.
- SBA Communications: site lease and site development for more than 16,500 communication towers in the United States, Canada, and Central and South America.
- Macquarie Infrastructure Group: diversified infrastructure, including airport services, airport parking, energy, and gas production and distribution.

Another example of privatization of U.S. infrastructure includes the Indianapolis airport, which has complete third-party management. Other firms manage the retail stores at major international airports including Pittsburgh, Boston Logan, and Baltimore/Washington (RREEF 2006b). Other countries including Australia, New Zealand, the United Kingdom, Canada, and China have privatized their airports. Airport privatization has been slow to develop in the United States even though Congress established the Federal Aviation Administration's Airport Privatization Pilot Program in 1997. Although under national control in other countries, airports are typically operated locally in the United States. Besides, airlines decisively influence the major aspects of airport development and management. These different conditions from other countries suggest the United States may have difficulty following the apparent lead of other countries in airport privatization (De Neufville 1999; Edwards 2009).

Several global infrastructure investors are potentially seeking full U.S. stock market listing to reduce local concerns over foreign ownership of infrastructure. Some U.S. and international infrastructure funds are available from Goldman Sachs, Credit Suisse/GE, and Carlyle (UBS 2006c). Analysts expect future opportunities in the United States for private infrastructure investors, particularly with the ongoing growth in pension funds and successful examples of PPPs.

INFRASTRUCTURE IN EUROPE

Despite the high quality of European infrastructure as shown in Table 11.6, government spending on infrastructure in Europe has declined. In 2006, infrastructure spending as a percentage of GDP was 3 percent in the United Kingdom and Germany and 6 percent in France. These proportions are considerably below those in 1970: 12 percent in the United Kingdom and 9 percent in France (Mercer 2005; Macquarie 2006). The EU may need to invest between €1.5 trillion and €2 trillion in infrastructure by 2020. Preliminary estimates suggest that implementing the Trans-European Transport Network (TEN-T) program required €500 billion. The member states need to allocate €1.1 trillion to the energy sector including €500 billion to upgrade and build new generation capacity, €400 billion on distribution networks and smart grids, and €200 billion to transmission networks and storages (OECD 2011).

The scale of the European infrastructure market currently is similar to the commercial property market at 30–40 percent of European equity and bond markets (Hobbs 2007). Analysts estimate the total European infrastructure market to be about €4.5

Table 11.6 **European Infrastructure Quality and Competitiveness**

	Infrastructure Quality					*Competitiveness*	
Country	*Overall*	*Road*	*Air transport*	*Port*	*Railroad*	*Infrastructure*	*Business*
United Kingdom	24	24	22	12	16	6	24
Netherlands	10	11	4	1	9	7	10
Sweden	19	25	20	11	21	19	6
France	5	1	10	26	4	4	23
Finland	3	9	11	7	6	23	4
Germany	9	10	7	9	7	3	11
Denmark	13	19	19	13	19	16	16
Austria	8	7	31	44	12	15	20
Ireland	37	31	32	30	31	25	35
Belgium	17	13	14	6	13	21	22
Spain	18	31	17	14	8	10	36
Switzerland	1	6	5	37	1	5	2
Norway	39	84	13	25	47	27	9
Italy	82	57	67	89	40	28	51
Portugal	11	4	35	40	26	24	40
Czech Republic	28	77	21	54	23	38	44
Hungary	51	69	91	83	42	50	55
Poland	79	124	105	108	77	73	61
Slovak Republic	70	38	124	82	25	56	62
Greece	61	71	45	66	69	43	98
Russia	101	136	104	93	30	47	53
Slovenia	30	38	72	33	54	35	39
Turkey	34	43	36	63	53	51	57
Romania	132	142	121	137	83	97	90

Source: Authors' compilation from World Economic Forum 2012.

trillion, with non-government ownership at 30 percent or €1.4 trillion. Listed companies hold the majority of this €1.4 trillion private infrastructure market.

The proportions of private infrastructure in Europe by market size are: Germany (14 percent), the Czech Republic, Hungary, Poland, and Slovakia or CE4 (13 percent), France (12 percent), Spain (10 percent), the United Kingdom (9 percent), and Italy (8 percent). The major areas for private infrastructure in Europe are railways (20 percent), roads (20 percent), airports (4 percent), and ports (3 percent). Within utilities, infrastructure includes electricity (23 percent), water and sewerage (13 percent), gas (13 percent), and oil (4 percent) (Hobbs 2007).

European countries are classified for their mature stage infrastructure investment attractiveness as:

- highly attractive (the United Kingdom, France, Germany, Spain, and Italy);
- attractive (Portugal, Austria, the Netherlands, Belgium, and Nordic countries);
- opportunistic (Greece, Poland, Czech Republic, and Slovakia); and
- limited (Baltics) (RREEF 2006b).

Roads and airports are the dominant infrastructure sectors in Europe for private involvement and this activity has increased substantially. Table 11.7 shows the major European listed infrastructure companies and funds. Many of these European infrastructure companies are among the largest in the world including Vinci, Abertis Infraestructuras, Autostrade, and Grupo Ferrovial. These firms diversify by having European and international infrastructure portfolios.

Table 11.7 **Leading European Listed Infrastructure Companies/Funds**

Company/Fund	*Sector*[a]	*Country*[b]
Vinci	Toll roads	France
Abertis Infrastructuras	Toll roads	Spain
Autostrade	Toll roads	Italy
Grupo Ferrovial	Toll roads	Spain
Brisa-Auto Estradas de Portugal	Toll roads	Portugal
Eutelsat	Communications	France
Fraport	Airports	Germany
Societe Des Autoroutes Paris-Rhone	Toll roads	France
Cintra Concesiones de Infrts	Toll roads	Spain
Inmarsat	Communications	UK
Forth Ports	Ports	UK
Kobenhaven Lufthave	Airports	Denmark
Autostrade Torino-Milan	Toll roads	Italy
Flughafen Wien	Airports	Austria
Unique Zurich Airport	Airports	Switzerland
SIAS	Toll roads	Italy
Brisa Auto Estradas	Toll roads	Portugal
Europistas CESA	Toll roads	Spain
Digital Multimedia Tech.	Communications	Italy
SAVE	Airports	Italy

[a] Sector represents major infrastructure activity.

[b] Country represents country of listing; some have international portfolios.

Source: Newell and Peng 2008b.

The importance of these European infrastructure companies in the toll road sector is evident, particularly in Spain, Germany, Portugal, Italy, and France. The more recent involvement in the airport sector is apparent. European governments are looking at other ways to reduce public debt since the crisis in 2010. This opens further potential opportunities for investors to access infrastructure portfolios (Colonial First State Global Asset Management 2012). Over 10 infrastructure assets of rail, electricity, airport, port, water, and gas sectors expect to be progressively readied for sale from 2011 to 2015.

Global Infrastructure Performance Indexes

The four main global listed infrastructure performance series are the: (1) UBS Global Infrastructure and Utilities Index, (2) Macquarie Global Infrastructure Index, (3) S&P Global Infrastructure Index, and (4) Dow Jones Brookfield Global Infrastructure Index.

UBS GLOBAL INFRASTRUCTURE AND UTILITY INDEX

Established in 2006, the UBS Global Infrastructure and Utilities Index tracks global infrastructure and utilities performance since 1990 (UBS 2006a). The 83 indexes cover a range of sub-indexes for regions, countries, subsectors, region by subsector, and country by subsector. Start dates for these various series range from January 1990 to December 1999. Specific infrastructure subsector series include toll roads, airports, communications, ports, and diversified infrastructure.

As of January 2006, the UBS Global Infrastructure and Utilities indexes comprised 242 companies and funds, with a total market cap of $1,321 billion. The UBS index includes 242 infrastructure and utilities companies and funds. Global utilities with 93.3 percent of the market cap dominate the index. Global infrastructure accounts for the remaining 6.7 percent. Europe (62 percent) is the major component in the global infrastructure series. Toll roads (50 percent) and airports (27 percent) are the major subsectors. North American utilities (47 percent) and European utilities (39 percent) constitute the major components in the global utilities series. Integrated (53 percent) and integrated regulated (29 percent) make up the major utilities subsectors.

MACQUARIE GLOBAL INFRASTRUCTURE INDEX

The equivalent Macquarie Global Infrastructure Index started in 2005 and comprises 248 global infrastructure and utilities companies with a market capitalization (cap) of $1.4 trillion in 2011; 14 subsector/regional sub-indexes are produced. The inception date of the S&P Global Infrastructure Index was July 2000. Of the 248 infrastructure and utilities companies or funds in the Macquarie index, U.S. companies or funds (38.40 percent by market cap) dominate the index, followed by the United Kingdom (7.60 percent), France (5.75 percent), Germany (5.48 percent), and Canada (5.46 percent).

S&P GLOBAL INFRASTRUCTURE INDEX

The S&P Global Infrastructure Index was announced in 2007. The S&P index consists of 75 infrastructure and utilities companies with $792 billion in market cap as of May 2011.

Of the 75 infrastructure and utilities companies in the S&P index, the transportation sector (40.7 percent) dominates, followed by utilities (38.5 percent), and energy (20.8 percent). U.S. companies (24.1 percent in country weight) are the major components in the index, with Canada (10.6 percent), France (9.3 percent), Germany (7.9 percent), Italy (7.6 percent), and Australia (7.5 percent) being the major contributors.

DOW JONES BROOKFIELD GLOBAL INFRASTRUCTURE INDEX

The Dow Jones Brookfield Global Infrastructure Index started in 2008. A total of 18 indexes are produced with a range of sub-indexes produced for regions, countries, and subsectors. The inception date for these various series is December 2002. The index comprises 121 infrastructure components. North American infrastructure companies or funds dominate the index accounting for 69.1 percent including the United States (56.3 percent) and Canada (12.8 percent), followed by the United Kingdom (8.0 percent), Australia (3.4 percent), and Spain (3.0 percent). In terms of sectors, oil, gas storage, and transportation (37.4 percent) account for the largest portion.

To trace the performance and diversification benefits of global unlisted infrastructure investment is difficult due to the lack of a reliable performance index. Previous research on regional unlisted infrastructure investment typically applied the indexes provided privately by an investment consultancy (Peng and Newell 2007; Newell, Peng, and De Francesco 2011). IPD has produced an Australian unlisted infrastructure index providing various return segmentations. In December 2012, the index comprised 15 unlisted infrastructure investment funds domiciled within Australia with A$19 billion in gross asset value (GAV).

Previous Infrastructure Research

Only limited research focuses on infrastructure as a separate asset class. Most infrastructure research concentrates on articulating its benefits and characteristics as a separate asset class (RREEF 2005; Macquarie 2006) or details on specific markets for the United States (RREEF 2006b; UBS 2006c), Europe (RREEF 2006a), and Asia (RREEF 2006c). Only limited empirical analysis assesses the risk-adjusted performance and portfolio diversification benefits of listed infrastructure in a portfolio (Liem and Timotijevic 2005; Macquarie 2006; RREEF 2006a; Peng and Newell 2007; Newell and Peng 2008a, b; Newell et al. 2011). Only Liem and Timotijevic (2005) and Peng and Newell (2007) consider unlisted infrastructure performance in an Australian investment context. Unlisted infrastructure provides returns at low risk, with substantial portfolio diversification benefits as compared with real estate and stocks (Peng and Newell 2007; Newell et al. 2011).

The Performance of Infrastructure Investment

The lack of unlisted infrastructure performance series in the United States and the United Kingdom prevents the fuller assessment of the diversification benefits of infrastructure. Most analyses assessing these diversification benefits use listed or modified listed infrastructure series. A review of long-term infrastructure investment performance draws from Australian experience, risk-adjusted and with portfolio diversification benefits. This section presents the impact of the global financial crisis (GFC) on infrastructure investment performance.

RISK-ADJUSTED RETURNS

Newell et al. (2011) evaluate Australian infrastructure investment performance. As Table 11.8 shows, the authors analyze listed and unlisted infrastructure performance with other major asset classes over Q3:1995–Q2:2009. The annual returns of listed (16.74 percent) and unlisted infrastructure (14.07 percent) are greater than global listed infrastructure (9.07 percent), direct property (10.56 percent), and Australian Real Estate Investment Trusts (A-REITs) (4.85 percent), as well as stocks (9.11 percent). The annual standard deviation for unlisted infrastructure (6.27 percent) is below that for listed infrastructure (24.64 percent), but exceeds that for direct property (3.00 percent). This evidence reflects the unlisted infrastructure and direct property series being valuation-based. As Figure 11.1 shows, different stages of infrastructure of mature, growth, and developing display higher risk compared with institutional-grade assets comprising the Australian direct property index.

On a risk-adjusted basis, only direct property (Sharpe ratio = 1.63) outperforms unlisted infrastructure (Sharpe ratio = 1.34), exceeding listed and global listed infrastructure performance. This result confirms the substantial risk-adjusted performance of unlisted infrastructure over this period.

An equivalent analysis occurs for U.S. and European listed infrastructure, as well as for China and India (Newell and Peng 2008a, b; Newell et al. 2009; Singhal, Newell, and Nguyen 2011). Over the 2000–2006 period, European infrastructure with an annual average return of 20.9 percent and Sharpe ratio of 1.26 outperforms European stocks. The return on stocks is 5.81 percent annually with a Sharpe ratio of 0.17, so infrastructure outperforms on both an absolute and risk-adjusted basis. Similar results apply to infrastructure performance in China and India. U.S. infrastructure presents an opposite

Table 11.8 **Australian Infrastructure Performance Analysis, Q3:1995–Q2:2009**

	Average Annual Return (%)	*Annual Risk (%)*	*Sharpe Ratio*[a]
Listed infrastructure	16.74	24.64	0.45 (3)
Unlisted infrastructure	14.07	6.27	1.34 (2)
Global infrastructure	9.07	17.55	0.19 (6)
Direct property	10.56	3.00	1.63 (1)
A-REITs	4.85	17.47	−0.05 (7)
Stocks	9.11	13.85	0.25 (5)
Bonds	7.04	4.64	0.30 (4)

[a] Risk-adjusted rank given in brackets.

Source: Newell et al. 2011.

result over the same period, reflecting the maturity and risk in different markets. This outperformance in most regions reflects substantial infrastructure growth, large investment by institutional investors, and increased maturity in the private market.

PORTFOLIO DIVERSIFICATION

To assess the portfolio diversification benefits of Australian infrastructure, Table 11.9 presents the inter-asset correlation matrix over Q3:1995–Q2:2009. Infrastructure sectors provide portfolio diversification benefits across all other asset classes, particularly those that are unlisted. This includes listed infrastructure ($r = 0.37$), global listed infrastructure ($r = 0.35$), direct property ($r = 0.23$), and stocks ($r = 0.15$). Unlisted and listed infrastructure ($r = 0.37$) offer more diversification benefit than direct property and A-REITs ($r = 0.46$). With financial assets, unlisted infrastructure with stocks ($r = 0.15$) provides more diversification benefits than direct property with stocks ($r = 0.38$). Unlisted infrastructure provides diversification benefits with bonds ($r = 0.06$). Listed infrastructure provides diversification benefits with stocks ($r = 0.48$) and bonds ($r = 0.09$), but not as significant as unlisted infrastructure.

Infrastructure sectors providing diversification benefits also apply to the infrastructure investment in other countries. Between 2000 and 2006, European infrastructure provides substantial diversification benefits with European stocks ($r = 0.60$). The result is similar in China where the infrastructure correlation with stocks is also 0.6 during the 1995–2006 period. India and U.S. infrastructure show less diversification benefits with stocks ($r = 0.70$ and $r = 0.95$, respectively). However, U.S. infrastructure provides large diversification benefits as compared with the property equivalents.

Table 11.9 **Australian Infrastructure Inter-asset Correlation Matrix, Q3:1995–Q2:2009**

	Infrastructure						
	Listed	*Unlisted*	*Global Listed*	*Direct Property*	*A-REITs*	*Stocks*	*Bonds*
Listed infrastructure	1.00						
Unlisted infrastructure	0.37*	1.00					
Global listed infrastructure	0.54*	0.35*	1.00				
Direct property	0.26	0.30*	0.39*	1.00			
A-REITs	0.57*	0.23	0.51*	0.46*	1.00		
Stocks	0.48*	0.15	0.61*	0.38*	0.57*	1.00	
Bonds	0.09	0.06	–0.17	–0.09	–0.02	–0.41*	1.00

Note: This table presents the inter-asset correlation matrix, which shows low correlations between Australian infrastructure sectors and other major asset classes. This indicates the portfolio diversification benefits provided by infrastructure sectors.

* Significant correlation ($p < 0.05$)

Source: Newell et al. 2011.

Overall, these results highlight the portfolio diversification benefits of infrastructure in a mixed-asset portfolio. In the Australian experience, the diversification benefits by unlisted infrastructure are more significant than those provided by listed infrastructure and direct property. This further reinforces the position of many pension funds for viewing infrastructure as a separate asset allocation in their alternate assets' portfolio.

IMPACT OF THE GFC ON UNLISTED INFRASTRUCTURE

Table 11.10 presents the impact of the GFC on infrastructure risk-adjusted performance over Q2:2007–Q2:2009. The impact of the GFC is evident, particularly across the listed sectors. Unlisted infrastructure (8.16 percent annually) is clearly the best performing asset class, along with direct property (3.30 percent annually). Both listed infrastructure sectors, namely, A-REITs and stocks, deliver negative returns over this volatile period. Although potential valuation lag issues are present for both unlisted infrastructure and direct property performance, they outperform the various listed sectors in the GFC.

Unlisted infrastructure has a similar standard deviation during the GFC of 6.65 percent annually to the 6.27 percent over Q3:1995–Q2:2009. This contrasts with the large increase in risk for global listed infrastructure (23.51 percent versus 17.55 percent), stocks (21.46 percent versus 13.85 percent), and A-REITs (31.64 percent versus 13.85 percent). On a risk-adjusted basis, unlisted infrastructure is the best-performing asset class during the GFC (Sharpe ratio = 0.32). Direct property and the various listed sectors deliver negative Sharpe ratios by underperforming the risk-free rate. This evidence highlights the robustness of unlisted infrastructure during the high market volatility of the GFC.

Table 11.11 presents the impact of the GFC on portfolio diversification benefits of unlisted infrastructure over Q2:2007–Q2:2009. The portfolio diversification benefits of unlisted and listed infrastructure are enhanced ($r = 0.31$ in GFC versus $r = 0.44$). The

Table 11.10 **Australian Infrastructure Performance Analysis, Q2:2007–Q2:2009**

	Average Annual Return (%)	*Annual Risk (%)*	*Sharpe Ratio*[a]
Listed infrastructure	–23.86	22.97	–1.30 (6)
Unlisted infrastructure	8.16	6.65	0.32 (1)
Global infrastructure	–10.51	23.51	–0.70 (4)
Direct property	3.30	5.80	–0.47 (3)
A-REITs	–35.75	31.64	–1.32 (7)
Stocks	–13.21	21.46	–0.90 (5)
Bonds	7.06	6.92	0.15 (2)

Note: This table presents the impact of the GFC on Australian infrastructure risk-adjusted performance. Over Q2:2007–Q2:2009, unlisted infrastructure outperformed other major asset classes.

[a] Risk-adjusted rank given in brackets.

Source: Newell et al. 2011.

Table 11.11 **Australian Infrastructure Inter-asset Correlation Matrix, Q2:2007–Q2:2009**

	Infrastructure						
	Listed	*Unlisted*	*Global*	*Direct property*	*A-REITs*	*Stocks*	*Bonds*
Listed infrastructure	1.00						
Unlisted infrastructure	0.31	1.00					
Global listed infrastructure	0.81*	0.29	1.00				
Direct property	0.26	0.68	0.38	1.00			
A-REITs	0.84*	0.16	0.64	0.25	1.00		
Stocks	0.93*	0.24	0.79*	0.25	0.77*	1.00	
Bonds	–0.78*	–0.10	–0.69	–0.08	–0.45	–0.81*	1.00

Note: This table presents the impact of the GFC on the portfolio diversification benefits of Australian infrastructure. The portfolio diversification benefits of unlisted and listed infrastructure were enhanced during the GFC.

* Significant correlation ($p < 0.05$)

Source: Newell et al. 2011.

diversification benefit of unlisted infrastructure and stocks is stable during the GFC (r = 0.24 versus r = 0.27). In contrast, listed infrastructure with stocks shows further loss of diversification benefits during the GFC (r = 0.93 versus r = 0.77). Overall, the GFC reinforced the robustness of unlisted relative to listed infrastructure performance.

Summary and Conclusions

Institutional investors include property in their core portfolios when they seek more stable or income-oriented returns. Recent years reflect not only economic and social changes for rising interest rates and skilled labor shortages but also demographic changes.

Due to the compression of property yields, pension funds and institutional investors have moved beyond the traditional property sectors to consider higher risk alternative property-related assets such as added-value property and infrastructure. This chapter presents the general concepts of infrastructure investments including their investment characteristics, vehicles, and an overview of markets. The chapter also presents an empirical analysis of infrastructure investment regarding its performance. In recent years, infrastructure sectors show enhanced returns and reduced risk leading to greater portfolio diversification benefits with all major asset classes around the world.

Finally, infrastructure investment has potential for growth both in local and international markets, particularly as investors seek new markets for these capital inflows. With the rapidly expanding market in recent years, the strong performance and volatility of infrastructure investment has been moderate, reflecting a maturing market. Successfully participating in these infrastructure investment markets requires adequate knowledge and experience.

Discussion Questions

1. Discuss the investment characteristics of infrastructure.
2. Discuss the investment risk factors of infrastructure.
3. Explain why infrastructure should be considered as a separate asset class from property in terms of investment.
4. Identify the advantages and disadvantages of direct infrastructure investment.

References

American Society of Civil Engineers. 2013. *2013 Report Card for America's Infrastructure*. Reston, VA: ASCE.

Australian Prudential Regulatory Authority. 2013. *Statistics: Quarterly Superannuation Performance: December 2012*. Canberra: APRA.

Blundell, Lynne. 2005. "Sparking Up Change." *Property Australia* 19:9, 36–39.

Blundell, Lynne. 2006. "Infrastructure Investment: On the Up." *Property Australia* 20:9, 20–22.

Central Intelligence Agency. 2013. *World Factbook 2013*. Washington, DC: CIA.

Colonial First State Global Asset Management. 2007. *Property Research Note: Risk-Reward Space and Australian Property Investment*. Sydney: CFSGAM.

Colonial First State Global Asset Management. 2012. *European Infrastructure: Themes and Opportunities*. Sydney: CFSGAM.

DB RREEF. 2005. *The Issues in Managing a Real Estate Portfolio*. Sydney: DB RREEF.

De Neufville, Richard. 1999. "Airport Privatization Issues for the United States." Working Paper, Massachusetts Institute of Technology.

Edwards, Chris. 2009. *Privatization*. Washington, DC: CATO Institute.

Hobbs, Peter. 2007. "Infrastructure Investing." *Journal of the Investment Property Forum* 6, 10–11.

Hopkins, Sheila. 2007. "The Structure of Infrastructure." *Institutional Real Estate Letter Europe* 1:3, 1–10.

Inderst, Georg. 2010. "Infrastructure as an Asset Class." *EIB Papers* 15:1, 70–104.

Infrastructure Australia. 2010. *State of Australian Cities 2010*. Canberra: Infrastructure Australia.

ING. 2008. *Global Vision*. Hague: ING Real Estate Investment Management.

Jones Lang LaSalle. 2012. *Real Estate Transparency Index*. Chicago.

J. P. Morgan Asset Management. 2010. *Infrastructure Investing: Key Benefits and Risks*. London: J. P. Morgan.

Larsen, Chris. 2005. "A Matter of Definition." *Property Australia* 19:11, 20–23.

Macquarie. 2006. *Infrastructure: The Cinderella Asset Class*. Sydney: Macquarie.

McCarthy, John. 2006. "All Aboard Europe's Infrastructure Train." *Professional Investor*, Summer, 10–13.

Mercer. 2005. *Infrastructure—Going Global and Listed. Mercer Investment Consulting*. Sydney: Mercer.

Newell, Graeme. 2008. "The Significance of Property in Superannuation Funds." *Australian and New Zealand Property Journal* 1, 670–677.

Newell, Graeme, and Hus Wen Peng. 2006. "The Significance of Emerging Property Sectors in Property Portfolios." *Pacific Rim Property Research Journal* 12:2, 177–197.

Newell, Graeme, and Hsu Wen Peng. 2008a. "The Role of US Infrastructure in Investment Portfolios." *Journal of Real Estate Portfolio Management* 14:1, 21–33.

Newell, Graeme, and Hsu Wen Pen. 2008b. "European Infrastructure Investment: A Valuable Addition to the Mixed-Asset Portfolios." London: Fibre Series, RICS.

Newell, Graeme, and Hsu Wen Peng. 2008c. "Assessing the Significance of Motivating Factors and Risk Factors in Infrastructure Funds Management." *Pacific Rim Property Research Journal* 14:4, 399–411.

Newell, Graeme, Kwong Wing Chau, and Siu Kei Wong. 2009. "The Significance and Performance of Infrastructure in China." *Journal of Property Investment and Finance* 27:2, 180–202.

Newell, Graeme, and Hsu Wen Peng, and Anthony De Francesco. 2011. "The Performance of Unlisted Infrastructure in Investment Portfolios." *Journal of Property Research* 28:1, 59–74.

OECD. 2006. *OECD Economic Outlook #80*. Paris: OECD.

OECD. 2011. *Pension Funds Investment in Infrastructure: A Survey*. Paris: OECD.

Peng, Hsu Wen, and Graeme Newell. 2007. "The Significance of Infrastructure in Investment Portfolios." *Pacific Rim Property Research Journal* 13:4, 423–450.

Rakowski, Arthur. 2003. "On the Rails." *IPE*, September, 25.

Rakowski, Arthur. 2004. "Infrastructure Investments Offer Unique Appeal." *Pensions Week*, January, 12.

RREEF. 2005. *Understanding Infrastructure*. London: RREEF.

RREEF. 2006a. *European Infrastructure Market: Explaining Current Trends in a Changing Market*. London: RREEF.

RREEF. 2006b. *Opportunities in Private Infrastructure Investment in the US*. San Francisco: RREEF.

RREEF. 2006c. *Asian Infrastructure Markets: Explaining Current Trends in a Changing Market*. London: RREEF.

Russell Investment Management. 2007. *Infrastructure: A Public Good for Private Investment*. London: Russell Investment Management.

Russell Investment Management. 2012. *Australians and Infrastructure Investment*. Sydney: Russell Investment Management.

Singhal, Shaleen, Graeme Newell, and Thi Kim Nguyen. 2011. "The Significance and Performance of Infrastructure in India." *Journal of Property Research* 28:1, 15–34.

UBS. 2006a. *S&P Calculated Benchmark for Global Infrastructure & Utilities*. Sydney: UBS.

UBS. 2006b *Asset Bubble, Structural Change or Fundamental Re-Rating?* London: UBS.

UBS. 2006c. *Toll Road Opportunities in the US*. Sydney: UBS.

World Bank. 2006. *Connecting East Asia: New Framework for Infrastructure*. Washington, DC: World Bank.

World Economic Forum. 2012. *The Global Competitiveness Report 2012–2013*. Geneva: World Economic Forum.

Part Three

AGENCY, SUSTAINABILITY, AND REGULATION

12

Appraisal and Valuation

JOHN A. KILPATRICK
Managing Director, Greenfield Advisors

Introduction

According to the Securities Industry and Financial Markets Association (2013), as of the first quarter 2013, outstanding U.S. residential mortgages totaled $13.1 trillion, down from $14.8 trillion in 2008. More than half of this amount or about $8.6 trillion was in residential mortgage-backed securities (RMBS), with new issuances topping $2 trillion in 2012.

An *RMBS* consists of many small, individual loans with diverse maturities and interest rates. A *mortgage* is any promissory note secured by residential real estate. The document pledging the real property as collateral may be a mortgage or deed of trust depending on state laws.

In the United States, the typical mortgage is issued for 30 years, with fixed payments and complete amortization of principal over the life of the loan, and a fixed interest rate or varying via a formula typically tied to LIBOR or some other common index. Conventional residential mortgages in the United States do not contain a prepayment penalty. In the absence of penalties, borrowers can refinance when interest rates fall with low cost. These arrangements lead to embedded assumptions about prepayment of mortgages and related securities, including those in the Public Securities Association (PSA) standard prepayment model, The proportion pre-paid each month rises by 0.2 percentage points per month for the first 30 months and then remains at 6 percent per month for the duration of the mortgage pool. In practice, any of the features can vary widely. A major function of the securitization process is to provide some level of standardization to the anticipated cash flows.

A critical RMBS feature is the quality level of the underlying mortgages, which dictates the credit rating and hence the pricing of tranches. Two pricing factors derive directly from the appraisal process: (1) the quality of the underlying collateral and (2) the loan-to-value (LTV) ratio. Both the aggregate and individual LTV ratios influence the rating and hence the price of the RMBS. For example, a typical representation or certification made for an RMBS may state that the average LTV ratio for the pool of mortgages is 80 percent, and none of the individual mortgages exceeds 100 percent. Decreasing LTV ratios have direct and material effects on default rates. As Hatchondo, Martinez, and Sanchez (2011) show, increasing down payments from 15 to 25 percent results in halving the default rate. Noordewier, Harrison, and Ramagopal (2001), Chiang, Liu, and Chow (2002), and Qi and Yang (2009) provide similar results on down payments and reduced default. Hence, both the collective LTV of the security and the individual LTVs of the constituent mortgages are important determinants of RMBS pricing.

Ben-Shahar (2008) shows the LTV ratio is the most important determinant of default risk. According to Chomsisengphet and Pennington-Cross (2006), lenders fail to trade-off LTV ratios and the credit score. During the run-up to the recession, the lowest LTV ratios were for borrowers in the highest category of credit score and for the lowest category of credit score (FICO < 500). LTV ratios trended slightly upward during the period leading up to the recession.

The appraisal describes the security for the bondholder in the event a mortgage defaults. Unlike corporate bonds, an RMBS rarely defaults in its entirety. Some level of default is assumed in the individual mortgages and the security is priced accordingly. If the appraisals are systematically inaccurate, the anticipated ex post settling up may not occur in the expected fashion and the market for RMBS may falter. If the appraisals are unreliable and expected to be inaccurate, the security will be down-rated and priced accordingly. Krainer (2001) finds that default is likelier under a high-LTV mortgage, implying the lender should seek a higher yield to compensate for the higher default risk.

Defaults and foreclosures are more likely to happen in down markets when, as Krainer (2001) notes, residential real estate liquidity is restricted. Noordewier et al. (2001) find a direct relationship between appraisal uncertainty and the likelihood of default. Hence, a high degree of credibility in the appraisal process is key, both to the pricing of each specific security as well as the marketability of future securities.

This chapter focuses primarily on the U.S. market. However, valuation methods are global, albeit with subtle differences that will be explored. The remainder of this chapter examines three issues. The first issue involves the regulatory environment governing mortgage loan appraisals, with a particular emphasis on the Financial Institutions Reform, Recovery, and Enforcement Act of 1989 (FIRREA). Subsequent legal references are to sections of the legislation. Congress enacted FIRREA after the collapse of the real estate market in the late 1980s, partly attributable to tightening in the 1986 Tax Reform Act of previously favorable provisions favoring the property market. These provisions included accelerated depreciation and deductibility of unlimited real estate losses against other income. The resulting overbuilding led to foreclosures and failures of lenders. Some contended that the crisis and failure were attributable to over-valuation of properties by loose or inconsistent appraisal. Tightening regulation of valuation and requiring a formal licensing of appraisers would prevent future real estate downturns. The second issue is the methodological basis for the appraisal process, focusing on the evolution of the body of knowledge. The third is the current state of the profession, examining moves to integrate across global boundaries.

History of the Appraisal Profession in the United States

During the 1980s, in response to the impending savings and loan crisis, the governing appraisal bodies and the system for administering appraisal standards were overhauled. In 1986, the leading appraisal organizations in the United States and Canada formed the Ad Hoc Committee on the Uniform Standards of Professional Appraisal Practice (USPAP). This joint task force established a set of minimum industry standards that ultimately became those used and updated biennially. The Committee established The Appraisal Foundation (TAF), which gave rise to the Appraisal Standards Board (ASB), to implement these standards. The first version of USPAP went into effect on January 30, 1989, and has remained the standard of generally accepted professional appraisal practice (The Appraisal Foundation 2013c). The Appraisal Foundation develops and advocates professional appraisal standards with governing bodies at the state and federal level, users in related industries, and the public. It oversees the activities of its boards and advisory councils: the Appraisal Practices Board (APB), the Appraisal Standards Board (ASB), and the Appraisal Qualifications Board (AQB). USPAP promotes and maintains public trust in appraisal by establishing minimum standard requirements for the profession. Every state has adopted these procedures.

Title XI of FIRREA was enacted to protect both the public and financial institutions with a uniform set of appraisal standards as well as to expand oversight from governing bodies. It provides that "real estate appraisals utilized in connection with federally related transactions [be] performed in writing, in accordance with uniform standards, by individuals whose competency has been demonstrated and whose professional conduct will be subject to effective supervision" (12 U.S.C. § 3331). Congress does not directly interfere with the appraiser licensing bodies of individual states, but sections of FIRREA work together to require appraisers to meet minimum USPAP standards.

FIRREA creates a distinction between state licensed appraisers, who have met certain requirements set by the state in which they reside, and state certified appraisers (12 U.S.C. § 3345). State certified appraisers, though also receiving a license through their state authorities, are required to meet heightened standards set by FIRREA to qualify for federally related work. They are required to be familiar with and follow USPAP standards. FIRREA requires that virtually all federally related appraisal transactions be performed by state certified appraisers (12 U.S.C. § 3342).

Furthering USPAP's reach, FIRREA established the Appraisal Subcommittee (ASC) to monitor and regulate state appraisal licensure bodies. The ASC is tasked with overseeing the "practices, procedures, activities, and organizational structure of the Appraisal Foundation" (12 U.S.C. 3332).

The Appraisal Foundation helps to carry out FIRREA's goals through two main groups. The ASB is responsible for the development, interpretation, and amendment of USPAP (The Appraisal Foundation 2013b). Before 2006, the ASB promulgated USPAP updates annually. USPAP standards that were replaced in 2006 applied until January 1, 2008. USPAP has been updated biennially since 2008. The Appraisal Qualifications Board (AQB) establishes the minimum education, experience, and examination requirements for state certification under FIRREA (The Appraisal Foundation 2013a).

Although Title XI applies only to appraisers who appraise properties for federally related real estate transactions, by increasing the standards required to access this desirable work, FIRREA places a heavy burden on states to prescribe and enforce appraiser standards to ensure the eligibility of its appraisers for federal work.Through the efforts of the boards in creating a uniform standard that satisfies FIRREA, USPAP is the de facto standard for appraisers.

INTERAGENCY APPRAISAL AND EVALUATION GUIDELINES—REGULATION OF BANKS

Title XI of FIRREA standardizes the appraisal industry through the federal banking system. FIRREA calls on the federal financial regulatory agencies, the Board of Governors of the Federal Reserve System, Federal Deposit Insurance Corporation, Office of the Comptroller of the Currency, Office of Thrift Supervision, and National Credit Union Administration to prescribe standards for the performance of real estate appraisals in connection with federally related transactions. At a minimum, these agencies are to require that real estate appraisals be in writing and USPAP-compliant. Even if an appraiser were licensed in one of the few states that does not mandate USPAP compliance, the appraiser would still be required to follow USPAP for any work on behalf of a federal lender. Title XI applies to all "federally related transactions," which was broadly defined as any real estate-related transaction requiring an appraisal that a federal financial institutions regulatory agency or the Resolution Trust Corporation engages in directly, contracts for, or simply regulates (U.S. Congress, 2090, FIRREA, 12 U.S.C. § 3350(4)).

Each agency separately enacted a set of regulations in 1992, but they ultimately came together to issue the *Interagency Appraisal and Evaluation Guidelines*. These guidelines were adopted by each regulatory agency including the Board of Governors of the Federal Reserve System (1994). All the financial regulatory agencies issued the same regulations at the same time. The Federal Reserve is used only as a reference case. The 2010 amendment (Board of Governors of the Federal Reserve System 2010, 75 Fed. Reg. 77,450), in which the National Credit Union Association joined, superseded the 1994 guidelines. These interagency guidelines provide guidance to residential real estate lenders regarding appraisals, explaining in detail how FIRREA affects their relationships with appraisers.

The interagency guidelines set five minimum appraisal standards. The 2010 revision (Board of Governors of the Federal Reserve System 2010) further explained, but did not change these minimum standards. First, the appraisal must conform to USPAP and to the principles of safe and sound banking. For example, an appraiser should not hold an interest in a property being appraised. Second, the appraisal report must be written and contain sufficient information and analysis to support the institution's decision to engage in the transaction. Third, the appraisal report must analyze and report appropriate deductions and discounts for proposed construction or renovation, partially leased buildings, non-market lease terms, and tract developments with unsold units. Fourth, the appraisal must use the definition of market value as defined in the relevant agency's regulations. Fifth, a state licensed or certified appraiser must perform the appraisal.

LICENSURE

In 1991, the AQB adopted three primary real property appraiser classifications: licensed residential, certified residential, and certified general (The Appraisal Foundation 2008). The AQB adopted separate classification for trainees in 1993. Since then, the basic requirements for each classification continue: all classifications are subject to USPAP, have minimum experience and education requirements, require continuing education in the field beyond the date of licensure, and require an examination before licensure of all non-trainee classifications. Adopted for implementation starting in 1998, the AQB increased the requirements in 1994 and 2003.

The Appraisal Body of Knowledge

The regulatory process sets normative standards but is generally silent as to methods of practice. For example, the International Association of Assessing Officers publishes various standards for conducting, measuring, and reporting mass appraisal that are methodological handbooks. On behalf of the U.S. Department of Justice and the Interagency Council on Federal Land Acquisition, The Appraisal Institute (2000) issued an updated version of the *Uniform Appraisal Standards for Federal Land Acquisition*, commonly known as the "Yellow Book." The Yellow Book purports to promulgate standards but is more of a methodological treatise with a particular focus on reporting. Instead, appraisers turn to the canonical texts in basic appraisal, such as *The Appraisal of Real Estate* (The Appraisal Institute 2012), training and coursework received in the licensure process, and the methodological guidance of such government-sponsored enterprises (GSEs) as Fannie Mae and Freddie Mac.

An obvious problem in this relatively disorganized body of knowledge is the inability to adapt methodology to meet changing times and the lack of an organized, cohesive process for disseminating such changes. Little agreement exists on a single authoritative source of methodological guidance. Although many view the Appraisal Institute as the leading professional organization in the world, it counts only about one-third of appraisers in the United States in its membership. That membership generally comes from commercial appraisers or residential appraisers who tackle more complex projects. The Appraisal Foundation (2013d) has taken steps to form an Appraisal Practices Board and codify the body of knowledge. However, many consider this effort as outside of the Foundation's core mission.

Fortunately, Fannie Mae and Freddie Mac have codified methods for appraisals that support loans sold to those two organizations. They have no specific legislatively defined jurisdiction in the appraisal process, but regulate what is acceptable to be sold to them. This puts the onus for proper appraisal methodology on the lenders and underwriters who sell loans or securities to these GSEs. Because Fannie Mae and Freddie Mac are a huge force in the industry, their methodological guidance has become ubiquitous for residential appraisal, even when the loan is not planned for sale. A residential mortgage is typically conducted in accordance with Fannie Mae and Freddie Mac guidelines and reported on their forms.

Federal Housing Authority (FHA) and Veterans Administration (VA) loans do not have to conform to Fannie Mae and Freddie Mac appraisal guidelines. These agencies, rather than being GSEs, are departments of the federal government. As such, they promulgate their own appraisal guidelines directly to the appraisers who are approved to work for them. Those guidelines tend to be compatible with the guidance from Fannie Mae and Freddie Mac. Before the market meltdown after the global financial crisis in 2007–2009, FHA and VA loans comprised a small proportion of the market. Since then, these loans constituted a much bigger slice.

Fundamentals of the Valuation Process

The appraisal exercise may result in different value determinations, such as distressed-sale value, value-in-use, and investment value. USPAP is silent as to the specific type of value to be used, only that the appraiser must disclose the type and source of that definition.

When a mortgage loan is made, sold, or securitized, the presumption is that the appraiser determined the market value of the collateral. This market value is the most probable price at which the property will sell under normal conditions of sale.

Many definitions of market value or fair market value are available. As used in federally related mortgage transactions, *market value* refers to the most probable price that a property should bring in a competitive and open market under all conditions requisite to a fair sale. This definition implies that the buyer and seller each act prudently and knowledgeably and the price is unaffected by undue stimulus. Implicit in this definition are the consummation of a sale as of a specified date and the passing of title from seller to buyer under the following conditions.

- The buyer and seller are motivated.
- Both parties are well informed or well advised, and acting in what they consider their own best interests.
- A reasonable time is allowed for exposure in the open market.
- The buyer makes payment in terms of cash in U.S. dollars or in comparable financial arrangements.
- The price represents the normal consideration for the property sold unaffected by special or creative financing or sales concessions granted by anyone associated with the sale.

If so, then the appraiser must also examine the current use of the property and the highest and best use. The highest and best use may be very different from the current use. For example, a fully depreciated house is probably a candidate to be torn down and rebuilt. The site may be more valuable as a vacant building lot than in its current use. A site zoned for commercial development but currently used as residential may be a candidate for economic repositioning. To value this collateral in its current use would result in a value-in-use rather than a market-value appraisal. Determining the correct highest and best use is critical to determining the correct market comparable data and the appropriate analytical techniques.

Valuation methodologies are generally categorized within three approaches to value: cost, sales comparison, and income. Not all approaches are applicable in all situations, but the appraiser is obligated to use all applicable approaches or to offer an explanation in the appraisal report.

The hedonic pricing model is a variant of the sales comparison approach. Most variants of the income approach apply net present value (NPV) determination, with discount rates extracted either empirically from the market or through a risk-adjustment determination. Ironically, the capital asset pricing model (CAPM) is rarely used in the real estate appraisal process. According to Lentz and Wang (1998), the sales adjustment grid, the most common form of the sales comparison approach found in residential mortgage appraisals, is a generalized version of a weighted-least-squares regression.

In a single-family residential appraisal, the sales comparison approach and the cost approach are most common. The income approach is rarely applicable, and data to support such an approach are sparse and inconsistent. For a condominium or co-op apartment, the cost approach is rarely used because the allocation of site value and common areas can be problematic. Small income properties such as duplexes, triplexes, and four lexes are usually valued using all three approaches. The final determination of value is typically some weighted average of these three approaches, called *reconciliation.*

Basis and Background for the Valuation Process

In a residential appraisal, the most common method is the adjustment grid process, which is part of the sales comparison approach. This is the model generally found on the Fannie Mae Form 1004 and Freddie Mac Form 70. Although this technique has been in practice for generations, Colwell, Cannaday, and Wu (1983) outline the theoretical underpinnings. They start with the hedonic regression used in pricing physical characteristics, where the price is the dependent variable. This procedure underlies automated appraisal. The authors take into account the traditional adjustment grid model commonly used by residential appraisers. This grid compares a subject property with three comparable recent transactions. The subject property appraisal is on a price-difference model. Colwell et al. (1983) show that a hedonic regression is consistent with the price-differences model. These two models are in Equations 12.1 and 12.2, respectively. Equation 10.1 shows the model for the hedonic regression:

$$SP_i = f_0 + f_1X_{1i} + f_2X_{2i} + \ldots + f_jX_{ji} + \varepsilon_i \tag{12.1}$$

where *SP* is the selling price of the ith property; X_{ji} is the jth attribute of the ith property; f_j is the adjustment factor associated with the jth attribute; and ε is the error term associated with the ith property.

This is a traditional hedonic multiple regression model and allows for a direct estimation of the marginal values of the various attributes. Conversely, the price-differences model more directly measures the marginal differences between the comparables and the subject property, and is a better representation of the actual workings of the sales adjustment grid:

$$SP_S - SP_i = f_1(X_{1S} - X_{1i}) + f_2(X_{2S} - X_{2i}) + \ldots + f_j(X_{jS} - X_{ji}) \tag{12.2}$$

where SP_S is the forecasted selling price of the subject house (i.e., appraised value); SP_i is the selling price of the ith comparable; X_{ji} is the jth attribute of the ith property; and f_j is the adjustment factor associated with the jth attribute.

The price-differences model does not have an error term. The hedonic model is constructed such that the standardized error has a mean of zero and a constant standard deviation. This requirement is regularly violated with pricing models, requiring a weighted least squares regression to compensate. In the latter, the errors in the valuation equation are heuristically adjusted through the process of estimating the factors.

The price-differences equation is implicitly applied for each comparable, and the typical residential appraisal has at least three. This requires reconciling the three or more valuation results. Problems arise in the weighting of the comparables. As Colwell et al. (1983) point out, the weights are non-negative and must sum to unity. Although that is correct in practice, no particular mathematical or theoretical reason exists for the non-negative requirement. Yet, the authors note that mystery shrouds the derivation of these weights. Hence, a substantial level of regulation is required in order to systematize the risk assessment to an extent that is useful in the securitization of mortgages.

EMPIRICAL PROBLEMS WITH THE SALES ADJUSTMENT GRID

Palmquist (2005) identifies several other critical empirical issues to be addressed in appraisal oversight. One is the issue of multicollinearity. Although this is more of an issue in hedonic models, sales adjustment grid data selection is based on the most comparable properties. Factors such as the number of bathrooms, number of bedrooms, and square footage are all highly correlated both with one another and among properties that are comparable. However, the price-differences model requires some degree of difference in order to measure the marginal price of each component. Identical comparable properties will give little in the way of sensitivity analysis in the face of changing market preferences as often happens when markets face systematic problems such as declining conditions. In practice, using multiple approaches to value or the sales adjustment grid cross-checked by use of a cost approach is the preferred solution.

Palmquist (2005) discusses the related problem of spatial autoregression. Other neighboring houses heavily influence the price or value of a given house. Again, in a sales adjustment grid analysis, little opportunity is available for sensitivity analysis. In the case of condominiums, regulators require that appraisals have at least one comparable from outside of the subject property's project.

Schill and Wachter (1993) emphasize the importance of neighborhood characteristics in the risk assessment of mortgages. Appraisers recognize and take advantage of the collinearity of values in a given neighborhood. Automated valuation models take advantage of sector analysis to examine this phenomenon at a more granular level. According to Schill and Wachter, neighborhoods have differential appreciation paths over time, which have important implications for risk assessment. Appraisal standards, consistent with federal regulation, prohibit using demographic characteristics as a basis for an appraisal decision. Consideration of neighborhood variables must be on a non-discriminatory basis and meet a legitimate business concern.

AGENCY ISSUES

As early as Lentz and Wang (1998), appraisal theorists were concerned with the issue of appraiser pressure. This arises from a distinct agency cost problem: the mortgage loan officer and the real estate broker have incentives to close the deal, and they are in the position of selecting the appraiser and potentially blacklisting those who undervalue the property. Related to pressure are agency issues of appraisal smoothing and low dispersion. After Lentz and Wang and during the housing bubble run-up of the early 2000s, various researchers addressed this problem including Wolverton and Gallimore (1999),

Gwin, Ong, and Spieler (2005), Amidu, Aluko, and Hansz (2008), Aycock and Black (2008), and Diaz and Hansz (2010).

Following FIRREA, a widespread belief was that USPAP and mandatory licensing and education would be crucial to correcting prior appraisal abuse problems. However, current research into the rise of the most recent housing burst suggests that the problem of appraiser pressure materially contributed to the housing bubble. Some have taken major practical steps to address this, including appraisal management companies as intermediaries between lenders and appraisers.

Agency leads to appraisal smoothing and low dispersion. Real estate markets are illiquid and few transactions generate comparable sales. Because commercial property frequently requires periodic appraisal, a tendency exists to use the most recent valuation. Appraisals become positively serially correlated, with the implied prices either rising or falling in sequence for extended periods. Another issue is that during the appraisal process, the appraiser receives information on the proposed price in a purchase and sale agreement. An incentive exists to hit the numbers, which in this case is the proposed price. In a majority of transactions, the appraisal valuation is very close to this proposed price leading to low dispersion.

These appraisal issues condense and truncate price distributions and understate the volatility and ultimately risk of investing in real estate. The measured risk-adjusted returns are higher than corrected for appraisal smoothing and low dispersion.

GSES AND INTERAGENCY GUIDELINES

After the global financial crisis of 2007–2009, nearly all U.S. mortgage securitization occurs at the GSE or federal level. Understanding the methodological focus of Fannie Mae and Freddie Mac and other agencies that issue, guarantee, and insure federally related mortgages is critically important.

Two documents can be viewed as canonical with respect to appraisal methods in the mortgage market. These are the interagency appraisal and evaluation guidelines or interagency guidelines and the Fannie Mae selling guide.

The former pertains to all appraisals for real estate loans originated or purchased by a regulated institution, either for the institution's own portfolio or as assets held for sale. The federal financial regulatory agencies jointly issue the guidelines. Regulated institutions include such entities as banks, savings and loans, and credit unions. The interagency guidelines are issued pursuant to the requirements of FIRREA Title XI as well as the parallel FDIC Improvement Act of 1991.

The latter, from Fannie Mae, provides guidance for appraisals on loans intended to be sold to it, Freddie Mac or be securitized. Resulting RMBS are sold to one of these GSEs. Because these entities are required to purchase any conforming loans, including from non-regulated sources, the Fannie Mae Guide provides additional direction in those circumstances. Loans from regulated entities intended for securitization or direct sale may fall under both sets of guidelines. Finally, many loans are made directly through the auspices of the FHA or VA. These agencies have their own sets of appraisal guidelines, which are generally compatible with the interagency guidelines.

The interagency guidelines more directly address the appraisal process, while the Fannie Mae guide views the appraisal within the larger context of the underwriting and selling. The interagency guidelines focus on appraisal management. They require regulated institutions to put appraisal supervision and evaluation systems in place. These systems provide for appraiser independence, performance evaluation, regulatory compliance, informational content, using reviews, and monitoring of collateral values. The guidelines specifically cite adherence to USPAP. The current issue of the guidelines (Board of Governors of the Federal Reserve System 2010) incorporates certain requirements of the Wall Street Reform and Consumer Protection Act (2010), or Dodd-Frank Act, on collateral evaluation, particularly with respect to higher risk loans.

The guidelines have other key elements. The appraisal is based on the definition of market value in the appraisal regulations. The appraisal considers actual physical condition, use, and zoning of the property as of the effective date. If the loan is for construction or renovation, an opinion of both the as-is value as well as the prospective when finished value.

The appraiser must be licensed or certified. All applicable approaches to value must be included. The subject property sales history is discussed. The highest and best use analysis has support. A prohibition exists against using restricted reports. Under USPAP, a restricted report or restricted use report is designed to be used only by the client, who is assumed to be knowledgeable about the property and therefore will not need much information normally included in the report.

The guidelines provide an exemption from these requirements for transactions less than $250,000 and business loans of less than $1 million when the loan does not depend on the sale or rental of real estate for repayment. An extension of a line of credit takes place when obvious or material change has occurred in either market conditions or the condition of the property and no new money is being advanced. In these cases, an evaluation may generally be substituted for a formal appraisal, unless certain other conditions are present, including:

- loans with combined LTVs greater than supervisory thresholds;
- atypical properties;
- properties outside the traditional lending market;
- extensions of credit with substantial risk; or
- borrowers with high-risk characteristics.

The interagency guidelines also provide for appraisal review. In the case of one to four family residences, when properties are securitized, the reviews should reflect a risk-focused approach on LTV ratios. Lower-risk loans may be sampled if pre-funded, but higher risk loans should be reviewed in a manner commensurate with the size, type, and complexity of the underlying credit transaction. If lenders find deficiencies in the underwriting process, these can be addressed via a second appraisal or a USPAP-compliant review performed by a qualified and competent state certified or licensed appraiser before the final credit decision.

One risk amelioration technique that has become fashionable as a means of reducing appraiser pressure is using an appraisal management company as an intermediary. An appraisal management company intermediates between owners or buyers and appraisers. The company administers independent contract appraisers and receives requests for real property appraisal services from clients. For a fee paid by the client, it enters into an agreement with one or more independent appraisers to perform the real property appraisal or serves as a third party liaison for appraisal management services. Some evidence suggests that these solutions have backfired. At least one such firm, RE Evaluation Solutions has declared bankruptcy, leaving the appraisers unpaid. Another, LSI Appraisal LLC faces legal and regulatory issues over the dissolution of the thrift lender Washington Mutual.

Some states are raising the amount of surety bond to be posted by appraisal management companies, and the guidelines have put lenders and their appraisers on notice. The institutions are accountable for ensuring that any services performed by a third party comply with applicable laws and regulations and are consistent with supervisory guidance. Regulated institutions should have internal controls for identifying, monitoring, and managing the risks associated with using a third party arrangement for valuation services.

The guidelines provide for the use of automated valuation models in the evaluation process. Institutions should ensure that staff has the requisite expertise and training to manage the selection use, and validation of these analytical methods or tools. Third-party expertise may be employed if such is lacking in-house.

When selecting an appraiser, the lender is cautioned to obtain an independent, disinterested examination and valuation, and be aware of and in full compliance with state licensing laws. Lenders should ensure that appraisers have the requisite knowledge and access to the necessary data sources. Lenders are responsible for the representations and warranties related to the value, condition, and marketability of the subject property.

When an extended loan-processing period exists, the appraisal may need to be updated. Fannie Mae requires that if the appraisal report is more than four months old, the appraiser must re-inspect the exterior of the property and review current market data. If the appraiser determines that the market value has declined, the underwriter must order an additional appraiser.

Table 12.1 **Fannie Mae and Freddie Mac Appraisal Forms**

	Fannie Mae	*Freddie Mac*
Uniform Residential Appraisal Report (URAR)	1005	70
Exterior only	2055	2055
Manufactured home	1004C	70B
Individual condominium	1073	465
Exterior only condominium	1075	466
Individual co-op interest	2090	N/A
Exterior only co-op interest	2095	N/A
Small income-producing property	1025	72
Appraisal update	1004D	442
Market conditions addendum	1004MC	71

Source: Fannie Mae 2012.

Appraisals are submitted on one of several pre-approved forms. Table 12.1 has a list of appraisal forms that may be found in the files of loans securitized through Fannie Mae or Freddie Mac. The use of Fannie Mae and Freddie Mac forms is so ubiquitous in the industry that finding these forms in files of any residential mortgage loans is common.

The GSEs require special appraisal considerations for homes affected by environmental hazards. Certain disclosures must be made and some environmental hazards render a property ineligible to be used as collateral, hence ineligible to be securitized. For example, an environmental condition may have a material effect on the value of the subject property, but the impact or diminution in value is not measurable with comparable sales, contracts, or active listings because the hazard is so serious or so recently discovered. Private well water is specifically noted, and if suspected of contamination, a well certificate may be required.

Fannie Mae provides a standardized property conditions rating as shown in Table 12.2. The ranking order ranges from a high of C1 (new construction) to a low of C6 (substantial damage requiring rehabilitation). As Table 12.3 shows, Fannie Mae provides a similar ranking or taxonomy of construction quality, ranging from a high of

Table 12.2 **Fannie Mae Condition Ratings**

Rating	*Description*
C1	The dwelling has been very recently constructed and has not been occupied. The entire structure and all components are new and the dwelling features no physical depreciation.
C2	The dwelling has no deferred maintenance, little or no physical depreciation, and requires no immediate repairs. Virtually all building components are new or have been recently repaired, refinished, or rehabilitated. Any outdated components and finishes have been updated and/or replaced with components meeting current standards.
C3	The dwelling is well maintained and evidences limited physical depreciation from to normal wear and tear. Some components, but not every major building component, has been recently updated or rehabilitated. The structure appears well maintained.
C4	There is some minor deferred maintenance and physical deterioration due to normal wear and tear. The dwelling has been adequately maintained and requires only minimal repairs to building components, mechanical systems, and cosmetic repairs. All major building components have been maintained and are functionally adequate.
C5	There are obvious items of deferred maintenance and some significant repairs are needed. Functional utility and overall livability is diminished, but the dwelling remains usable as a residence.
C6	The dwelling evidences substantial damage or deferred maintenance with deficiencies that are sufficiently severe to affect the safety, soundness, or structural integrity. Many or most major components require repair.

Source: Fannie Mae 2012.

Table 12.3 **Fannie Mae Construction Quality Ratings**

Rating	*Description*
Q1	These are unique structures, individually designed by an architect for a specified user. Such residences are typically constructed from detailed architectural plans and specifications and feature an exceptionally high level of workmanship and materials throughout the interior and exterior of the structure, high-quality exterior and interior refinements.
Q2	Such dwellings are often custom designed for construction on an individual property owner's site. However, dwellings in this quality grade are also found in high-quality tract developments featuring residences constructed from individual plans or from highly modified or upgraded plans. Designs features detailed, high-quality exterior ornamentation and interior refinements.
Q3	These are higher quality residences built from either individual or readily available designer plans in above-standard residential tract developments or on an individual property owner's site. Designs include significant exterior ornamentation and well-finished interiors. Workmanship exceeds acceptable standards and many materials and finishes have been upgraded from "stock" standards.
Q4	These homes meet or exceed applicable building code requirements. Standard or modified standard building plans were used, and designs include adequate fenestration, some exterior ornamentation, and some interior refinements. Materials, workmanship, finish, and equipment are of stock or builder grade and may feature some upgrades.
Q5	Economy of construction and basic functionality as main considerations for these homes. They feature a plain design based on readily available or basic floor plans with minimal fenestration, basic finishes, minimal exterior ornamentation, and limited interior detail. The homes meet minimum building codes and are constructed with inexpensive, stock materials.
Q6	These are basic quality and lower cost homes, some of which may not be suitable for year-round occupancy. They are often built with simple plans or without plans, utilizing the lowest quality building materials. Often, these are often built or expanded by persons who do not have professional skills or who or possess only minimal construction skills. Electrical, plumbing, and other mechanical systems and equipment may be deficient or nonexistent. Older dwellings may have one or more substandard or nonconforming additions to the original structure.

Source: Fannie Mae 2012.

Q1 (unique, architecturally built homes) to Q6 (basic quality that may be unsuitable for year-round residence).

Fannie Mae makes a point of noting that the appraiser must identify and describe physical deficiencies that could affect a safety, soundness, or structural integrity. If any such deficiencies are noted, the property must be appraised subject to completion of the specific repairs or alterations. In that case, the quality ratings reflect the quality of the property based on the hypothetical condition that the repairs or alterations have been completed.

Often, the appraiser will not be qualified to evaluate the alterations or repairs needed. In that case, the appraiser must identify and describe the deficiencies. The property requires an appraisal by a qualified professional and must pass a satisfactory inspection. The appraisal may have to be revised based on the results of the inspection. If so, the report must indicate the impact on the final opinion of value. A certification of completion is required to ensure the completion of the necessary alterations or repairs before sale or securitization of the mortgage.

Fannie Mae and Freddie Mac will buy or securitize loans collateralized by manufactured, modular, or other types of prefabricated homes under the following conditions: (1) if the home is designed as a one-family dwelling; (2) it assumes the same characteristics as site-built housing; (3) it can be legally classified as real property; (4) it is permanently affixed to an appropriate foundation system that is appropriate to the site; and (5) it meets all local building codes. For mixed-use properties, the market value of the property must primarily be a function of the residential characteristics rather than the business use. The mixed use must be permissible under local zoning requirements.

Appraisers give particular consideration to properties in special assessment or community facilities districts. They must investigate the financial health of the district. Appraisers must take into account the financial difficulty that has an effect on the value of the subject property and potential liabilities. This should be accomplished by examining current and expired listings within the district, pending contract sales, and recent closed sales. If financial difficulty is so severe that no comparable sales are available, the mortgage cannot be sold or securitized until an active market develops.

Leasehold interests also require special consideration. Appraisers are required to develop a thorough, clear, and detailed narrative identifying the terms, restrictions, and conditions regarding lease agreements or ground leases and include this information as an addendum to the appraisal report. The report must discuss any effect the lease agreement or ground lease has on the value and marketability of the subject property. The sales comparison approach must use comparable sales with similar leasehold interests. If enough closed comparable property sales with similar leasehold interests are available, the appraiser should use them in the sales adjustment grid.

When a co-op interest is financed and sold or securitized, Fannie Mae Form 1074 (Request for Cooperative Project Information) is an information-gathering tool. Comparables used to value co-ops should be from similar types of co-op projects. However, appraisers may use condominium comparables if co-op sales are unavailable, along with an explanation. The appraisal must adjust the condo comparables to reflect any reference for condo ownership in the subject market area.

After each appraisal is submitted, a review or underwriting analysis is required. The lender is required to make note of the current contract for sale for purchase money transactions. It must use current listings or comparable sales for both purchase and refinance transactions. Underwriting uses the current ownership and the appraiser analysis of the sale or transfer history of the subject property and of comparable sales.

In summary, the interagency guidelines and the Fannie Mae selling guide provide the guidance and direction for residential appraisals in the United States. Although different reasons led to the development of these two documents, they are generally compatible with one another, and in many cases, both will apply.

Globalization of Appraisal Standards and Methods

The International Valuation Standards (IVS) arose from talks in the 1970s between U.S. and U.K. valuation professionals. This led to the International Asset Valuation Standards Committee in 1981, eventually renamed the International Valuation Standards Council (IVSC). The IVSC includes representatives from more than 50 countries and provides a mechanism for valuation standards to complement the International Financial Reporting Standards (IFRS).

In 2006, the Madison Agreement called for reconciliation of USPAP and IVS. However, reconciliation still waits, partly due to the deep integration of USPAP into FIRREA and both state and federal legislation. Kilpatrick (2012) examines the issues in comparing international evaluation standards. For example, USPAP's Rule 9 is almost a verbatim restatement of Internal Revenue Service (IRS) Ruling 59–60. This same language appears in the American Society of Appraisers' Business Valuation Standards, in the Institute of Business Appraisers Professional Standards, and in the National Association of Certified Valuation Analysts Development Standards. The Uniform Appraisal Standards for Federal Land Acquisition specifies USPAP and uses it as a starting point.

Other challenges arise from the different development histories of USPAP and IVS. USPAP arose from a single body of knowledge and evolved as an integrated part of a highly fragmented regulatory climate. An alternative to USPAP would require legislative changes in at least 54 jurisdictions plus shifts at the federal level. States continue to require USPAP recertification every two years by instructors certified by the Appraisal Foundation and do not accept IVS course work. In some jurisdictions questions arise as to whether IVS training is acceptable, depending on the type of instruction offered.

Wolverton (1996) and Gallimore and Wolverton (1997) examine cultural differences between American appraisers and English valuers, focusing on comparable sale selection. In two highly related cultures, the professionals operate in very different task environments. American residential appraisers use pre-approved, standardized forms, notably the Uniform Residential Appraisal Report or Freddie Mac Form 70 to report the analysis and the value conclusion. Conversely, English valuers have minimal reporting requirements and hence use various reporting options. Valuers rarely identify or describe comparable sales and adjustments in a manner similar to their American counterparts. American appraisers on residential property use multiple listing service (MLS) data because most American sales pass through those databases and MLS provides a comprehensive sample of market data in most American markets. Because English valuers have no comparable databases on which to rely, they typically rely on fewer comparable sales. Finally, English lenders do not provide a pending sales price to the valuer, finessing the issue of limited appraisal-price differentials. This one difference can result in statistically significant and material differences in value outcomes. As Diaz and Hansz (2002) note, this difference in task environment alone does not completely explain or account for the observed differences in the two professional cultures. They cite education and licensing differences as other important considerations.

Progress is being made toward reconciliation of procedures in the USPAP and IVS. The U.S. Appraisal Institute originally required USPAP coursework for all members, but will accept IVS for members working exclusively abroad. Conversely, Canada is moving toward domestic standards incorporating IVS. To varying degrees, Latin America and the Caribbean nations recognize IVS as authoritative for valuation, but all have different regulatory climates. The United States, with about 80,000 licensed and certified appraisers, continues to be the one region in the world where reconciliation is a challenge.

Summary and Conclusions

Residential mortgage loans in the United States are aimed toward securitization and the appraisal process is a critical element in the risk assessment. Because these mortgages typically flow through regulated financial institutions such as banks and credit unions, or GSEs, the appraisal methodological guidance proffered by these conduits takes on a canonical role.

Since the early 1990s, with the passage of FIRREA, licensure at the state level has been the norm for appraisers. Both state license laws and methodological regulations mandate adherence to USPAP, which directs appraisers to use generally accepted methods. A background of globalization of appraisal standards and methods exists. Substantial barriers continue to exist to globalization, including regulatory entrenchment and professional differences across cultures.

Discussion Questions

1. Discuss the major difference between the Fannie Mae selling guide and the interagency appraisal guidelines.
2. Identify two key impediments to globalization of appraisal standards.
3. Explain the difference between construction quality and dwelling condition from an appraisal perspective.
4. Identify the party ultimately responsible for adherence to appraisal guidelines.
5. Discuss the circumstances under which a federally regulated lender can make a real estate loan without an appraisal.

References

Amidu, Abdul-Rasheed, Bioye Tajudeen Aluko, and J. Andrew Hansz. 2008. "Client Feedback Pressure and the Role of Estate Surveyors and Valuers." *Journal of Property Research* 25:2, 89–106.

Appraisal Foundation, The. 2008. *A Guide for Understanding the 2008 Real Property Appraiser Qualification Criteria*. Washington, DC: The Appraisal Foundation.
Appraisal Foundation, The. 2013a. *Appraisal Qualifications Board*. https://netforum.avectra.com/eweb/DynamicPage.aspx?Site=&WebCode=AQB.
Appraisal Foundation, The. 2013b. *Appraisal Standards Board*. https://netforum.avectra.com/eweb/DynamicPage.aspx?Site=taf&WebCode=ASB.
Appraisal Foundation, The. 2013c. *Real Property Appraiser Qualification Criteria*. https://netforum.avectra.com/eWeb/dynamicPage.aspx?Site=TAF&WebCode=RPCriteria.
Appraisal Foundation, The. 2013d. *History of the Foundation*. http://www.appraisalfoundation.org.
Appraisal Institute, The. 2000. *Uniform Appraisal Standards for Federal Land Acquisition*. 5th edn. Chicago: The Appraisal Institute.
Appraisal Institute, The. 2012. *The Appraisal of Real Estate*. 14th edn. Chicago: The Appraisal Institute.
Aycock, S. Alan, and Roy T. Black. 2008. "Special Master Bias in Eminent Domain Cases." *Real Estate Issues* 33:2, 53–58.
Ben-Shahar, Danny. 2008. "Default, Credit Scoring, and Loan-to-Value: A Theoretical Analysis of Competitive and Non-Competitive Mortgage Markets." *Journal of Real Estate Research* 30:2, 161–190.
Board of Governors of the Federal Reserve System. 1994. *Interagency Appraisal and Evaluation Guidelines*. Washington, DC: Board of Governors of the Federal Reserve System.
Board of Governors of the Federal Reserve System. 2010. *Interagency Appraisal and Evaluation Guidelines*. Washington, DC: Board of Governors of the Federal Reserve System.
Chiang, Ramond C., Ming Liu, and Ying Foon Chow. 2002. "Residential Mortgage Lending and Borrower Risk: The Relationship between Mortgage Spreads and Individual Characteristics." *Journal of Real Estate Finance and Economics* 25:1, 5–24.
Chomsisengphet, Souphala, and Anthony Pennington-Cross. 2006. "The Evolution of the Subprime Mortgage Market." *Federal Reserve Bank of St. Louis Review* 88:1, 31–56.
Colwell, Peter F., Roger E. Cannaday, and Chunchi Wu.1983. "The Analytical Foundations of Adjustment-Grid Methods." *Real Estate Economics* 11:1, 11–29.
Diaz, Julian, and J. Andrew Hansz. 2002. "Behavioral Research into the Real Estate Valuation Process: Progress toward a Descriptive Model." In Ko Wang and Marvin Wolverton, eds., *Real Estate Valuation Theory*, 3–29. Northwell, MA: Kluwer.
Diaz, Julian, and J. Andrew Hansz. 2010. "A Taxonomic Investigation of Valuation Bias in Residential Real Estate Appraisals." *International Journal of Strategic Property Management* 14:1, 3–17.
Fannie Mae. 2012. *Uniform Mortgage Data Program*. Washington, DC: Fannie Mae. http://www.fanniemae.com/content/technology_requirements/uad-standardization-requirements.pdf.
Gallimore, Paul, and Marvin Wolverton. 1997. "Price Knowledge Induced Bias: A Cross Cultural Comparison." *Journal of Property Investment and Valuation* 15:3, 261–273.
Gwin, Carl R., Seow-Eng Ong, and Andrew C. Spieler. 2005. "Real Estate Appraisal and Bid Price: An Empirical Evaluation of Alternative Theories." *Urban Studies* 42:12, 2245–2259.
Hatchondo, Juan Carlos, Leonardo Martinez, and Juan Sánchez. 2011. "Mortgage Defaults." Federal Reserve Bank of St. Louis Working Paper 2011–2019A.
Kilpatrick, John A. 2012. "Reconciling IVS and USPAP." Presented to the American Real Estate Society Annual Meeting, St. Petersburg, Florida.
Krainer, John. 2001. "A Theory of Liquidity in Residential Real Estate Markets." *Journal of Urban Economics* 49:1, 32–53.
Lentz, George H., and Ko Wang. 1998. "Residential Appraisal and the Lending Process: A Survey of Issues." *Journal of Real Estate Research* 15:1/2, 11–39.
Noordewier, Thomas G., David M. Harrison, and K. Ramagopal. 2001. "Semivariance of Property Value Estimates as a Determinant of Default Risk." *Real Estate Economics* 29:1, 127–159.
Palmquist, Raymond B. 2005. "Property Value Models." In Karl-Goren Maler and Jeffrey Vincent, eds., *Handbook of Environmental Economics*, Volume 2, 764–819. Amsterdam: North-Holland.

Qi, Min, and Xiaolong Yang. 2009. "Loss Given Default of High Loan-to-Value Residential Mortgages." *Journal of Banking and Finance* 33:5, 788–792.

Schill, Michael H., and Susan M. Wachter. 1993. "A Tale of Two Cities: Racial and Ethnic Geographic Disparities in Home Mortgage Lending in Boston and Philadelphia." *Journal of Housing Research* 4:2, 245–275.

Securities Industry and Financial Markets Association (SIFMA). 2013. *U.S. Mortgage-Related Securities*. New York: SIFMA. http://www.sifma.org/research/statistics.aspx.

U.S. Congress. 1989. *Financial Institutions Reform, Recovery and Enforcement Act of 1989*. http://www.fdic.gov/regulations/laws/rules/8000-3100.html. Public Law No. 101–173, Stat. 513, effective August 9, 1989, codified to 12 USC 3331–3351.

Wolverton, Marvin. 1996. "Investigation into Price Knowledge Induced Comparable Sale Selection Bias." PhD dissertation, Department of Real Estate, Georgia State University.

Wolverton, Marvin, and Paul Gallimore. 1999. "Client Feedback and the Role of the Appraiser." *Journal of Real Estate Research* 18:3, 417–433.

13

Real Estate Brokerage

G. DONALD JUD
Professor Emeritus, Bryan School of Business and Economics, University of North Carolina at Greensboro

Introduction

Most people employ a real estate agent or broker to help them when they buy or sell a house. The buyer wants to locate the best house at the lowest price in the shortest possible time. Alternatively, the seller wants to sell at the highest price in the shortest possible time. Brokers provide buyers and sellers with market information that may be too time-consuming or expensive for them to produce on their own.

Brokers, which is a generic term used to describe licensed agents, advise buyers about the properties currently for sale that may meet their housing needs and financial circumstances. This chapter uses the terms "brokers" and "agents" interchangeably to describe state licensees receiving compensation for arranging real estate transactions including sales, leases, and property management. They provide help with matters including mortgage qualification, home inspections, contract negotiation, and closing arrangements. Likewise, brokers advise sellers on the best listing price, advertising strategy, home staging, contract negotiation, and closing arrangements. The real estate broker is usually involved in almost every aspect of a housing purchase or sale. The utility of real estate agents and brokers is attested to by the fact that they assist 89 percent of all buyers and 88 percent of all sellers of houses, according to a 2012 survey by the National Association of Realtors (2012b).

Beginning in the 1990s, focus and attention on the real estate brokerage industry accelerated along with housing prices. Benjamin, Jud, and Sirmans (2000a, b) published two literature reviews of the brokerage industry and Zietz and Sirmans (2011) have provided an updated review since 2000. This chapter synthesizes and extends the review of brokerage literature and provides a larger institutional framework for understanding the industry.

The remainder of the chapter is organized as follows. The next section reviews employment trends. It is followed by a discussion of the historical development of the industry. The legal environment is sketched next. Educational, training, and licensure requirements are discussed in the section that follows. Trends in earnings are discussed next. The subsequent section looks at commercial real estate brokerage. Next, the structure of the brokerage industry is examined followed by sections on franchise affiliation and information technology. The next two sections examine the competitive environment extant in the industry and how brokers affect the terms of sale in a real estate transaction. The following section surveys the global environment for real estate brokerage. A final section provides an overall summary.

Employment

According to the Bureau of Economic Analysis (BEA) (2013), the real estate sector, defined by the North American Industrial Classification System (NAICS) as code 531, employed 1,416,000 persons full or part-time in 2012. This sector includes firms primarily engaged in renting or leasing real estate to others; managing real estate for others; selling, buying, or renting real estate for others; and providing other real estate related services, such as appraisal. Real estate sector (NAICS code 531) employment accounted for 1.1 percent of total national employment in 2012. From the start of the housing downturn in 2006, real estate employment fell 6.3 percent through 2011, compared to a decline in overall national employment of 3.1 percent. Since the end of 2011, employment in real estate has begun to rebound, rising 1.0 percent in 2012, based on data from the Bureau of Labor Statistics (BLS) as shown in Figure 13.1.

Most real estate professionals are members of the National Association of Realtors (NAR), the largest trade association in the country with almost 1 million members and 1,379 local associations in 2012. NAR membership peaked in 2006 and by 2012 had fallen by 26 percent, reflecting the housing market crash as shown in Figure 13.2 (National Association of Realtors, 2013a).

A total of 57 percent of NAR members are licensed as sales agents, while 27 percent are licensed brokers. Among real estate sales personnel, brokers and agents perform the same kind of work for their clients. Sales agents work under the direction of a real estate broker. Both brokers and agents are licensed by the state or states in which they operate,

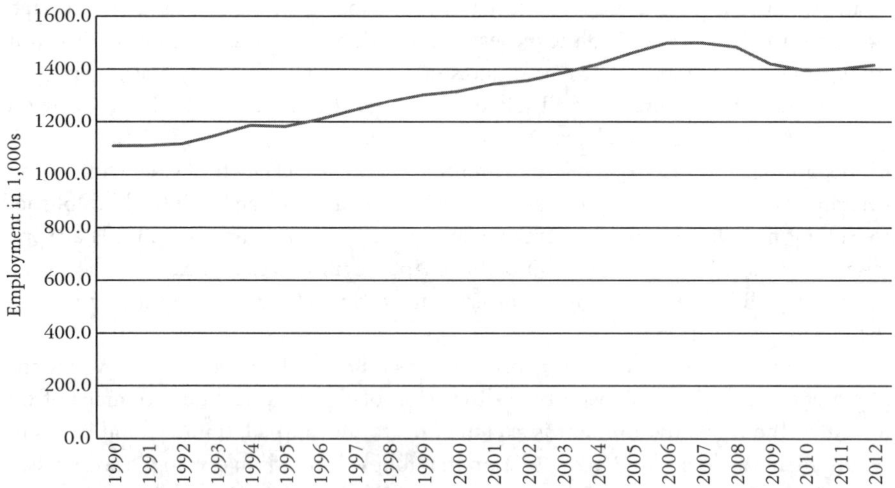

Figure 13.1 Real Estate Sector Employment, 1990–2012. Source: BLS.

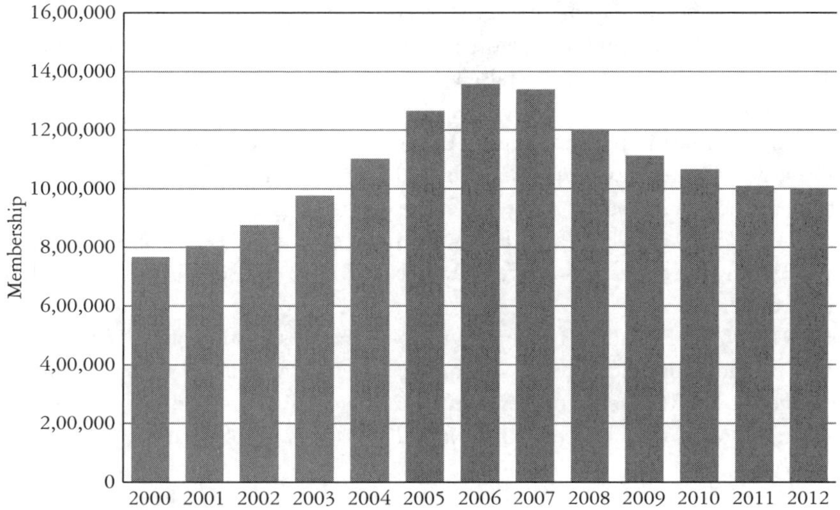

Figure 13.2 NAR Membership: 2000–2012. Source: NAR.

but brokers have more rigorous licensing requirements and are allowed to manage their own real estate businesses.

The Bureau of Labor Statistics (BLS) (2012) projects employment of real estate brokers and sales agents to grow a little more than 1 percent annually from 2010 to 2020, about as fast as the average for all occupations. However, job growth is highly dependent on the health of the housing sector and the overall economy. Employment typically expands rapidly along with rising housing prices and sales and tends to decline rapidly during market downturns.

History

The buying and selling of real estate has always been part of the American tradition. Attorneys and surveyors were initially the main professionals assisting property transfers. However, increasing urbanization added to the complexity of real estate transactions for both buyers and sellers. Many buyers and sellers needed to spend additional time and resources to obtain market information necessary for more optimal decisions. As a result, buyers and sellers began to turn increasingly to real estate specialists, or agents and brokers, to provide the information they needed. As the numbers of real estate brokers increased, some began to organize the market more formally by creating local boards of exchange to list properties available for sale and lease.

Davies (1958) provides a comprehensive discussion of the early development of the brokerage industry. A real estate board was organized in New York City in 1847 but lasted only one year. It was subsequently reorganized in 1885. Others organized similar boards in Baltimore, Birmingham, Buffalo, Chicago, Cleveland, Denver, Minneapolis, Richmond, San Jose, and St. Louis between 1860 and 1900. The National Association of Real Estate Exchanges (NAREE) was founded in 1908 in Chicago, following three earlier attempts beginning in 1891. NAR records show 120 founding members representing 19 local boards and one state association. NAREE adopted a professional code of ethics in 1913 in an attempt to raise the standards of professionalism and service in the industry.

Among the most important items in the code was the strong advocacy of the use of exclusive listings. In an *exclusive listing*, the seller agrees not to sell the property directly. Instead, a specific real estate broker shows the property and is entitled to a commission when the property is sold. In a *net listing*, the seller demands a set price, and the broker keeps anything the buyer pays above that price. The 1913 code of ethics discouraged the practice of net listings.

In 1916, NAREE changed its name to the National Association of Real Estate Boards (NAREB) and adopted the term "realtor" to distinguish NAREB members who subscribed to the NAREB's code of ethics. In 1972, the name of the National Association of Real Estate Boards was changed to the National Association of Realtors (NAR).

The Legal Environment

Real estate brokers, seeking to advance their professional image and perhaps also raise their commission rates, began to stress that they acted as "agents" for the property seller or buyer. They began to demand "exclusive" listing contracts before agreeing to help owners sell their properties. Under the terms of an exclusive contract, the broker usually agrees to help market the property through advertising, listing the property with the local multiple listing service (MLS) maintained by the local board of realtors, arranging open houses, helping determine a listing price, negotiating a sales price, and helping arrange the closing. To expedite a sale, many brokers also provide help with home inspections, mortgage financing, repairs, and other issues related to the sale.

As compensation, listing brokers are normally paid as commission a predetermined percentage of the sales price of the property at closing. To facilitate the sale, the listing broker may agree to give a portion of the sales commission to another agent responsible for bringing and showing the property to the ultimate buyer. If the listing broker finds the buyer, then the listing broker keeps the entire sales commission. Often the listing broker works for a firm owned by another broker. In this case, the listing broker has to share some of the sales commission with the firm. The share taken by the firm may be as much as 50 percent but is usually much less for experienced brokers. Under some arrangements, more experienced agents negotiate to keep 100 percent of the commission and simply pay the firm a fixed overhead fee to cover the cost of office space, phones, computers, and other office expenses.

Because real estate brokers have historically claimed to be "agents" of the seller or the buyer, not merely intermediaries facilitating the transaction, they have become subject to the general law of agency, which imposes duties on agents with regard to their principals (National Association of Realtors 2006). These duties include: (1) loyalty and obedience, (2) skill, care, and diligence, (3) disclosure of information, and (4) accounting. As Grohman (1987) and others show, buyers and sellers often are confused about their relationship with the real estate broker. Buyers frequently view the broker is their "agent," when in fact the broker normally works for the seller.

Most states apply agency law to real estate brokerage (Association of Real Estate License Law Officials 2012). Only six states (Arkansas, Massachusetts, Oklahoma, Utah, Vermont, and West Virginia) do not. In these states, the broker is most often described as a "transaction broker" and is not an agent for either the buyer or the seller. A transaction broker has less of a legal duty to clients than does an agent to a principal.

Many states require that brokers notify potential buyers and sellers about their agency options, often on the first substantial contact and in writing. A total of 44 states require a written notice be given to potential brokerage customers explaining to them the agency options they have available. A potential buyer searching for a new house might want to employ a buyer's agent. Alternatively, the listing agent might be empowered to serve as a dual agent by acting also as the buyer's agent.

Gardiner, Heisler, Liu, and Kallberg (2007) examine the impact of such disclosure laws. Drawing on data from Hawaii, they look at state legislation passed in 1984 that required the disclosure in writing of dual agency. *Dual agency* is where the broker serves as the agent for both the buyer and the seller. Before the legislation, dual agency resulted in an average 8 percent lower selling price and 8.5 percent less time on the market. After the legislation, dual agency fell from 44 percent to 28 percent of all transactions and its impact fell to a 1.4 percent lower selling price. Marketing time for dual agency transactions remained about 8.1 percent shorter. Turnbull and Dombrow (2007) report similar results. Homes listed and sold by different agents in the same firm sell for less, again suggesting that dual agency has a negative effect on price.

Historically, the legal doctrine of *caveat emptor*, or buyer beware, required only that home sellers and their brokers tell the truth when communicating with potential buyers about a property (National Association of Realtors 2006). A broker had no obligation to disclose to potential buyers who they did not represent anything unfavorable about properties available for sale.

Most states have enacted a tighter disclosure standard. Sellers and their brokers are obligated to disclose known property defects. Consumer protection and deceptive trade practice laws extend to real estate transactions. Many states have enacted disclosure requirements that obligate the seller and the broker to disclose certain specified information about the property such as environmental hazards. They may be held legally liable if they do not do so.

Anti-discrimination statutes, or fair housing laws, is another area in which real estate agents and brokers are subject to federal, state, and local laws (National Association of Realtors 2006). The most important of these laws are the Civil Rights Act of 1866 and the Civil Rights Act of 1968. Together, these laws do not permit brokers to refuse to rent, sell, or otherwise discriminate against anyone on the basis of religion, color, national origin, sex, or handicap status race, familial status. The courts have interpreted these acts as making it illegal to discriminate by (1) refusing to rent or sell, (2) steering or trying to influence a buyer's choice of housing, (3) blockbusting or trying to create panic selling in areas undergoing racial transition, and (4) advertising that shows a preference for or against a certain class of buyers. The federal government has empowered the Department of Housing and Urban Development (HUD) with broad powers to enforce federal fair housing laws. Likewise, state fair housing laws give substantial powers to state agencies to enforce anti-discrimination laws in individual states.

Education, Training, and Licensure

Real estate brokers and sales agents must be knowledgeable about the market in their area, and they need to be aware of mortgage financing options, government programs, and real estate, zoning, and fair housing laws. Because of the complexity of the real estate market, many agents and brokers specialize either in residential or commercial transactions. A total of 83 percent of NAR members specialize in residential sales, while only 2 percent specialize in commercial sales and leasing. Others concentrate in property management, land development, and other areas.

Brokers and agents normally must have a high school diploma and many have college degrees. In 2012, 91 percent reported some education beyond high school, and 48 percent reported they had a bachelor's degree or higher.

Entry into the real estate brokerage industry is relatively easy, allowing industry employment to swell when the housing market is on the upswing and decline sharply on the downswing. The Association of Real Estate License Law Officials (ARELLO) publishes an annual report of a survey of real estate licensing laws and standards in the United States and Canada. Their data for the United States show 2,889,619 licensed agents and brokers in 2012. Of these, 909,307 (31 percent) held brokers licenses. Many of these were on inactive status. The data on inactive licensees are incomplete for all states. In Florida, 7.6 percent of brokers and 14.2 percent of sales agents were inactive compared with 29.5 percent of brokers and 21.4 percent of agents in Nevada. Large numbers of inactive agents and brokers suggest that the supply of brokerage services in the industry could easily expand if the pace of housing activity were to increase.

All states and the District of Columbia require that agents and brokers be licensed in order to sell, lease, or manage real estate for others. Among the basic licensing requirements are that candidates (1) complete a minimum number of hours of classroom instruction, (2) pass an exam, and (3) obtain a minimum level of experience. Most areas require a minimum number of hours of annual continuing education.

The education requirements for industry entry are not high. In 2012, Massachusetts required 24 hours of pre-licensing education, while California had the highest with a requirement of 135 hours of classroom instruction. Most states impose additional education and experience requirements plus the passage of another exam to become a licensed broker. The average pass rate on the broker's exam is usually above 50 percent. In 2012, the Association of Real Estate License Law Officials (2012) reported pass rates on the brokerage exams for 18 states. The median pass rate was 64 percent, with a range from 34 to 88 percent.

Earnings

The 2012 NAR Membership Survey reports that 60 percent of members are female, 86 percent white, 6 percent Hispanic, 4 percent black, and 3 percent Asian or Pacific Islanders. Of these NAR members, 11 percent were born outside the United States. A total of 48 percent have a bachelor's degree or higher, while only 9 percent report having only a high school education. NAR members frequently have careers in other fields before

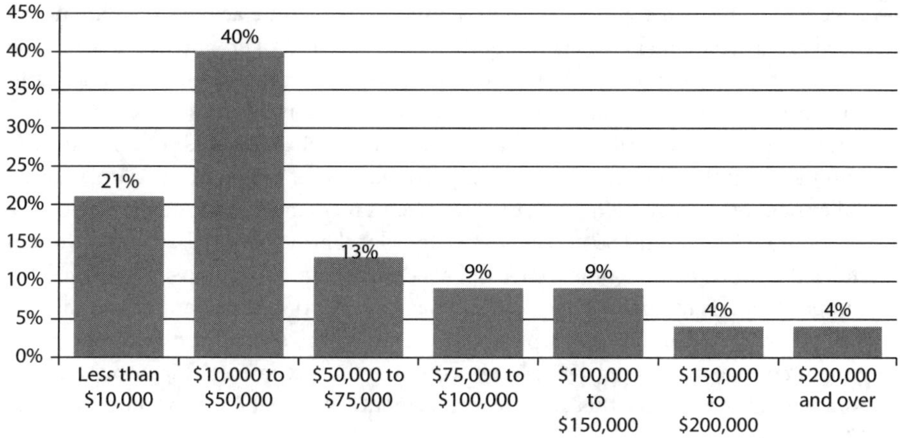

Figure 13.3 Distribution of Realtor Income: 2011. Source: NAR.

entering the real estate business. The most common areas of prior work experience are management, business, finance, sales, and retail. Only 5 percent of members entered the real estate field as a first career (National Association of Realtors 2012a).

The Bureau of Economic Analysis (2013) reports the average annual compensation for both full- and part-time persons in the real estate sector was $55,064 in 2011, compared to $60,524 for all workers. Since 2004, average compensation in the real estate sector has risen 19.0 percent unadjusted for inflation, lagging the growth of average compensation for all industries of 23.9 percent.

The overwhelming percentage of NAR members are paid primarily on the basis of commissions earned on the properties they sell. Only 2 percent of members in 2012 receive a salary. The average NAR member earned $34,900 in 2011, up 2 percent from 2010 and the first year-over-year increase since 2002. As Figure 13.3 shows 61 percent of NAR members earned less than $50,000. Managers, brokers, and appraisers not directly involved in the selling of real estate earned higher incomes on average than those members who are primarily involved in sales. Higher earnings are related strongly to experience and hours worked per week. More experienced individuals and those working longer hours earn substantially more.

A recent NAR membership survey reveals that 69 percent of NAR members are employed under a percentage commission split agreement, while only 17 percent worked with a 100 percent commission contract. A 100 percent commission agreement is more popular with brokers (23 percent) than sales agents (12 percent) and with those with greater work experience (National Association of Realtors 2012a).

Commercial Real Estate Brokerage

Some 230,000 NAR members report that they are active in commercial real estate, including commercial sales and brokerage, leasing, development of land, office, industrial, multifamily, retail space, and property management. Older, more experienced brokers and agents are more likely to engage in commercial real estate activity than are newly licensed agents (National Association of Realtors 2013b). Brokers and agents who deal in commercial property must be trained and conversant in the language of finance to effectively represent and communicate with commercial buyers and sellers.

On average, commercial realtors have been in the real estate field for 25 years and in commercial real estate for 15 years. Sixty-five percent of commercial realtors have a bachelor's degree or higher. In 2012, they reported a median annual income of $90,200. Most commercial realtors (56 percent) work for a local firm. Fifty-eight percent work in an office that has a mix of commercial and residential agents. The most common form of compensation is the percentage commission split. Forty-five percent of commercial agents are employed under this type of arrangement. The second most common employment arrangement is the 100 percent commission agreement. Thirty-four percent of commercial agents have this kind of arrangement (National Association of Realtors 2013b).

A total of 46 percent of commercial realtors earned 50 percent or more of their income from the commissions they earned on the sale of commercial properties. Twenty-two percent earned 50 percent or more of their income from commissions on commercial leases they negotiated. Just 8 percent earned 50 percent or more of their income from property management (National Association of Realtors 2013b).

Much of the consumer protection legislation that has been applied to residential transactions does not apply to commercial real estate. Commission rates are more open to negotiation and the kinds of listing contracts are more varied.

Historically, commercial real estate has been slow to develop an analog to the residential MLS for sharing local market information on the properties available for sale and lease. However, this gap has begun to be filled over the past decade. National firms such as CoStar have developed nationwide commercial real estate information exchanges, and NAR has developed a national exchange on its website CommercialSource.com. Local NAR affiliates operate 66 commercial information exchanges (CIEs) across the country. CIEs differ from traditional MLSs in that listing brokers do not offer to cooperate on the same terms will all buyer brokers. Instead, co-brokerage agreements must be negotiated for each transaction.

Increasing globalization has made international business of growing importance in commercial real estate. Twenty-four percent of commercial realtors report that international transactions are an important part of their business, and 16 percent report that their international business transactions are growing (National Association of Realtors 2013b).

The Structure of the Real Estate Brokerage Industry

Two annual surveys provide detailed information about the structure of the real estate brokerage industry. The annual Real Trends survey provides extensive information on the operations of brokerage firms. The annual NAR membership survey has detailed information about brokers and sales agents.

As Table 13.1 shows, most real estate offices are small. In 2012, the average brokerage office closed $87 million in sales and earned $2.35 million in gross commission income.

Table 13.1 **The Average Real Estate Brokerage Office**

	2011	*2010*	*% Change*
Closed sales volume	$87,041,511	$85,821,406	1.4
Gross commission income	$2,351,685	$2,261,366	4.0
Average commission rate (%)	2.7	2.6	2.5
Number of transaction sides	351	345	1.7
Number of agents	45	46	–2.2
Full-time	36	31	16.1
Part-time	9	15	–40.0
Average commission per agent	$38,392	$36,193	6.1
Transaction sides per agent	7.8	7.5	4.0
Firms franchise affiliated (%)	56	Unavailable	Unavailable

Source: Real Trends 2012.

The average commission rate earned on sales was 2.7 percent. Because a brokerage firm earns commission income when it sells a listing or closes a buyer-agent sale, the average commission figure represents just half of the total commission generated by a real estate transaction, with the sides split equally.

Each real estate transaction has two sides: one paid by the seller (the commission to the listing agent) and the other paid by the buyer (the commission to the buyer agent). The average real estate office assisted in 351 transaction sides and employed 45 agents, 36 full-time and 9 part-time. On average, agents assisted in 7.8 transaction sides per year and earned an average of $38,392 in commission income.

The small size of brokerage firms is reflected in the way they are legally organized. Fifty-three percent of real estate brokerage firms are organized as S-corporations, 27 percent are limited liability corporations (LLCs), and 3 percent are sole proprietorships. Only 7 percent are organized as C-corporations. The average number of shareholders per firm is 3.5. Beck, Scott, and Yelowitz (2012) find market concentration levels are low, indicating no tendency toward domination by a single firm or group of firms.

Franchise Affiliation

Because real estate firms tend to be small, many seek competitive advantage through affiliation with a national or regional franchise. Real Trends (2012) reports that 56 percent of brokerage firms were franchise affiliated in 2012. The NAR survey finds that only 38 percent of NAR members were affiliated with a franchise, while 59 percent worked for an independent company (National Association of Realtors 2012a).

The Real Trends (2012) survey reports that franchise-affiliated firms have higher commission income and sales volume but lower net incomes. In 2012, the average commission income for franchise-affiliated firms was 5.5 percent higher than non-affiliated firms, but because expenses were higher for affiliated firms, their average net operating income was lower. Franchise-affiliates had a net operating income to sales ratio of 0.3 percent, while independent firms reported a ratio of 1.7 percent.

Information Technology

The rapid increase in information technology continues to have a dramatic impact on the real estate brokerage industry. A NAR survey reveals that more than 90 percent of members use email and desktop computers daily (National Association of Realtors 2012a). Additionally, 78 percent have smart phones with wireless email and Internet capabilities that they employ in daily use, and 93 percent report that email is their preferred method for communicating with clients and customers. Ten percent of members have a blog and 54 percent actively use social and professional networking websites.

Nearly two-thirds of NAR members have a website on which they provide information about their listings, buying and selling of real estate, mortgage rates, local schools, and other information. Members spend an average of just $200 to maintain their websites, but those who spend more get a larger percentage of their business through web traffic.

The Real Trends (2012) survey reports that the average real estate brokerage website drew 358,014 unique visitors in 2012. Of this traffic, 47.8 percent came from search engines such as Google, 30.7 percent came by the visitor typing in the URL of the brokerage firm, and 21.4 percent came from referring sites such as Trulia.com, Craigslist.org, Facebook.com, and Realtor.com. The 2012 NAR homebuyer survey reveals that 89 percent used the Internet to assist them in their housing search (National Association of Realtors 2012b). This percentage is up from 71 percent in 2002.

Competition in Real Estate Brokerage

The structure of competition in the real estate brokerage industry has become a topic of interest to policymakers and others interested in the functioning of the brokerage market. The Federal Trade Commission (FTC) (2007) notes that commission rates tend to be stable and the industry has little price competition. Because commission rates are relatively stable, a real estate agent's income will differ dramatically based on the price of the house. This is despite the effort expended by the agent to sell a more expensive house being little more than that required to sell a less expensive one.

Little data are available on average commission rates in the real estate industry. The data that exist are from the annual *Brokerage Performance Report* published by Real Trends, which obtains these data by a survey of brokerage firms across the country. Its 2012 report (containing data from 2011) reflects results from a survey of over 650 U.S. brokerage offices. Figure 13.4 plots average the commission rates reported by Real Trends between 1991 and 2011. From 1991 through 2005, average rates fell 17.7 percent. Since 2005, the trend in rates has turned up, with average rates rising 7.6 percent.

The pattern of commission rates shown in Figure 13.4 suggests a negative correlation between commission rates and real housing prices. As real home prices rose from 1991

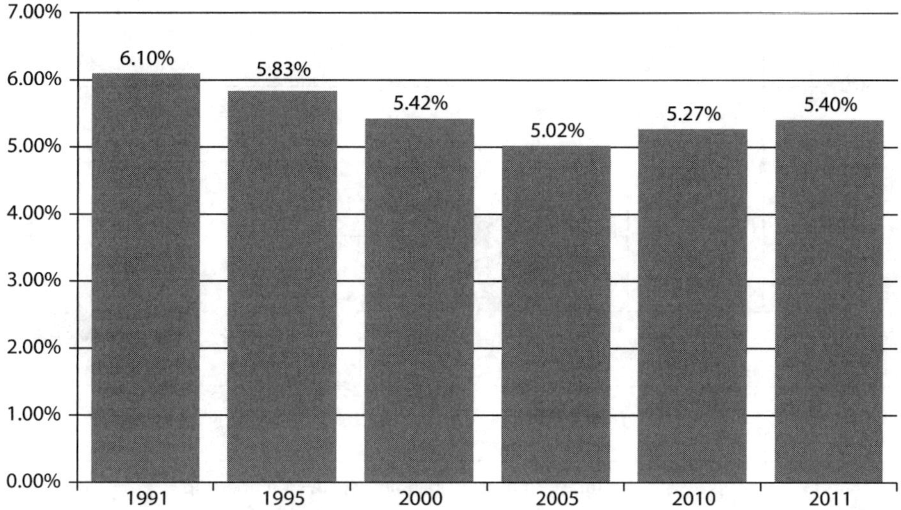

Figure 13.4 Average Commission Rates: 1991–2011. Source: Real Trends.

through 2005, the average commission rate fell, but when housing prices turned down following 2005, brokerage commission rates started to rise.

As the Federal Trade Commission (2007) notes, the variation in real housing prices has been greater than the variation in commission rates (see Table 13.2). From 1991 through 2005, real housing prices rose 49.5 percent, but real home prices have fallen 19.4 percent since 2005. The real price that homebuyers and sellers paid for brokerage services rose when home prices went up during 1991–2005 and did not fall proportionally when home prices fell after that year.

Table 13.2 **Commission Rates, Home Prices, and NAR Membership, 1991–2011**

Year	*Average Commission (%)*	*Median Existing Home Prices (in $2006)*	*Average Real Commissions*	*Existing Home Sales*	*Total Real Commission Income*	*NAR Membership*
1991	6.1	$153,925	$9,389	3,146,000	$29,537,794,000	763,965
1995	5.8	$155,365	$9,058	3,849,000	$34,864,242,000	719,673
2000	5.4	$172,427	$9,346	5,173,000	$48,346,858,000	766,560
2005	5.0	$230,059	$11,549	7,080,000	$81,766,920,000	1,265,367
2011	5.4	$185,337	$10,015	4,260,000	$42,663,301,587	1,009,940

Note: The table shows the calculation of total commission income, which is estimated by multiplying the average commission rate times home price times the number of existing home sales.

Source: FTC.

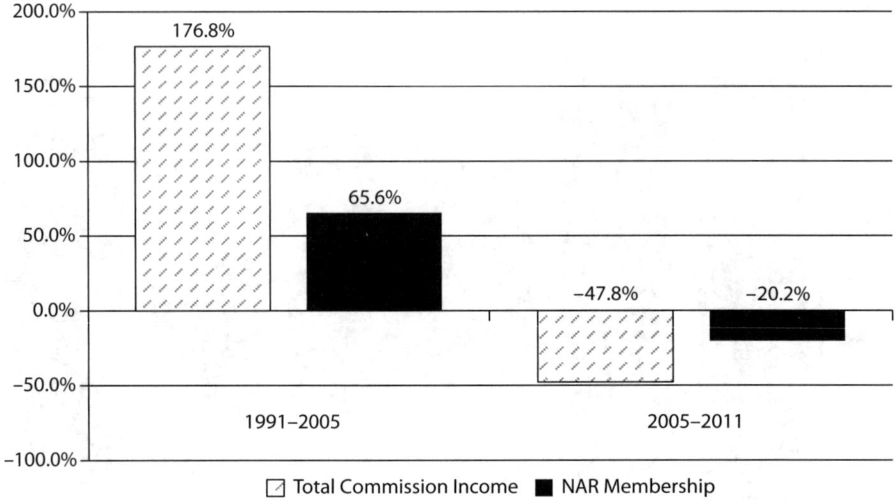

Figure 13.5 Real Estate Brokerage Industry Income and NAR Membership: 1991–2011
Source: National Association of Realtors (2013a).

Because commission rates are relatively inflexible and housing market sales and prices volatile, corresponding volatility exists in total brokerage income over the housing cycle. Figure 13.5 plots the percentage changes in total commission income and NAR membership from table 13.2. From 1991 through 2005, brokerage industry income rose 176.8 percent, but it fell 47.8 percent after 2005. This wide fluctuation in brokerage industry income is associated with a correspondingly wide fluctuation in industry employment, as agents and brokers enter and leave the industry. From 1991 through 2005, NAR membership rose 65.6 percent but has dropped 20.2 percent since 2005.

Questions of economic efficiency and equity have motivated research on the brokerage industry. According to Hsieh and Moretti (2003), the market for brokerage services is economically inefficient with relatively fixed commission rates and low barriers to entry. Buyers and sellers pay more for brokerage services in cities where housing prices are higher, although the quality of services remains relatively the same. Real estate agents in more expensive cities are no better off because the higher price of brokerage services stimulates the entry of more agents who compete away any gains in income. The higher commissions paid by buyers and sellers in more expensive cities are simply wasted through the entry of more agents who could be engaged productively elsewhere. In more expensive housing areas (1) agents and brokers comprise a larger fraction of the total labor force, (2) agent productivity (homes sold per agent) is lower, and (3) the real wages of brokers are no higher. Similar criticisms of the inefficiency of the brokerage industry are offered by Wachter (1987), Lande and Marvel (2000), Yavas (2001), and Miceli, Pancak, and Sirmans (2007) who show that fixed commission rates and low barriers to entry help foster the inefficiency.

Many observers believe that fixed commissions reflect monopolistic collusion among brokers by their joint involvement in local boards and the associated MLS (Federal Trade Commission 2007). In contrast, Bruce and Santore (2006) contend that higher-fixed commission rates arise because buyers and sellers cannot observe the level of effort or the quality of service provided by the broker. As a result, the market's normal price mechanism cannot work. Because the home seller cannot observe how efficiently the broker works and how much effort is expended, the seller faces a trade-off. A lower commission rate may allow the seller to keep a higher percentage of the sales price, but cause the broker to work less diligently resulting in a lower sales price or a longer time on the market. Therefore, the optimal commission rate is a balance between these two considerations. Competition among brokers does not reduce average commission rates because home sellers are worse off by insisting on lower rates. A lower rate leads to inferior service. On the other hand, brokers do not benefit over the longer term from higher rates. Increased entry and non-price competition tend to eliminate the broker's economic profit.

The traditional assumption has been that commissions are relatively fixed and reflect market failure. Others question the assumption of fixed rates. Sirmans and Turnbull (1997) find that the commission rate responds to changes in housing market conditions and agent costs, as in a competitive market. Schnare and Kulick (2009) examine the variation in buy-side commission rates across markets from 2000 through 2007 in seven metropolitan statistical areas. Commission rates are market determined, not fixed. Rates fall in more active markets and rise with agent experience.

Brokerage, Price, and Time on the Market

Many academic studies examine the question of how the buyer's or seller's use of a real estate agent affects the terms of a real estate transaction. Jud and Frew (1986) investigate housing prices paid in the broker-assisted portion of the market versus the for-sale-by-owner market in Charlotte, North Carolina. Homes sold with broker assistance, through the MLS, sold for an average of 3 percent more, controlling for differences in housing quality. Sellers can shift part of the real estate commission to buyers because broker-listed properties are easier to find, resulting in a saving in buyer search costs. Salant (1991) and Yavas (1992) report similar results.

Huang and Rutherford (2007) examine the impact of the realtor designation on homes sold through an MLS. Realtor properties sell at higher prices and with shorter marketing times. The realtor designation appears to provide a signal of quality to homebuyers.

Baryla and Zumpano (1995) find that homebuyers who use real estate brokers have shorter search times. Brokers act as effective market intermediaries. Elder, Zumpano, and Baryla (1999) show that brokers reduce buyer search time by increasing the intensity of search. Rutherford, Springer, and Yavas (2001) investigate whether exclusive agency contracts produce different price outcomes and marketing times than the standard exclusive right to sell contract. In the exclusive right to sell contract, the seller agrees to sell only through one particular agent and not to sell directly to a buyer. Exclusive agency contracts (where the owner retains the right to sell directly to a buyer) are associated with lower prices and shorter marketing times.

Benefield, Pyles, and Gleason (2011) examine how using increasingly popular limited-service brokers as compared with traditional full-service brokers affects housing transactions. Limited-service listings sell for more and quicker than traditional full-service listings. The effects differ by price category. Higher priced homes sell more quickly but not at relatively higher prices. Lower priced homes sell for higher prices but do not sell more quickly.

Rutherford and Yavas (2012) study the effects on price and time on the market when a seller selects a discount broker. Houses listed by discount brokers sell at prices similar to non-discount brokerage listings. These houses are less likely to sell, and remain on the market three days longer when they do sell. Lower transaction costs do not affect prices in the housing market, but affect liquidity or marketing time.

Munneke and Yavas (2001) explore whether the most productive agents self-select into 100 percent commission contracts with their firms. If so, they generate higher selling prices and shorter time on the market for their clients. More productive agents are more likely to select the 100 percent contract. Empirical tests show no differences in the selling prices or marketing times generated by 100 percent commission agents versus other agents employed under more traditional arrangements.

Johnson, Zumpano, and Anderson (2008) compare 100 percent versus traditional split-commission agents in terms of selling price and time on the market. Standardizing for home quality, 100 percent commission agents obtain higher selling prices with lower selling times than split-commission agents.

Turnbull and Dombrow (2007) examine how characteristics of the individual agent and firm affect price and time on the market. The gender of the agent has no influence on either price or time on the market. Salter, Mixon, and King (2012) find that female agents are associated with significantly higher selling prices.

The characteristic that Turnbull and Dombrow (2007) finds most important is the degree of specialization of the agent and the firm. Agents who specialize in obtaining listings produce higher selling prices, while those more specialized in buyer representation obtain lower prices. Firms that specialize in listing and selling properties in particular geographic areas produce higher selling prices for houses sold in that area. Brastow, Springer, and Waller (2012) report similar results for geographic specialization. Brokers become more efficient if they concentrate their marketing efforts in a limited geographic area of a city. Sellers who list properties within a broker's geographic area of expertise are rewarded with higher selling prices and shorter marketing times.

Rutherford, Springer, and Yavas (2005) maintain that the fixed percentage commission system induces agents to reduce effort. They compare sales of agent-owned properties with those sold by agents on behalf of clients. They find no significant difference in selling time, but agent-owned properties sell at a higher price. Levitt and Syverson (2008) report similar findings. Agent-owned properties sell at a 4–5 percent premium but were on the market for a longer time. These results are similar to those by Rutherford, Springer, and Yavas (2007) involving condominium sales. Agents who sell their own condominiums receive a 3–7 percent premium but experience marketing times that are 3 percent longer.

Another way that real estate agents influence the terms of a transaction is through their physical attractiveness. Salter, Mixon, and King (2012) study the impact of agent beauty on the prices of the houses they sold. More attractive agents are associated with higher selling prices, suggesting that prettier agents receive higher wages per transaction.

Global Real Estate Brokerage

The rules governing agency arrangements, buyer and seller representation, agent and broker liability, government regulation, the use of auctions, and the fees and commissions differ among countries. Although many differences are well known, no one has undertaken a systematic cataloging of country differences.

Miceli (1988) reports a major difference between the United States and Great Britain in market arrangements. The local MLS prevalent in the United States is largely absent in Great Britain. The use of auction sales is another area where wide differences exist. Auction sales are more common in Australia and New Zealand than in the United States, where their use is associated with distressed sales. Dotzour, Morehead, and Winkler (1998) show that auction sales produce above average prices in countries where they are widely used. In the United States, auction sales normally produce lower sales prices (Mayer 1998). However, Ashenfelter and Genesove (1992) report that auctions of condominiums generate higher prices, andQuan (2002) finds that auctions of vacant lots also produce higher prices.

Delcoure and Miller (2002) survey real estate commission rates in 30 countries in 1999. Figure 13.6 shows a frequency diagram of the results. The median commission rate is 4.8 percent but the reported U.S. rate is 6 percent. Rates tend to be lower in advanced countries and where the number of sales per agent is higher. When Delcoure and Miller apply their model to the United States, the conclusion is that rates are too high. Rates in the United States should be closer to the 3 percent average reported in Belgium, Japan, and the United Kingdom.

Globalization is leading individuals and firms to buy and sell property across international boundaries. This may lead to greater uniformity of practice in the brokerage industry internationally, resulting in the formulation of a global framework for rules of

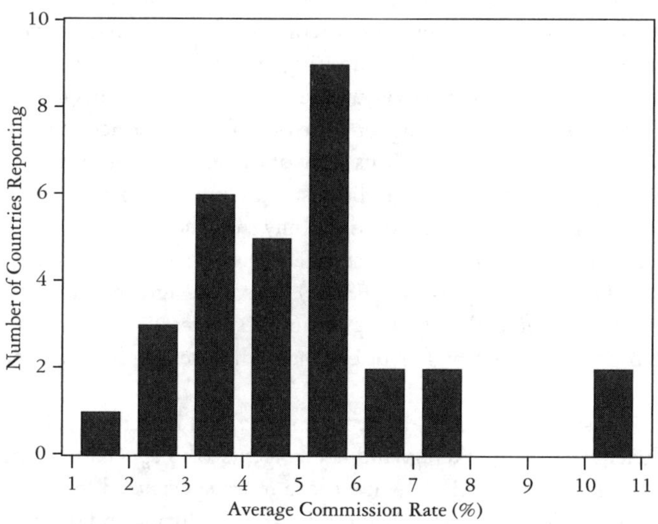

Figure 13.6 International Variation in Average Brokerage Commission Rates: 1999.
Source: Delcoure and Miller (2002).

best practice in the delivery of brokerage services. This trend is already apparent in the Royal Institute of Chartered Surveyors (RICS) developing an international code that outlines how real estate brokers and agents should conduct their business. The efforts of internationally franchised brokerage firms to push for uniformity of practice in the countries in which they operate are also evident.

Summary and Conclusions

Buyers and sellers need brokers and agents to assist with real estate transactions because they lack market information that is too time-consuming or expensive to acquire on their own. In 2012, the real estate sector of the economy employed 1.4 million full- or part-time individuals, and the National Association of Realtors reported a membership of 1.0 million.

Real estate brokers and agents are subject to a comprehensive set of federal and state laws that require them to treat their customers fairly, not to discriminate, and to fully disclose all relevant information that may affect the value of a property transaction. All states and the District of Columbia require that agents and brokers be licensed in order to sell real estate. Among the basic licensing requirements are that candidates complete a minimum number of hours of classroom instruction, pass an exam, and obtain a minimum level of experience. Additionally, most areas require a minimum number of hours of annual continuing education.

Because real estate firms tend to be small, many seek competitive advantage through affiliation with a franchise. Franchise-affiliated firms have higher commission income and sales volume but lower net incomes.

The structure of competition in the real estate brokerage industry has become a keen topic of interest. According to the FTC, commission rates tend to be stable and little price competition is evident. With relatively fixed commission rates and low barriers to entry, the market for brokerage services is economically inefficient. Buyers and sellers pay more for brokerage services where housing prices are higher, although the quality of brokerages services remains relatively the same. Real estate agents in more expensive cities are no better off because the higher price of brokerage services stimulates entry to compete away any gains in income. This view of the brokerage industry is not universally accepted. Competing evidence indicates that commission rates are not fixed and the market may not be as inefficient as commonly supposed.

General agreement exists that the use of an agent results in a higher selling price when compared to for-sale-by-owner (FSBO) sales. Less agreement exists on whether agents consistently generate the highest price in the shortest period of time. Agents who sell their own properties get higher prices than when they sell similar properties for clients.

The degree of specialization of the agent and the firm is an important characteristic affecting efficiency in the brokerage industry. Agents who specialize in obtaining listings produce higher selling prices, while those more specialized in helping the buyer obtain lower prices. Firms and brokers concentrating on listing and selling properties in particular geographic areas produce higher selling prices and lower marketing times for houses sold in their local area.

Institutional arrangements governing the transfer of real estate internationally differ widely, including agency arrangements, buyer and seller representation, agent and broker liability, government regulation, the use of auctions, and the level of fees and commissions. Research comparing commission rates suggests that those in the United States may be too high and should be closer to rates in Belgium, Japan, and the United Kingdom. Increasing globalization leads individuals and firms to buy and sell property across international boundaries. Over time, globalization is likely to foster more uniformity of practice in the brokerage industry internationally and result in the formulation of a global framework for rules of best practice in the delivery of brokerage services.

Discussion Questions

1. Discuss the level of employment and income in the real estate brokerage industry.
2. Describe the major factors influencing employment and income in the brokerage industry.
3. Explain what licensing requirements are needed to work in the real estate brokerage industry.
4. Discuss the economic structure of the real estate brokerage industry.
5. Explain whether the real estate brokerage industry operates in an economically efficient manner.

References

Ashenfelter, Orley, and David Genesove. 1992. "Testing for Price Anomalies in Real Estate Auctions." *American Economic Review* 82:2, 501–505.

Association of Real Estate License Law Officials. 2012. *Digest of Real Estate License Laws and Current Issues*. Chicago: Association of Real Estate License Law Officials.

Baryla, Edward A., and Leonard V. Zumpano. 1995. "Buyer Search Duration in the Residential Real Estate Market: The Role of the Real Estate Agent." *Journal of Real Estate Research* 10:1, 1–14.

Beck, Jason, Frank Scott, and Aaron Yelowitz. 2012. "Concentration and Market Structure in Local Real Estate Markets." *Real Estate Economics* 40:3, 422–460.

Benefield, Justin D., Mark K. Pyles, and Anne Gleason. 2011. "Sale Price, Marketing Time, and Limited Service Listings: The Influence of Home Value and Market Conditions." *Journal of Real Estate Research* 33:4, 531–564.

Benjamin, John D., G. Donald Jud, and G. Stacy Sirmans 2000a. "Real Estate Brokerage and the Housing Market: An Annotated Bibliography." *Journal of Real Estate Research* 20:1/2, 217–278.

Benjamin, John D., G. Donald Jud, and G. Stacy Sirmans 2000b. "What Do We Know about Real Estate Brokerage?" *Journal of Real Estate Research* 20:1/2, 5–30.

Brastow, Raymond T., Thomas M. Springer, and Bennie D. Waller. 2012. "Efficiency and Incentives in Residential Brokerage." *Journal of Real Estate Finance and Economics* 45:4, 1041–1061.

Bruce, Donald, and Rudy Santore. 2006. "On Optimal Real Estate Commissions." *Journal of Housing Economics* 15:2, 156–166.

Bureau of Economic Analysis. 2013. *Income & Employment by Industry*. Tables 6.2D and 6.4C. http://www.bea.gov/iTable/iTable.cfm?ReqID=9&step=1#reqid=9&step=1&isuri=1.

Bureau of Labor Statistics. 2012. *Occupational Outlook Handbook*. Washington, DC: Bureau of Labor Statistics.

Davies, Pearl. 1958. *Real Estate in American History*. Washington, DC: Public Affairs Press.
Delcoure, Natalya, and Norman G. Miller. 2002. "International Residential Real Estate Brokerage Fees and Implications for the US Brokerage Industry." *International Real Estate Review* 5:1, 12–39.
Dotzour, Mark G., Everard Morehead, and Daniel T. Winkler. 1998. "The Impact of Auctions on Residential Sales Prices in New Zealand." *Journal of Real Estate Research* 16:1, 57–71.
Elder, Harold W., Leonard V. Zumpano, and Edward A. Baryla. 1999. "Buyer Brokers: Do They Make a Difference? Their Influence on Selling Price and Search Duration." *Real Estate Economics* 26:2, 337–362.
Federal Trade Commission. 2007. *Competition in Real Estate Brokerage*. Washington, DC: Federal Trade Commission.
Gardiner, J'Noel, Jeffrey Heisler, Crocker H. Liu, and Jarl G. Kallberg. 2007. "The Impact of Dual Agency." *Journal of Real Estate Finance and Economics* 35:1, 39–55.
Grohman, Joseph M. 1987. "A Reassessment of the Selling Real Estate Broker's Agency Relationship with the Purchaser." *St. John's Law Review* 61:4, 560–590.
Hsieh, Chang-Tai, and Enrico Moretti. 2003. "Can Free Entry be Efficient? Fixed Commissions and Social Waste in the Real Estate Industry." *Journal of Political Economy* 111:5,1076–1122.
Huang, Biqing, and Ronald C. Rutherford. 2007. "Who Are You Going to Call? Performance of Realtors and Non–realtors in a MLS Setting." *Journal of Real Estate Finance and Economics* 35:1, 77–93.
Johnson, Ken H., Leonard V. Zumpano, and Randy I. Anderson. 2008. "Intra–firm Real Estate Brokerage Compensation Choices and Agent Performance." *Journal of Real Estate Research* 30:4, 423–440.
Jud, G. Donald, and James Frew. 1986. "Real Estate Brokers, Housing Prices, and the Demand for Housing." *Urban Studies* 23:1, 21–31.
Lande, Robert H., and Howard P. Marvel. 2000. "The Three Types of Collusion: Fixing Prices, Rivals, and Rules." *Wisconsin Law Review* 2000:941, 1–44.
Levitt, Steven D., and Chad Syverson. 2008. "Market Distortions When Agents Are Better Informed: The Value of Information in Real Estate Transactions." *Review of Economics and Statistics* 90:4, 599–611.
Mayer, Christopher J. 1998. "Assessing the Performance of Real Estate Auctions." *Real Estate Economics* 26:1, 41–66.
Miceli, Thomas J. 1988. "Information Costs and the Organization of Real Estate Brokerage Industry in the United States and Great Britain." *AREUEA Journal* 16:2, 173–188.
Miceli, Thomas J., Katherine A. Pancak, and C. F. Sirmans. 2007. "Is the Compensation Model for Real Estate Brokers Obsolete?" *Journal of Real Estate Finance and Economics* 35:1, 7–22.
Munneke, Henry J., and Abdullah Yavas. 2001. "Incentives and Performance in Real Estate Brokerage." *Journal of Real Estate Finance and Economics* 22:1, 5–21.
National Association of Realtors. 2006. *Real Estate Brokerage Essentials: Managing Legal and Business Issues*. Washington, DC: National Association of Realtors.
National Association of Realtors. 2012a. *Membership Profile*. Washington, DC: National Association of Realtors.
National Association of Realtors. 2012b. *Profile of Home Buyers and Sellers*. Washington, DC: National Association of Realtors.
National Association of Realtors. 2013a. *Historical Membership Statistics*. Washington, DC: National Association of Realtors. http://www.realtor.org/membership/historic-report.
National Association of Realtors. 2013b. *Commercial Member Profile*. Washington, DC: National Association of Realtors.
Quan, Daniel C. 2002. "Market Mechanism Choice and Real Estate Disposition: Search versus Auction." *Real Estate Economics* 30:3, 365–384.
Real Trends. 2012. *Brokerage Performance Report*. http://www.realtrends.com.
Rutherford, Ronald C., Thomas M. Springer, and Abdullah Yavas. 2001. "The Impact of Contract Type of Broker Performance." *Real Estate Economics* 29:3, 389–409.

Rutherford, Ronald C., Thomas M. Springer, and Abdullah Yavas. 2005. "Conflicts between Principals and Agents: Evidence from Residential Brokerage." *Journal of Financial Economics* 76:3, 627–665.

Rutherford, Ronald C., Thomas M. Springer, and Abdullah Yavas. 2007. "Evidence of Informational Asymmetries in the Market for Residential Condominiums." *Journal of Real Estate Finance and Economics* 35:1, 23–38.

Rutherford, Ronald C., and Abdullah Yavas. 2012. "Discount Brokerage in Residential Real Estate Markets." *Real Estate Economics* 40:3, 508–535.

Salant, Stephen W. 1991. "For Sale by Owner: When to Use a Broker and How to Price the House." *Journal of Real Estate Finance and Economics* 4:2, 157–174.

Salter, Sean P., Franklin G. Mixon, Jr., and Ernest W. King. 2012. "Broker Beauty and Boon: A Study of Physical Attractiveness and Its Effect on Real Estate Brokers' Income and Productivity." *Applied Financial Economics* 22:10, 811–825.

Schnare, Ann, and Robert B. Kulick. 2009. "Do Real Estate Agents Compete on Price? Evidence from Seven Metropolitan Areas." In Edward L. Glaeser and John M. Quigley, eds., *Housing Markets and the Economy: Risk, Regulation and Policy. Essays in Honor of Karl E. Case*, 308–347. Cambridge, MA: Lincoln Institute of Land Policy.

Sirmans, C. F., and Geoffrey K. Turnbull. 1997. "Brokerage Pricing under Competition." *Journal of Urban Economics* 41:1, 102–117.

Turnbull, Geoffrey K., and Jonathan Dombrow. 2007. "Individual Agents, Firms, and the Real Estate Brokerage Process." *Journal of Real Estate Finance and Economics* 35:1, 57–76.

Wachter, Susan M. 1987. "Residential Real Estate Brokerage: Rate Uniformity and Moral Hazard." In Austin J. Jaffe and Richard O. Zerbe, Jr., eds., *Research in Law and Economics* 10, 189–210. Greenwich, CT: JAI Press Inc.

Yavas, Abdullah. 1992. "A Simple Search and Bargaining Model of Real Estate Markets." *AREUEA Journal* 20:4, 533–548.

Yavas, Abdullah. 2001. "Impossibility of a Competitive Equilibrium in the Real Estate Brokerage Industry." *Journal of Real Estate Research* 21:3, 187–200.

Zietz, Emily Norman, and G. Stacy Sirmans. 2011. "Real Estate Brokerage Research in the New Millennium." *Journal of Real Estate Literature* 19:1, 5–40.

14

Green Buildings

SANDY BOND
Professor of Property Studies, Commerce Faculty, Lincoln University

ELAINE WORZALA
Director and Professor, Carter Real Estate Center, School of Business, College of Charleston

Introduction

Commercial real estate investors have always been aware of the need to take environmental matters into account. Legislation such as the Clean Air Act of 1970, which is administered by the U.S. Environmental Protection Agency (EPA), makes it a legal requirement. Since then, environmental concerns related to energy and resource conservation have become increasingly important.

Some estimates indicate that buildings contribute around 30 percent, on average, of greenhouse gas emissions globally, although this varies substantially from country to country. Estimates of greenhouse gas emissions from buildings indicate the United Kingdom as the highest (42 percent), followed by the United States (38 percent), Australia (23 percent), and New Zealand (17 percent) (World Green Building Council 2010). According to the Australian Greenhouse Office (1999), renamed the Department of Resources, Energy and Tourism after 2007, electricity is responsible for the majority of emissions in buildings. In terms of operational energy applications, cooling, air handling, lighting, and heating account for around 84 percent of commercial building greenhouse gas emissions. Improving energy efficiency of buildings is the quickest and most cost-effective way of reducing greenhouse gas (GHG) emissions (Creyts, Derkach, Nyquist, Ostrowski, and Stephenson 2007).

Both supply and demand factors have driven the movement toward a more sustainable environment. Companies, tenants, and occupiers, as well as investors and landlords, have begun to demand real estate that is green certified. On the supply side, regulations are being put in place that require owners to measure and disclose the energy performance of their buildings, reduce their energy consumption, and minimize detrimental impacts on the environment. The pace of change differs widely across the globe, with Australia, New Zealand, the United Kingdom, and Europe leading the way.

These forces are causing major changes in the real estate marketplace. If an owner or investor is not strategically looking at the green footprint of their investments, those assets will quickly become obsolete and lose value. An understanding of sustainability and sustainable design features and how these factors affect the value of commercial property is an important requirement for property investors. This requirement covers those who have sustainable property in their investment portfolios or have a desire to do so, and property appraisers involved in valuing such property.

This chapter briefly reviews the beginnings of the international environmental movement, reports on regulations developed across the globe to reduce energy use and carbon dioxide (CO_2) emissions, and summarizes the growth of the green building rating and certification systems that have been put in place since 2000. The regulations and the rating systems are constantly evolving, so the chapter provides examples to motivate the discussion. As with many of the externalities affecting a real estate investment, investors must stay constantly tuned to changes in policies and regulations. The final section of the chapter reviews some recent research that investigates the economic case for green buildings and outlines the implications for real estate investors. The chapter also addresses more recent trends going forward including the development of performance measurement systems designed to help change behavior.

Sustainability Concepts

This section provides a brief history of sustainability and its meaning. It also discusses some institutional investment drivers for green buildings.

HISTORY AND DEFINITIONS

The laudable pursuit of global economic growth, an agenda developed by the World Bank in the mid-1940s, led to rapid industrialization, but with it came a degradation of the environment and a reduction in scarce natural resources. To address these issues and harmonize prosperity with ecology, the World Commission on Environment and Development (WCED) was established in 1983. This organization later became known as the Brundtland Commission, to unite countries to pursue sustainable versus economic development together. The Brundtland Commission officially dissolved in December 1987 after releasing the *Brundtland Report*, also known as *Our Common Future* (World Commission on Environment and Development 1987). The most common definition for sustainable development was a byproduct of this report.

"Sustainable development is the kind of development that meets the needs of the present without compromising the ability of future generations to meet their own needs" (World Commission on Environment and Development 1987, 43).

In 1994, the term *triple bottom line* began to be used to describe sustainability in terms of the balance between the economy, environment, and social aspects of economic development. The term is commonly associated with both corporate social responsibility (CSR) and sustainable development (SD) (Elkington and Robins 1994). The various Earth Summits (1992 Rio Summit, 1997 Earth Summit + 5, 2002 United Nations World Summit on Sustainable Development, and 2012 Rio + 20) were aimed at developing a global action plan for sustainable development. This plan has become part of the global climate change agenda. More recent meetings have highlighted that implementation efforts have largely been unsuccessful (United Nations Economic and Social

Council 2002). Matthews and Hammill (2009, 1119) note that the main problem since the 1992 Rio Summit has been "in designing the move from theory to practice."

Understanding sustainable or green buildings and how these can contribute positively to climate change is the major focus of this chapter. According to the U.S. Environmental Protection Agency (EPA) (2012), *sustainable development* is the practice of creating structures and using processes that are environmentally responsible and resource-efficient throughout a building's life-cycle. For a new building, this would include all phases from planning to design, construction, operation, maintenance, renovation, and deconstruction.

INSTITUTIONAL INVESTMENT DRIVERS FOR GREEN BUILDINGS

According to Foliente, Delsante, Ren, Ton, Ambrose, Higgins, and White (2009), while the building sector is not the largest contributor to GHG emissions, it is one of the fastest-growing. In 2002, eight countries responded to concerns about the impact of the property sector on the environment by establishing the World Green Building Council (WorldGBC). One of the more advanced Green Building Councils is the U.S. Green Building Council (USGBC) formed in 1993. According to the USGBC website (U.S. Green Building Council 2013a), the mission is to "transform the way buildings and communities are designed, built and operated, enabling an environmentally and socially responsible, healthy, and prosperous environment that improves the quality of life."

Trying to reduce the impact of buildings on the environment involves understanding the main features that contribute to making a building energy efficient or an energy hog. Table 14.1 on the next page details those features that can substantially reduce energy consumption. According to the Green Building Council of Australia (2008) in its matrix of cost versus sustainability, the following items are considered to be the lowest cost and to have the highest sustainability benefit.

- Building user training program
- Automatic heating, ventilation, and air conditioning (HVAC) switch off
- Passive solar orientation
- Fire test water retention
- Reduction in photocopiers/printers due to dedicated rooms
- T5 fluorescent lighting
- Xeriscape landscaping
- Zero ozone depleting potential building insulation
- Energy use targets and monitoring

Regulations

The real estate community has seen a substantial increase in environmental legislation and regulations that affect the built environment, as governments trying to meet GHG emissions reduction targets to combat climate change. Several countries have been leaders in this arena including the European Union (EU), Australia, and New Zealand. These trends are discussed below.

Table 14.1 **Features Contributing to the Energy Efficiency of a Building**

Building Design and Materials	*Water Use*	*Heating/Cooling*	*Ventilation/Air Quality*	*Lighting/Daylight*	*Use of Renewable Energy Sources*
Specialized glazing (e.g., low emissivity; double glazing)	Flow restrictors and/or efficient fixtures/fitting	Specialized glazing (low emissivity; double)	Low volatile organic compounds (VOC) materials	Specialized glazing (Low emissivity; double) T5 lighting	Photo-voltaic arrays
Solar passive	Waterless urinals	Chilled beams	Fresh air	Maximize natural light by placement of building	Solar panels
Large floor plates/ campus style/ open plan	Rainwater capture	External and internal shading blinds	CO_2 levels constantly monitored	External and internal shading blinds (some sensor controlled)	Wind turbines
Recycled timber; or sustainability harvested timber	Leak detection systems	Multi-zone tenant controlled	Opening windows	Motion light sensors	Harbor heat rejection system

Table 14.1 **continued**

Building Design and Materials	*Water Use*	*Heating/Cooling*	*Ventilation/Air Quality*	*Lighting/Daylight*	*Use of Renewable Energy Sources*
Recycled materials	Sensor taps	Thermal massing (e.g., limestone wall)	Indoor plants	Open plan to maximize daylight penetration	Gas powered co-generation plant
Reduction in use of PVC piping	Multi-cycle systems for cooling towers	Perimeter water pipes to assist cooling			Fuel cell
Low volatile organic compound materials	Grey-water or black-water recycling systems	Solar chimneys (heat extraction and draw in fresh air); solar panels; photo-voltaic (PV) cells			
No polyvinyl chloride (PVC) backing on carpet tiles		Separate air handling units for each façade and interior zone			
Fit-out to match building		Vertical planting for shading			

Source: Bond 2010.

The European Union's Energy Performance of Buildings Directive (EPBD) was the first mandatory system for energy labeling of buildings. The stated goals of the EU are to reduce energy consumption and eliminate wastage that will, among other things, help the EU meet its Kyoto Protocol commitments. The directive came into force in 2006 and required the 27 member states to comply with the following four requirements by 2009:

1. general framework for a methodology to calculate the integrated performance of buildings (Article 3);
2. setting minimum standards in new and existing buildings (Articles 4, 5, 6);
3. energy certification of buildings (Article 7); and
4. inspection and assessment of heating and cooling installations (Articles 8, 9) by independent experts (Article 10).

However, many countries encountered difficulty in implementing the Directive. After the launching of the Concerted Action (CA) EPBD designed to support the sharing of information and experiences from national adoption and implementation between member states (Concerted Action EPBD 2013), the Directive was recast in 2010 (Directive 2010/31/EU).

Member states such as England and Wales sequentially implemented the requirements for the certification of buildings between August 2007 and October 2008. For non-domestic buildings, energy performance is shown as a single CO_2 based index, based on a scale of A to G, with A being very efficient and G being least efficient. The Energy Performance Certificate (EPC) also shows the energy rating of the building. An accredited assessor conducts the assessments. Public buildings greater than 1,000 square meters (about 11,000 square feet) require a Display Energy Certificate (DEC). The DEC shows the actual energy consumption for the current year in the form of an operational rating (OR) as well as the performance over the previous three years (Concerted Action EPBD 2011).

Haydock and Arbon (2009) studied the implementation of the EPBD in Europe. They identify various barriers to implementation and those relating to the United Kingdom, including:

- Difficulty in identifying, training, and re-educating all parties in the building chain, from architects to engineers to auditors on regulations and requirements of the EPBD.
- Basing energy certificates for existing buildings on calculations using consumption data is problematic for old building complexes that may be comprised of buildings of widely varying types, with different heating types and joint metered supplies.
- Interpreting the Directive and subsequent consultations within government as to how it should be implemented has caused delays and frustration. The lack of clarity with the wording has led to numerous interpretations within the three distinct governing bodies of the United Kingdom (England and Wales, Northern Ireland, and Scotland) and consequently, major differences occur in delivery methodology and requirements.
- Incorporating high specification energy efficiency has met with resistance by developers concerned about initial capital costs. Their focus is on selling the asset upon completion.

On January 16, 2012, the EU adopted the Delegated Regulation (EU) No. 244/2012 supplementing Directive 2010/31/EU and Directive 2002/91/EC on the energy performance of buildings by establishing a comparative methodology framework for calculating cost-optimal levels of minimum energy performance requirements for buildings and building elements. The Buildings Performance Institute Europe (BPIE 2010) analyzed the status of implementation of EPC schemes across selected member states. It identified various challenges and issues and found that many individual EU member states encounter difficulties in implementing EPCs within their national legal frameworks. Member states have varying implementation solutions: the chosen calculation methods, the registration procedures, promotional activities undertaken, and quality control mechanisms and enforcement systems. These differences lead to discrepancies between countries in the ability of EPCs to effect change and bring about energy efficiency improvements in buildings across Europe. The report identifies factors that could enhance the effectiveness of implementation such as: involving multidisciplinary stakeholders in the design; learning from the experience and knowledge of others; ensuring the implementation approach fits with everyday practice; developing a registration system suitable for monitoring and evaluation; raising public awareness of the EPC through promotion and communication; and designing a sound system for the enforcement of EPC obligations.

In Australia, the National Strategy on Energy Efficiency (NSEE) was introduced in 2009 and updated in 2010 to accelerate energy efficiency efforts and help businesses prepare for the introduction of a carbon 'price' or tax. New buildings and major renovations will be designed and constructed according to increasingly stringent energy efficiency standards in the Building Code of Australia (BCA). Efficiency provisions for HVAC systems and for artificial lighting are designed to lead to a reduction in energy consumption. After the NSEE, the Building Energy Efficiency Disclosure Act 2010 established the Commercial Building Disclosure (CBD) Program. The program requires energy efficiency information to be provided when commercial office space of 2,000 square meters or more (about 21,500 square feet, or more) is offered for sale or lease (Australian Government Department of Resources, Energy, and Tourism 2103). The aim of this legislation is to improve the energy efficiency of Australia's largest office buildings and to ensure prospective buyers and tenants are informed about conservation efforts. Building owners must obtain a Building Energy Efficiency Certificate (BEEC) before the building goes on the market for sale, lease, or sublease. A BEEC is valid for 12 months and is undertaken by accredited assessors. The process includes:

- the building's National Australian Built Environment Rating System (NABERS) (2013) Energy Star rating;
- a tenancy lighting assessment of the relevant area of the building; and
- general energy efficiency guidance.

In an efficient market, consumers make informed choices about the buildings they buy and lease, showing preference for the good performers and it is hypothesized that building owners and investors will respond by investing in the more energy efficient buildings (Council of Australian Governments 2010).

New Zealand has long recognized that the environment needs to be protected and resources conserved. The Resource Management Act (RMA), passed in 1991, was the first statutory planning regime to incorporate the principle of sustainability (Smith 1997). It incorporated sustainable management as an explicitly stated purpose that directs all other policies, standards, plans, and decision-making under the RMA. Subsequently, Prime Minister Helen Clark in a term from 1999 to 2008 was pro-active in addressing climate change and environmental issues. Under her leadership, New Zealand became a party to the Kyoto Protocol.

To meet its Kyoto Protocol commitments, the New Zealand government introduced a raft of sustainability initiatives including in 2001 the New Zealand Energy Efficiency and Conservation Strategy (NZEECS) (Energy Efficiency and Conservation Authority and Ministry for the Environment 2001). According to the EECA (EECA 2007, 10), the NZEECS is "a detailed action plan for increasing the uptake of energy efficiency, conservation and renewable energy programmes across the economy and to make doing so part of the normal behavior of New Zealanders."

A second version of the NZEECS, published in 2007 (EECA 2007), focused on actions and set targets. Related to commercial buildings, these included increased stringency of lighting and HVAC performance requirements in the building code, development of the Building Energy End Use Project (BEEP), designed to research how and where commercial buildings use energy, and finally, the investigation of a building energy rating scheme for New Zealand (EECA 2007).

The third edition of the five-year NZEECS 2011–2016 (EECA 2011) was changed to advocate a market-driven approach. The strategy avoids specifying a list of government energy efficiency initiatives. It states that the government will support market-based solutions such as the use of building performance rating tools. In addition, the New Zealand government's procurement reform provides an important lever to support public sector agencies in making energy efficient choices in the purchase and lease of energy efficient buildings. As such, "local government has a significant role in providing community leadership" (EECA 2011, 27).

In the United States, mandatory energy performance disclosure is on a state by state basis. For example, following similar moves in other cities and states, from July 1, 2013, California commercial building owners must comply with California Public Resources Code, §25,402.10, first enacted as AB 1103 (Saldana) in 2007. This regulation requires owners to track and disclose detailed information about energy consumption of each building in excess of 50,000 square feet.

Green Rating Systems and Other Assessment Tools

While the above discussion provides details about regulations for the measurement of the energy performance of buildings, other rating tools have been developed to measure a wider range of sustainable features than just energy consumption. The Building Research Establishment Environmental Assessment Method (BREEAM), which measures environmental performance, not just energy use, was the first building rating system to be established globally in 1990. This rating system covers 10 categories (Building Research Establishment 2012). Over the next two decades other countries adopted rating systems. Table 14.2 shows the main commercial building rating systems available

Table 14.2 **Description of Alternative Green Rating Systems by Country**

Rating System	*Year*	*Country*	*Description*
BREEAM Building Research Establishment (BRE) Global Ltd	1990	United Kingdom	First global building rating system. Used to assess both new and existing buildings. BREEAM uses a percentage scoring system that equates to a star rating: • Unclassified < 10; Acceptable ≥ 10 to < 25 (1 star) • Pass ≥ 25 to < 40 (2 star); Good ≥ 4 to < 55 (3 star) • Very Good ≥ 55 to < 70 (4 star); Excellent ≥ 70 < 85 (5 star) • Outstanding ≥ 85 (6 star) (BRE 2012) Categories: management; health and wellbeing, energy, transport, water, materials, waste, land use and ecology, and pollution (Inbuilt 2010)
LEED USGBC. Green Building Certification Institute	2000	United States	LEED certification is available for all building types, new and existing. Categories in the rating include: sustainable sites, water efficiency, energy and atmosphere, materials and resources, indoor environmental quality, and innovation in design. Four levels out of a total 100 points: • Certified 40–49; Silver 50–59; Gold 60–79; Platinum 80 and above (U.S. Green Building Council 2013)
Energy Star Environmental Protection Agency (EPA)	2000	United States	The rating is based on utility bill data and building information. This data is entered into Portfolio Manager, EPA's free online tool for measuring and tracking energy use, water use, and greenhouse gas emissions. The tool calculates a 1 – 100 ENERGY STAR score. Buildings that score a 75 or higher are eligible to apply for ENERGY STAR certification. The information within the application must be verified as accurate by a professional engineer or registered architect.
Green Star Green Building Council of Australia (GBCA)	2002	Australia	Green Star evaluates the environmental design and construction of new and refurbished buildings based on categories similar to the BREEAM rating system. Points are awarded for 3 levels: Best Practice 45–59 (4 star); Australian Excellence 60–74 (5 star); and World Leaders 75 + (6 star)

Table 14.2 **continued**

Rating System	*Year*	*Country*	*Description*
National Australian Built Environment Rating System (NABERS) New South Wales Office of Environment and Heritage	2005	Australia	Measures the environmental performance of buildings and tenancies: energy efficiency, water usage, waste management, and indoor environment quality. Takes into account the net rentable area of the building, number of computers, and hours of operation. Converted into a scale from one to six stars, with 6 stars market-leading performance (NABERS 2011)
Green Star New Zealand Green Building Council (NZGBC)	2005	New Zealand	Non-residential property only, rating tools are available for the following property types/categories: office, interiors, industrial, and education. Home Star was introduced in 2010 to cater for residential buildings. In 2012, BASE (Building a Sustainable Environment) was introduced specifically for the Christchurch rebuilding efforts after the earthquakes. It is an introductory-level green building assessment tool to benchmark the environmental features. For Green Star rated buildings, the categories and point system are the same as for Australia (NZGBC 2011a, b)
NABERSNZ Administered by NZGBC.	2013	New Zealand	The Energy Efficiency and Conservation Authority (EECA) is the principal sponsor for the introduction and use of NABERS in New Zealand. EECA is the licensee of NABERSNZ launched in New Zealand in June 2013 (EECA 2013)

today. Reed, Bilos, Wilkinson, and Schulte (2009) offer a more complete discussion of the evolution of these rating systems internationally.

The most common type of measure or rating scheme used to evaluate environmental performance detailed in Table 14.2 is that a building can be certified that it has attained a given score/level in terms of its green attributes. For example, a Leadership in Energy and Environmental Design (LEED) rated building, which is part of the USGBC rating scheme, will be certified as silver, gold, or platinum depending on the number of points that are captured in the whole building rating scheme. Alternatively, Energy Star is a rating scheme developed by the U.S. Environmental Protection Agency (EPA) that focuses on the actual measurement of energy consumption in buildings.

Impact on the Financial Performance and Value of Real Estate

Since 2000 the real estate industry has begun to look at the built environment and its role in reducing greenhouse gas emissions as well as examining the business case for building new or retrofitting existing buildings that are sustainable. Many empirical studies have directly tried to isolate promised benefits of the green movement including higher prices or rental rates, lower operating expenses, lower occupancy rates, and other performance measures often associated with a real estate investment. The majority of this work centers on the office sector in major U.S. cities using primarily the CoStar database. A few studies involve other countries including Australia (Newell, MacFarlane, and Kok 2011; Gabe and Rehm 2013), and the United Kingdom (Chegut, Eichholtz, and Kok 2011; Fuerst and McAllister 2011a). Table 14.3 provides a summary of some of this research for countries other than the United States. Table 14.4 summarizes results inside the United States. Christensen (2013) and Robinson (2013) offer a detailed review of studies in this area and Hyland, Lyons, and Lyons (2012) provide a review of some research in the residential real estate sector.

A summary of the most relevant findings, include:

1. An increase in sales prices for both LEED and Energy Star rated buildings. Researchers studied LEED buildings more often and tended to find higher impacts, up to a 26 percent price increase for a building with LEED certification (Fuerst and McAllister 2011b), although the more common premiums were in the 7–10 percent range.
2. An increase in rental rates or net operating income (NOI) for properties that have a LEED certification. In most cases, the researchers report increases between 3 and 7 percent, although one study finds an increase as high as 17 percent (Wiley, Benefield, and Johnson 2010).
3. A minor decrease in capitalization (cap) rates.
4. An increase in occupancy rates up to 18 percent, but the more common result is around 10 percent.
5. Lower energy consumption that often translates to lower occupancy costs, lower vacancy rates, and higher worker productivity (Chappell and Corps 2009; Dorsey and Reid 2012).

Table 14.3 **Sustainable Real Estate Results: Outside United States**

Reference	*Country*	*Data/Time Period*	*Findings*
Chappell and Corps (2009)	Canada	Three studies of the impact of high performance construction on valuations	High performance buildings compared to market have lower energy consumption, operating costs, and vacancy rates. More marketability
Chegut, Eichholtz, and Kok (2011)	United Kingdom	CoStar 2000–2009, BREEAM	21 percent higher rental rates and 26 percent higher sales prices for green buildings
Fuerst and McAllister (2011b)	United Kingdom	IPD appraised values, rental rates and yields	No impact on the performance of green properties
Kok and Jennen (2011)	Holland	Proprietary databases of real estate companies Lease transactions	Buildings rated as energy inefficient have 7 percent lower rents
Newell, MacFarlane, and Kok (2011)	Australia	Jones Lang LaSalle and CBRE Green Star and NABERS rated office buildings	• 5 percent higher gross rent, 12 percent higher sales price, 0.6 percent lower vacancy rate, and 0.02 percent lower cap rate for Green Star Rating • 0.6 percent higher gross rent, 9 percent higher price, 6 percent lower vacancy rate and 0.15 percent lower cap rate for NABERS 5-Star Rating • 0.2 to (−0.3) percent higher gross rent, 2.5 percent higher sales prices, 5–7 percent lower vacancy rate and 0.05 percent lower cap rate in NABERS 3–4.5 Star Rating
Op't Veld and Vlasveld (2013)	Holland	CBRE managed retail properties with energy labels	Found green properties had lower rents and higher vacancies than non-green properties until more traditional attributes such as location and size are considered, then the difference attributed to the label disappears
Gabe and Rehm (2013)	Australia	489 Lease transactions in 76 NABERS energy certified buildings in Sydney	Found no difference in rents between highly rated green buildings and poorly rated green buildings. Conclude that green price premiums are paid by the owner not the tenant

Table 14.4 **Sustainable Real Estate Results: United States**

Reference	*Data/Time Period*	*Findings: impact of green features on property performance*
Miller, Spivey, and Florance (2008)	CoStar 2008 Energy Star and LEED buildings compared with noncertified buildings	• Absorption: faster rates for LEED-rated buildings, except 2006 2Q • Price: 10 percent premium for LEED, 6 percent premium for Energy Star • Rent: $2.50 per sq. ft. annual premium for LEED
Fuerst and McAllister (2009)	CoStar Energy Star and LEED	Occupancy: 8 percentage points higher for LEED and 3 percent higher for Energy Star rated buildings
Miller, Pogue, Gough, and Davis (2009)	CoStar 2010 sales Class A	• Rents and Prices: higher for LEED • Vacancy: Not conclusive for LEED, lower for Energy Star
Eichholtz, Kok, and Quigley (2010)	CoStar 2004–2007 Energy Star and LEED buildings compared with noncertified buildings	• Occupancy: 11 percent higher rates for LEED • Rent: face rents 3 percent higher for LEED, effective rents 7 percent higher • Prices: 16–17 percent higher for Energy Star
Pivo and Fisher (2010)	NCREIF 1999–2008 for LEED	• Occupancy: 1 percent higher, plus 20 basis points more in regeneration zone of CBDs • Prices: 9 percent higher, plus 7 percent higher prices in CBDs, 9 percent higher prices when near transit in CBDs • NOI: 3 percent higher plus 8 percent higher NOI in CBDs.; utility costs 13 percent lower • Cap rate: 5.2 basis points lower
Wiley, Benefield, and Johnson (2010)	CoStar January 2008 Energy Star and LEED buildings compared with noncertified	• LEED: 5–17 percent higher rent, 16–18 percent higher occupancy rates and $129 higher sales price • Energy Star: 7–9 percent higher rent, 10–11 percent higher occupancy rates and $29.71 higher prices

Table 14.4 **continued**

Reference	*Data/Time Period*	*Findings: impact of green features on property performance*
Das, Tidwell, and Ziobrowski (2011)	CoStar 2007–2010 San Francisco and Washington, DC	• Rents: higher for LEED • 2.4 percent in recession, 0.1 percent in expansion
Fuerst and McAllister (2011a)	CoStar 1999–2008 Energy Star and LEED buildings compared with noncertified buildings	• LEED: 4–5 percent higher rent and 25 percent higher price; depends on level • Energy Star: 4 percent higher rental, 1–3 percent higher occupancy and 26 percent higher prices
Reichardt, Frantz, Rottke, and Zietz (2012)	CoStar 10 largest metros 2000–2010 Energy Star	• Rents: 2.5–2.9 percent higher • Occupancy: higher
Dorsey and Reid (2012)	Case Study of Duke building in Charlotte, NC, energy conservation	• Energy use: down 22 percent; water down 75 percent • Worker productivity: up 2 percent • Construction costs: up 3 percent, paid back in 10 years
Eichholtz, Kok, and Quigley (2013)	CoStar tenant 2004–2009	3 percent higher rental rates, 8 percent higher effective rents and 13 percent higher sales prices for LEED
Robinson (2013)	CoStar Leases 2011 Sales 2001–2011	Rents and prices higher for Energy Star buildings and Dual Energy Star/LEED buildings
Das and Wiley (2013)	CoStar Comps 2004–2011	Price: up 10.6 percent for LEED and 16.4 percent for Energy Star, though depends on the property type and geographic market

6. Green premiums disappear when the research moves away from broad building-level data and examines individual leases and individual appraisals (Gabe and Rehm 2013; Op't Veld and Vlasveld 2013; Robinson 2013). In all three studies, once other variables are added to the models to account for characteristics including location and size, the green premiums were no longer significant. This research suggests a lack of a complete understanding of the relationship between green features in a building and its performance for an investor or owner.

The majority of the studies in this area before 2008 were more general and focused on the case for sustainability and how green features should be incorporated into valuation reports (Lützkendorf and Lorenz 2005; Ellison, Sayce, and Smith 2007; Lowe and Chappell 2007; Lorenz and Lützkendorf 2008). Sayce, Sunderberg, and Clements (2010) provide an extensive review of studies on sustainable real estate that were completed before the more recent set of empirical studies. The researchers identify 128 studies that examine real estate sustainability. Since 2008, there has been a shift in emphasis and studies have focused on ways to incorporate the impact of individual sustainability features on the value of a piece of property (Myers, Reed, and Robinson 2007; Chappell and Corps 2009; Muldavin 2010; Runde and Thoyre 2010).

Impact on Employee Productivity and Satisfaction

Yudelson (2010) outlines the drivers for green building, other than financial performance, including:

- increased occupier productivity, due to improved health of tenants and reduced absenteeism;
- marketing benefits, especially for developers and building owners;
- public relations benefits, especially for developers, building owners, and managers;
- recruitment and retention of key employees; and
- demonstration of commitment to sustainability and environmental stewardship.

According to Ang and Wilkinson (2008), regulation is the tool government uses to drive the market toward more energy efficient buildings. Additionally, many public sector agencies are leading by example. For example, the General Services Administration (GSA) in the United States have incorporated mandatory LEED certified buildings in their Request for Proposals (RFPs) for space. Large corporations in the private sector are also providing leadership in green buildings (Bond 2010; Nelson, Rakau, and Dorrenberg 2010; Christensen 2013). Many companies have a strong environmental focus and a sustainability policy at the core of their business, leading them to occupy green space. This behavior is commonly called corporate social responsibility (CSR). Some investment firms are taking on socially responsible property investment strategies (Pivo and McNamara 2005). Pivo (2008) finds that the top ranked criteria for real estate investment decisions are energy efficiency and conservation, high level of public transport services, transit-oriented development, daylight and natural ventilation, and development that contributes to higher density, mixed-use walkable places. In their survey of 56 New Zealand based property professionals, Bond and Perret (2012) report similar results showing the top three drivers for sustainable development in New Zealand are a benefit to the environment, tenant demand, and corporate social responsibility.

According to the Green Building Council of Australia (2008), tenants have become less focused on savings in operating costs, and are placing a higher value on the intangible benefits such as productivity, staff attraction and retention, and reduced sick leave and absenteeism. Miller, Spivey, and Florance (2008) estimate the productivity benefits from environmentally sustainable building designs to be as much as 10 times the energy savings from strategies to include green features in a building.

A major problem with using these intangible factors for making the business case for green buildings is that productivity and health benefits are harder to assess and measure with any degree of accuracy than quantifiable energy and water savings from these buildings. However, a correlation exists between improvements in indoor air quality, better lighting and building comfort, and worker health and productivity (Kats 2003).

The benefits of green development, including the intangible ones mentioned above, are only evident over time. For example, a post-occupancy study by Paevere and Brown (2008) of the CH2 building in Melbourne, Australia, finds that productivity increased 10.9 percent by moving from the former building CH1 to CH2. The study includes physical indoor environmental quality (IEQ) measures as well as evaluation of occupant health, well-being, and productivity based on occupant questionnaires, spot health symptoms questionnaires, focus group interviews, sick leave (absenteeism), and staff turnover data. The occupant surveys yielded results from more than 260 employees in CH1 and CH2. The 10.9 percent productivity increase translates to an annual cost saving of $2.4 million (AU). The energy saving of $370,000 reduces the payback time for the increased costs of going green to between five and seven years. Choi (2009) recommends constant documentation and communication about the costs, benefits, and performance.

Barriers to Investing in Green Buildings

Despite the advantages of sustainable buildings, many barriers exist to investing in green buildings (Urban Land Institute 2009; Bond 2010; Yudelson 2010) including:

- *Financial considerations.* A big barrier to investing in green buildings is the perception that they cost more compared to conventional buildings. Most studies show the true cost to be negligible (Matthiessan and Morris 2004, 2007; Ciochetti and Gowan 2010) but some tabulate the cost to be as high as 7 percent (Kats 2003; Miller et al. 2008). The most successful green building strategies result from using a holistic approach to design, allowing the design team to innovate solutions by involving the builder, tenant, facility manager, and contractors early in the design process. Further, using tried and tested technologies, ensuring the interior fit-out matches the base building, and requiring all relevant contractors to stay involved during the commissioning and tuning process (at least 12 months) as well as providing the necessary documentation to aid the certification process ensured successful outcomes, while helping to control the costs involved in green building development (Bond 2010).

- *Split incentives.* Landlords are responsible for investing in green buildings but it is the tenants that benefit through reduced energy and water costs and increased employee productivity. If the leases are written with the landlord responsible for the green features but the tenants receive the benefits, landlords have difficulty rationalizing the investment if the payback period is long or is not captured in the market place with increased rents. Kahn, Kok, and Quigley (2013) find that tenants whose utilities are bundled into the rent consume more electricity than identical tenants who pay their own bills. If the marginal cost of energy to the tenant is zero, building managers are more likely to be required to keep energy consumption of the building in check. Thus, the party paying for the energy matters.
- *Lack of owner and tenant knowledge and experience.* A lack of practical understanding and misconceptions exist among building owners about energy efficiency and green buildings. Commonly, they overestimate the initial cost premium, which hinders the implementation of sustainability measures. Further, users and tenants need to be educated in how to best use the green features or attributes incorporated into their space.
- *Lack of incentives.* Incentives are not strong enough to change behavior. For example, energy prices are very low in many countries. Tax and other political incentives are insufficient to change behavior. Mandatory reporting regimes are aimed at addressing this, with the incentive being market-driven.

Summary and Conclusions

Since 1990 the green building movement has grown in importance. The demand for buildings that are energy efficient and kind to the environment has increased. Conversely, socially responsible investors and tenants are rejecting buildings that are carbon emitters. To remain competitive, new Class A commercial developments are striving to gain LEED or other certifications, and existing buildings are being retrofitted to similar standards. Driving this activity are regulations that mandate making energy performance data available to investors and tenants. Further, the majority of recent research shows that investors and tenants are willing to pay a premium for high performance buildings, yet others question these findings. Despite this controversy, green buildings have typically benefited from lower occupancy costs and vacancy rates.

Tracking energy performance and certifying green buildings are expected to become more prevalent as economies grapple with their environmental footprints and work to meet carbon emission reduction targets.

In conclusion, the challenge for the green building investor is to balance the need to reduce energy and resource consumption of commercial real estate with the need for a financial return on that investment. The perception that green buildings cost more than comparative non-green buildings and that these extra costs are difficult to recoup within a reasonable timeframe has tempered enthusiasm. More research and education are necessary to clearly demonstrate that the benefits outweigh the costs when considering the entire life cycle of a building and the productivity gains from employees occupying the space. This information needs to be widely disseminated if green buildings are to become the benchmark for the commercial real estate industry.

Discussion Questions

1. List the main drivers for green buildings.
2. Define sustainable development.
3. Discuss the extent to which buildings contribute to greenhouse gas emissions and its most common cause.
4. What factors or features in a building does the Australian Green Building Council consider to have the lowest cost but the highest sustainability benefit?
5. What is the main green rating tool used for commercial buildings in the United States and what does it measure?

References

Ang, Su Li, and Sara J. Wilkinson. 2008. "Is the Social Agenda Driving Sustainable Property Development in Melbourne, Australia?" *Property Management* 26:5, 331–343.

Australian Government Department of Resources, Energy, and Tourism. 2013. "What Is CBD?" http://cbd.gov.au/overview-of-the-program/what-is-cbd.

Australian Greenhouse Office 1999. *Australian Commercial Building Sector Greenhouse Gas Emissions 1990–2010: Executive Summary Report.* http://ee.ret.gov.au/energy- efficiency/strategies-and-initiatives/national-construction-code/greenhouse-gas-emissions/australian-commercial-building-sector-greenhouse-gas-emissions-1990-2010-executive-summary-report.

Bond, Sandy. 2010. "Lessons from the Leaders of Green Designed Commercial Buildings in Australia." *Pacific Rim Property Research Journal* 16:3, 314–338.

Bond, Sandy, and Guy Perret. 2012. "The Key Drivers and Barriers to Sustainable Development of Commercial Property in New Zealand." *Journal of Sustainable Real Estate* 4:1, 48–77.

Building Performance Institute Europe (BPIE). 2010. "Energy Performance Certificates across Europe: From Design to Implementation." http://www.buildup.eu/system/files/content/BPIE_EPC percent20report percent202010.pdf.

Building Research Establishment (BRE). 2012. "Operational Guidance for the BREEAM In–Use Scheme." http://www.breeam.org/filelibrary/BREEAM percent20In percent20Use/SD096_-Rev_21_BREEAM_In-Use_Scheme_Document.pdf.

Building Research Establishment Environmental Assessment Method (BREEAM). 2013. "Schemes." http://www.breeam.org/podpage.jsp?id=54.

Chappell, Theddi Wright, and Chris Corps. 2009. "High Performance Green Building: What's It Worth? Investigating the Market Value of High Performance Green Buildings." Seattle: Cascadia Chapter of the U.S. Green Building Council. http://www.capitalmarketspartnership.com/UserFiles/admin percent20GBValueStudy.pdf.

Chegut, Andrea, Piet Eichholtz, and Nils Kok. 2011. "The Value of Green Buildings: New Evidence from the United Kingdom." Working Paper for the Sustainable Investment Research Platform sponsored by Umea University in Sweden. http://www.sirp.se/getfile.ashx?cid=280784&cc=3&refid=34.

Choi, Chris. 2009. "Removing Market Barriers to Green Development: Principles and Action Projects to Promote Widespread Adoption of Green Development." *Journal of Sustainable Real Estate* 1:1, 107–138.

Christensen, Pernille. 2013. "Key Strategies of Sustainable Real Estate Decision-Making in the United States: A Delphi Study of the Stakeholders." PhD dissertation, Clemson University, Planning, Design and the Built Environment.

Ciochetti, Brian, and Mark McGowan. 2010. "Energy Efficiency Improvements: Do They Pay?" *Journal of Sustainable Real Estate* 2:1, 305–333.

Concerted Action EPBD. 2011. "Implementation of the EDBD in England and Wales, Scotland and Northern Ireland: Status in 2010." http://www.epbd-ca.org/Medias/Downloads/CA_Book_Implementing_the_EPBD_Featuring_Country_Reports2010.pdf.

Concerted Action EPBD. 2013. "Concerted Action Energy Performance of Buildings." http://www.epbd-ca.eu/.

Council of Australian Governments (COAG). 2010. *"National Strategy on Energy Efficiency: Updated 2010."* http://www.coag.gov.au/sites/default/files/nsee_update_july_2010.pdf.

Creyts, Jon, Anton Derkach, Scott Nyquist, Ken Ostrowski, and Jack Stephenson. 2007. *Reducing U.S. Greenhouse Gas Emissions: How Much at What Cost?* McKinsey, December. http://www.mckinsey.com/~/media/mckinsey/dotcom/client_service/sustainability/pdfs/reducing percent20us percent20greenhouse percent20gas percent20emissions/us_ghg_final_report.ashx.

Das, Prashant, Alan Tidwell, and Alan Ziobrowski. 2011. "Dynamics of Green Rentals of Market Cycles: Evidence from Commercial Office Properties in San Francisco and Washington, DC." *Journal of Sustainable Real Estate* 3:1, 1–22.

Das, Prashant, and Jonathan A. Wiley. 2013. "Determinants of Premia for Energy-Efficient Design in the Office Market." *Journal of Property Research*. http://dx.doi.org/10.1080/09599916.2013.788543.

Dorsey, Thomas, and Dustin Reid. 2012. "Best Practices in High-Performance Office Development: The Duke Energy Center in Charlotte, North Carolina." *Real Estate Issues* 37:2/3, 26–30.

Eichholtz, Piet, Nils Kok, and John Quigley. 2010. "Doing Well by Doing Good? Green Office Buildings." *American Economic Review* 100:5, 2492–2509.

Eichholtz, Piet, Nils Kok, and John Quigley. 2013. "The Economics of Green Building." *Review of Economics and Statistics* 95:1, 50–63.

Elkington, John, and Nic Robins. 1994. "Company Environmental Reporting. A Measure of the Progress of Business and Industry towards Sustainable Development, Technical Report No. 24." Nairobi: UNEP Industry and Environment Office.

Ellison, Louise, Sarah Sayce, and Judy Smith. 2007. "Socially Responsible Property Investment: Quantifying the Relationship between Sustainability and Investment Property Worth." *Journal of Property Research* 24:3,191–219.

Energy Efficiency and Conservation Authority (EECA) and Ministry for the Environment. 2001. "National Energy Efficiency and Conservation Strategy. Energy Efficiency and Conservation Authority." Wellington: Energy Efficiency and Conservation Authority.

Energy Efficiency and Conservation Authority (EECA). 2007. *The New Zealand Energy Efficiency and Conservation Strategy (NZEECS): Making It Happen*. http://www.eeca.govt.nz/sites/all/files/nzeecs-07.pdf.

Energy Efficiency and Conservation Authority (EECA). 2011. *New Zealand Energy Strategy: Developing our Potential and the New Zealand Energy Efficiency and Conservation Strategy 2011–2016*, August. http://www.eeca.govt.nz/sites/all/files/nz-energy-strategy-2011.pdf.

Energy Efficiency and Conservation Authority (EECA). 2013. *Office Building Rating Scheme Coming to New Zealand*. http://www.eecabusiness.govt.nz/content/office-building-rating-scheme.

Energy Star. 2012. "Energy Star: Celebrating 20 Years." http://www.energystar.gov/ia/about/20_years/ES_20th_Anniv_brochure_spreads.pdf?fc60-a3c1.

Foliente, Greg, Angelo Delsante, Zhengen Ren, T. Ton, Michael Ambrose, Andrew Higgins, and S. White. 2009. "AusZEH Roadmap: Developing Pathways toward Zero-Emission Housing in Australia." CSIRO Report USP2007/054, March.

Fuerst, Franz, and Patrick McAllister. 2009. "An Investigation of the Effect of Eco-Labeling on Office Occupancy Rates." *Journal of Sustainable Real Estate* 1:1, 49–64.

Fuerst, Franz, and Patrick McAllister. 2011a. "The Impact of Energy Performance Certificates on the Rental and Capital Values of Commercial Property Assets." *Energy Policy* 39:10, 6608–6614.

Fuerst, Franz, and Patrick McAllister. 2011b. "Green Noise or Green Value? Measuring the Effects of Environmental Certification on Office Values." *Real Estate Economics* 39:1, 45–69.

Gabe, Jeremy, and Michael Rehm. 2013. "Who Pays Green Office Premiums: Owners or Renters?" Working Paper, American Real Estate Society Meetings, Hawaii, April.

Green Building Council of Australia (GBCA). 2008. *The Dollars and Sense of Green Buildings 2008*. http://www.gbca.org.au/docs/dollars-sense08.

Green Building Council of Australia (GBCA). 2013. *Green Star Overview*. Available at http://www.gbca.org.au/green-star/green-star-overview/.

Haydock, Heather, and Jo-Anne Arbon. 2009. "Study on Energy Performance of Buildings." A study requested by the European Parliament's Committee on Industry, Research and Energy (ITRE), IP/A/ITRE/ST/2008–2010. http://www.europarl.europa.eu/committees/en/studiesdownload.html?languageDocument=EN&file=24491.

Hyland, Marie, Ronan Lyons, and Sean Lyons. 2012. "The Value of Domestic Building Energy Efficiency—Evidence from Ireland." Working paper 614, Department of Economics Discussion Paper Series, University of Oxford, June.

InBuilt. 2010. "BREAM versus LEED." http://www.ukpassivhaus.org/media/406565/breeam-vsleed.pdf.

Kahn, Matthew, Nils Kok, and John Quigley. 2013. "Energy Consumption and the Durable Building Stock: The Capital Vintage Paradox." http://www.corporate-engagement.com/files/file/KKQ percent20Commercial percent20050513.pdf.

Kats, Gregory. 2003. "Green Building Costs and Financial Benefits." Boston: Massachusetts Technology Collaborative. http://www.dcaaia.com/images/firm/Kats-Green-Buildings-Cost.pdf.

Kok, Nils, and Maarten Jennen. 2011. "The Impact of Energy Labels and Accessibility on Office Rents." *Energy Policy* 46:July, 489–497.

Lorenz, David, and Thomas Lützkendorf. 2008. "Sustainability in Property Valuation—Theory and Practice." *Journal of Property Investment & Finance* 26:6, 482–521.

Lowe, Tim, and Theddi Wright Chappell. 2007. "Special Consideration in the Value of Sustainable Properties." *PREA Quarterly* 11:2, 38–44.

Lützkendorf, Thomas, and David Lorenz. 2005. "Sustainable Property Investment: Valuing Sustainable Buildings through Property Performance Assessment." *Building Research and Information* 33:3, 212–234.

Matthews, Richard A., and Anne Hammill. 2009. "Sustainable Development and Climate Change." *International Affairs* 85:6, 1117–1128. http://onlinelibrary.wiley.com/doi/10.1111/j.1468-2346.2009.00852.x/pdf.

Matthiessan, Lisa Fay, and Peter Morris. 2004. "Costing Green: A Comprehensive Cost Database and Budgeting Methodology." Davis Langdon. http://www.usgbc.org/Docs/Resources/Cost_of_Green_Full.pdf.

Matthiessan, Lisa Fay, and Peter Morris. 2007. "Cost of Green Revisited: Reexamining the Feasibility and Cost Impact of Sustainable Design in the Light of Increased Market Adoption." Davis Langdon. http://www.davislangdon.com/upload/images/publications/USA/2004 percent20Costing percent20Green percent20Comprehensive percent20Cost percent20Database.pdf.

Miller, Norman, David Pogue, Quiana Gough, and Susan Davis. 2009. "Green Buildings and Productivity." *Journal of Sustainable Real Estate* 1:1, 65–89.

Miller, Norman, Jay Spivey, and Andrew Florance. 2008. "Does Green Pay Off?" *Journal of Real Estate Portfolio Management* 14:4, 385–400.

Muldavin, Scott. 2010. "Value Beyond Cost Savings: How to Underwrite Sustainable Properties. Green Building Finance Consortium." http://www.greenbuildingfc.com/Documents/Value%20Beyond%20Cost%20Savings—Final.pdf.

Myers, Georgia, Richard Reed, and Jon Robinson. 2007. "The Relationship between Sustainability and the Value of Office Buildings." 13th Annual Pacific Rim Real Estate Society (PRRES) Conference, January 21–24, Fremantle, Australia.

National Australian Built Environment Rating System (NABERS). 2011. *Fact Sheet 4: Preparing for NABERS Office Rating Applications*. http://www.nabers.gov.au/public/WebPages/DocumentHandler.ashx?docType=3&id=15&attId=0.

National Australian Built Environmental Rating System (NABERS). 2013. *Sustainability Initiatives Using NABERS: Green Star*. http://www.nabers.gov.au/public/WebPages/ContentStandard.aspx?module=10&template=3&include=programs.htm.

Nelson, Andrew J., Oliver Rakau, and Phillipp Dorrenberg. 2010. "Green Buildings: A Niche Becomes Mainstream." Deutsche Bank Research. http://www.dbresearch.com/PROD/DBR_INTERNET_EN-PROD/PROD0000000000256216.pdf.

Newell, Graeme, John MacFarlane, and Nils Kok. 2011. *Building Better Returns*. Sydney: Australian Property Institute.

New Zealand Green Building Council (NZGBC). 2011a. *Who We Are*. http://www.nzgbc.org.nz/index.php?option=com_content&view=article&id=62&Itemid=32.

New Zealand Green Building Council (NZGBC). 2011b. *New Zealand Green Building Council: Home*. http://www.nzgbc.org.nz/.

Op't Veld, Hans, and Martijn Vlasveld. 2013. "The Effect of Sustainability on Retail Investment Performance: International Evidence." Paper presented at the American Real Estate Society Meetings in Hawaii, April.

Paevere, Phillip, and Steven Brown. 2008. "Indoor Environment Quality and Occupant Productivity in the CH2 Building: Post Occupancy Summary." Report No. USP2007/23. http://www.melbourne.vic.gov.au.

Pivo, Gary. 2008. "Responsible Property Investment Criteria Developed Using the Delphi Method." *Building Research and Information* 36:1, 20–36.

Pivo, Gary, and Jeffrey Fisher. 2010. "Income, Value and Returns on Socially Responsible Property Investment." *Journal of Real Estate Research* 32:2, 243–269.

Pivo, Gary, and Paul McNamara. 2005. "Responsible Property Investment." *International Real Estate Review* 8:1, 128–143.

Reed, Richard, Anita Bilos, Sara Wilkinson, and Karl-Werner Schulte. 2009. "International Comparison of Sustainable Rating Tools." *Journal of Sustainable Real Estate* 1:1, 1–22.

Reichardt, Alexander, Fuerst Franz, Nico Rottke, and Joachim Zietz. 2012. "Sustainable Building Certification and the Rent Premium: A Panel Data Approach." *Journal of Real Estate Research* 34:1, 991–926.

Robinson, Spenser. 2013. "Measuring Well by Managing Good: The True Story of Sustainable Real Estate Premiums." Working Paper presented at the American Real Estate Meetings, Hawaii, April.

Runde, Timothy, and Stacy Thoyre. 2010. "Integrating Sustainability and Green Building in the Appraisal Process." *Journal of Sustainable Real Estate* 2:2, 221–248.

Sayce, Sarah, Anna Sunderberg, and Billy Clements. 2010. "Is Sustainability Reflected in Commercial Property Prices? A Review of the Evidence Base." London: RICS Research.

Smith, Gordon. 1997. "The Resource Management Act 1991—'A Biophysical Bottom Line' vs. 'A More Liberal Regime' A Dichotomy?" *Canterbury Law Review* 6:3, 499–538.

U.S. Environmental Protection Agency (EPA). 2012. *Green Building*. http://www.epa.gov/greenbuilding/pubs/about.htm.

U.S. Green Building Council (USGBC). 2013a. *About USGBC*. Available at http://www.usgbc.org/about.

U.S. Green Building Council. 2013b. *FAQ: LEED Green Building Certification System*. http://www.usgbc.org/sites/default/files/Docs3330.pdf.

United Nations Economic and Social Council. 2002. *Implementing Agenda 21: Report of the Secretary-General*. Commission on Sustainable Development acting as the preparatory committee for the World Summit on Sustainable Development, Second preparatory session, January 28–February 8, 2002. New York: United Nations Economic and Social Council.

Urban Land Institute. 2009. *Retrofitting Office Buildings to be Green and Energy-Efficient: Optimizing Building Performance, Tenant Satisfaction, and Financial Return*. Washington, DC: Urban Land Institute.

Wiley, Jonathan A., Justin Benefield, and Ken Johnson. 2010. "Green Design and the Market for Commercial Office Space." *Journal of Real Estate Finance and Economics* 41:2, 228–243.

World Commission on Environment and Development (WCED). 1987. *Our Common Future*. Oxford: Oxford University Press.

World Green Building Council. 2010. *Tackling Global Climate Change: Meeting Local Priorities, A World Green Building Council Special Report*, September. http://gbcbrasil.org.br/sistema/referencia/1_(201109265257)WORLDGBC.pdf.

Yudelson, Jerry. 2010. *Greening Existing Buildings*. New York: McGraw Hill.

Discussion Questions and Answers

Chapter 2 Institutional Real Estate Markets

1. Outline the major steps that institutional investors take in developing a real estate strategy.

   In developing a real estate strategy, institutional investors typically take the following steps: (1) allocate to the real estate asset class; (2) hire consultants and managers to develop the real estate strategy; (3) set property type, city, submarket, and property quality targets; (4) develop leverage strategy and limits; and (5) create implementation guidelines and targets.
2. Explain the major players in the institutional real estate investment process and their functions.

   The institutional real estate investment process involves three major players. First, institutional investors include pension funds, endowments, and real estate investment trusts (REITs). They allocate money to be invested in real estate for their constituents. Second, consultants provide advice, guidance, and oversight of the investment process. They help in developing the investment strategy, setting criteria for choosing investment managers, and selecting investment managers. Consultants provide performance measurement and monitor the investment managers. Third, managers receive investment commitments from the institutional investors and implement the client's investment strategy by finding, acquiring, managing, and disposing of real estate investments. They provide property-level accounting and performance measurement of properties they manage.
3. Identify the major reasons institutional investors include real estate in their portfolios.

   Institutional investors add real estate to their portfolios to increase potential returns, hedge against inflation, and gain portfolio diversification. Real estate has a relatively low correlation with other investments.
4. List and describe the main property-type risk categories institutional investors might consider in their real estate portfolios.

The main property-type risk categories are:

- Core properties. High quality properties in institutional grade markets.
- Core plus properties. High quality properties that need a small amount of upgrade or re-tenanting.
- Value added properties. Properties that need some rehabilitation or re-tenanting.
- Opportunistic properties. Good locations that need substantial rehabilitation, re-positioning, and full leasing or re-leasing.
- REITs. Public companies purchased for dividend income and price appreciation that are the liquid portion of the real estate allocation.
- Debt. Mortgages on residential or commercial buildings that produce income, or commercial mortgage backed securities (CMBS) that sell bonds backed by a pool of commercial mortgages.

Chapter 3 Real Estate Cycles: International Episodes

1. What determines housing price movement in a particular country or geographical area?

   The asset price of housing, at a given location and given time period, consists of two components—its fundamental value (F_t) and a shock (B_t). Conceptually speaking, F_t represents the discounted present value of expected rental income per period, *R*, in all future time periods. The expected rental growth rate can be construed as a depository of all effects of demand- and supply-side housing market fundamentals or their expected trends at time *t*. As such, realized and expected changes in demographic characteristics such as aging, baby boomers retirement and fertility, macroeconomic conditions, demand-supply mismatch either nationally or locally, credit supply, and even government regulations. The shock component (B_t), on the other hand, represents a non-measurable component in housing price based on market fundamentals. When the shock is positive ($B_t > 0$), the housing asset is overvalued, and vice versa. Some view its persistence as the main cause of cyclical housing price movement. A rational investor is still willing to buy even with a positive *B*, so long as there is an expectation of over-valuation growing over time at a rate at least equal to the time value of money. Here $E_t[B_{t+1}] = B_t \geq (1 + i_t) B_t$, where *i* is the appropriate discount rate in a rational bubble.
2. What are similarities and dissimilarities among the housing markets in the United States, Korea, and China?

   Different market fundamentals are at work in different countries over different periods. Emerging markets such as Korea and China often experience high levels of housing price volatility in the course of rapid industrialization and urbanization. Furthermore, the liberalization of mortgage lending in these countries often amplifies the cycle, generating spillovers to the macro-economy and financial system. Main public policy issues in the mortgage market differ between emerging market countries such as Korea and China and the United States. In the United States, high loan-to-value (LTV) and other affordable mortgage products are available to consumers, for which proper risk management through various prudential regulations is a critical policy issue. Mortgage lending is more conservative and tightly regulated in Korea and China through debt-to-income (DTI_ and LTV limits. The consequence is that mortgage loans are less available to borrowers constrained by income or wealth.

3. What are the main contributing factors to the contagious housing price cycles from the real (or non-financial) side of the housing sector?

   The main contributing factors to the contagious housing price cycles include rapid urbanization and chronic shortage of affordable housing (as in the case of Korea and China), consumer expectations of strong and sustained future housing price appreciation, land use and other development constraints (through their effects on housing supply elasticity), and over-supply by home builders during a booming period.

4. How can financial deregulation and pro-cyclical mortgage lending amplify housing price cycles?

   Evidence shows that both mortgage lending volume and borrowing constraints measured by LTV and DTI react to changes in housing prices with a positive correlation. Lenders pro-cyclically change lending constraints by raising volume and relaxing borrowing constraints during ebullient times as the rising asset prices reduce perceived default risk. This lending increases the share of natural or optimistic buyers and will bid up asset value. During the downturn, however, they reduce lending volume and make the underwriting criteria more restrictive exacerbating downward trends of housing prices and construction activity.

Chapter 4 Behavioral Real Estate

1. Identify several misconceptions about behavioral real estate.

   The greatest misconception about behavioral real estate is that behaviorists assume people are irrational. Behavioral studies can relate to rationality but they mainly differ in their definition of utility maximization. A second misconception is that behavioral real estate is an alternative to traditional real estate. More accurately, it is a different way of looking at a problem. Finally, researchers often think that behavioral real estate cannot be combined with a traditional approach but this belief is false. Several studies use otherwise traditional methods and incorporate transactions data but also supplement the analysis by using an experimental approach.

2. When would someone want to use a behavioral real estate concept instead of relying on purely traditional transactions data?

   Using a behavioral real estate concept instead of relying on purely traditional transactions data would be appropriate when:

   - Field data are inaccurate or have been intentionally manipulated.
   - Transactions data do not tell the whole story (i.e., the researcher has questions that go deeper than what transactions data can reveal).
   - No existing data set has been collected on the problem currently being investigated, which is often the case with behavioral studies.

3. Provide several examples of how behavioral real estate has been used to answer real estate research questions.

   Examples of how behavioral concepts have been employed to answer real estate research questions include when:

   - testing behavioral-specific concepts such as loss aversion, prospect theory, mental accounting, false reference points, familiarity bias, and regret aversion;
   - examining portfolio allocation questions;
   - examining financial market behavior relating to herding and preference for skewness in financial returns;
   - determining "just compensation" as it relates to eminent domain cases;
   - understanding strategic mortgage default considerations;
   - examining mortgage foreclosure contagions; and
   - determining why lenders rarely modify loans.

4. List some technologies being used in behavioral real estate research.

   Technologies used to complete behavioral real estate research projects include:

   - functional Magnetic Resonance Imaging (fMRI);
   - Agent-Based Modeling (ABM);
   - game theoretic based simulations;
   - experimental market software (like Z-Tree);
   - on-line experiments using existing data venders to access sample participants;
   - electroencephalography (a technology that measures contemporaneous brain activity during real estate decision-making processes);
   - ocular tracking (a device that measures the exact location where people are looking while evaluating a real estate decision on a computer screen); and
   - physiology equipment to measure Galvanic Skin Response (GSR) and pulse rate.

5. Identify fields from which behavioral real estate has borrowed ideas.

   Behavioral real estate has borrowed ideas from each of the following fields in order to answer real estate research questions: psychology, medicine, finance, economics, law, marketing, engineering, modeling and simulation, and natural sciences.

Chapter 5 Multifamily Investment

1. Explain why multifamily property may be a preferred investment for both institutional and small investors.

   The multifamily investment market is divisible, including property as small as duplex units or encompassing properties that span many acres with thousands of units. The units may be in high and midrise buildings or garden-style apartments. The rental rate is re-priced to the market level over a relatively short period of time. Multifamily property generates a cash flow that is more stable over time than many other property types because any one individual tenant or lease has less impact on overall valuation. The attractiveness of multifamily investment to the spectrum of investors is related to the transparency of operations, recurring mark-to-market of rents, potential substantial diversification of tenants and resulting stability in revenues, access to debt markets, and reduction in legal risk associated with tenant-landlord conflicts. The residential lease is one of the least complicated of real estate contracts. Standardized leases are the norm and the lease duration is short.

2. Identify the primary determinants of cap rates in the multifamily sector and indicate whether these rates are more or less known with certainty.

   The conventional cap rate is net operating income (NOI) divided by the value. The value is the NOI divided by the cap rate. For a Gordon growth model over time, the value is the NOI divided by a denominator. The denominator is the cap rate less the growth in NOI. This cap rate depends on submarket, property hedonics or physical characteristics, and macroeconomic variables. Researchers have been unable to determine the cap rate with accuracy in these models.

3. Discuss the role of the natural vacancy rate in multifamily investment.

   Each market and submarket has a *natural vacancy rate,* which is that rate where rent increases are zero. The rent growth is negative and falls when vacancy is above the natural rate. Alternative definitions of the natural vacancy rate are where rent increases are expected or are equal to the rate of inflation.

4. Explain what shifts rental rates, expenses, and returns.

   Multifamily rents are related to demographicsincluding population, density, and income. Neighborhood effects and amenities including location, access to transit, and distance away from noise are also important.

5. Identify the factors that affect per unit prices in multifamily investment.

   Both the characteristic of the property and owner affect prices. For property characteristics, size, number of units, location, and neighborhood factors influence price. For owner characteristics, evidence shows that out-of-towners, tax deferred exchangers, condominium converters, REITs, institutional investors providing additional capital, value-added investors, owners of foreclosed properties, and other clienteles pay different transaction prices. Capital structure and access also influence price.

Chapter 6 Retail Real Estate

1. The origin-destination (OD) survey used to model shopping destination choices includes only weekdays (Monday to Friday) but stores are also open on weekends. What is the effect of such a data bias on the model reliability and how could it be handled?

   A substantial share of all retail sales occurs during the weekend, often as family activities and from 9 a.m. to 6 p.m. Thus, not accounting for such sales may result in a distortion of shopping trip patterns derived from OD surveys. A solution to this problem is to include weekend trips in the survey.

2. For the same independent variables, odds ratios between big-box stores versus regional shopping centers can differ. How can these differences be explained and how do they relate to the independence of irrelevant alternatives (IIA) issue?

The IIA principle implies that introducing additional choice alternatives in the model should not affect the preference ranking already obtained. As Table 6.4 shows, trips to big-box stores and power centers are much more likely to be done by car than by bus. The likelihood of bus trips doubles when considering commercial streets and neighborhood centers as well as community centers as destination choice alternatives. This difference occurs because additional pairs of odds ratios must be considered for maximum likelihood computation.

3. What is the key concept underlying the existence and development of shopping centers and how does this concept apply to them?

    The existence and development of shopping centers rest on the concept of agglomeration economies, which also grounds urban spatial structure theories. In a shopping center, anchor tenants, usually located at each end of the mall so as to generate a sustained traffic flow, act as magnets for customers. Non-anchor retailers located in between feed on the agglomeration economies generated.

4. Why was the Herfindahl index initially developed and how is it operationally defined here for measuring retail concentration in shopping centers?

    The Herfindahl index was initially developed for measuring the degree of concentration of industrial production. Here, the Herfindahl index is defined as the sum of squares of stores' gross leasing area (GLA) shares for a given retail category in a given shopping center.

5. What do regression findings from this case study suggest about the influence that retail concentration exerts on shopping center unit base rents?

    Findings suggest that while raising intra-category retail concentration has an overall negative impact on base rents, the impact varies markedly depending on the retail category considered. For stores in categories with high barriers to entry and facing harsh competition on prime locations, the agglomeration economies they generate outweigh the bargaining power effect, with a higher level of retail concentration resulting in higher base rents. The reverse occurs for stores with few barriers to entry and facing extensive online competition. These stores benefit from a rent discount as retail concentration increases.

Chapter 7 Healthcare Facilities

1. Discuss whether hospital and nursing home beds are rising or falling in the United States.

    Hospitals and nursing homes are investable real estate assets because they obtain revenue and expenses at a specific facility. The occupancy of hospitals has been falling over time, even as the population ages. Shifts to nursing homes, copayments, and insurance restrictions on the length of stay are factors. Hospital beds and the number of facilities have been declining in the United States since 1980. Nursing home beds and nursing home facilities have been declining in the United States since 2000. Both have occurred even as the population has been rising.

2. In the presence of price controls and regulation, discuss whether excess demand or supply for healthcare facilities would exist.

Price control on healthcare utilization and facilities should suggest excess demand. Rent control is an example. But with healthcare facilities, excess supply occurs. Some view the unused capacity as providing facilities to deal with disaster surges.

3. Identify the major issues regarding demand and pricing for healthcare facilities.

   Public or private insurance pays the bill from the hospital or nursing home. The user faces a limited copayment and does not see the full charge that is made. By paying a relatively low price based on copayments and deductibles that reflect only a portion of total billing, patients increase their demand. Demand increases with the nature and extent of insurance coverage.
4. Identify the methods for managing the construction of hospitals and beds.

   The construction of new hospitals and beds is limited by state regulation for certificates of need. Under these restrictions, even adding beds at an existing hospital requires approval from a state agency.

Chapter 8 Healthcare Providers

1. Identify two behavioral issues leading to increased demand for healthcare.

   Behavioral issues leading to increased demand for healthcare include action and regret bias. Action bias involves requesting that providers make and take decisions. Patients often view not receiving a prescription on a doctor visit as a bad outcome even though many prescriptions are unnecessary and 25 percent are never filled. Regret bias is having too many choices available, making suboptimal decisions and then second-guessing afterwards.
2. Discuss how the U.S. healthcare system rewards facilities.

   The U.S. healthcare system rewards facilities. In a complex arrangement involving a coding system labeled as Current Procedural Terminology (CPT), the healthcare system pays higher fees at upgraded facilities including hospitals. The reimbursement is based on three factors: the work and skill of doctors, facility expenses, and malpractice. Of the two types of facility expenses, those at hospitals are better compensated.
3. Explain how patients and physicians inflate the demand for real estate in healthcare in the United States.

   Patients in the United States do not face the true cost of healthcare because they pay only 10 percent of the total cost out-of-pocket. As a result, their demand is much higher than would be expected in a true market. For their part, physicians rarely have to confront the costs of healthcare. Their power over the allocation of health resources—through their ability to admit patients, write prescriptions, and order tests—can raise healthcare expenditures well beyond what would occur in a market. This behavior of patients and physicians generates outsized demand for more healthcare facilities—hospitals, ambulatory care centers, and physician offices.
4. Discuss the locational differences in healthcare costs.

   A geographic cost price index (GCPI) is used to adjust medical care costs for reimbursement. This system is in place to reward parts of the country on the East and

West coasts that have higher expenses for supplies, equipment, and real estate. Yet, compensation of doctors is higher in areas away from the two coasts.

Chapter 9 Corporate Real Estate

1. How do firms not in real estate make their decisions to buy property and why are these decisions flawed?

   Most firms currently lease space if the present value of future rent is less than the present value of the cost of self-ownership, net of depreciation benefits and expected property appreciation. The correct model for the own-versus-lease decision must compare the present value of profits the corporation expects if it leases with the present value of expected profits if it decides to own real estate.
2. Why did firms not in the real estate business own property?

   In an era of industrial and manufacturing companies, a high proportion of corporate real estate was idiosyncratic properties such as factories, workshops, and industrial plants. Because a competitive rental market for the bulk of these properties did not exist, companies set up corporate real estate departments. Since product life cycles were long and relatively little merger and acquisition (M&A) activity occurred, the long-term nature of corporate real estate ownership provided a reasonable match with respect to duration for both product and corporate life cycles.
3. Why has the rationale for operating businesses owning real estate changed?

   Rapidly changing consumer preferences, new technologies, global competition, and M&A activity have reduced both product and corporate life cycles. The emergence of the service sector and the explosion of professional jobs have shifted the nature of corporate real estate usage toward general-purpose buildings, which are available in increasingly competitive leasing markets. Capital markets increasingly reward firms that create shareholder value by focusing their capital on the areas of company core competence.
4. What alternatives exist for selling off real estate?

   Large real estate companies including REITs focus primarily on the efficient operation of existing assets rather than on the development of new assets. Major real estate owner-operators can efficiently raise large amounts of debt and equity. Future sales of corporate real estate will not be mere sale-leaseback financing transactions by financially challenged companies, but rather sales of general-purpose real estate by strong operating companies to strong real estate companies.

Chapter 10 Mineral Rights

1. What is different about mineral rights ownership in the United States versus other countries?

   In virtually all countries, the owner of the surface land for a house, building, or farmland has no rights to mineral ownership. The central government owns such rights. By contrast, the owner of the surface land in the United States also has the rights to extract minerals from underneath that land. Consequently, private holders from the surface land or transfers own much of the mineral rights across the United States, as opposed to governments.

2. Discuss the bundle of rights that a U.S. farmland holder has.

   A U.S. farmland holder has the right to farm, to use the land for grazing, and to offer hunting rights. The owner also has royalty and overriding royalty rights and geothermal and wind rights. In many areas they also own the subsurface water rights. The farmland owner has the ability to grant easements for pipelines, oil and gas access roads and drilling pad-sites, injection wells, subsurface water rights, and fracking ponds. Fee simple ownership includes the surface and subsurface rights.

3. How is net revenue interest used to value the mineral rights in land?

   Net revenue interest (NRI) is equivalent to net operating income (NOI) in traditional real estate investments. Consider a NRI of $1,000 annually paid to the owner by the mining firm annually. Using the 10 percent equivalent cap rate and viewing the payment to be for the oil and gas royalty after wells are drilled and producing, the value of the mineral rights is $10,000 per acre.

4. Identify some specific risk factors in mineral rights.

   Due diligence should but does not always detect an ability to develop the mineral estate. There are additional local zoning or permitting ordinances. A risk comes from a drop in commodity prices below the current long-term market trend lines. Associated economic risks include overdevelopment and finding natural gas that is more economical to produce. Another risk is anticipated changes in federal and state taxing rules and regulations. Proposed changes in governmental environmental rules and regulations involving various technologies pose additional risk. These technologies include hydro-fracking, water disposal, noise, and air pollution of rigs that could limit or shut down drilling. The subsurface land rights holder faces risks of the mining company performing on the contract. One risk is operator bankruptcy and unscrupulous operators. The company may not pay the agreed-on royalty, or make unsubstantiated claims such as the difficulty of extraction. Other risks include financial shenanigans, theft, and other forms of business fraud. Another risk involves a challenge to the title of mineral rights owned.

Chapter 11 Infrastructure

1. Discuss the investment characteristics of infrastructure.

   Infrastructure has many distinctive investment characteristics that differ from property or financial assets. Infrastructure assets have barriers to entry due to large investment scale and high regulatory control by government. This means that infrastructure is characterized by monopolistic, inelastic demand, and long duration. With these attractive investment characteristics, institutional investors such as pension funds include infrastructure in their portfolios to produce predicable and stable cash flows over the long term.

2. Discuss the investment risk factors of infrastructure.

   Although infrastructure investment provides attractive investment characteristics, investors should consider the risk factors of infrastructure investment. Rising interest rates have been a major concern in the infrastructure investment market.

Due to high leverage levels, a rise in interest rates will result in decreasing performance of infrastructure investment. Another major key risk factor for investors is the consistency of the regulatory system over time given that the government often regulates infrastructure assets.. Other key issues about investing in infrastructure include increasing competition for quality assets, over-valuation of assets, life stage of the projects, and liquidity.

3. Explain why infrastructure should be considered as a separate asset class from property in terms of investment.

   The similarities between infrastructure and property include predictable cash flows, high yields, competition for quality assets, limited liquidity, and valuation-based performance. The differences between infrastructure and property include different structures and investment packaging, ownership of the property versus the right to operate the infrastructure, and the larger investment scale for infrastructure. Infrastructure and property are also likely to behave differently. Empirical studies whos that infrastructure is not highly correlated with other assets such as property, stocks, and bonds. This brings potential diversification benefits to a mixed-asset portfolio.

4. Identify the advantages and disadvantages of direct infrastructure investment.

   Recent years have seen institutional investors join together to increase investment power for direct infrastructure investment. Such investment involves both advantages and disadvantages. The major advantages include the potential for constructing a portfolio that better matches the assets and liability structure of an investor, accessing a board seat, and adding to control and influence over an investment. The disadvantages of direct infrastructure include requiring appropriate government structures, incurring headline risk, having a concentrated allocation, experiencing single asset risk, and handling the demands of managing direct investment.

Chapter 12 Appraisal and Valuation

1. Discuss the major difference between the Fannie Mae selling guide and the interagency appraisal guidelines.

   Although the Fannie Mae selling guide provides requirements for loans to be sold to that entity, the requirements do not carry the force of law or regulation. Conversely, federal agencies issue the interagency guidelines and carry the force of law.

2. Identify two key impediments to globalization of appraisal standards.

   The main impediments to globalization of appraisal standards are regulatory entrenchment and professional differences across cultures.

3. Explain the difference between construction quality and dwelling condition from an appraisal perspective.

   The construction quality of a dwelling is generally established when it is built or substantially renovated or rebuilt. The condition of that dwelling is a function of its maintenance and upkeep over time. A home initially built to top-quality standards may be in poor condition and vice versa.

4. Identify the party ultimately responsible for adherence to appraisal guidelines.

The underwriter that is attempting to sell the loan or security is required to adhere to appraisal guidelines.

5. Discuss the circumstances under which a federally regulated lender can make a real estate loan without an appraisal.

   Real estate loans do not require an appraisal under several circumstances: (1) when the transaction is less than $250,000; (2) if it is a business loan of less than $1 million when the loan does not depend on the sale or rental of real estate for repayment; and (3) if the transaction is an extension of a line of credit when no obvious or material change has occurred in either market conditions or the condition of the property and no new money is being advanced.

Chapter 13 Real Estate Brokerage

1. Discuss the level of employment and income in the real estate brokerage industry.

   Employment in the real estate sector of the economy totaled 1.5 million full- and part-time workers in 2011. Total National Association of Realtors (NAR) membership was about 1.0 million. Earnings in the industry averaged $55,064 in 2011, compared to an average for all workers of $60,524.

2. Describe the major factors influencing employment and income in the real estate brokerage industry.

   Employment and income in the brokerage industry are highly dependent on conditions in the housing market. Rising housing sales and prices generate greater employment and income in the industry. Because entry is relatively easy, when housing sales and prices rise, more people enter the industry limiting the average earnings of industry workers. Other factors that influence worker earnings are education, experience, hours worked, and the use of information technology.

3. Explain what licensing requirements are needed to work in the real estate brokerage industry.

   All states and the District of Columbia require that agents and brokers be licensed in order to sell real estate. Among the basic licensing requirements are that candidates complete a minimum number of hours of classroom instruction, pass an exam, and obtain a minimum level of experience. Most states also require a minimum number of hours of annual continuing education.

4. Discuss the economic structure of the real estate brokerage industry.

   Most real estate firms in the United States are small and legally organized as S-corporations. Market concentration levels across the country are low, indicating no tendency toward domination by a single large firm or group of firms. Because real estate firms tend to be small, many seek competitive advantage through affiliation with a national or regional franchise.

5. Explain whether the real estate brokerage industry operates in an economically efficient manner.

   The Federal Trade Commission concludes that commission rates tend to be stable and the industry has little price competition. Relatively fixed commission rates and low barriers to entry lead the market for brokerage services to be socially inefficient. Homebuyers and sellers pay more for brokerage services in cities where housing prices are higher, although the quality of brokerages services remains relatively the same. Real estate agents in more expensive cities are no better off because the higher price of brokerage services stimulates the entry of more agents who compete away any gains in agent income. Competing evidence indicates commission rates are not really fixed. Nevertheless, a fixed-commission system may be efficient because the buyer and seller cannot observe and properly evaluate the effort expended by the broker. Because the client cannot observe how efficiently the broker works and how much effort is expended, buyers and sellers may accept higher rates to stimulate the broker to work more diligently.

Chapter 14 Green Buildings

1. List the main drivers for green buildings.

   The main drivers for green buildings are to:

   - deal with climate change including the need to reduce CO^2 emissions and energy use;
   - reduce operational costs of running a building by installing and using materials that are energy efficient;
   - enhance rental levels and values due to increased demand for high performance, energy efficient real estate;
   - improve employee productivity;
   - reduce vacancies and turnover due to high demand and tenant satisfaction;
   - comply with increased regulation and legislation requiring certification or mandatory energy performance reporting; and
   - meet increased user demand due to corporate social responsibility statements and associated reporting regimes.

2. Define sustainable development.

   Sustainable development is the kind of development that meets the needs of the present without compromising the ability of future generations to meet their own needs.
3. Discuss the extent to which buildings contribute to greenhouse gas emissions and its most common cause.

   Buildings contribute about 30 percent of global greenhouse gas emissions but this proportion varies by country. Electricity is responsible for the majority of emissions in buildings. In terms of the operational energy applications, cooling, air handling, lighting, and heating account for about 84 percent of commercial building greenhouse gas emissions.
4. What factors or features in a building does the Australian Green Building Council consider as having the lowest cost but the highest sustainability benefit?

   The following are factors or features in a building that the Australian Green Building Council considers to have the lowest cost but the highest sustainability benefit.

   - Passive solar orientation
   - Building user training program

- Automatic HVAC switch off
- Fire test water retention
- Reduction in photocopiers and printers
- T5 fluorescent lighting
- Xeriscape landscaping
- Zero Ozone Depleting Potential (OPD) building insulation
- Energy use targets and monitoring

5. What is the main green rating tool used for commercial buildings in the United States and what does it measure?

   The main green rating tool used for commercial buildings in the United States is Leadership in Energy and Environment Design (LEED). The rating has five categories: (1) sustainable sites; (2) water efficiency, energy, and atmosphere; (3) materials and resources; (4) indoor environmental quality; and (5) innovation in design.

Index

N

T